HARRAP

British Dates

MINI DICTIONARY

by

Rodney Castleden

HARRAP

EDINBURGH PARIS

Published 1993 by Chambers Harrap Publishers Ltd
43-45 Annandale Street, Edinburgh EH7 4AZ

British Library Cataloguing in Publication Data

A catalogue record for this book is available from the British
Library

ISBN 0 245 60350 6

Typeset by O'Connor, Parkstone, Poole
Printed in England by Clays Ltd, St Ives plc

For John and Anthea
their sort of book

Acknowledgements

Thanks are due to my father-in-law, John Dee, for supplying useful dates in the history of transport, and the historian Jeffery Davis for supplying additional information and for his scrupulous checking of the draft text.

BC

8000 The last glaciers in Britain finally melt as the climate becomes warmer. The sea is still about 30m below its AD 1991 level, but rising rapidly. The Straits of Dover and the southern North Sea bed are dry land; people and animals can walk to and from the mainland of Europe. A totem pole is raised on the site of the Stonehenge car park: the place is already a ritual centre of some kind.

6500 The land bridge joining Britain to Europe is flooded, so that Britain becomes an island.

4800 Beginning of agriculture, in small forest clearings.

4070 Flint is mined at Church Hill near Worthing.

3840 A timber trackway, the Sweet Track, is built across the Somerset Levels.

3600 The neolithic enclosure at Maiden Castle is built.

3200 Stonehenge is laid out as an earth circle consisting of an outer ditch and inner bank. It has a round timber building at the centre and a pair of portal stones – of which only the Heel Stone survives – marking the midsummer sunrise. Stone houses are built at Skara Brae, Orkney.

3000 Flint mining begins at Grime's Graves in Norfolk.

2700 Silbury Hill near Avebury is built.

2600 Avebury's stone circles are completed at about this time.

2520 A large wooden enclosure is laid out on the site of Dorchester.

2300 The neolithic village of Skara Brae is abandoned when a storm engulfs it in sand.

2250 85 bluestones are transported from the Preseli Mountains in Wales to Stonehenge, where an unusual double stone circle is begun but not completed.

2200 The bluestone project at Stonehenge is abandoned. The bluestones are moved off-site so that work can begin on a circle made of larger sarsen stones with running lintels, and a horseshoe arrangement of colossal trilithons. The large sarsens are brought from the hills near Avebury.

2000 The bluestones are reincorporated into Stonehenge, set as a circle and a horseshoe among the sarsen settings.

1900 Cairnpapple Hill, Lothian, is laid out as an egg-shaped henge with an arc of 24 standing stones. The hill continues to be a focus for ritual activity until the time of Christ.

1200 Mam Tor, Derbyshire, is occupied; it is one of the highest and oldest hillfort sites to be developed.

1100 Large-scale religious cult activity begins at Flag Fen near Peterborough: for the next 900 years it will be one of the major sacrificial centres of Europe.

450 South Barrule hillfort, Isle of Man, is occupied.

325 Pytheas of Massilia (Marseilles) refers to Ireland and Britain as the Pretanic (or Britannic) Islands: this is thought to be the earliest reference to Britain in documented history.

150 East Anglia, Kent and the Thames Basin are gradually settled from this time on by Belgic people from northern France. Maiden Castle is refortified, apparently against the Belgae.

100 Danebury and other hillforts of southern England are given additional defences because of the threat from Belgic tribes to the east.

55 The Roman Invasion of Britain (55 BC - 45 AD) begins with Julius Caesar's first (reconnaissance) expedition to Britain.

54 Julius Caesar's second expedition, with 800 ships, 5 legions and 2000 cavalry. Cassivellaunus, King of the Catuvellauni, is elected overall war leader in command of a huge confederate Celtic army raised to meet the Roman threat. Caesar crosses the Thames to strike at Cassivellaunus. Cassivellaunus defends the oppidum of Ravensburgh Castle (Hexton, Hertfordshire) against Caesar's forces, but the British army disintegrates.

44 Julius Caesar is murdered in Rome.

27 Octavian becomes Emperor, taking the title Augustus; renewed plans for the Roman conquest of Britain come to nothing.

20 Tincommius becomes King of the Atrebates, whose territory centres on Hampshire; it is possible that Tincommius was a Romanizing influence.

10 Tincommius, King of the Atrebates, is deposed by his own tribesmen. He flees to Rome and is succeeded by his brother Epillus.

8 Camulodunum (Colchester), the capital of the Trinovantes tribe, is captured by the neighbouring (Hertfordshire) Catuvellauni tribe under their leader Tasciovanus, although this conquest is short-lived.

6 Addedomarus, King of the Trinovantes, reclaims his capital.

1 Epillus is deposed and takes refuge in Kent; he is succeeded as King of the Atrebates by Verica.

AD

1 Addedomarus, King of the Trinovantes, dies and is probably buried in the Lexden Tumulus at Colchester; he is succeeded by Dubnovellaunus.

9   Tasciovanus, King of the Catuvellauni, is succeeded by his son Cunobelinus, who recaptures Camulodunum.

10   Cunobelinus reigns over much of south-east England from his headquarters at Camulodunum, as a tributary ally of the Roman emperors.

20   Epillus, ex-King of the Atrebates, is driven out of his Kentish refuge by Cunobelinus.

40   Cunobelinus dies and is succeeded by his sons Togodumnus and Caractacus.

41   The invasion of Britain planned by the Emperor Gaius (Caligula) comes to nothing; the expedition peters out in shell-collecting on the French beaches.

42   Verica is deposed and exiled; he is the third successive King of the Atrebates to be ousted.

43   The Romans invade Britain under Aulus Plautius, on the orders of the Emperor Claudius. Waves of defensive activity, including the refortification of hillforts like Mount Caburn, spread through England. Nevertheless, 11 kings throw in their lot with Rome straight away.

44   In the campaign of 43-44, the Romans, under Vespasian, attack and slight over 20 hillforts in southern England. This is the probable date of the massacres at Maiden Castle and Spettisbury and the ballista attack on Hod Hill in Dorset. The Catuvellauni, Trinovantes and Cantiaci, forming a confederation, probably switched their headquarters from Verulamium (St Albans) where there were no defensive earthworks to Camulodunum (Colchester) where there were defences.

47   Roman armies now occupy Britain as far west as the Severn and as far north as the Trent. The Roman military zone is extended to include Devon and Cornwall. The conquest of

Britain is progressing so easily and rapidly that a tendency towards Romanization even before the invasion seems likely.

48 British resistance to the Roman occupation nevertheless continues in the territories of the Catuvellauni and Trinovantes, led by the war-leader, Caractacus (correctly Carataccus). Midsummer Hill fort is burnt down by Ostorius Scapula when he attacks the Decangi tribe. Sutton Walls hillfort is similarly attacked and its occupants are massacred.

49 Caractacus continues his guerilla war into Wales. The Romans found Colchester.

50 Caractacus is finally defeated in battle; he flees to the Brigantes. At the large hillfort of Stanwick in North Yorkshire, Venutius prepares his Brigantian supporters for revolt against the Romans. At about this time the Romans found London.

51 Caractacus is handed over to the Romans by Cartimandua, Queen of the Brigantes, and taken to Rome as a prisoner.

58 Quintus Veranius arrives in Britain with new orders to conquer the whole island, a significant expansion of Rome's ambition.

60 Boudicca's East Anglian revolt against Rome begins. A Roman force occupies Sudbrook Camp in Gwent, using it as a base from which the Silures tribe may be subdued.

61 Colchester, St Albans and London are sacked by the Iceni under their queen, Boudicca. The suppression of the Druids in Britain.

62 Boudicca is defeated; she escapes from the field of battle and commits suicide by taking poison.

70 The British Governor Petillius Cerialis attacks Venutius and his followers at Stanwick. The Brigantes are unable to withstand the Roman onslaught.

76 The Emperor Hadrian is born.

78 Gnaeus Julius Agricola's campaigns to subdue northern Britain begin.

80 Scotland, as far north as the Forth and Clyde, is conquered by Roman forces.

84 The final, decisive defeat of the British at Mons Graupius, on the Moray Firth. The British, under the Caledonian war-leader Calgacus, suffer 10,000 casualties. Calgacus tells them just before the battle that they are 'the last men on earth, the last of the free'. Agricola's campaign against the tribes of Scotland is complete.

100

100 At about this time Roman forces temporarily lose control of Scotland; the northern frontier is for a time marked by the Tyne-Solway line.

117 Hadrian becomes Emperor.

121 Hadrian visits Britain and personally surveys the line of the frontier wall which he planned, and which is named after him.

122 Beginning of the building work on Hadrian's Wall (Tyne-Solway) under the supervision of Aulus Platorius Nepos.

138 Emperor Hadrian dies.

140 The Antonine advance into Scotland.

142 Building of the Antonine Wall (Forth-Clyde) under the supervision of Quintus Lollius Urbicus.

163 Hadrian's Wall is restored.

193 Septimius Severus becomes Emperor, and Clodius Albinus is proclaimed governor of Britain.

196 Clodius Albinus withdraws forces from Britain in his attempt to become Emperor; as a result, the northern frontier of Britain is overrun.

200

208 Emperor Septimius Severus visits Britain himself, to oversee the re-conquest of Scotland.

211 Septimius Severus dies at Eboracum (York).

274 Britain is taken back under central government, and ruled direct from Rome.

287 Carausius, a senior Roman officer charged with clearing the English Channel of pirates, attempts to found an independent 'Empire of Britain'. For a time Britain is under the rule of a local emperor.

293 Carausius loses his foothold on the European mainland when the siege of Boulogne ends. Carausius is deposed and then murdered by Allectus, one of his own men.

296 Constantius Chlorus, Caesar in the West, resumes the conquest of Britain, arriving with a force of Roman troops.

297 Allectus is defeated, and the 'Empire of Britain' comes to an end.

300

304 St Alban is executed at Verulamium; a Roman legionary, he sheltered the Christian Amphibalus and was converted by him. Amphibalus is caught by the Romans four miles away, on Watling Street, and he too is executed.

306 Constantine the Great proclaims himself Emperor at Eboracum (York), and then leaves Britain to fight for his throne. Campaign of Constantius I in Scotland.

343 The Emperor Constans crosses the Channel to Britain.

360 The Mildenhall Treasure is buried, probably by the family of the Roman general Lupicinus following his arrest.

363 Five years of instability begin; repeated attacks from Saxons.

364 A large-scale 'barbarian' raid.

367 The great barbarian invasion; the Romans in Britain are successfully attacked by Picts, Scots and Saxons.

369 Roman authority is restored in Britain by Theodosius.

382 Magnus Maximus, the military commander of Britain, wins a victory over the Picts.

383 Magnus Maximus revolts against Rome's authority.

388 The fall of Magnus Maximus.

400

401 The Roman legions begin to leave Britain. Local defence forces are created. South Cadbury Castle is reoccupied, remaining an important centre for 200 years to come.

406 The usurper Constantine III withdraws Roman forces from Britain to support his claims. This event probably marks the end of the Roman military occupation of Britain.

409 The Saxons renew their attacks on Britain. The British rebel against Constantine III's administration, breaking with Roman rule. From now on, Britain is free of Roman rule.

410 Rome is sacked by the Goths under their leader Alaric. The Emperor Honorius tells the Britons that they must organize their own defence.

418 The Romans gather all the gold-hoards in Britain; some are taken to Gaul and some are buried in Britain.

429 The Roman control of Britain continues to diminish, although the Christian Church maintains close links with Rome until

455. St Germanus, a prominent Gallo-Roman bishop, visits Britain to combat heresy, debating publicly at Verulamium with British leaders.

430 Palladius is sent by Pope Celestine to preach Christian baptism to the Scots.

446 The Britons make a last appeal to Rome to send troops to defend them, but the Romans refuse to help because of their war with the Huns. The Britons also appeal to the Angles.

448 Angles under Hengist and Horsa are invited to Britain by King Vortigern to help defend the country against its enemies.

455 Hengist and Horsa turn against King Vortigern at Aylesford in Kent: Horsa is killed.

456 Hengist and his son Aesc lead a battle against the Britons at Crayford in Kent, killing four companies and putting the rest to flight.

477 The Saxon Aelle and his three sons, Cymen, Wlencing and Cissa, sail to Sussex in three ships, landing at Selsey and killing many Britons.

485 Aelle and his men fight against the Britons at the Battle of Mearcredesburna (Seaford?).

491 A Saxon force under Aelle besieges the Roman fort of Anderida (Pevensey), killing all the Britons inside it.

495 Cerdic, a Saxon leader and ancestor of Alfred, arrives in Wessex.

500

501 The Saxons Port, Bieda and Maegla land at Portsmouth and seize land.

515 Battle of Mount Badon: the West Saxon advance is halted by the Britons, perhaps under Arthur as war-leader.

519 Cerdic and his son Cynric gain control of what is to become the kingdom of Wessex; Cerdic becomes King of the West Saxons.

530 Cerdic and Cynric gain control of the Isle of Wight.

534 Cerdic, King of Wessex, dies, succeeded by Cynric, his son or grandson. Cynric gives the Isle of Wight to Stuf and Wihtgar, his kinsmen.

547 Ida becomes King of Bernicia (part of Northumbria). He builds Bamburgh, first enclosing it with a stockade, then with a rampart.

559 Ida, King of Bernicia, dies and is succeeded by Glappa.

560 Ceawlin, great-grandson of Cerdic, becomes King of Wessex on the death of Cynric, his father. Ceawlin organizes a confederation to drive the Britons out of Wessex and becomes second overlord of the Southern English. Ethelbert, later overking, becomes King of Kent on the death of his father, Eormenric. Glappa, King of Bernicia, dies and is succeeded by Adda.

563 The Irish St Columba founds a monastery on the island of Iona.

568 Ceawlin and Cutha fight against Ethelbert and drive him into Kent. They kill two Kentish princes, Oslac and Cnebba, at Wibbandum (Wimbledon?). Adda, King of Bernicia, dies and is succeeded by Aedilric.

571 Cutha, the brother of King Ceawlin, fights against the Britons at Biedcanford (unidentified), capturing the villages of Limbury, Aylesbury, Benson and Eynsham. Later in the year Cutha dies.

572 Aedliric, King of Bernicia, dies and is succeeded by Theodric.

574 Columba anoints and inaugurates Aidan as King of Dal Riada.

575 Columba accompanies Aidan, King of Scots, to Ireland and plays a prominent part in the council held at Druim Ceata.

577 Battle of Dyrham, at which Cuthwine and Ceawlin fight against the Britons, killing three of their kings, Coinmail, Condidan and Farinmail. The West Saxon advance is resumed. Cuthwine and Ceawlin also capture Gloucester, Bath and Cirencester.

579 Theodric, King of Bernicia, dies and is succeeded by Friduuald.

582 King Penda of Mercia, son of Pybba, is thought to have been born in this year.

585 Friduald, King of Bernicia, dies and is succeeded by Hussa.

591 There is a bloody battle at Adam's Grave, Alton Priors, and Ceawlin is deposed; he is succeeded as King of Wessex by Ceol. Hussa, King of Bernicia, dies and is succeeded by Ethefrith.

593 Ceawlin, deposed King of Wessex, dies. Aethelfrith, son of Aethelric, succeeds to the kingdom of Northumbria.

596 Pope Gregory instructs Augustine to go to Britain.

597 St Augustine lands in Kent; he has been sent by the Pope to convert Ethelbert, King of Kent and overking of Southern England. St Columba dies (8 Jun) on Iona; pilgrims begin arriving within days to see his books, stone pillow, pastoral staff and grave. Augustine becomes Archbishop of Canterbury. Ceol, King of Wessex, dies and is succeeded by Ceolwulf.

600

601 Pope Gregory sends Augustine more assistants. Augustine makes Paulinus Bishop of York, reviving the old Romano-British see of York.

604 Augustine consecrates two bishops, Mellitus and Justus, to
preach to the East Saxons. Mellitus is given the see of
London, Justus the newly-founded see of Rochester.
Aethelfrith, King of Northumbria, kills countless Britons at
Chester, including 200 priests who came to pray for the
British host; the British leader was Scrocmail, who was one of
the few to escape.

607 Aethelfrith, King of Northumbria, defeats the Welsh in a
great battle at Chester.

611 Ceolwulf, King of Wessex, dies and is succeeded by
Cynegils.

612 Oswiu is born, son of Aethelfrith, King of Northumbria.

616 Aethelfrith, King of Northumbria, dies and is succeeded by
Edwin, who becomes the fifth overlord of the English.
Aethelberht, King of Kent, dies, succeeded by his son
Eadbald. Eadbald reverts to paganism, but is converted by
Archbishop Laurentius, Augustine's successor. Redwald,
King of East Anglia, takes an army through Mercia and
defeats the Northumbrians on their own frontier.

617 Aethelfrith, King of Northumbria, is killed by Redwald, King
of East Anglia; he is succeeded by Edwin, under whom
Northumbrian power and influence increase. Edwin is
acknowledged as bretwalda, or overlord.

619 Archbishop Laurentius dies and is buried beside Augustine;
he is succeeded by Mellitus as Archbishop of Canterbury,
but when Mellitus leaves London the city reverts to
paganism.

624 Archbishop Mellitus dies; Honorius becomes Archbishop of
Canterbury.

625 Redwald of East Anglia and overlord of England dies and is
buried at Sutton Hoo. The famous ship burial uncovered in
1938-9 is thought to be his.

626   Eomer, a West Saxon assassin, fails to kill King Edwin.
            Edwin promises Paulinus that he will give his newly-born
            daughter to God if Paulinus will, by prayer, enable him to
            overthrow the enemy who sent the assassin. Edwin journeys
            to Wessex and kills a great number of people. Paulinus
            baptizes Edwin's daughter on Whit Sunday in the wooden
            church at York.

627   Edwin, King of Northumbria, is baptized at Easter by
            Paulinus.

632
Oct   [14] The allied forces of Penda of Mercia and Cadwallon of
            North Wales defeat the Northumbrian army at Hatfield.
            Edwin, King of Northumbria and fifth overlord of the
            Southern English, is killed in the battle with his son Osfrith;
            Osric, son of Aelfric, succeeds Edwin. Penda becomes King
            of Mercia.

633   Osric dies and is succeeded by Oswald.

634   Birinus begins preaching Christianity to the West Saxons
            under King Cynegils. Wilfrid begins his education at the
            court of Oswald, King of Northumbria; Oswald becomes
            overking.

635   Cynegils, King of Wessex, is baptized by Birinus; Oswald,
            King of Northumbria, stands sponsor for him. Birinus is
            given the old Roman fort at Dorchester-on-Thames to found
            his see.

636   Bishop Aidan chooses the island of Lindisfarne as his base,
            within sight of King Oswald's Bamburgh Castle.

640
Jan   [20] Eadbald, King of Kent, dies and is succeeded by his son
            Earconberht.

641   King Oswald of Northumbria, sixth overlord of the Southern
            English, is canonized after his death in battle against Penda

at Maserfield (Oswestry?). King Oswald is buried at Bardney and is succeeded by Oswy.

643 Cenwalh succeeds to the kingdom of Wessex after Cynegils' death.

644 Archbishop Paulinus dies in Rochester (Oct 10). Oswine, son of Osric, becomes King of Deira, after Northumbria's division into two kingdoms, Deira and Bernicia.

645 Cenwalh, King of Wessex, is driven from his kingdom by King Penda.

648 St Peter's church in Winchester, founded by King Cenwalh, is completed and consecrated.

650 *The Book of Durrow*, the earliest known example of the new Celtic Christian art, dates from about this time.

651
Aug [20] Oswine, King of Deira, dies and is succeeded by Ethelwald, son of King Oswald. [31] Bishop Aidan dies in the parish church at Bamburgh; at the same moment Cuthbert, a shepherd in the Lammermuir Hills, sees a vision of a host of angels, which he later connects with Aidan's death and interprets as a call to serve God.

653
Sep [30]Archbishop Honorius dies.

654 Anna, King of East Anglia, dies and is succeeded by Aethelhere.

Nov [15] Oswy, brother of Oswald, destroys Penda's last alliance in the Battle of Winwaed. Penda and 30 other princes and kings are killed, including Aethelhere of East Anglia, who is succeeded by Ethelwold. Oswiu, King of Bernicia, rules Mercia for three years.

655 Oswiu, King of Bernicia, annexes the Kingdom of Deira and becomes overking. Deusdedit becomes Archbishop of Canterbury.

656 King Peada of Mercia is killed and is succeeded by Wulfhere, son of Penda.

657 The monastery at Whitby is founded. Wulfhere, son of Penda, becomes King of Mercia and overlord of the Southern English.

658 King Cenwalh fights with the Britons at Penselwood.

660 The Augustinian monastery at Canterbury is founded. Bishop Aegelbriht leaves the court of King Cenwalh to receive the bishopric of Paris.

661 Wulfhere, son of Penda, attacks the Isle of Wight and gives the island over to Ethelwold, King of Sussex.

663 Oswiu, King of Northumbria, holds the Synod of Whitby, to resolve the dispute over the date of Easter; Roman Christianity prevails over Celtic Christianity in England.

May [3] Eclipse of the sun. Plague sweeps Britain. Bishop Tuda dies. Earconberht, King of Kent, dies and is succeeded by his son Egbert I. Ethelwold, King of East Anglia, dies and is succeeded by Aldwulf. Archbishop Deusdedit dies.

667 Oswiu and Ecgbryht send the priest Wigheard to Rome to be consecrated there as Archbishop of Canterbury, but he dies on arriving in Rome.

668 Pope Vitalianus consecrates Theodorus as Archbishop of Canterbury and sends him to Britain. Theodorus introduces a strictly Roman parochial system and a centralized episcopal system, which will later become a model for the secular state. There is also a revival of Greco-Roman culture.

669 St Wilfrid, the great art patron, is reinstalled as Bishop of Northumbria. St Chad resigns from the bishopric of Lindisfarne to make way for Wilfrid: Wilfrid chooses York as the centre of his diocese.

670
Feb [15] The death of King Oswiu ends the Northumbrian supremacy: he is succeeded by Egfrith.

672 Cenwalh, King of Wessex, dies and is succeeded by his Queen, Seaxburg, for a year. St Chad dies. A synod at Hertford establishes guidelines for the government of the Church.

673 Aescwine succeeds to the throne of Wessex. The Venerable Bede is born; his *Ecclesiastical History of the English Nation* is the main source of information about preceding centuries. St Ethelthryth founds the monastery at Ely. Etheldreda, daughter of Anna, King of East Anglia, founds the convent at Ely.

Jul [4] Egbert I, King of Kent, dies.

674 The bishopric of Winchester is founded. Building work begins on Hexham Abbey under Wilfrid's direction, using stones from the Roman camp at Corbridge. Wulfhere, King of Mercia, dies and is succeeded by Ethelred, son of Penda.

678
Aug A comet appears, shining for three months like a sunbeam. Bishop Wilfrid is driven from his bishopric by King Egfrith: he sets out for Rome by way of the Netherlands.

679 Queen Etheldreda dies of cancer of the throat.

680 Wilfrid tells Pope Agatho of the founding of the monastery of Peterborough; the Pope sends a deed for the monastery back to Ethelred. Wilfrid returns with vestments and ornaments for his new church at Hexham. Theodorus, Archbishop of Canterbury, presides over a synod at Hatfield. Hilda, Abbess of Whitby, dies.

685 A 'bloody rain' (probably coloured by Saharan dust) falls on Britain. Centwine, King of Wessex, is deposed and is succeeded by Ceadwalla. The Battle of Nectansmere ends Northumbrian dominance in England. At York, Theodorus consecrates Cuthbert as Bishop of Hexham, at the command of Egfrith.

Feb [6] Hlothere, King of Kent, dies and is succeeded by his son Eadric.

May [20] King Egfrith is killed with many of his men; he is succeeded by his brother Aldfrith.

686 Eadric, King of Kent, dies and is succeeded by Oswini.

687 Caedwalla, King of Wessex, launches a second attack on Kent, where his brother Mul is burnt to death.

Mar [20] St Cuthbert dies on Farne Island.

688 Caedwalla abdicates and goes to Rome. Ine becomes King of Wessex, establishing his line as kings of the 'West Saxons', in control of Dorset, Wiltshire and Hampshire. Ine draws up the earliest substantial code of British laws to survive. In Rome, Caedwalla is baptized Peter by Pope Sergius; seven nights later he dies in his baptismal robes and is buried in St Peter's.

690 Archbishop Theodorus, the last Roman archbishop, dies and is buried at Canterbury. Wihtred, son of King Egbert I, becomes King of Kent.

692
Jul [1] Brihtwold, Abbot of Reculver, is chosen archbishop; he is the first English Archbishop of Canterbury.

693
Jun [29] Brihtwold is enthroned as archbishop.

694 The people of Kent confer with Ine, offering to pay compensation for killing Mul.

695 Abbess Sexburga, St Etheldreda's sister, transfers the saint's body to a shrine in the abbey church at Ely.

697 The Mercians kill Osthryth, Ethelred's queen and daughter of Oswy, King of Northumbria.

698 *The Lindisfarne Gospels* are written and illuminated at about this time.

700

704   Cenred becomes King of Mercia in place of Ethelred, who abdicates and becomes a monk. Aldfrith, King of Northumbria, dies and is succeeded by Eadwulf.

709   His mother murdered and his father a monk, Ceolred becomes King of Mercia. Cenred and Offa journey to Rome, Cenred remaining in Rome until his death. Bishop Wilfrid dies at Oundle and is buried at Ripon.

710   Acca, Wilfrid's chaplain, receives Wilfrid's bishopric. Ine and Nun wage war against Geraint, the Welsh king.

713   Aldwulf, King of East Anglia, dies and is succeeded by Alfwold.

714   St Guthlac dies at his hermitage in the Fens.

715   Ine, King of Wessex, and Ceolred, King of Mercia, fight at Adam's Grave.

716   Osred, King of Northumbria, is killed and is succeeded by Cenred. Ceolred, King of Mercia, dies and is buried at Lichfield; he is succeeded by Ethelbald. Ethelred, ex-King of Mercia, dies. Crowland Abbey is founded on the site of St Guthlac's hermitage.

718   Ine's brother Ingild dies; their sister Cuthberg founds the religious community at Wimborne. Cenred, King of Northumbria, dies and is succeeded by Osric, son of King Aldfrith.

721   The kindly John, Archbishop of York, dies in retirement at Beverley.

722   Queen Ethelburg destroys Taunton, which the King of Wessex built.

725 Wihtred, King of Kent, dies after ruling for 34 years, succeeded by his son, Ethelbert II. Ine fights with the South Saxons.

726 Ine, King of Wessex, dies in Rome and is succeeded by Aethelheard.

729 Two comets appear.

May [9] Osric, King of Northumbria, dies and is succeeded by Ceolwulf.

731 Archbishop Beorhtweald dies; Tatwine succeeds him as Archbishop of Canterbury.

734
Jul Archbishop Tatwine dies.

735 The death of Bede marks the close of a golden age of Northumbrian art and learning. Nothelm becomes Archbishop of Canterbury.

740 Aethelheard, King of Wessex, dies and is succeeded by Cuthred. Cuthbert succeeds Nothelm as Archbishop of Canterbury.

741 York is burnt down.

743 Ethelbald, King of Mercia, and Cuthred, King of Wessex, fight the Welsh.

744 There are many shooting stars.

746 The First Council of Clofesho (Brixworth?) begins.

747 The Council of Clofesho ends.

748 Cynric, atheling of Wessex, is killed. Eadbriht, King of Kent, dies and is succeeded by Ethelbriht.

749 Alfwold, King of East Anglia, dies; his kingdom is divided among Hun, Beonna and Alberht.

752 Cuthred, King of Wessex, fights with Ethelbald, King of Mercia, and puts him to flight.

756 Cuthred, King of Wessex, dies and is succeeded by Sigeberht. Canterbury is burnt. Ethelbald, King of Mercia and overlord of the Southern English, is killed at Seckington and buried at Repton.

757 Offa seizes the kingdom of Mercia, uniting most of England under his rule; Offa governs England south of the Humber and his son-in-law rules Northumbria. Offa becomes overlord of the Southern English, assuming the title 'rex totius Anglorum patriae'. Sigeberht, King of Wessex, is deposed and killed, and is succeeded by Cynewulf.

758 Edbriht, King of Northumbria, becomes a monk and is succeeded by his son Osulf, who is killed by his own household.

760 Archbishop Cuthbert dies.

761 Moll Ethelwold becomes King of Northumbria. Breguwine becomes Archbishop of Canterbury.

762 Ethelbert of Kent dies and is succeeded by his son Eardwulf.

763 A hard winter.

764 Ceolwulf, King of Northumbria, dies. Breguwine is succeeded by Jaenbeorht as Archbishop of Canterbury.

765 Alhred becomes King of Northumbria.

774 At Easter, the Northumbrians drive their king, Alhred, from York, taking Ethelred I, son of Moll, as their lord.

776 Mercian and Kentish forces meet in battle at Otford in Kent. Strange adders are seen in Sussex.

779 Cynewulf, King of Wessex, and Offa, King of Mercia, fight near Benson (in Oxfordshire): Offa takes the town.

780 Ethelberht, Archbishop of York, dies and is succeeded by Eanbald. Bishop Ealhmund of Hexham dies, succeeded by Rilberht. Bishop Cynewulf of Lindisfarne resigns and is succeeded by Higbald.

783 Cyneheard kills Cynewulf, King of Wessex, and is himself killed; Brihtric becomes King of Wessex.

787 A contentious synod is held at Chelsea. The first Viking raids. King Offa has his son Egfrith solemnly consecrated as King of the Mercians.

789 Brihtric, King of Wessex, takes Offa's daughter Eadburg for his wife. A dispute arises between Offa and Charlemagne; as a result, Frankish ports are closed to English merchants. The first three ships of the Danes come to England.

790 Osred, King of Northumbria, is betrayed and driven out of his kingdom and is succeeded by Ethelred.

792 King Offa, who lives at Sutton Walls near Hereford, has Ethelbert, King of East Anglia, beheaded. Ethelbert is a suitor for the hand of Offa's daughter Alfrida, and later Offa is stricken with remorse; this leads him to order a tomb for Ethelbert housed in a church, which eventually becomes the Saxon cathedral of Saints Mary and Ethelbert. Jaenbeorht, Archbishop of Canterbury, dies.

793 Athelheard becomes Archbishop of Canterbury. Offa founds St Albans Abbey as a monastery. There are unusual weather phenomena: whirlwinds, lightning storms and 'fiery dragons in the sky' (aurora borealis?): there is also famine. 'Heathen men' ravage and destroy the church at Lindisfarne; this is the earliest report of a Viking raid. King Osred of Northumbria returns from exile, only to be taken and killed: he is buried at Tynemouth. Vikings ransack Egfrith's monastery at Jarrow, but many are later drowned when their ships break up in bad weather; some survivors manage to swim ashore, but they are killed by Northumbrians at Tynemouth.

795 Viking raid on Iona.

796 Eadbert becomes King of Kent. Osbald accedes to the Northumbrian throne but is deposed after a reign of only 27 days, succeeded by Eadwulf, who is crowned on May 26.

Jul   [29] Offa, King of Mercia, dies: his death marks the end of Mercian dominance in England.

Dec   [17] Offa's son and successor Egfrith dies and is succeeded by Cenwulf.

798   Cenwulf, King of Mercia, ravages Kent, stamping out the attempted Kentish coup against him. The Kentish King Eadbert is taken to Mercia, where his eyes are put out and his hands cut off; the Kentish dynasty is ended, and Cenwulf governs Kent through his brother Cuthred.

800

800   Three Viking raids on Iona are reported at about this time: 68 monks are killed by Vikings at Martyrs' Bay.

802   Brihtric, King of Wessex, dies and is succeeded by Egbert.

803   Higbald, Bishop of Lindisfarne, dies and is succeeded by Egbert.

805   Archbishop Athelheard dies.

806   Wulfred becomes Archbishop of Canterbury. Eardwulf, King of Northumbria, is deposed and expelled, and succeeded by Elfwald.

807   Cuthred, King of Kent, dies; his successor is unknown.

808   Elfwald, King of Northumbria, dies and is succeeded by Eanred, son of King Eardwulf.

814   Archbishop Wulfred journeys to Rome with Wigbriht, bishop of Essex.

815   Wulfred returns to Kent with the Pope's blessing. Egbert, King of Wessex, ravages Cornwall.

821 Cenwulf, King of Mercia, dies and is succeeded by Ceolwulf. Cenwulf's seven-year-old son is murdered and buried beside his father at Winchcombe Abbey in Gloucestershire.

823 Ceolwulf, King of Mercia, is deposed and expelled, and succeeded by Beornwulf.

825 Battle of Ellandun, Wiltshire: Egbert of Wessex defeats the Mercians under Ceolwulf and Wessex becomes the dominant kingdom in England, with suzerainty over Kent, Sussex and Essex. The men of Cornwall fight the men of Devon at Galford. The East Angles kill Beornwulf, King of the Mercians; he is succeeded by Ludecan. Vikings burst into the church on Iona, killing the bishop and several monks, then setting fire to the buildings. Baldred, King of Kent, is deposed and expelled by Egbert, King of Wessex; from now on Kent, Sussex and Essex are to be ruled by the kings of the West Saxons, initially under Egbert's son Ethelwulf as sub-king.

827 Ludecan, King of Mercia, is killed together with his five ealdormen; he is succeeded by Wiglaf. King Egbert conquers Mercia, controlling all England south of the Humber. He is the eighth king to achieve this; the others were Aelle, King of Sussex; Ceawlin, King of Wessex; Aethelbryht, King of Kent; Redwald, King of East Anglia; Edwin, Oswald and Oswy, Kings of Northumbria. Egbert leads his troops against the Northumbrians, who offer him submission and a treaty, which he accepts.

830 The deposed Wiglaf again becomes King of Mercia. King Egbert leads his troops into North Wales and subdues it.

832 Archbishop Wulfred dies; Feologild becomes Archbishop of Canterbury.

833 Ceolnoth becomes Archbishop of Canterbury.

835 The Danes begin to raid the Kentish coast.

836 Egbert's forces are defeated by an army of 25 shiploads of Danes at Carhampton in Somerset.

838 A large force of Danes arrives by sea in Cornwall. Egbert defeats the Danes and their Cornish allies at Hingston Down, putting them to flight.

839 Egbert, King of Wessex, dies after reigning for 37 years; he is succeeded by his son Athelstan as sub-king of Kent, Essex, Sussex and Surrey, and by his son Ethelwulf as King of Wessex. The Pictish king is killed by Danes.

840 In this year the Danes are reported as landing and wintering on the coasts of Britain. Ealdorman Wulfheard fights against 37 ship-companies of Danes at Southampton, and succeeds in beating them off. Ealdorman Aethelhun fights the Danes at Portland: Aethelhun is killed and the Danes hold the field. Wiglaf, King of Mercia, dies and is succeeded by Beorhtwulf. At about this time the Stone of Destiny is removed, probably from Iona, to Scone Abbey by King Kenelm II.

841 Ealdorman Herebryht is killed by Danes, and many of the people of Romney Marsh with him. The same Danish force is responsible for killing many more people in Kent, East Anglia and Lincolnshire. The Danes found Dublin as a trading station and power base in Ireland. Eanred, King of Northumbria, dies and is succeeded by his son Ethelred II.

842 The Danes kill many in London and Rochester.

844 Kenneth MacAlpin becomes King of Picts as well as Scots, forming the Kingdom of Alba.

845 A Saxon force consisting of men from Somerset under ealdorman Eanulf and men from Dorset under ealdorman Osric meets a Danish army in battle at the mouth of the River Parrett: the Danes are defeated.

849 King Alfred is born, the fifth son of Ethelwulf, at Wantage. Wystan, heir to the Mercian throne, is murdered by his godfather.

850 Ethelred II, King of Northumbria, dies and is succeeded by
Osbert.

851 Danes overwinter in southern England. 350 shiploads of
Danes sail into the Thames estuary and sack London. The
Danes pillage Canterbury and put to flight King Beorhtwulf
of Mercia and his troops. After this they advance into Surrey,
where they are met by West Saxon troops under Ethelwulf
and his son Ethelbald; a great battle follows resulting in a
major Saxon victory. Later in the year Athelstan fights a sea
battle with the Danes off Sandwich, capturing nine ships and
scattering the rest.

852 Beorhtwulf, King of Mercia, dies and is succeeded by
Burgred.

853 Alfred visits Rome and is honoured by the Pope. With the
aid of King Ethelwulf, King Burgred of Mercia defeats the
Welsh. On Thanet, the men of Kent under Ealhere and the
men of Surrey under Hutha fight against the Danes; many
are killed on both sides, including the two ealdormen. King
Burgred of Mercia marries King Ethelwulf's daughter.

855 Alfred makes a state visit to Rome with his father, King
Ethelwulf: they remain in Rome for 12 months. The Danes
spend their first winter on the Isle of Sheppey. Edmund
becomes King of East Anglia.

856 On his return journey from Rome, Ethelwulf marries Judith,
the daughter of Charles the Bold, King of the Franks.

858
Jan   [13] Ethelwulf, King of Wessex, dies and is succeeded by his
son Ethelbald, who has been his co-ruler for three years and
who marries his stepmother, Judith.

860 Ethelbald, King of Wessex, dies and is buried at Sherborne;
he is succeeded by his brother Ethelbert. The Danes attack
Winchester.

863 Aelle becomes King of Northumbria.

865 Ethelbert, King of Wessex, dies and is buried at Sherborne; he is succeeded by his brother Ethelred. The Danish force remains in Thanet and makes peace with the Kentish; the Kentish promise them payment for the truce, but the Danes steal out at night and ravage eastern Kent. The Danish 'Great Army' under the command of Halfdan and Ivarr the Boneless lands on the coast of East Anglia.

866 The 'Great Army' of Danes moves across England.

867 The 'Great Army' takes control of York and ravages Northumbria and Mercia. Alfred marries Elswitha of Mercia. Aelle, King of Northumbria, is murdered by Ragnar Lothbrok; Egbert I is set up as a puppet king by the Danes.

868 Alfred goes with his elder brother King Ethelred in an attempt to dislodge the Vikings from Nottingham.

869 The Great Army descends again on East Anglia.

870 Archbishop Ceolnoth dies and is succeeded by Ethelred as Archbishop of Canterbury.

Nov [20] The Danes murder Edmund, King of East Anglia, when he refuses to become their subject; he is succeeded by Oswald, the last English king of East Anglia. The Danes move further south and penetrate up the Thames valley as far as Reading, camping there in readiness for an invasion of Wessex.

871 Battle of Ashdown: King Ethelred of Wessex and Alfred, his younger brother, lead the Wessex armies to victory over the Danes under Kings Bagsac and Halfdan. King Ethelred dies in April of his battle wounds and is succeeded by Alfred as King of Wessex.

872 The Danes occupy London. Egbert I, the puppet king of Northumbria, is driven out.

873   The Danish occupation of north-east England continues.
Ricsige becomes King of Northumbria.

874   Mercia falls to the Danes and Burgred, King of Mercia, is
driven out; he goes to Rome, where he dies. Burgred is
succeeded by Ceolwulf II.

875   The Danes make renewed attacks on the east coast of
England. The monks of Lindisfarne put the bones of St Aidan
and the head of St Oswald into St Cuthbert's coffin and set
off, with the *Lindisfarne Gospels*, to wander about
Northumbria and Galloway for the next eight years. The
Danes under their leaders Guthrum, Oscytel and Anund turn
south and attack Wessex.The Viking kingdom of York is
founded by Halfdan.

876   Ricsige, King of Northumbria, dies and is succeeded by
Egbert II.

877   A Danish fleet of 120 ships is wrecked at Peveril Point,
Swanage.

878   The Danes agree to depart from Exeter and Wareham, but
this turns out to be a piece of deception. Guthrum makes a
surprise attack on Alfred at Chippenham; Alfred takes refuge
at Athelney. Battle of Edington: Alfred, leading troops from
all over southern England, succeeds in defeating the Danish
forces under Guthrum. Egbert II, King of Northumbria north
of the Tyne, dies; he is the last recorded king of
Northumbria.

879   Treaty of Wedmore, between Alfred and Guthrum; Guthrum
is baptized, and Alfred cedes England north of Watling
Street to the Danes.

880   Shaftesbury Abbey is founded. The Viking army settles on
the land in East Anglia under their leader Guthrum, who
assumes the name Athelstan at his baptism.

883 The monks of Lindisfarne settle at Chester-le-Street. Mercia is now ruled by ealdorman Ethelred, who acknowledges the overlordship of Alfred, King of Wessex.

886 Alfred takes and and occupies London. A treaty with Guthrum formally recognizes the Danelaw, the area of eastern England between Thames and Tees under Viking control; the line of Watling Street from London to Chester is taken as the frontier. Alfred begins to learn Latin.

889 Archbishop Ethelred dies.

890 Plegmund becomes Archbishop of Canterbury. Guthrum dies, possibly succeeded by Eric as ruler of the Danish kingdom of East Anglia.

892 A large Viking force under Haesten invades England, landing in the Thames estuary, but it has only a limited success.

893 At about this time, Pope Formosus (891-6) writes to the Archbishop of Canterbury complaining that 'the abominable rites of the pagans' have been revived in Britain: 'we were minded to cut you off from the body of the Church'.

896 Haesten's Viking invasion force disperses.

899
Oct [26] Alfred the Great dies and is succeeded by Edward the Elder, his son, as King of Wessex.

900

900
Jun [8] Coronation of Edward the Elder.

902 Eric, ruler of the Danish kingdom of East Anglia, dies at the Battle of the Holme.

903 Monks receive what they believe to be the body of King Edmund, who was murdered in 870, and bury the remains at Beodricsworth (later renamed Bury St Edmunds).

910 Asser, bishop of Sherborne, dies. The reconquest of the Danelaw begins.

914 Archbishop Plegmund dies, succeeded by Athelhelm as Archbishop of Canterbury.

917 Aethelflaed, King Edward the Elder's sister, takes Derby; the northern frontier of England now runs from the Wash to the Dee estuary.

918 Edward conquers East Anglia and southern England and receives the 'submissions' of the Welsh kings of Dyfed and Gwynedd.

919 Ragnald becomes ruler of the Viking kingdom of York; in the same year he acknowledges the overlordship of Edward the Elder.

920 Edward the Elder now rules England and Scotland as far north as the Forth and Clyde.

921 Edmund, the son of King Edward and Eadgifu, is born.

923 The King of Scots makes his submission to King Edward. Athelhelm dies and Wulfhelm becomes Archbishop of Canterbury.

924
Jul [17] King Edward the Elder dies and is succeeded by his son Athelstan.

926 Athelstan compels Welsh, Danish and Scots under-kings to renew the oaths of allegiance they made to his father.

927 The effective northern frontier of England is marked by the River Tees. Athelstan establishes direct rule over the Danes of York.

937 The Battle of Brunanburh, regarded as Athelstan's crowning victory; his English army defeats a combined force of Danes, Scots and Welsh. The West Saxon kings now have clear control over England.

939
Oct [27] King Athelstan of Wessex dies and is succeeded by his half-brother Edmund I.

940 Dunstan begins the refoundation of Glastonbury as a monastic house.

942 Wulfhelm dies and is succeeded by Oda as Archbishop of Canterbury.

943 Edgar, son of King Edmund and Aelfgifu, is born.

945 Edmund suppresses a Danish rebellion in Mercia and Northumbria and forms a loose alliance with Malcolm, King of Scots.

946
May [26] King Edmund I is murdered by the outlaw Leofa in his hall at Pucklechurch in Gloucestershire; he is succeeded by his brother Edred.

947 York once again falls to the Danes, under Eric Bloodaxe.

948 Eric Bloodaxe establishes himself as King of York, but is driven out in the same year.

952 The Danes drive Anlaf Sihtricson out of York, and take Eric Bloodaxe back as their leader.

954 King Edred invades Northumbria, driving Eric Bloodaxe out of York. King Eric and his household make for Solway Firth, but they are ambushed and killed in the Stainmore Pass in the Pennines. England is formally and permanently unified from this time onwards.

955 King Edred dies and is succeeded by Edwig the All-Fair, his nephew.

957 Edwig's brother Edgar leads a rebellion against him and is proclaimed King of Mercia. Dunstan becomes Bishop of London.

958 Oda dies, succeeded by Alfsige as Archbishop of Canterbury; Alfsige also dies, succeeded by Beorhtelm, who is deposed.

959 Edwig dies, succeeded by Edgar the Peaceable, who reunites England. Dunstan leads the movement for monastic reform.

960 Dunstan becomes Archbishop of Canterbury.

965 Westminster Abbey is founded.

966 Crowland Abbey is founded at about this time.

973 Edgar's supremacy as Emperor of Britain is asserted by a solemn coronation by Dunstan at Bath on May 11. The antiphon 'Zadok the Priest' is sung – as it has been at all subsequent coronations. Edgar sails with his fleet to Chester to meet eight British or Welsh sub-kings, who swear fealty to him and row him on the River Dee while Edgar holds the rudder.

975
Jul [8] Edgar the Peaceable dies and is succeeded by his 13-year-old son, Edward the Martyr.

979
Mar [18] King Edward the Martyr is murdered at Corfe Castle; he is succeeded by Ethelred II (the Unready or Ill-advised). Edward is revered as a martyr.

980 From this year, there are increasing numbers of Danish raids. They succeed because of Ethelred's inability to unite the English. Anlaf, King of the Danes in the area round Dublin, abdicates and goes to live as a penitent on Iona.

986 Danes raid Iona, killing the abbot and six monks on the White Sands.

988 Dunstan dies and is succeeded by Athelgar as Archbishop of Canterbury.

990 Athelgar dies and is succeeded by Sigeric Serio as Archbishop of Canterbury.

991 Battle of Maldon: Byrhtnoth of Essex is defeated by the Danes; this is the first Danish victory over the English for 100 years. There are renewed Viking raids on England. 10,000 pounds of silver are paid as Danegeld.

994 The Danish king Sweyn (or Sven) leads an attack on England. Archbishop Sigeric dies.

995 The Lindisfarne community, driven south by the Danes, resettles in Durham, building 'a little church of wands and branches'. Aelfric becomes Archbishop of Canterbury.

997 Another Viking raid.

1000

1002 Ethelred marries Emma, daughter of Richard Duke of Normandy. Massacre of St Brice's Day: Ethelred, motivated by fear and suspicion, attempts to exterminate the Danes in England. The Danes in Oxford take refuge in St Frideswide's minster church, but the citizens burn it down. Among the casualties are Gunhild, Sweyn's sister, and her family.

1003 King Sweyn leads an invasion of England, prompted by the massacre of Danes. After landing on the East Anglian coast, Sweyn sacks Norwich.

1005 King Sweyn leaves England, returning to Denmark. Lanfranc, Archbishop of Canterbury, is born. Alphege becomes Archbishop of Canterbury.

1006 King Sweyn returns, leading his army through Berkshire, Hampshire and Wiltshire.

1009 80 ships of the new English fleet are burnt through the treachery of an English captain. A Danish army lands, led by Hemming and Thorkill the Tall.

1010 Thorkill's force burns Oxford and then moves across into East Anglia.

1012 The Danes raid Kent, burning Canterbury Cathedral; Archbishop Alphege is taken prisoner by the Danes and held at Greeenwich.

Apr [19] During a drunken feast, the Danes murder Alphege. Thorkill, disgusted by his troops' brutality in murdering Alphege, changes sides and brings 45 ships into Ethelred's service.

1013 King Sweyn lands at Sandwich in Kent and establishes his rule over all England. The men of the Danelaw welcome a Danish king and accept Sweyn almost immediately. King Ethelred flees to Normandy. King Sweyn (Forkbeard) sails in triumph up the River Trent to Gainsborough, where he receives the submission of the Northumbrians, the men of Lindsey, and the Danish settlers of north-east Mercia. Lyfing becomes Archbishop of Canterbury.

1014 Battle of Clontarf: Brian Boru, the Irish king, defeats Danish raiders decisively. From this time on, the Danes settle to peaceable trading with the Irish. King Sweyn dies and Ethelred is restored, but the Danish army in England elect Cnut (also spelt Canute) as their king.

1016 Ethelred ravages the old kingdom of Lindsey (part of Lincolnshire), for its complicity in the Danish invasions.

Apr [23] Ethelred dies and is succeeded by his son Edmund II, Ironside. Edmund and Cnut fight for the kingdom. Edmund comes to an agreement with Cnut whereby he secures Wessex and leaves Cnut in possession of the rest of England.

Nov [30] Edmund is murdered, probably at the instigation of Edric Streona. Cnut, son of Sweyn Forkbeard, becomes King of England.

1017 Cnut I divides England into four earldoms. Edric Streona is executed and succeeded as ruler of Mercia by Leofric. Gloucester Abbey is founded.

1018 The Oxford assembly accepts Cnut as king. Buckfast Abbey is founded.

1020 Bury St Edmunds Abbey is founded. Lyfing dies, succeeded by Åthelnoth as Archbishop of Canterbury.

1022 Harold Godwinson is born.

1025 At about this time King Cnut's sister runs a lucrative white slave trade, selling English girls to Scandinavia.

1027 William the Conqueror is born in Normandy. Cnut makes a pilgrimage to Rome, demonstrating his alliance with the Church.

1028 In addition to his existing kingdoms, Cnut becomes King of Norway, including Greenland, Orkney, Shetland, Hebrides, Isle of Man; he is now in effect head of a huge Scandinavian empire.

1031 Cnut travels to Scotland and compels Malcolm, King of Scots, to acknowledge his overlordship.

1032 A new stone abbey is dedicated at Bury St Edmunds, on Cnut's orders.

1033 St Anselm is born. The bones of St Alphege are transferred by Cnut from St Paul's Cathedral to Canterbury Cathedral.

1034
Nov [25] Malcolm II of Scotland dies and is succeeded by Duncan I.

1035 William becomes Duke of Normandy.

Nov [12] Cnut I dies at the age of 40, and his empire disintegrates. Harold I, Cnut's son by Aelgifu of Northampton, becomes Regent of England while his half-brother delays in Denmark. England splits once more into the old pattern of Northumbria and Mercia against Wessex.

1036 Alfred and Edward, the sons of Ethelred, return to England from Normandy. On Harold's orders, Alfred is seized and savagely blinded: he dies at Ely. Edward returns to the safety of Normandy.

1037 Archbishop John, who died in 721, is canonized; his body is reburied in a gold-plated shrine at Beverley Minster. The Witan makes Harold I, Cnut's illegitimate son, king.

1038 Eadsige becomes Archbishop of Canterbury.

1040

Mar [17] Harold I dies and is succeeded by Harthacnut (or Cnut II), the son of Cnut by Emma.

Aug [14] Macbeth murders Duncan, King of Scotland: Macbeth himself becomes king.

1041 The men of Worcester murder Harthacnut's tax collectors. Danes burn the monastery at Worcester; Bishop Wulfstan begins rebuilding on a larger scale. Edward the Confessor resides with King Harthacnut, who seems to regard Edward as his successor.

1042

Jun [8] Harthacnut dies and Edward the Confessor, son of Ethelred the Unready, becomes King of England; the English line of kings is restored.

1043

Apr [3] Edward the Confessor is crowned.

1045

Jan [23] King Edward marries Edith, daughter of Earl Godwin.

1051 Duke William of Normandy visits England. Edward welcomes him and promises the English succession to him, during a quarrel with Edward's father-in-law, Earl Godwin, over the King's preference for Norman courtiers. Godwin is exiled. Robert Champert of Jumièges becomes Archbishop of Canterbury.

1052 Westminster Abbey is founded by Edward the Confessor. Earl Godwin dies, choking on a crust at a banquet, and is succeeded by his son Harold; Harold, now leader of the army, is in favour with the King. Archbishop Robert is expelled: Stigand becomes Archbishop of Canterbury as well as Bishop of Winchester.

1054 Malcolm III succeeds to the Scottish throne.

1055 Siward, Earl of Northumberland, dies; Harold's untrustworthy brother Tostig is elevated to the earldom in his place.

1056 Harold Godwinson wages a campaign against Griffith ap Llewellyn, the ruler of Wales.

1057
Aug [15] Macbeth, King of Scots, dies and is succeeded by his stepson Lulach. Leofric, Earl of Mercia, dies and is succeeded by his son Aelfgar, who surrenders the earldom of East Anglia. East Anglia is bestowed on Harold's brother Gurth. Another of Harold's brothers, Leofwine, is given an earldom made up of the counties north and south of London.

1058 A Norwegian expedition against England is repulsed.
Mar [17] Lulach, King of Scots, dies and is succeeded by Malcolm III (Canmore), the son of Duncan I.

1060 Waltham Abbey is completed and consecrated.

1062 Aelfgar, Earl of Mercia, dies and is succeeded by his young son Edwin.

1063 Harold Godwinson wages his second campaign against the aggressions of Griffith ap Llewellyn, King of North Wales. Griffith is killed by his own men.

1064 Harold is shipwrecked on the Normandy coast and falls by chance into the hands of Duke William; he is apparently forced to swear an oath promising William the English Crown.

1065
Nov   Northumbria rebels against Earl Tostig, who is forced into
      exile: he becomes Harold's enemy because Harold does not
      support him.

1066
Jan   [5] Edward the Confessor dies; Harold Godwinson, Earl of
      Wessex, is chosen by the Witan to succeed him the next day.
Sep   [25] Tostig invades Northumbria with a Norwegian army.
      Battle of Stamford Bridge: Harold's English army defeats an
      army led by Harold Hardrada, King of Norway, and Tostig,
      the English king's brother. [28] William Duke of Normandy
      disembarks in Pevensey Bay. Harold begins the march south
      to meet him.
Oct   [14] Battle of Hastings: the English lose the battle partly
      because they leave their strong position on the crest of a
      ridge, and partly because they are exhausted by Stamford
      Bridge and the long march south. The Witan chooses Edgar
      Atheling, grandson of Edmund Ironside, as king. William
      circles London and approaches from the north. At
      Berkhamsted, Edgar and other Saxon notables meet William
      and offer him the Crown.
Dec   [25] William is crowned King in Westminster Abbey.

1067   William is absent in Normandy from February to December.
           Battle Abbey is founded to commemorate his victory. The
           Saxon cathedral at Canterbury is burnt down. A rebellion
           against William in Kent, led by Eustace of Boulogne, is easily
           suppressed.

1068   Henry I is born, son of William I and Matilda.

1069   Rebellion against the Norman invasion breaks out in Mercia
           and Northumbria; William's troops devastate the north in
           retaliation.

1070   Council at Winchester summoned and presided over by the
           King: Stigand is deposed and Lanfranc becomes Archbishop
           of Canterbury.

1071 Revolt of Hereward the Wake in the Fens.

1072 William extends his conquest to Scotland. St Margaret orders the abbey on Iona to be rebuilt. A Council at Winchester settles the controversy over the primacy of Canterbury. The Normans capture Ely.

1079 Robert of Normandy rebels against his father in an attempt to gain possession of Normandy for himself. He is defeated by his father, the Conqueror, and reconciled to him.

1080 Pope Gregory VII demands that William should do him homage as his vassal, but William refuses on the grounds that it has not been offered by any of his predecessors.

1083 William's queen, Matilda of Flanders, dies.

1086 The Domesday Book is compiled.

1087
Sep [9] William the Conqueror dies at Rouen, as a result of injuries sustained in a horse-riding accident. [26] Coronation of William II of England.

1088 Rebellion in support of Robert Curthose.

1089
May [28] Archbishop Lanfranc dies: the archbishopric remains vacant for four years.

1090 William II wages war on his brother Robert in Normandy.

1091 Malcolm III of Scotland invades England, but is horrified at the English army that confronts him: he readily agrees to offer William homage and acknowledge him as overlord. William is absent from England from February to August. In the Treaty of Caen, William II and Robert of Normandy agree terms: whichever survives will succeed to the dominions of his brother.

1093 Anselm becomes Archbishop of Canterbury.

Nov [13] Malcolm III of Scotland dies, succeeded by Donald Bane, his brother. Queen Margaret, widow of Malcolm III, dies.

1094 Rebellions by the Welsh and by the English barons. William II is absent March-December.

May King Donald Bane is deposed and Duncan II, son of King Malcolm, becomes King of Scots.

Nov [12] Duncan II dies and Donald Bane is reinstated.

1095 William II calls a council at Rockingham to settle the dispute between himself and Anselm. To William's consternation Anselm appeals to Rome, arguing that he may not be tried in a secular court.

1096 William II is absent in France from September. The First Crusade begins.

1097 King Donald Bane of Scotland is deposed; with William's intervention he is succeeded by Edgar, son of Malcolm III. Archbishop Anselm, frustrated by powerlessness, seeks to confer with the Pope; he sails from Dover, leaving the Canterbury estates in the King's hands.

1098 William II is absent from England all year.

1099 The First Crusade ends. William returns to England in April, absent again June-September.

1100

1100
Aug [2] William II dies in a New Forest hunting accident. Henry I becomes King of England, taking possession immediately of the treasury at Winchester. [5] Henry I is crowned at Westminster Abbey.

1101
Jul Duke Robert of Normandy lands at Portsmouth; many barons flock to his side, but Henry I is also strongly supported. Negotiation at Alton results in Robert's withdrawal on a pension of £2000 a year, on condition that he renounces his claim to the English throne.

1102 Henry I orders Edward the Confessor's tomb to be opened, and the rumour that the body has not decayed is found to be true. Bishop Gundulf of Rochester is strongly rebuked by Abbot Crispin for trying to pull out some tufts of hair from King Edward's white beard, which he wanted to take home as a relic.

1104 The bones of St Cuthbert are buried in the still-incomplete Durham Cathedral.

1106 Battle of Tinchebrai: Henry I acquires Normandy and captures his brother Robert, who remains a captive for the rest of his life in Cardiff Castle.

1107
Jan [8] King Edgar of Scotland dies and is succeeded by his brother Alexander I.

1109
Apr [21] Archbishop Anselm dies, and his archbishopric remains vacant for five years.

1114 Ralph, Bishop of Rochester, becomes Archbishop of Canterbury.

1117 Magnus (St Magnus), Earl of Orkney, is murdered on the island of Egilsay in Orkney.

1118 Henry I spends the whole year in Normandy, fighting the forces of the French King, the Count of Anjou and the Count of Flanders; while he is overseas, England is governed by a vice-regal committee. Henry's queen, Matilda, dies.

Dec [21] Thomas Becket is born at a house in Cheapside.

1119 The Order of Knights Templars is founded.

1120 The wreck of the *White Ship*; William, the heir to the English throne and Henry I's only legitimate son, is drowned.

1122 Archbishop Ralph of Canterbury dies. Henry I remarries, with the aim of producing a new heir, but the marriage proves childless.

1123 William of Corbeil becomes Archbishop of Canterbury.

1124

Apr   [25] Alexander I dies; his brother David I succeeds to the Scottish throne.

1125 Edgar the Atheling, grandson of the Saxon king Edmund II (Ironside) dies.

1128 Henry I's only surviving legitimate child, Matilda, is married to the 14-year-old Geoffrey Plantagenet. Henry compels the English barons to swear to receive Matilda as their queen on his death.

1131 Henry I again insists that his barons swear to recognize Matilda as his successor.

1133

Mar   [5] Henry II is born at Le Mans, the son of Geoffrey, Count of Anjou and Matilda, Henry I's daughter.

1134 Duke Robert of Normandy dies.

1135

Dec   [1] Henry I dies near Rouen. [22] Coronation of King Stephen, followed by civil war between supporters of Stephen and supporters of Matilda. The Scots invade England.

1136 William of Corbeil, Archbishop of Canterbury, dies. The King's castle at Norwich is attacked and captured by the Earl of Norfolk.

1137 The Earl of Gloucester, an illegitimate son of Henry I, begins plotting on his half-sister Matilda's behalf.

1138 Battle of the Standard: Thurston, Archbishop of York, organizes an English army to resist the attack of David, the Scots' king, who tries to invade England. It is a resounding English victory. Archbishop Thurston carries with him into battle the banner of St John of Beverley, together with those of St Cuthbert, St Peter of York and St Wilfrid, 'all suspended from one pole like the mast of a ship. The pole was stepped in a four-wheeled cart, on which the bishop stood'.

1139 Theobald of Bec becomes Archbishop of Canterbury. Matilda lands in England, openly supported now by the Earl of Gloucester; the civil war between Stephen and Matilda continues.

1140 St William of Norwich, a 12-year-old skinner's apprentice, is murdered; the citizens of Norwich assume that he has been sacrificed by Jews, which starts a wave of anti-Semitism in England and France.

1141
Feb Battle of Lincoln: Stephen is captured and later exchanged for Robert, Earl of Gloucester. The civil war is resumed.

1143 William the Lion, King of Scots, is born.

1147 Matilda's main supporter, Robert of Gloucester, dies. The Second Crusade begins.

1148 Disheartened, Matilda leaves England never to return.

1149 Northumbria is ceded to David, King of Scots. The Second Crusade ends.

1151 King Stephen's wife Matilda dies. Count Geoffrey of Anjou dies, succeeded by Henry, who for a time is diverted from English affairs to deal with his estates in France.

1152 Henry of Anjou, later Henry II, marries Eleanor of Aquitaine, following her divorce from Louis VII. King Stephen's son Eustace dies. Geoffrey of Monmouth, author of *History of the Kings of Britain*, dies.

1153 William, son of Henry of Anjou and Eleanor, is born. Henry invades England to claim his inheritance, and is promised the English succession in the Treaties of Wallingford, Winchester and Westminster.

1154
Oct [10] Roger of Pont L'Eveque becomes Archbishop of York.
[24] King Stephen dies and is buried at Faversham.
Dec [4] Nicholas Breakspear becomes the first and only English
pope – Adrian IV. [8] Henry of Anjou arrives in England. [19]
Henry II of Anjou is crowned King and immediately appoints
Thomas Becket his chancellor, apparently on Archbishop
Theobald's recommendation. The founding of the House of
Plantagenet (Angevin) (1154-1399).

1155
Feb [28] Henry, son of Henry II, is born. The composer Berbart
de Ventadorn visits England. The beginning of Henry II's
struggle to reduce clerical encroachment on the Royal Courts.

1156 Prince William dies. Matilda, third child and first daughter of
Henry II, is born.

1157
Sep [8] Richard I, Duke of Aquitaine, is born at Oxford, the son of
Henry II and Eleanor of Aquitaine. Henry regains
Northumbria from King David of Scotland.

1158
Sep [23] Geoffrey, Duke of Brittany, is born, the son of Henry II
and Eleanor of Aquitaine.

1159
Sep [1] Pope Adrian IV, Nicholas Breakspear, dies.

1161 Eleanor, the sixth child of Henry II, is born.
Apr [18] Theobald of Bec, Archbishop of Canterbury, dies.

1162
Jun [3] Henry II appoints his Chancellor, Thomas Becket, as
Archbishop of Canterbury.

1163
Oct [13] The remains of Edward the Confessor are translated to a
new shrine built at Henry II's orders. The still-undecayed
body is carried to the new tomb by Archbishop Thomas
Becket, Henry II and the Abbot of Westminster.

1164

Jan [13] Council of Clarendon: Henry II obtains ratification for a code based on the practices of Henry I, 'The Constitutions of Clarendon'. Thomas Becket, supported by his bishops, rejects the Constitutions because they limit the power and freedom of the Church. The rift between King and Archbishop widens.

Oct [6] Council of Northampton: this develops into a trial at which Becket is pronounced guilty of feudal disobedience: in fear of his life, Becket rides away to Grantham in the middle of the night.

Nov [2] Becket leaves England and goes into voluntary exile.

1165

Oct Joan, Henry II's seventh child, is born. The Welsh revolt.

Dec [9] Malcolm IV of Scotland dies, succeeded by his brother William the Lion.

1166 Assize of Clarendon: Henry II orders an enquiry into all the crimes committed since the beginning of his reign.

1167 Oxford University is founded at about this time. The Empress Matilda dies.

Dec [24] King John is born at Beaumont Palace in Oxford, the last child of Henry II and Eleanor of Aquitaine.

1168 Princess Matilda marries Henry the Lion, Duke of Saxony.

1169 The dispossessed King of Leinster seeks help in recovering his Crown. Strongbow, Earl of Pembroke, invades Ireland with a small force of Norman adventurers; this is the beginning of Anglo-Norman rule in Ireland.

1170

Jun [14] Coronation of the young king, Prince Henry; he uses the style 'King of the English' and is actually referred to by some chroniclers as 'Henry III'.

Dec [2] Thomas Becket returns to Canterbury from his exile. [29] Thomas Becket is murdered in Canterbury Cathedral by four of Henry II's knights, Reginald Fitzurse, William de Tracy, Hugh de Morville and Richard le Breton – on Henry II's orders.

1171 Benedict, the custodian of Thomas Becket's shrine in the crypt at Canterbury, records 14 miraculous cures among the pilgrims approaching the shrine; a cult begins. Strongbow becomes King of Leinster, which arouses Henry II's suspicions. Henry embarks in person on the conquest of Ireland, landing at Waterford and meeting no opposition.

1173 Rebellion against Henry II: William the Lion, King of Scots, invades the north of England. Henry resorts, for the only time in England, to the use of mercenary troops in the suppression of this feudal revolt.

1174
Apr   [7] Richard of Dover becomes Archbishop of Canterbury.
Sep   [4] The Choir of Canterbury Cathedral is gutted by fire. The rebuilding of the Choir marks the first appearance in England of the pointed arch. William the Lion is taken prisoner at Alnwick.

1176 Princess Eleanor marries Alphonso VIII, King of Castile. Assize of Northampton: England is divided into six circuits, each with its own itinerant justices.

1177 A great fire destroys much of Rochester in Kent. A monk steals the bones of St Petroc from Bodmin Priory and takes them to Brittany; Henry II instigates a search for them and they are returned.

1178
Jun   [18] A violent explosion is seen on the moon; later astronomers calculate that this may have been the meteor impact that created the crater known as Giordano Bruno.

1181 The Assize of Arms: a major reorganization of the English militias.

1183 Death of the young king, Prince Henry, of a fever.

1184 Glastonbury Abbey is badly damaged by fire; rapid rebuilding begins at once.

Dec [16] Baldwin becomes Archbishop of Canterbury.

1185 Lincoln Cathedral is destroyed by an earthquake.

1186 The rebuilding of Lincoln and Chichester Cathedrals begins. A great fire sweeps through Chester. Aaron the Jew dies at Lincoln, leaving a fabulous fortune which is seized by the King.

Aug [19] Prince Geoffrey, Henry II's third son, dies at a tournament.

1188
Jul [10] Henry II leaves England for the last time.

1189 Princess Matilda, Henry II's daughter, dies.

Jul [6] Henry II dies at Chinon, succeeded by his son Richard I, Coeur de Lion.

Aug [29] Prince John marries Isabella of Gloucester.

Sep [3] Coronation of Richard I in Westminster Abbey. The Third Crusade is launched, led by Frederick Barbarossa, Philip Augustus of France and Richard I of England.

1190
Jul Richard I leaves for the crusade; William Longchamp, Bishop of Ely, is appointed Justiciar.

1191 A Glastonbury monk sees a vision of the coffin of Arthur and Guinevere buried between two pyramids in the Glastonbury burial ground.

May [12] Richard I marries Berengaria of Navarre. Acre is captured by the crusaders.

1192 The Third Crusade ends without regaining Jerusalem. Richard I is seized and held to ransom in Austria on his return journey.

1193 Hubert Walter becomes Archbishop of Canterbury.

1194 At a cost of 100,000 marks, Richard I is ransomed and released.

Mar   Richard returns to England.

Apr   [16] King Richard I takes a bath. The Judicial Inquiry: a
       questionnaire is sent to all local jurors to assess how local
       government is working.

1198

Aug   [24] Alexander II, King of Scotland, is born, the son of
       William I and Ermengarde. The New Fiscal Assessment:
       Hubert Walter reintroduces the idea of a land tax, based on
       100-acre units of arable land, but the scheme is not fully
       worked out or applied.

1199

Apr   [6] Richard I dies from a crossbow wound received while
       besieging Chaluz Castle.

May   [27] John becomes King of England. Establishment of
       Chancery Rolls.

1200

1200

May   Treaty of Le Goulet: the French king recognizes John's
       French possessions, in return for which John surrenders the
       Vexin, pays 20,000 marks, and acknowledges King Philip as
       his overlord in France.

1202 Queen Eleanor, widow of Henry II, dies.

1204 England loses Normandy to France when Philip II of France
       calls King John to account for the murder of Arthur, John's
       nephew. Beaulieu Abbey is founded.

1205 On the death of Archbishop Hubert, the Canterbury monks
       fail to agree on a successor: some favour Reginald, others
       John de Grey. They appeal to Rome to settle the dispute.

1207 Pope Innocent III sets aside both Canterbury candidates.

Jun   [12] Stephen Langton becomes Archbishop of Canterbury.
       King John makes a pilgrimage, in great state, to the shrines
       of Saints Oswald and Wulfstan at Worcester.

Oct [1] Henry III, the son of King John, is born at Winchester.

1208 Simon de Montfort is born. King John refuses to allow
Stephen Langton, elected Archbishop of Canterbury in
Rome, into England; the Pope, Innocent III, places England
under interdict.

1209 Cambridge University is founded at about this time.

Jan [5] Prince Richard, son of King John, is born. Pope Innocent
III excommunicates King John and declares him deposed.

1210 Llewellyn's revolt in Wales.

Jul [22] Joan, daughter of King John, is born.

1213

May Pope Innocent III authorizes the French King Philip to
prepare an invasion to enforce John's deposition. John
surrenders to this pressure, accepting the Pope as overlord,
and the interdict is lifted. A great fire destroys Southwark.

Aug Stephen Langton summons a select meeting of barons and
prelates in St Paul's to discuss a formula that will provide
redress for grievances without open conflict.

1214 Isabella, daughter of King John, is born. Roger Bacon is born
at about this time. Battle of Bouvines, in which the French
are victorious; this is followed by open rebellion against King
John in England. At Bury St Edmunds the barons swear to
compel John to grant a charter of rights and liberties, by force
if necessary.

Dec [4] William the Lion, King of Scotland, dies, succeeded by his
son Alexander II.

1215 Eleanor, daughter of King John, is born. At Brackley the
barons assemble and restate their demands before advancing
to London to confront the King.

Jun [15] Magna Carta: King John is compelled by his barons and
prelates to sign the Great Charter at Runnymede.

1216 The barons invite King Philip's son Louis to take the English
throne. Many of the barons desert John for Louis. John

prepares to march on London, but while crossing the Nene estuary he loses his treasure when a rising tide cuts off his baggage train. There are French raids on the south coast of England.

Oct   [19] King John dies unexpectedly at Newark, of a fever, and is succeeded by Henry III. [28] Coronation of Henry III; the Earl of Pembroke is appointed Governor during the King's minority.

1217

May   Battle of Lincoln.

Aug   Battle of Dover. The French under Louis, later Louis VIII, are driven out of England. Treaty of Lambeth: Louis is able to exact reasonable terms for himself and his supporters before withdrawing to France.

1219

May   Earl of Pembroke dies, leaving the direction of the Great Council of magnates to Hubert de Burgh, Peter des Roches, Bishop of Winchester and the new papal legate, Pandulf.

1220

Jul   [7] In Canterbury Cathedral, Henry III and a host of bishops, abbots, lords and ladies witness the translation of St Thomas; Archbishop Stephen Langton carries the bones of Thomas Becket up from the old shrine in the crypt to a magnificent new shrine in the newly-built Trinity Chapel.

1221 Dominican and Franciscan friars begin arriving in England.

Jun   [19] Princess Joan, King John's daughter, marries Alexander II of Scotland.

1224 Eleanor, daughter of King John, marries William Marshal, Earl of Pembroke. An important Great Council of magnates is convened, when the King is declared formally of age.

Jul   [19] The foundation stone of Elgin Cathedral is laid.

1225 Thomas Aquinas is born.

1228

Jul   [9] Stephen Langton, Archbishop of Canterbury, dies.

1229
Jun   [10] Richard Grant becomes Archbishop of Canterbury.

1230 Queen Berengaria of Navarre, Richard the Lionheart's widow, dies.

1232 Hubert de Burgh falls from favour. Lacock Abbey, Wiltshire, is founded.

1234
Apr   [2] Edmund Rich becomes Archbishop of Canterbury.

1235
Jun   [11] Isabella, daughter of King John, marries Emperor Frederick II. Matthew Paris, monk of St Albans and a friend of Henry III, begins compiling the *Historia Maior*, covering world history; in the section dealing with the years 1235-59, he succeeds in producing a work of original research in which he glorifies England and all things English.

1236
Jan   [20] Henry III marries Eleanor of Provence.

1238
Jan   Eleanor, daughter of King John and widow of the Earl of Pembroke, marries Simon de Montfort, Earl of Leicester.

1239
Jun   [17] Edward I is born at Westminster.

1240 Edmund, Archbishop of Canterbury, dies. Llewellyn ap Iorworth, who united Wales and won independence from both the English kings and the Marcher lords, dies; his wife, Joan, was an illegitimate daughter of King John: she predeceased him in 1237.

Sep   [29] Margaret, daughter of Henry III, is born. At about this time the great council begins to be called 'Parliament'. Knights of the Shire are summoned sometimes to share in its discussions, but its membership and specific functions are far from precisely defined at this stage.

1242
Jun [25] Beatrice, daughter of Henry III, is born. Henry III launches an expensive and unsuccessful war to regain the lost English possessions in France.

1245
Jan [15] Boniface of Savoy becomes Archbishop of Canterbury. [16] Edmund 'Crouchback', son of Henry III, is born.

1246 Queen Isabella, King John's widow, dies.

1249 University College, Oxford, is founded.

Jul [8] Alexander II of Scotland dies, succeeded by his son Alexander III.

1252
Dec [26] Margaret, daughter of Henry III of England, marries Alexander III of Scotland.

1254 Henry III accepts the Pope's offer of the throne of Sicily. Prince Edward, later to be Edward I, marries Eleanor of Castile.

1255 A child is found drowned in a cesspool in Lincoln; 'Little St Hugh' is assumed to be a child-sacrifice, a victim of the Jewish community, and canonized, reinforcing the 'blood libel' against the Jews.

1257
Jan [13] Prince Richard, King John's second son, is elected King of the Romans.

1258 The Provisions of Oxford; the barons under Simon de Montfort force reforms on Henry III: his favourites are to be expelled from England and a committee of 24 appointed to reform the government.

May In the Treaty of Paris Henry III renounces those provinces in France that he has already lost, and becomes vassal of the French king for fiefs in the south-west of France that are still left to him.

Sep [20] Consecration of the newly-completed Salisbury Cathedral.

1259 Matthew Paris, chronicler and miniaturist, dies.

1260 Beatrice, daughter of Henry III, marries John de Dreux, later Duke of Brittany.

1261 The Pope absolves Henry III from his oath to keep the Provisions of Oxford.

1264

May Battle of Lewes: Simon de Montfort's troops defeat those of Henry III and Prince Edward. Henry III is captured and Simon's party becomes England's rulers.

Jun Eleanor, daughter of Prince Edward, is born. Simon de Montfort proposes a new form of government, the Forma Regiminis, by which a Council of Nine would be appointed to advise the King in his choice of ministers.

1265 Simon de Montfort's Parliament; burgesses are called as representatives of certain boroughs for the first time.

Aug [4] Battle of Evesham: defeat, death and dismemberment of Simon de Montfort. The battle is the first recorded occasion when a British commander – in this case Prince Edward – exploits an inferior position by taking on one at a time, and defeating, sections of a divided enemy force.

Oct [26] Edmund 'Crouchback' is created Earl of Leicester.

1266 Dictum of Kenilworth, restoring Henry III's full authority and annulling the Provisions of Oxford. The Isle of Man and Hebrides are ceded to the Kingdom of Scotland by Norway.

Jun [10] John, son of Prince Edward, is born.

1267 Treaty of Montgomery: Henry III recognizes Llewellyn ap Gruffyd as Prince of Wales.

Jun [30] Edmund 'Crouchback' is created Earl of Lancaster.

1268 Balliol College, Oxford, is founded.

Oct [13] Edward the Confessor's body is translated to an even more magnificent new shrine, built at Henry III's orders.

1270 Elgin Cathedral is burnt.

1272 Prince Richard, King of the Romans, dies. William Wallace, the Scottish patriot, is born.

Nov [16] Henry III dies at Westminster, succeeded by his eldest son, Edward I. Edward is in Sicily as the time of his father's death, and stays abroad until August 1274; the country is ruled by regents during this time: Walter Giffard, Archbishop of York, Roger Mortimer and Robert Burnel.

1274
Jul [11] Robert Bruce is born at Turnberry in Ayrshire.
Aug [2] Edward I arrives back in England.

1275
Sep [11] Margaret, daughter of Edward I, is born.
Feb [19] John Pecham becomes Archbishop of Canterbury.

1276 First Welsh War begins.

1277 Roger Bacon is imprisoned for heresy. The Welsh War ends.

1279 Statute of Mortmain: the Church is forbidden to inherit any lay person's property without royal licence.

1282 Rebellion in Wales against English rule. Llewellyn is killed. Edward I succeeds in conquering Wales. Llewellyn's brother Dafydd is captured, tried and executed as a traitor.

1284 The completion of Edward I's conquest of Wales. The Statute of Wales is enacted at Rhuddlan; Wales is formally annexed to England and henceforth subject to the same laws.

Apr [25] Edward II is born at Caernarvon Castle, the third son of Edward I. Peterhouse at Cambridge is founded.

1285 Statute of Winchester: the completion of Henry II's Assize of Arms, providing also for the appointment of Justices of the Peace.

1286
Mar [19] Alexander III, King of Scotland, dies after a fall from his horse, and he is succeeded by Margaret, 'Maid of Norway',

the daughter of Eric II of Norway, and Margaret the daughter of Alexander III. Edward I leaves England for Gascony.

1289   Edward I returns from Gascony.

1290   Queen Eleanor of Castile, Edward I's wife, dies. John Schorne becomes rector of North Marston, Buckinghamshire, achieving fame as an exorcist and miracle worker. Statute of Quia Emptores, intended to preserve the rights of lords over their tenants, but in fact it becomes the means of ending tenure by means of knight service.

Jul   [8] Margaret, Edward I's daughter, marries John, Duke of Brabant.

Sep   [26] Margaret, Queen of Scotland, 'Maid of Norway', dies at the age of seven in Orkney on her way to marry the six-year-old Edward of Caernarvon, which would have united the Crowns of England and Scotland. The first Scottish interregnum begins. Edward I begins his attempt to rule Scotland. Until now the Jews have been protected by kings as important sources of loans; but public opinion has turned against the Jews, and certain Italian houses are ready to finance royal loans instead. Expulsion of Jews from England.

Nov   [1] Massacre of Jews at York Castle.

1291   Queen Eleanor, Henry III's widow, dies. Edward asserts his overlordship of Scotland, persuading the Scots to place the principal Scottish castles in his hands.

1292
Nov   [17] The first interregnum in Scotland comes to an end. John Balliol succeeds to the Scottish throne, selected out of 13 competitors by Edward I.

1293
May   An Anglo-Gascon fleet defeats a larger Norman-French fleet off the coast of Brittany, and then sacks La Rochelle.

1294   Roger Bacon, the founder of experimental science, dies.
May   War with France begins.

Sep   [12] Rebellion breaks out again in Wales. [12] Robert
       Winchelsey becomes Archbishop of Canterbury.

1295 The Earl of Warwick's troops defeat those of the principal
       Welsh leader, Madog ap Llewellyn, breaking the back of the
       Welsh rebellion. The 'Model Parliament' of Edward I; two
       knights and two burgesses are called from each shire to vote
       taxes for him.

Oct   [23] Franco-Scottish alliance.

1296
Mar   John Balliol, the Scots' king, sends his defiance to Edward I
       and renounces his homage. Edward musters a large army at
       Newcastle in readiness for an invasion of Scotland.
Apr   [27] Edward I's advance guard defeats the Scottish host at
       Dunbar.
Jul   [10] John Balliol abdicates, forfeiting the throne for
       contumacy. Edward I takes the government of Scotland into
       his own hands in the second interregnum; he also, in a
       symbolic act, takes the Stone of Destiny from the Abbey at
       Scone to Westminster Abbey. Edward comes into conflict
       with the Church.

1297 The rights of the English Parliament to approve taxes and
       customs dues are confirmed, and also the right to initiate
       legislation.

Aug   [22] Edward I sails for Flanders.
Sep   [11] Battle of Stirling Bridge; Scots troops under William
       Wallace defeat the English.
Oct   [10] In Edward I's absence overseas, his regent and council
       come to terms with opposition leaders. Edward achieves
       nothing in Flanders, and makes a truce with King Philip IV.

1298 Battle of Falkirk; Edward I's troops defeat Wallace's.

1299 King Edward I of England marries Margaret of France. In
       Scotland, John Comyn is placed at the head of a Regency for
       his absent uncle John Balliol.

1300

1300 The English Law Courts are organized into three parts: the King's Bench, the Court of Common Pleas and the Court of the Exchequer.

1301
Feb [7] Edward of Caernarvon and Earl of Chester, later to become Edward II, is created Prince of Wales.

1302
Nov [14] Humphrey, son of Edward I, is born.

1303 John Comyn and his army defeat an English army at Roslin. In retaliation, Edward I for the third time reduces Scotland, and then makes a treaty with Comyn. The Carta Mercatoria grants merchants full freedom of trade and safe conduct, in return for customs dues.

1304 Scotland formally submits to Edward I.

1305
Aug [3] William Wallace, the Scots patriot and army commander, is betrayed. Sir John Menteith and 60 men surprise Wallace in his sleep at Robroystoun, capture him and take him to Carlisle. Wallace is given a show trial by the English. [23] Wallace is executed in London by hanging, drawing and quartering.
Sep An ordinance of Edward I sets out the planned shape of Scotland's future goverment.

1306
Feb [10] Robert Bruce meets John Comyn in the church at Dumfries and kills him: his motive is not known.
Mar [25] The second interregnum in Scotland ends. Robert Bruce is crowned King of Scotland; a revolt against Edward I begins.
Apr [5] Furious that his plan for Scotland has been circumvented, Edward I appoints Aymer de Valence as his personal lieutenant in Scotland.

Jun   Valence defeats Bruce at the Battle of Methven: many of
      those captured are afterwards executed. Bruce becomes a
      fugitive.

1307
May   Bruce defeats Valence at Loudon Hill.
Jul   [7] Edward I dies in the arms of his attendants at
      Burgh-on-Sands near Carlisle, during the march north to
      Scotland. [8] Edward I is succeeded by his son Edward II.
      Piers Gaveston, a Gascon knight previously banished by
      Edward I, is recalled by Edward and created Earl of
      Cornwall.

1308   The death of Duns Scotus.
Jan   [10] The Templars are suppressed in Britain. [25] Edward II
      marries Isabella, the daughter of Philip IV of France. While
      Edward II is in France, Piers Gaveston, Earl of Cornwall, is
      Regent.
Feb   [25] Coronation of Edward II.
Mar   In Parliament the earls demand that the King banish
      Gaveston. Gaveston leaves for the Lieutenancy of Ireland. In
      Scotland, Robert Bruce consolidates his position against his
      Scottish rivals.

1309   Robert Bruce holds his first Parliament at St Andrews.

1310   Edward II leads an English army into Scotland, but to no
      effect. Parliament appoints Lords Ordainers, 21 bishops and
      peers, to reform the government and regulate the King's
      household.

1311   Robert Bruce leads raids across the English border.

1312   Robert Bruce attacks Durham and Hexham. Piers Gaveston,
      the King's favourite, is recalled, seized by the Earl of
      Warwick and murdered.
Nov   [13] Edward III is born at Windsor Castle, the son of Edward
      II. [24] The King's new son is created Earl of Chester.

1313   Walter Reynolds becomes Archbishop of Canterbury.

Apr John Balliol, the ex-King of Scotland, dies.

1314 The war between England and Scotland begins again. The Buckinghamshire miracle-worker, John Schorne, dies; pilgrims flock to his tomb at North Marston.

Jun [24] Battle of Bannockburn: the victory of Robert Bruce's army over Edward II's much larger army secures Scotland's independence. Edward II escapes with difficulty to Dunbar and then sails to Berwick. Heavy rains ruin the grain harvests, causing a famine.

1315 Great famine, resulting from a second poor harvest. The Scots raid County Durham and lay siege to the city of Durham.

1316

Aug John, son of Edward II, is born. The food shortage continues.

1317 Food shortage continues: prices remain high.

1318

Apr The Scots take Berwick and threaten to conquer the whole of northern England.

Aug The Treaty of Leake: the English magnates succeed in imposing a programme of reform on the royal household, appointing a formal council.

1319 A truce is agreed between England and Scotland.

1320 Hugh Despenser and his son rise in favour at Edward II's court.

1321

Jan The Despensers put their castles into a state of defence.

Apr Civil war breaks out in England.

May [24]The Earl of Lancaster calls an assembly of the chief magnates of northern England; they promise to act together to preserve the peace and defend the realm.

Aug [19] Parliament passes formal judgement on the Despensers; they are sentenced to total forfeiture and banishment.

1322 The English-Scottish truce expires, and Scots cross the border
to raid northern England as far south as Preston.

Feb   Thomas, Earl of Lancaster, is denounced as a rebel.

Mar   [16] Edward II defeats his opponents at Boroughbridge. [22]
Edward II orders the execution of the Earl of Lancaster at
Pontefract. This is the first time a summary sentence of death
and forfeiture for high treason has ever been passed on a
peer of the realm.

May   [2] Statute of York, revoking the earlier Ordinances.

1323

May   [30] A 13-year truce is agreed between England and Scotland
at Bishopthorpe.

1324 William of Wykeham is born.

1325 Queen Isabella, Edward II's wife, crosses to France on a
pretext; once there, she refuses to return to Edward's court
unless he will get rid of the Despensers.

1326

Sep   [25] Queen Isabella, Roger Mortimer and Prince Edward land
at Orwell in Suffolk and assume royal power. The
Despensers are captured and hanged.

Oct   [26] Edward, the King's son, is proclaimed Keeper of the
Realm.

1327 The Treaty of Corbeil re-establishes the 'auld alliance' of
France and Scotland.

Jan   [13] A group of bishops and magnates takes an oath at the
Guildhall in London to uphold the Queen's cause. [15] The
Archbishop of Canterbury announces in Westminster Hall
that the King is deposed. [16] Edward II is kept as a prisoner.
[20] Edward II agrees to abdicate at Kenilworth. [25] He is
succeeded by his son, Edward III. During the summer two
attempts are made to rescue the ex-king.

Sep   [21] Edward II is secretly murdered in Berkeley Castle on
Mortimer's orders.

1328 Treaty of Northampton formally recognizes Robert Bruce as Scotland's ruler and Scotland as an independent kingdom.

Jan   [24] Edward III of England marries Philippa, daughter of William I, Count of Hainault.

Jun   [5] Simon Mepham becomes Archbishop of Canterbury.

1329 Edward III crosses to Amiens to pay homage to Philip IV of France.

Jun   [7] Robert Bruce, King of Scotland, dies of leprosy at Cardross Castle, succeeded by his five-year-old son David II.

1330

Jun   [15] Edward of Woodstock, the Black Prince, is born.

Oct   [19] The 18-year-old Edward III enters Nottingham Castle by a subterranean passage and surprises and arrests Roger Mortimer. [20] Edward III takes the reins of England's government, assuming personal rule for the first time since his accession. Edward keeps his mother, Isabella, imprisoned at Castle Rising in Norfolk for the remainder of her life.

Nov   [29] Roger Mortimer is hanged as a traitor at Tyburn.

1331 Edward III confirms in writing that it was *liege* homage that he swore to Philip IV in 1329. Edward crosses to France in disguise to discuss with Philip at Pont St Maxence the terms of a lasting peace between England and France.

Sep   [24] Edward Balliol is enthroned at Scone as King of Scotland.

1332 The first record of the English Parliament dividing into two Houses, Lords and Commoners.

Jun   [16] Isabella, daughter of Edward III, is born.

Dec   [19] Edward Balliol is surprised at Annan by the Earl of Moray and Sir Archibald Douglas, supporters of David Bruce, and he flees for his life.

1333

Mar   [18] Edward the Black Prince is created Earl of Chester.

May   Edward III blockades Berwick.

Jul [19] Battle of Halidon Hill; the Scottish army is defeated by Edward III, demonstrating for the first time the full potential of the English longbow. Edward supports the cause of Edward Balliol and places him on the Scottish throne.

Nov [26] John Stratford becomes Archbishop of Canterbury.

1334 Edward III leads an army into Scotland. David II, newly installed as the Scottish king, is offered refuge by the French.

Jun [19] Edward Balliol offers homage to Edward III at Newcastle.

1335 Edward III puts the English Channel ports into a state of defence, anticipating a French intervention in the planned English invasion of Scotland. The French support David Bruce.

Jul The Archbishop of Rouen declares that 6000 French troops will be sent to help the Scots.

1336 Edward III invades Scotland again. Philip IV's Mediterranean crusading armada appears in the English Channel; there is fighting between English and French at sea.

1337 Edward III leads a smaller army into Scotland, but returns because of fears of an invasion by the French. The beginning of the Hundred Years War between England and France, prompted by rumours that a French fleet has been sighted, preparing to sail to Scotland.

Oct [7] Edward III describes himself as King of France and England, reopening the question of the French succession and making it clear that he is not prepared to compromise.

Dec Edward III agrees to suspend hostilities against the French until March, at the request of papal representatives.

1338

May [6] After a French attack on Portsmouth and the Isle of Wight, Edward III announces that the December truce is no longer binding; the Hundred Years War now begins in earnest. Edward forms an alliance with Flanders.

Nov [29] Lionel, son of Edward III, is born.

1339 Edward III invades France for the first time, without success.

1340

Jan [26] At Ghent, Edward solemnly assumes the arms and title of King of France, mainly to regularize the position of Flemish towns, which have allied themselves to the English cause.

Mar John of Gaunt (Ghent), Edward III's son, is born.

Jun Battle of Sluys; Edward III defeats a superior French fleet of 200 ships. Much of the fighting is hand-to-hand, from the castle on one ship to that on another. England loses Edinburgh to the Scots.

Sep Edward agrees to a one-year truce with France, at Esplechin.

Nov [30] Edward returns to England. Geoffrey Chaucer is born.

1341 The Trial of Peers: in a clash between Edward III and Archbishop John Stratford the King accuses Stratford of wasting the King's money. The Lords demand that henceforth a peer may only be tried by his Peers in Parliament; Edward III agrees.

1342

Jun [30] Edmund of Langley, son of Edward III, is born.

Sep [20] John of Gaunt is created Earl of Richmond.

1343 A truce is declared between England and France.

1344 Peace conference at Avignon, presided over by Pope Clement. The English bid for sovereignty over Gascony, but the conference ends without a settlement.

1346

Jul Edward III decides to lead an army into France on a second campaign, sailing from Portchester, and creating his son a knight.

Aug [26] Battle of Crecy; Edward III leads an army of dismounted men-at-arms and archers to destroy a French army of mounted men-at-arms under King Philip: it is the first use of the English longbow in continental warfare.

Sep [4] Edward and his army begin the siege of Calais. Battle of Neville's Cross; the Scots attack northern England and are beaten near Durham. King David II of Scotland is taken prisoner.

1347
Aug [4] Calais surrenders to the English. In celebration, the first English gold coin is minted: Calais is shortly to become an English colony.

Sep A new truce between England and France is declared at Calais, with England in a position of strength.

1348 The Order of the Garter is founded, to encourage chivalry and military adventure. Black Death in England: the first outbreak of the plague.

1349 Black Death sweeps England.
Jul Black Death reaches its peak. [19] Thomas Bradwardine becomes Archbishop of Canterbury.
Aug [25] Thomas Bradwardine dies.
Dec [20] Simon Islip becomes Archbishop of Canterbury.

1350 Owen Glendower is born. Black Death reaches Scotland.

1351 First Statute of Labourers; the English Parliament attempts to freeze wages. Statute of Provisors; this recognizes the King as 'patron paramount' of the English Church, as a check against papal control.

1352 First Statute of Treason; this makes the position of the magnates more secure by giving treason a narrower definition, involving an 'open act' aimed at compassing the King's death.

1354 Treaty of Guines; mediated terms are proposed for a peace between England and France based on Edward renouncing his claim to the French throne, in return for which he will receive in full sovereignty Poitou, Aquitaine, Anjou, Maine,

Touraine and Calais, yet the treaty is never ratified. Edward refuses to renounce his claim.

1355

Jan   Thomas of Woodstock, son of Edward III, is born.

1356 The Third English Campaign in France.

Sep   [18] Cardinal Talleyrand's mediation between Henry of Lancaster and King John fails. [19] Battle of Poitiers; Edward the Black Prince defeats the French largely because the French foot soldiers are sent up a hill against the English archers. The Black Prince captures the French king, John II. The victory leads to the Treaty of Bretigny of 1360.

1358 Queen Isabella, Edward II's widow, dies.

1360 Treaty of Bretigny, ending the first stage of the Hundred Years War. Edward III makes great territorial gains in France and appears content with the settlement. King John, the French monarch, is to be freed on payment of a huge ransom of three million gold crowns. Henry Yevele becomes disposer of the King's works of masonry at Westminster Palace and the Tower.

Apr   [14] 'Black Monday': reported as 'so full dark of mist and hail and so bitter cold that many men died on their horsebacks with the cold'.

1361 Second major outbreak of plague, lasting until 1362.

1362 Wool Staple established at Calais. English becomes the official language in Parliament and the Law Courts instead of French.

1364 King John of France, unable to raise his ransom, dies a prisoner in London.

1365

Jul   [27] Isabella, Edward III's daughter, marries Enguerrand de Coucy, later Earl of Bedford.

1366
Apr   Henry IV, son of John of Gaunt and Blanche, is born.
Nov   Simon Langham becomes Archbishop of Canterbury.

1367   Civil war breaks out in Castile. England and France support
          rival candidates for the Castilian throne, leading to renewed
          hostilities between England and France. The Black Prince
          leads an expedition to Spain to support Pedro the Cruel in
          his attempt to regain the Castilian throne.
Jan   [6] Richard II is born at Bordeaux.
1368
Oct   [17] Lionel, Duke of Clarence, dies.

1369   Fourth Campaign in France: Charles V renews the Hundred
          Years War with a series of damaging raids on the Channel
          coast of England. Queen Philippa, Edward III's wife, dies.
          The third outbreak of plague in Britain.
Jan   William Whittlesey becomes Archbishop of Canterbury.

1370   Massacre at Limoges; the Black Prince brutally puts 3000
          inhabitants of Limoges to death for deserting the English
          cause. His health permanently broken, the Black Prince has
          to resign his command in Aquitaine and return to England.

1371   Popular discontent, largely with the failure of the war in
          France, is voiced in the English Parliament.
Feb   [22] King David II of Scotland dies, succeeded by Robert II.
Sep   John of Gaunt marries Constance, daughter of Pedro the
          Cruel, and assumes the title King of Castile and Leon.

1372   The Castilian fleet destroys at sea an English force on its way
          to Aquitaine. The Black Prince returns from France.

1373   John of Gaunt leads a large army from Calais to the borders
          of Burgundy.

1375   Treaty of Bruges; a year-long truce between England and
          France.
Jun   [5] Simon Sudbury becomes Archbishop of Canterbury.

1376 The 'Good Parliament' meets, complaining of illegal profiteering, bribery and waste by named individuals, in particular Lord Latimer, the King's Chamberlain, and Alice Perrers, the King's mistress; this is the first instance of impeachment in English history. The Treaty of Bruges is renewed for another year.

Jun [8] Edward, the Black Prince, dies.

1377 The Spring Parliament grants a poll tax of 4d per head on the whole population between the ages of 12 and 60.

Jun [21] Edward III dies, succeeded by his ten-year-old grandson Richard II; no regent or chief councillor is appointed. [24] The Treaty of Bruges expires and the war between England and France resumes with England ill-prepared.

Jul [16] Coronation of Richard II of England; Thomas of Woodstock is created Earl of Buckingham. There are French raids on the Channel coast; Rye and Portsmouth are sacked. Robin Hood is mentioned for the first time.

1378 John of Gaunt besieges St Malo without success. There are further French raids on the Channel coast, especially in Cornwall.

1379 The Spring Parliament grants another poll tax, this time graded by rank, from 10 marks for the Duke of Lancaster down to 4d for a labouring man. New College is founded by William of Wykeham.

1380 The Spring Parliament agrees to another poll tax, this time one shilling a head for the entire male population, three times the 1377 tax; the tax is to be collected in two instalments, in January and June, 1381. The announcement leads to demonstrations of anger across England. There are more French raids on the Channel coast; Gravesend and Winchelsea are burned.

1381

Jan   The first instalment of the poll tax comes in and it is plain
      that large-scale evasion has taken place, so the
      Government decides to collect the second instalment straight
      away.

May   Poll-tax collectors are set upon and expelled from some
      towns.

Jun   [4] The Peasants' Revolt begins; rebels attack Dartford.
      [6]Rebels besiege Rochester. [7] Rebels enter Maidstone and
      choose Wat Tyler as their chief. [10] Rebels enter Canterbury
      under Tyler's leadership. [12] Essex rebels reach Mile End
      and Kentish rebels reach Blackheath. [13] The Essex and
      Kentish rebels enter London; the King withdraws to the
      safety of the Tower; the rebels ransack John of Gaunt's
      palace. [14] Richard II rides to Mile End to parley with
      rebels, who demand the abolition of serfdom and limitation
      of rents, and for the heads of Chancellor Sudbury,
      Treasurer Hales, John of Gaunt and others. Richard agrees to
      all but the executions. Meanwhile, Kentishmen are breaking
      into the Tower and beheading Sudbury and Hales. The
      deaths of the Treasurer and Chancellor, who is also
      Archbishop of Canterbury, are followed by a general
      massacre of Flemings in the City of London. [15] Richard II
      summons the Kentish rebels to Smithfield; Tyler meets the
      King, grows insolent and abusive, and is killed by Mayor
      Walworth.

Oct   [23] William Courtenay becomes Archbishop of
      Canterbury.

1382 John Wycliff, after surviving the heresy trials of 1377-8
      thanks to John of Gaunt's intervention, is finally condemned.
      The Statute de Heretico Comburendo forbids unlicenced
      preaching and allows obdurate heretics to be burned; this is
      aimed at suppressing the Lollards.

Jan   [20] Richard II marries Anne of Bohemia, the daughter of
      Charles VI of France.

1384 John Wycliff, critic of the Pope's supremacy and infallibility, has a stroke at Mass and dies. The Lollards are expelled from Oxford.

1385 Richard II leads an army into Scotland as far as Edinburgh, but fails to bring the Scots into battle. Joan of Kent, the Black Prince's widow and Richard II's mother, dies.

Aug [6] Edmund of Langley and Thomas of Woodstock, sons of Edward III, are created Duke of York and Duke of Gloucester.

1386 The Council of Eleven is appointed; the King is compelled to entrust the government of England to a Council of Eleven headed by the Duke of Gloucester. A large French army gathers at Sluys and an invasion of England seems imminent, but the army disbands.

Jul John of Gaunt sails for Galicia and is away for four years. The Autumn Parliament demands the dismissal and impeachment of Pole. Pole is sentenced to forfeiture of a large part of his estates and to imprisonment 'at the King's pleasure'.

1387 Richard II leaves Westminster taking with him a rival council to the Council of Eleven, or commission council.

Sep [16] Henry V is born at Monmouth Castle, the son of Henry IV and Mary Bohun.

Nov [17] The commission council appears before the King, 'appealing' (or requesting the arrest of) five of his favourites.

1388 The 'Merciless Parliament' meets; the appelant lords (Gloucester, Arundel, Warwick, Derby and Nottingham) appear arm in arm and dressed in cloth of gold, to impeach the King's favourites, de Vere, de la Pole (Earl of Suffolk) and others for high treason.

1389 Richard II, now 23, declares himself of age, dismisses his protectors and assumes authority.

May A three-year truce is arranged between England and France. John of Gaunt returns to England untainted, in the King's eyes, by the events of the previous year.

1390 The fourth outbreak of plague in Britain. Elgin Cathedral is burnt again.

Apr [19] Robert II, King of Scotland, dies, succeeded by Robert III, his son. John of Gaunt, already Duke of Lancaster and King of Castile and Leon, is created Duke of Aquitaine.

1392 An English deputation led by John of Gaunt is received in Amiens by Charles VI; terms for a final peace settlement are discussed.

1393 Richard II orders a cycle of sculptures to decorate the remodelled Westminster Hall. William of Wykeham founds Winchester College.

1394 Richard II grants Chaucer a pension of £20 a year for life. Richard leads an expedition to Ireland (ending in 1395).

Jun [17] Anne of Bohemia, Richard II's wife, dies.

1396 Anglo-French Treaty.

Mar [12] Richard II marries Isabella, daughter of Charles VI of France.

1397 Richard II makes himself an absolute monarch; the 'tyranny' begins. Richard Whittington, a wealthy merchant, becomes mayor of London.

Jan [11] Thomas Arundel becomes Archbishop of Canterbury, but is later transferred to St Andrews.

Sep [9] Thomas of Woodstock, Duke of Gloucester, is put to death at Calais at the instigation of his nephew Richard II. Other Lords Appellant also suffer; Arundel is beheaded and Warwick is imprisoned for life.

1398 Roger Walden becomes Archbishop of Canterbury.

Jan Parliament at Shrewsbury: all the acts of the Merciless Parliament are annulled. [30] Bolingbroke appears before the

King in Parliament with allegations of treason against
Mowbray. Investigations reveal no evidence.

Sep   [16] Mowbray and Bolingbroke are ordered to fight a judicial
       duel at Coventry to settle the matter; the King intercedes and
       banishes them both.

1399

Feb   [3] John of Gaunt dies. Richard extends Bolingbroke's
       banishment from ten years to life and takes the whole of his
       inheritance into his own hands.

May   Richard II goes to Ireland, giving the exiled Henry
       Bolingbroke the opportunity to return to England .

Jul   Bolingbroke returns to England to claim his father's estates.

Aug   [10] At Conway, Richard is assured that his throne will not
       be in jeopardy, so long as he restores Bolingbroke's estates to
       him; Richard agrees to these terms. [19] At Chester, Richard
       becomes a captive of Henry Bolingbroke, Duke of Lancaster,
       until his death.

Sep   [29] Richard II becomes the second British monarch to
       abdicate. [30] Henry Bolingbroke is chosen by Parliament to
       succeed Richard, as Henry IV.

Oct   [13] Coronation of Henry IV, the first Lancastrian king
       of England; founding of the House of Lancaster
       (1399-1461). [15] His son, later Henry V, is created Prince
       of Wales. [19] Archbishop Walden is deprived of his office,
       and Thomas Arundel is restored as Archbishop of
       Canterbury.

1400

1400   Rebellion of the Earls of Huntingdon, Kent, Rutland and
       Salisbury, to restore Richard to the throne; it is soon
       suppressed and Kent, Salisbury and Huntingdon are
       executed.

Feb   [10] Richard II disappears while imprisoned in Pontefract
       Castle; it is presumed that he is murdered at about this date.

His corpse is shortly afterwards displayed in London to prove that he is dead.

Sep   [16] The Owen Glendower revolt in Wales; Welsh landowners proclaim him Prince of Wales and there are attacks on the English in Flint and Denbigh. A punitive expedition to North Wales is launched by Henry IV.

Oct   [25] Geoffrey Chaucer, poet and story-teller, dies.

1401 Persecution of the Lollards; a new act permitting the burning of heretics is passed. William Sawtre, sometime Rector of Lynn, is burnt by royal command for preaching Lollard doctrines; he is the first to be executed for Lollard heresy.

1402 Rumours circulate that Richard is still alive somewhere in Wales or Scotland. A Scottish force led by the Duke of Albany invades England. On its way home it is heavily defeated by the Percies at Homildon Hill; many Scottish noblemen are taken prisoner.

Aug   [1] Edmund of Langley, Duke of York, dies.

1403 Rebellion of the Percies; Henry IV owes the Percies £20,000, so the Percies ally themselves with Owen Glendower, the Mortimers and the Scottish Earl Douglas.

Jul   [12] Henry IV hears the news that his former supporters the Percies are in revolt against him. [21] Battle of Shrewsbury; advancing towards Wales to join Glendower, Henry Hotspur is defeated and killed. The Prince of Wales is wounded in the face. Northumberland submits and is pardoned with a fine.

1404 William of Wykeham dies. The French form an alliance with Owen Glendower.

1405 Rebellion against Henry IV in North Wales, and a second rebellion led by Northumberland together with Archbishop Scrope and Mowbray; the Northumberland rebellion is in favour of Edmund Mortimer, Earl of March, who is Henry IV's prisoner. French forces join Glendower's in his great raid into England.

Apr   Northumberland makes a Treaty of Partition with Glendower
      and Sir Edmund Mortimer.
May   Prince Henry's force routs the Welsh near Usk; Owen's son
      Griffith is captured. Northumberland's rebellion is
      suppressed; Northumberland escapes to Scotland, but
      Archbishop Scrope and Mowbray are captured and executed.
      From this time on, Henry IV is often ill; his eldest son Prince
      Henry gradually assumes a dominating influence in the
      government.

1406 James, the Scottish King's son, is captured at sea by the
      English and held captive.
Apr   [4] Robert III, King of Scotland, dies; his successor, James, is
      still held by the English, so a Regency is assumed by the
      Duke of Albany. Richard Whittington is again Mayor of
      London.

1407 Plague strikes England for the fifth time.

1408 Northumberland's third rebellion against Henry IV.
Feb   At the Battle of Bramham Moor, the Earl of Northumberland
      is defeated, captured and executed. John Gower, the last of
      the Anglo-Norman poets, dies; he wrote in both Latin and
      French and later, perhaps as a result of Chaucer's influence,
      in English.

1409 Prince Henry, by virtue of his father's illness, is effective
      president of the King's Council.
Sep   [13] Queen Isabella, widow of Richard II, dies.

1410 Owen Glendower's revolt ends.

1412
Jun   Henry IV suspects the Prince of Wales of plotting to usurp
      the throne.
Jul   [9] Henry IV's second surviving son, Thomas, is created
      Duke of Clarence and Earl of Aumale.

1413 John Wycliff's writings are condemned by Pope John.

Mar [20] Henry IV dies of a stroke as he prays at Edward the Confessor's Shrine in the Jerusalem Chamber at Westminster Abbey. It had been prophesied he would die in Jerusalem. His elder son, Henry V, succeeds to the throne. [21] Henry V has James of Scotland put in the Tower as a precaution.

Jul Sir John Oldcastle, the King's friend, is found to be an obdurate heretic, arrested and condemned to be executed. Henry V requests a stay of execution so that he can reason with Oldcastle.

Oct [19] Oldcastle escapes from the Tower.

Dec Richard II's body is taken from Langley and reburied at Westminster.

1414

Jan [9] Lollards attempt to capture Henry V and seize the City of London, but the King's troops arrest them in St Giles' Field as they approach the city gates. [13] About 40 of the insurgents are hanged, though Sir John Oldcastle, the probable organizer, escapes.

May [30] Henry Chichele becomes Archbishop of Canterbury.

Dec The Commons plead with Henry V to negotiate a peaceful settlement instead of resorting to arms against France.

1415

Apr [16] At a great council meeting the Chancellor, Bishop Beaufort, announces that Henry V has decided to cross the Channel to recover his heritage; in his absence England will be governed by the Duke of Bedford.

Jul [31] A Lollard Plot to assassinate the King at Portchester on his way to embark for France is exposed. The conspirators (Richard, Earl of Cambridge, Lord Scrope and Sir Thomas Grey) favour Edmund Mortimer, Earl of March, as king. Grey is executed at once.

Aug [5] Cambridge and Scrope are executed at Southampton after trial by their peers. [11] Henry V sails with his army from Southampton. Hostilities between England and France are resumed in the second stage of the Hundred Years War.

Sep [22] Henry succeeds in taking Harfleur after a five-week
     siege; he needs to secure this port for his conquest of
     Normandy.
Oct [25] Battle of Agincourt; 20 miles inland from Boulogne,
     Henry V defeats a French army three times the size of his
     own, mounted and heavily armed, with a force of only 6000
     men, mostly archers.
Nov [23] Henry V's triumphant return to London.

1416 Owen Glendower dies. Henry V makes a pilgrimage to St
     Winifrede's Well at Shrewsbury.
May [1] Emperor Sigismund arrives in England to try to
     arrange an alliance between England, France and the
     Empire.
Aug [15] Treaty of Canterbury agreed between Henry V and
     Sigismund, a friendship treaty by which the Emperor
     promises England military support.

1417 Sir John Oldcastle is finally run to earth in Herefordshire,
     hung in chains and executed by burning.
Feb There is widespread rearmament in England (gathering
     goose-feathers for arrow flights).
Jul [23] English troops embark once more for France.
Sep [4] Henry V is victorious at the Battle of Caen. [11] Henry V
     takes Pontoise.

1418
Jan [20] The English army takes Louviers.
Jul [21] The English army takes Compiègne. [30] The Siege of
     Rouen begins.
Sep Cherbourg falls to English forces under Gloucester and
     Huntingdon. The Duke of Brittany tries unsuccessfully to
     bring the warring parties together to find a peace formula.
Nov Inconclusive discussions between the English and French
     leaders at Alençon.

1419 Richard Whittington is Mayor of London for the third time.

Jan	[19] The long siege of Rouen ends; Henry starves the inhabitants into submission. Remaining resistance to Henry V in Normandy crumbles. [20] Henry V enters Rouen.
Feb	[5] Mantes surrenders to the English. [8] Dieppe surrenders to the English.
May	[30] Henry V meets Duke John of Burgundy at Meulan and falls in love with the Princess Catherine.
Jul	[31] Gisors and Pontoise fall to the English.
Dec	[25] A formal treaty is agreed between England and France.

1420

Apr	[9] Treaty of Troyes; English claims to the French throne are recognized and Henry undertakes to marry a French princess; the English conquest of Normandy is complete.
Jun	[2] Henry V marries Catherine de Valois, daughter of Charles VI of France, in Troyes Cathedral.
Nov	[18] Henry V takes Melun after a siege.
Dec	[1] Henry makes a triumphal entry into Paris.

1421

Feb	[1] Henry V and Catherine land at Dover to an enthusiastic welcome; the barons of the Cinque Ports wade into the sea to carry them in on their shoulders. [23] Coronation of Catherine, followed by a royal tour of the kingdom that includes a visit to the shrine of St John of Beverley.
Mar	[22] Thomas, Duke of Clarence, is killed at Beaugé by the French.
Jun -Aug	A revival of French resistance causes Henry V to return to France.
Dec	[6] Henry VI, the only child of Henry V, is born at Windsor.

1422 William Caxton is born.

| May | [2] Meaux falls to the English army under Henry V. |
| Aug | [31] Henry V dies at Vincennes of dysentery, succeeded by his nine-month-old son, Henry VI. John, Duke of Bedford, acts as Protector of England and Regent in France during the King's minority; the claim of the Duke of Gloucester to the |

Regency is resisted. Under Bedford, the third stage of the Hundred Years War begins. The Paston letters, a remarkable collection of correspondence of a middle-class English family, begin in this year (and go on until 1509).

1423 Richard Whittington dies. In prison, King James of Scotland writes his *Kingis Quair*. The Duke of Bedford marries Anne, sister of Philip the Good, strengthening England's alliance with Burgundy.

Aug   [23] Battle of Verneuil; English and Burgundian forces defeat Franco-Scottish forces.

1424 James I returns to Scotland after his captivity in England. The Cambridge University Library now consists of 122 volumes.

1425 The Parliament of Bats: members are forbidden to carry arms, so they carry sticks and bats instead.

Sep   Henry Beaufort, Bishop of Winchester, gathers troops in London; England is close to civil war.

Oct   [30] There is a skirmish at London bridge between Beaufort's supporters and those of his rival, the Duke of Gloucester; Archbishop Chichele intervenes and arranges a truce.

1426 A reconciliation between Beaufort and Gloucester is organized by a committee of peers.

Mar   [13] After attempting to explain his conduct in a speech, Beaufort resigns as Chancellor and prepares to leave the country.

1427 Beaufort, now a Cardinal, leaves England for Bohemia as a legate for the Roman Curia.

1428 Richard Neville, Earl of Salisbury and Warwick, is born. English forces under Salisbury lay siege to Orléans, the key to the southern provinces of France; Salisbury himself is killed by a cannon-ball. Beaufort returns to England with a legatine commission to preach against the Hussites. There is a dispute in East Anglia between the Duke of Norfolk and the Earl of Huntingdon; serious rioting results.

1429 The Battle of Herrings; the French make an unsuccessful attack on Sir John Fastolf's convoy; he is carrying supplies of fish to those under siege.

Apr [28] Joan of Arc drives the English force away from Orléans. Joan's leadership saves Orléans and France from the English. At Pataye, Joan of Arc defeats Talbot and captures him.

Jul [17] The French Dauphin is crowned Charles VII.

Nov [5] Coronation of Henry VI of England.

1430 Joan of Arc is captured by the Burgundians at Compiègne and sold to the English.

Jan [5] Philippa, daughter of Henry IV, marries King Eric IX of Denmark.

Apr [23] Henry VI, a boy of eight, goes to France for two years; during his absence, Humphrey, Duke of Gloucester, is Regent.

Oct [16] James II of Scotland is born, the son of James I and Joan Beaufort.

1431 A Lollard rising is planned in England, but does not take place. Henry VI is crowned in Paris.

May [30] Joan of Arc is burnt as a witch at Rouen, by the English.

1432
Feb Henry VI returns to England.

1433 Henry VI makes a pilgrimage to Bury St Edmunds, where the monks present him with an illustrated *Life of St Edmund*.

1435
Aug Congress of Arras begins. The French offer to cede Normandy and Guienne if Henry VI will renounce his claim to the French throne.

Sep [6] The English reject the terms offered by the French and the peace conference ends inconclusively. [15] John, Duke of Bedford, dies.

1436 The French army takes Paris.

1437 English troops under John, Lord Talbot, take Pontoise from the French and threaten Paris. Catherine of Valois, Henry V's queen, dies. All Souls College, Oxford, is founded.

Feb [21] James I of Scotland is murdered, succeeded by his son, James II.

Nov [12] Henry VI is declared to be of age.

1439 A peace conference at Calais ends in failure.

1440

Oct [11] Eton College is founded by Henry VI.

1441 King's College, Cambridge, is founded by Henry VI. English troops under York and Talbot make significant gains in Normandy, breaking the French siege of Pontoise, but lack of money and reinforcements make it impossible for them to consolidate these successes.

Oct The Duchess of Gloucester is tried for traffic in sorcery and dealing with sorcerers. She admits the charges are true, but denies plotting to destroy the King by sorcery. She is sentenced to public penance followed by life imprisonment. The Duke of Gloucester's political influence is negligible from now on.

1442 It becomes clear that the English possessions in Calais, Normandy and Guienne may all be lost to the French.

Apr [28] Edward IV is born at Rouen, the son of Richard, Duke of York.

1443

Apr [12] Archbishop Henry Chichele dies. A decision is made to send an expedition to Guienne.

Jun [25] John Stafford becomes Archbishop of Canterbury.

1444

May It is agreed that Henry VI will marry Margaret of Anjou, in return for a two-year truce., the Truce of Tours.

1445 The French indicate that the cession of Maine to France would form the basis of a peace settlement.

Apr   [23] Henry VI marries Margaret of Anjou.
Dec   [22] Henry VI promises in a personal letter to Charles VII to
      deliver Maine to France.

1446 There is widespread anger in England and among the
      English in France, that Maine is to be ceded to France. The
      Duke of Suffolk is blamed, though it is really the King's fault.
      King's College, Cambridge (complete).

1447
Feb   The Spring Parliament is summoned to Bury. [18]
      Humphrey, Duke of Gloucester, arrives at Bury and is
      arrested and confined, apparently at Suffolk's instigation.
      [23] Gloucester dies; he may have been murdered or have
      died of heart failure brought on by the shock of arrest. It is
      widely assumed that he has been murdered on Suffolk's
      orders.

1449 The French overrun Normandy, partly because of the Duke
      of Suffolk's miscalculations; Normandy is finally lost to the
      French.

1450 Jack Cade's rebellion against Henry VI's government; the
      rebels demand the blood of the traitors who have lost the
      French possessions.

Feb   [7] The Commons in Parliament impeach the Duke of Suffolk
      for mismanaging the war and for fraud. Henry VI intervenes
      to save Suffolk's life by banishing him from England for five
      years.
Mar   Sir Thomas Kyriel lands at Cherbourg with a force of 3000
      men.
Apr   [15] Kyriel's troops are virtually annihilated by the French.
May   [1] Suffolk embarks for France, but his ship is run down in
      the Channel by another ship, the *Nicholas of the Tower*, and
      Suffolk is captured.
May   [2] The captain of the *Nicholas* orders Suffolk to be beheaded
      over one of the ship's boats.
Jun   The French close in on Somerset's troops at Caen.

Jul   [1] Somerset surrenders Caen. [4] Cade's rebels are in control of London. [5] There is fierce fighting on London Bridge between Cade's rebels and Lord Scales' troops; the rebels are dispersed after they are offered free pardons.

Aug Cherbourg is lost to the French, leaving the whole of Normandy under French control and exposing the south coast of England to attack by the French. Morale collapses in England.

1451 The French take Guienne.

Jan [7] Glasgow University is founded.

Sep The Earl of Devon lays siege to his old enemy Lord Bonville in Taunton Castle.

1452

May James III of Scotland is born.

Sep [6] John Kempe becomes Archbishop of Canterbury.

Oct [2] Richard III is born at Fotheringhay Castle.

1453 John Dunstable, composer, dies. The French overrun Gascony. The Battle of Chatillon; the final English defeat in France and the end of the Hundred Years War; the English withdraw entirely from France, except for the Channel Islands and Calais, which they retain. The Battle of Heworth, between the followers of the Nevilles and the Percies; this is the first skirmish leading to the Wars of the Roses.

Aug Henry VI loses his senses and his memory, the first attack of a periodic mental disorder.

Oct [13] Edward, son of Henry VI, is born and created Duke of Cornwall.

Dec Somerset is arrested and put in the Tower, probably for his own safety.

1454

Mar [15] Prince Edward is created Prince of Wales. [27] York is named Protector during the King's insanity, and chief of the council.

Aug [22] Thomas Bourchier becomes Archbishop of Canterbury.

Dec Henry VI recovers his sanity.

1455

Feb   Somerset is released from the Tower; York is dismissed from his Protectorship.

May   [22] First Battle of St Albans, marking the beginning of the Wars of the Roses, a struggle between the Dukes of York and Lancaster for the throne of England. Yorkist troops under the Duke of York and the Earls of Salisbury and Warwick break into the town, defeat the royal army and capture the wounded Henry VI; Somerset, the Earl of Northumberland and Lord Clifford die in action, although only 120 men altogether are killed.

1457

Jan   [28] Henry VII is born at Pembroke Castle, the son of Edmund Tudor, Earl of Richmond and Margaret Beaufort.

Mar   Henry VI attempts to reconcile the two sides in the civil war, but the reconciliation is a matter of form only.

Aug   The French raid the port of Sandwich.

1459   Queen Margaret prepares for war, raising troops in Cheshire.

Sep   [23] Battle of Blore Heath; Salisbury defeats a Lancastrian force. Bills of Attainder are passed against the Duke of York and his supporters.

Oct   [12] Battle of Ludford Bridge at Ludlow; the Yorkists are routed by Lancastrian forces headed by Henry VI.
      [13] Richard, Duke of York, and his son the Earl of Rutland escape to Wales and then to Ireland; Salisbury, Warwick and the Earl of March flee to Calais.

Nov   [20] Parliament of Devils meets at Coventry; an Act of Attainder convicts York, the Nevilles and their supporters, and legalizes the seizure of their lands.

1460

Jul   [10] Battle of Northampton; the Yorkists win and Henry VI is again taken prisoner by the Yorkist lords; he is taken to London in royal state.

Aug [3] King James II of Scotland dies, succeeded by James III, his
eldest son.

Oct [6] The Duke of York arrives back in England. [10] York
arrives with his army in London. [16] York's counsel submits
to Parliament York's claim to the throne, now publicly
mentioned for the first time. [25] The Lords' Act of Accord:
Henry VI should retain the Crown for his lifetime, but then
York and his heirs are to succeed; Henry VI agrees.

Dec [9] York and Salisbury set off for the north, pursued by the
Lancastrians. The poet John Skelton is born.

1461

Feb [2] Battle of Mortimer's Cross; the Yorkists are victorious,
capturing Owen Tudor and other Lancastrian lords. Owen
Tudor is beheaded. Queen Margaret advances south, with
promises of aid from Scotland and France. [17] Second Battle
of St Albans; Queen Margaret defeats the Earl of Warwick
and releases her husband, Henry VI, from captivity by the
Yorkist lords.

Mar [4] Henry VI is deposed, succeeded by Edward, Earl of
March, the late Duke of York's son, as Edward IV; the
founding of the House of York (1461-85). Edward sets off for
the North, seeking Margaret's army. [29] Battle of Towton;
the Yorkists win a particularly bloody battle between the
largest armies ever to have met on an English battlefield:
28,000 men die. The outcome of the battle confirms Edward's
position.

Jun [28] Coronation of Edward IV.

1462 Norway surrenders the Shetlands to the kingdom of
Scotland.

Oct Queen Margaret sails to north-east England from Boulogne
with 800 French troops.

1463 Henry Beaufort, Duke of Somerset, changes sides again,
deserting Edward IV and rejoining Henry VI in Scotland.

1464 Another outbreak of plague in Britain.

Apr [23] Robert Fayrfax, composer, is born.
May [1] Edward IV secretly marries Elizabeth Woodville at Grafton Regis. Somerset is captured and executed after a skirmish at Hexham.
Jun [1] Edward IV successfully negotiates a 15-year truce with Scotland, depriving the Lancastrians of a Scottish refuge. As a result, Henry VI becomes a fugitive.

1465
May Queen Elizabeth's Coronation.
Jul Henry VI is captured by Edward IV and kept prisoner until 1470.
Dec France declares war on England, although no action is taken.

1466 Princess Elizabeth, daughter of Edward IV, is born.

1468 Norway surrenders the Orkneys to the kingdom of Scotland.

1469 Rebellion of Richard, Earl of Warwick, and George, Duke of Clarence, against Edward IV.

Jul [11] Clarence marries Isabella Neville at Calais. [26] Battle of Edgecote; Warwick's forces defeat Edward IV. Edward IV is imprisoned by Warwick until the end of September, but then released. Warwick and Edward IV are reconciled.

1470 Rebellion breaks out against royal tax-gatherers in Lincolnshire, led by Sir Robert Wells. Edward IV defeats the rebels nears Empingham in a battle known as 'Lose Coat Field'.

May [5] Edward IV summons Warwick and Clarence. They realize that Edward knows of their treachery and escape to France, where they join Queen Margaret after a reconciliation effected by Louis XI; Warwick becomes a Lancastrian.
Sep [13] Warwick, Clarence and Queen Margaret return to England and dethrone Edward IV. Edward escapes from Lynn to the Netherlands.
Oct [3] Return and re-crowning of Henry VI.
Nov [2] Edward V, the son of Edward IV, is born.

1471 Londoners deride the spectacle of Henry VI being brought out in procession in an old blue velvet gown.

Mar [14] Edward IV returns to England.

Apr [11] Henry VI is deposed again. [14] Battle of Barnet; the Lancastrians are defeated and Warwick, 'the Kingmaker', is killed trying to escape from the battlefield.

May [4] Battle of Tewkesbury; Prince Edward, the son of Henry VI and Queen Margaret, is stabbed to death by Clarence and Gloucester after the battle. The Lancastrians are crushed. [21] The deposed king, Henry VI, who has been Edward IV's prisoner since April 11, is murdered in the Tower; Edward IV marches into London in triumph.

Jun [26] Edward IV's son Edward is created Prince of Wales. Sir Thomas Malory dies. St Wilfrid's remains are transferred to a large shrine in York Minster.

1472
Jul [12] Richard, Duke of Gloucester, marries Anne Neville, daughter of Richard, Earl of Warwick.

1473 Edward, Richard Duke of Gloucester's son, is born.

Mar [17] James IV of Scotland is born.

Aug [17] Edward IV's son Richard is born.

1474
May [28] Edward IV's son Richard is created Duke of York. William Caxton prints the first book in English, *The Recuyell of the Historyes of Troye*, in Bruges.

1475 Edward IV makes an alliance with the Duke of Burgundy against Louis XI, reviving the old claim to the French throne. John Schorne's body is transferred to St George's Chapel, Windsor. Clarence quarrels with his brothers, the Duke of Gloucester and the King, over property.

Jul [4] Edward IV begins a military expedition to France.

Aug [29] The Anglo-French Treaty of Pecquigny; Louis is to pay a yearly pension to Edward and a ransom for Queen Margaret.

1476 William Caxton sets up his printing press at Westminster.

1477
Feb Richard, Edward IV's son, is created Duke of Norfolk. In the summer, John Stacey and Thomas Burdett are executed for trying to kill the King by necromancy. The Duke of Clarence protests their innocence before the council at Westminster, confirming in the King's mind his untrustworthiness; Clarence is placed in custody.

Nov [18] William Caxton publishes the first book dated in England, *The Sayings of the Philosophers*.

1478
Jan The Duke of Clarence is attainted by Parliament, found guilty of high treason and sentenced to death.

Feb [7] Sir Thomas More, statesman and philosopher, is born in London. [15] Edward, Richard Duke of Gloucester's son, is created Earl of Salisbury. [18] Clarence is secretly executed in the Tower.

1479 An outbreak of plague.

1480 Caxton prints *The Chronicles of England*.

1482
Aug [25] Margaret of Anjou, widow of Henry VI, dies.

1483 Louis XI breaks off the marriage contract made by the Treaty of Pecquigny. Edward IV prepares to invade France again.

Apr [9] Edward IV dies suddenly and unexpectedly at the age of 40, succeeded by his 12-year-old son Edward V. [29] The Dukes of Gloucester and Buckingham join forces at Northampton. [30] Gloucester takes possession of Edward V at Stony Stratford as his Protector, and exercises effective control from this time on.

May Richard, Duke of Gloucester, arrives in London with Edward V and is recognized as Protector of the Realm.

Jun [16] Edward V and his brother are held in the Tower. [22] Bishop Stillington declares that the two boys are technically bastards, invalidating Edward's claim to the throne.

[25] Edward V is deposed. [26] Accession of Richard III; his son Edward is created Duke of Cornwall.

Aug [24] Prince Edward is created Prince of Wales; the Princes in the Tower are probably murdered at about this time.

Oct Rebellion of Henry, Duke of Buckingham.
William Orchard: Divinity School, Oxford.

1484

Mar [1] Elizabeth Woodville, Edward V's mother, is persuaded to come out of sanctuary.

Apr [9] Richard III's son Edward dies.

Aug Richard III orders the body of Henry VI to be removed from Chertsey Abbey to St George's Chapel, Windsor; the King's body is well preserved, although the face is 'somewhat sunken, with a more meagre appearance than ordinary'.

1485 James III of Scotland recovers Dunbar Castle.

Mar [16] Anne Neville, Richard III's queen, dies.

Aug [7] Henry Tudor lands at Milford Haven with 1800 French troops. [22] Battle of Bosworth Field; Richard III is killed and his army defeated, largely because sections of his army under the treacherous Stanley brothers defect during the battle. Henry Tudor, the victor, becomes Henry VII.

Oct [31] Coronation of Henry VII; the founding of the House of Tudor (1485-1603).

Dec [16] Catherine of Aragon, the first wife of Henry VIII, is born, the daughter of Ferdinand and Isabella.

1486

Jan [18] Henry VII marries Elizabeth, the daughter of Edward IV, uniting Yorkist and Lancastrian claims in his own dynasty.

Mar An attempted rising in North Yorkshire is led by Lord Lovell. It collapses as the King travels north to deal with it; Lovel flees abroad.

Jul [14] Queen Margaret, wife of James III of Scotland, dies. [16] Henry VII announces that the Princes in the Tower were murdered by Richard III.

Sep [19] Henry VII's son Arthur is born and created Duke of Cornwall.

Dec [6] John Morton becomes Archbishop of Canterbury.

1487 Henry VII founds the court subsequently known as the Court of the Star Chamber.

May [5] A party of Yorkists with German troops lands at Dublin.
[24] Lambert Simnel, an impostor, is supported by the Lord Deputy of Ireland, Lord Kildare, and crowned in Dublin as Edward V.

Jun [16] Battle of Stoke; Simnel's rising is crushed by the King's forces.

1488

Jun [11] Battle of Sauchieburn; King James III of Scotland is defeated and afterwards murdered, succeeded by his son, James IV.

1489 In Scotland, rebellions by Lennox in the west and Forbes in the east are suppressed by James IV. Thomas Cranmer, Archbishop of Canterbury, is born at Aslockton. The Treaty of Medina del Campo is agreed between Henry VII and Ferdinand of Aragon.

Nov [29] Henry VII's daughter Margaret is born; Arthur is created Prince of Wales.

1490 The Scottish alliance with France is renewed; Scotland is now bound to attack England in the event of an English-French war.

1491 William Caxton, who established the first printing press in London and published nearly 80 books, dies. Charles VIII of France annexes Brittany by compelling Anne, Duchess of Brittany, to marry him. Henry VII opposes this and lays siege to Boulogne. Perkin Warbeck arrives in Cork, calling himself Richard, Duke of York.

Jun [28] Henry VIII is born at Greenwich, the son of Henry VII and Elizabeth of York.

Dec [21] Truce between England and Scotland declared at Coldstream.

1492

Jun [8] Queen Elizabeth Woodville, widow of Edward IV, dies.

Nov By the Treaty of Etaples, Henry agrees to withdraw from Boulogne on promise of a payment of £149,000.

1493 Margaret, Duchess of Burgundy, receives Warbeck as her nephew, calling him the 'White Rose of England'.

1494 Sir William Stanley and other noblemen are arrested, charged with complicity in the Warbeck plot and executed.

Dec Poynings' Law (the Statute of Drogheda) is passed by Sir Edward Poynings, the King's Deputy in Ireland; the law states that no Irish Parliament shall be held and no legislation made without the consent of the English Parliament. The University of Aberdeen is founded.

1495 William Tyndale is born.

Aug Warbeck fails to take Waterford.

Nov Perkin Warbeck arrives in Stirling.

1496 Jesus College, Cambridge, is founded. John Colet begins to lecture at Oxford. Mary Tudor, daughter of Henry VII, is born. Henry VII issues a patent to John Cabot's syndicate, giving him permission to annexe and trade with any lands hitherto unknown on his voyage of exploration. Perkin Warbeck is warmly received at the court of James IV of Scotland; James gives Warbeck Lady Catherine Gordon in marriage.

Sep James IV crosses the English Border accompanied by troops and Perkin Warbeck, but the raid is unsuccessful. Magnus Intercursus; this treaty between Henry VII and Philip of Burgundy encourages the export of wool to the Netherlands but forbids the entry of rebels against Henry into Philip's domains.

1497 The Cabots reach Nova Scotia and return with reports that
lead to the development of the Newfoundland fisheries.
Rebellion in Cornwall; the Cornish object to paying taxes
for a war against Scotland. 15,000 rebels march on
London, camping at Blackheath. Many desert; the remaining
rebels are beaten by the King's troops and the leaders
executed.

Jul [6] Warbeck leaves Scotland. James IV fails to take Norham
Castle; a truce is negotiated. [26] Warbeck lands in Cork.
Landing in Cornwall, he fails to take Exeter and flees to
Beaulieu Abbey where he is captured.

1498 A war between England and Scotland is narrowly averted.
Perkin Warbeck escapes, but is recaptured.

1499 An epidemic of plague sweeps across Scotland.

Feb [22] Henry VII's son Edmund Tudor is born (dies 1500).
Jul The truce between England and Scotland is renewed at
Stirling.
Nov [23] Perkin Warbeck is hanged in the Tower of London. The
Earl of Warwick is also executed, and with his death the male
line of Edward IV becomes extinct.

1500

1500 Wynkyn de Worde sets up his printing press in Fleet Street,
London; this is the beginning of a long connection between
Fleet Street and printing.

Sep [15] John Morton, Archbishop of Canterbury, dies.

1501 Negotiations are made for the marriage of James IV of
Scotland to Margaret Tudor. A spectacular pageant is staged
to greet Catherine of Aragon's arrival in London.

Aug [2] Henry Deane becomes Archbishop of Canterbury.
Nov [14] Arthur, Prince of Wales, marries Catherine of Aragon,
forming a major diplomatic link between England and Spain
against France.

1502 Margaret, Countess of Richmond (Henry VII's mother), founds divinity professorships at the Universities of Oxford and Cambridge. James IV of Scotland marries Margaret, Henry VII's daughter.

Apr [2] Arthur, Prince of Wales, dies; Catherine of Aragon is espoused to Arthur's 11-year-old brother Henry, after papal dispensation is obtained.

1503 Sir Thomas Wyatt is born. Queen Elizabeth, Henry VII's wife, dies in childbirth: the King is heart-broken.

Feb [15] Archbishop Deane dies.

1504 Henry VII places guilds and companies under state supervision. Coins are minted bearing an accurate likeness of the King.

Jan [24] William Warham becomes Archbishop of Canterbury.
Feb [18] Prince Henry, who became Duke of Cornwall on his brother Arthur's death, is created Prince of Wales and Earl of Chester.

1505 Henry VII grants a new charter to the Merchant Adventurers Company which holds an export monopoly in English cloth to Germany and the Low Countries. Thomas Tallis, composer, is born. Christ's College, Cambridge, is founded. The Prince of Wales' engagement to Catherine of Aragon is broken off.

Apr James IV of Scotland threatens to declare war on England.

1506 By the Treaty of Windsor, Henry Prince of Wales is engaged to Margaret of Austria, the daughter of Archduke Philip. Philip extradited the Yorkist pretender to the English throne, Edmund Earl of Suffolk, from the Tyrol; Edmund is subsequently imprisoned in the Tower of London.

1507 London is ravaged by an epidemic of 'sweating sickness', an infectious disease similar to the plague.

1508 James IV declines to give Henry VII of England an undertaking not to renew his alliance with France.

Archbishop Warham opens the tomb of St Dunstan at
Canterbury. In a leaden case he finds the saint's bones and a
lead plate inscribed with Dunstan's name. Warham
triumphantly writes to Abbot Bere of Glastonbury of his
discovery, instructing him to abandon all claim to his ,
Bere's, obviously fake 'Dunstan' relics. The first book to be
printed in Scotland is produced: it is a volume of Chaucer.

1509 Sebastian Cabot leads an expedition to search for the
North-West Passage to Asia, but turns back in Hudson Bay
when confronted by ice. Erasmus visits England for the third
time and lectures at Cambridge.

Apr [21] Henry VII dies at Richmond; his death is greeted wth
feasting, dancing and general rejoicing. He is succeeded by
his 17-year-old son, Henry VIII.

Jun [11] Henry VIII marries Catherine of Aragon. [24] Coronation
of Henry VIII.

1510 John Colet founds St Paul's School, London. Erasmus
becomes Professor of Greek at Cambridge. Richard Empson
and Edmund Dudley are executed for alleged treason; they
were Henry VII's extortionate tax-gatherers and House of
Commons speakers, and their execution was a calculated bid
for popularity. *Everyman*, the morality play, is performed for
the first time.

1511 Henry VIII joins the Holy League against the French and
begins large-scale reforms of the Royal Navy. The Scottish
warship *Great Michael* is built. All men under the age of 40 are
required to possess bows and arrows, and practise archery.

1512 Henry VIII claims the French throne. Scotland renews its
alliance and England finds itself at war with both France and
Scotland. English troops are sent, unsuccessfully, into Spain.
For the first time in the English Royal Navy double-decked
warships are used; they displace one thousand tons and are
armed with 70 guns. An Act of Parliament is passed

removing benefit of clergy for many serious crimes.
Physicians and surgeons are required to obtain licences from
the Bishop of London in order to practise in London.
Parliament forbids the importing of foreign caps into
England.

Apr [10] Queen Margaret of Scotland gives birth to a son,
James V.

Dec Bitter anti-clerical feelings in London result in the arrest of
Richard Hunne on heresy charges and his murder in prison.

1513 The Scots renew their alliance with France and invade
England.

Sep [9] Battle of Flodden Field; King James IV of Scotland is
defeated and killed by English troops under Thomas
Howard, Earl of Surrey, and thousands of Scots are
slaughtered in the battle. James is succeeded by his son,
James V, with Queen Margaret as his guardian. The Scottish
Navy is sold to France. Henry VIII withdraws from the Holy
League. Edmund, Earl of Suffolk, is executed.

1514 England makes peace with Scotland and France. Mary
Tudor, Henry VIII's sister, marries Louis XII of France; Louis
dies three months later and Mary then marries the Duke of
Suffolk. Thomas Wolsey becomes Archbishop of York and
orders work to begin on Hampton Court Palace.

Aug Queen Margaret Tudor, Regent of Scotland, marries
Archibald Douglas, Earl of Angus. John Colet and Erasmus
visit and describe the Shrine of St Thomas at Canterbury;
Erasmus leaves Cambridge and returns to the Continent.
Fresh green peas become a fashionable ingredient in the
English diet.

1515 Laws are passed against the enclosure of common land.
Richard Kidderminster, Abbot of Winchcombe, and Dr
Henry Standish debate the independence of the English
Church. The 300-foot spire of Louth Church is completed at a
cost of £305.

May   The Duke of Albany captures the young James V and makes
      himself Protector of Scotland.
Sep   [30] Albany forces Margaret Tudor, the Queen Regent, to flee
      to England.
Dec   [24] Thomas Wolsey becomes Lord Chancellor of England
      and a cardinal.

1516
Feb   [18] Queen Mary I (Mary Tudor) is born at Greenwich Palace,
      the daughter of Henry VIII and Catherine of Aragon.

1517 The Duke of Albany goes to France and Queen Margaret
      returns to Scotland. 'Evil May Day' riots in London are
      brutally suppressed; on Wolsey's orders 60 rioters are
      hanged. Wolsey is made papal legate to England. The galley
      Virgin Mary is launched, with Henry VIII acting the role of
      the ship's master, blowing a large whistle 'almost as loud as a
      trumpet'. A printing press is set up for the first time in
      Oxford.

1518 The Peace of London is devised by Wolsey between England,
      France, the Pope, Maximilian I and Spain; now that he is
      papal legate Wolsey's authority exceeds that of the
      Archbishop of Canterbury. Authorized by Henry VIII,
      Thomas Linacre founds a college of physicians. Another
      epidemic of 'sweating sickness' sweeps England, killing large
      numbers in the towns. Queen Margaret of Scotland quarrels
      with her husband Angus.

1519 Henry VIII becomes a candidate in the election of a Holy
      Roman Emperor; his secretary, Richard Pace, is sent to
      Germany to represent him. The King's illegitimate son,
      Henry Fitzroy, is born. Queen Margaret of Scotland forms an
      alliance with the Earl of Arran, the enemy of her husband
      Angus. The Royal Exchange in London is founded by
      Thomas Gresham, a merchant.

1520 Henry VIII journeys to Otford Palace, then on to Canterbury,
      Dover and France for the 'Field of the Cloth of Gold', a

diplomatic meeting with the French King Francis I; the result is an Anglo-French commercial treaty, agreed at Dover and Canterbury. Bowling lanes are built in Whitehall at the King's orders. A printing press is set up at Cambridge. A religious discussion group sympathetic to Church reform meets regularly at the White Horse tavern in Cambridge; among its members are Thomas Cranmer, Hugh Latimer, John Firth and Miles Coverdale.

Nov [19] The Duke of Albany returns to Scotland.

1521 Henry VIII and Wolsey attempt to set up a National Company to promote trade and discovery, but are prevented by obstruction from the London Livery Companies. Pope Leo X confers the title 'Defender of the Faith' on Henry VIII. Henry orders the execution of Edward Stafford, Duke of Buckingham, on trumped-up charges of disloyalty.

May In London many foreign Lutheran books are ceremoniously burned in front of Cardinal Wolsey.

Oct [24] Robert Fayrfax, composer, dies.

1522 England declares war on France and Scotland. The Holy Roman Emperor Charles V visits Henry VIII in England and signs the Treaty of Windsor; the two monarchs agree to invade France. Wolsey faces increasing opposition and criticism as his power increases. Hugh Aston, composer, dies.

1523 Sir Thomas More is elected Speaker of the House of Commons, after Parliament meets at Blackfriars. Parliament rebels against Henry VIII's demands for extra funds and he is forced to abandon his request.

Apr An English army under Dorset invades Scotland.

Sep The Duke of Albany returns to Scotland from France.

1524 Queen Margaret governs Scotland in alliance with the Earl of Arran, her husband having left Scotland for France in 1522. English courtiers feast on turkeys brought from South America. William Tyndale leaves England for Germany.

Oct   [20] Thomas Linacre, physician to Henry VII and Henry VIII, dies.

1525 Wolsey founds Cardinal College, Oxford, and completes the suppression of 29 religious houses, transferring their revenues to his new college which is later to become Christ Church. Wolsey concludes a peace agreement with France. Hops are introduced into England from Artois. Wolsey is forced to abandon his Amicable Loan, which is in effect a tax without Parliamentary approval. Henry Fitzroy, the King's illegitimate son, is created Duke of Richmond and Somerset.

1526 The Earl of Kildare, who rules Ireland, is committed to the Tower; he is replaced by Sir William Skeffington. The authorities in England try to prevent Tyndale's Bible being distributed. The portrait painter Hans Holbein come to England.

1527 Copies of William Tyndale's English translation of the New Testament are publicly burnt in St Paul's Cathedral. The Royal Divorce crisis begins, as Henry VIII appeals to the Pope for permission to divorce Catherine of Aragon. Henry's sister Margaret divorces Angus, and secretly marries Henry Stuart, Lord Methven. Sir Hugh Willoughby sets sail to try to discover a North-East Passage to China; he gets little support from the King, who prefers to spend his money strengthening the Royal Navy. John Dee, scholar and alchemist, is born.

1528 England and France are at war with Spain. In Scotland, Angus falls from power and the Scottish Reformation begins. The Scots under James V conclude a five-year truce with England. Wolsey dissolves 22 religious houses to provide funds for the foundation of several colleges. Wolsey has several men prosecuted for distributing copies of the Tyndale testament. Kentish weavers riot when the English staple for wool moves from Antwerp to Calais.

1529 English Church reforms begin; Henry VIII summons the Reformation Parliament. The Peace of Cambrai is signed. Cardinal Wolsey fails to procure for Henry a divorce from Catherine of Aragon; he is stripped of his property and most of his official positions, but remains Archbishop of York. After the fall of Wolsey, Sir Thomas More succeeds him as Lord Chancellor. Kildare is released from the Tower and returns to Ireland. Another epidemic of 'sweating sickness' sweeps through England.

1530 22 abbots sign a petition to the Pope in support of the Royal Divorce; royal agents tour European universities seeking the support of scholars for the 'illegality' of Henry's marriage, in the hope that this will persuade the Pope. The King orders a Commission to examine the need for an English Bible; its report is favourable to the idea. Wolsey is accused of treason and summoned to London.

Nov [29] Wolsey dies at Market Harborough on his way from York to London.

1531 The appearance of Halley's Comet causes widespread panic. The English clergy recognize Henry VIII as Supreme Head of the English Church. John Hilsey and George Browne 'visit' all the friaries in the country; the Houses of Observant Friars are closed. Thomas Cromwell, formerly an agent of Wolsey's, joins the Privy Council. The building of sewers in London is to be regulated by law.

1532 The Act of Annates. Henry VIII steadily whittles away papal authority in England in his determination to divorce Catherine of Aragon and marry Anne Boleyn; as a result, More resigns as Chancellor. Anne Boleyn is created Marquess of Pembroke. Skeffington is succeeded by Kildare as Lord Deputy in Ireland and there is increasing disorder. Holbein decides to settle permanently in England. Thomas Cromwell takes charge of the machinery of government.

Aug [22] Archbishop Warham dies.

1533 The truce between England and Scotland is renewed. The
Act of Appeals proclaims Henry VIII's new imperial status.

Jan   [25] Henry VIII marries Anne Boleyn in secret at Whitehall.

Mar   [30] Thomas Cranmer becomes Archbishop of Canterbury.

May   [23] The King's marriage to Catherine of Aragon is formally
annulled. [28] The King's marriage to Anne Boleyn is
declared valid. [31] Coronation of Anne Boleyn at
Westminster; the crowds who watch are sullen and quiet.

Jun   [24] Mary, the King's sister, dies.

1534 The Act of Supremacy; Henry VIII formally asserts control
over the English Church, severing ties with Rome. The First
Act of Succession; the succession to the English throne is to
lie with the heirs of Henry VIII and Queen Anne, and it is
treason to dispute that succession. The Treason Act; the
definition of treason is extended to include verbal attacks on
the King. The Act in Restraint of Annates; the King is
empowered to appoint bishops. The Dispensations Act;
requests from clerics to hold more than one living are to be
submitted to the Archbishop of Canterbury, not the Pope.
The Act for the Submission of the Clergy; all measures of
Convocation are to be submitted to the King for approval,
and the ultimate appeal in any ecclesiastical disputes is to lie
with the Crown. Cranmer invites several bishops and
scholars to correct and modify Tyndale's Bible, but nothing
worthwhile comes of this initiative. In Antwerp, Miles
Coverdale starts work on his own translation of the Bible into
English. English farmers are forbidden by law to own more
than 2000 sheep. The manufacturing of woollen cloth begins
in Worcester. A peace treaty is signed between England and
Scotland.

Mar   The King's marriage to Catherine of Aragon is 'utterly
dissolved' by Act of Parliament.

Apr   Elizabeth Barton, the 'Nun of Kent' who denounced the
King's divorce, is arrested and hanged at Tyburn.

Nov   Anne Boleyn bears Henry VIII a son, but he dies in infancy.

1535 Thomas Cromwell is appointed Vicar General by Henry VIII and begins to put into effect his plan for the seizure of the Church's wealth; the visitation of all religious houses begins. The execution of Prior Houghton and other Carthusian monks for resistance. Miles Coverdale's Bible in English is printed in Zürich. Henry VIII authorizes the printing of Coverdale's complete English Bible in London, by the printer James Nicholson. Lectures in civil law are substituted for those in canon law in English universities.

Jul [6] Sir Thomas More is executed on Tower Hill for treason; John Fisher is also executed.

1536 Parliament passes an Act for the Dissolution of the Smaller Monasteries, those with an annual income of less than £200, instigated by Henry VIII and Thomas Cromwell. Suppression of Robert Aske's Catholic rebellion. The Union of England and Wales. William Tyndale, the English Protestant and translator of the New Testament from Greek into English, is lured out of his safe house at Vilvorde and burnt at the stake as a heretic. Holbein is appointed Court painter to Henry VIII.

Jan [1] Lord Leonard Grey succeeds Skeffington as Lord Deputy in Ireland. [8] Catherine of Aragon dies at Kimbolton Palace.
May [17] The King's marriage to Anne Boleyn is declared invalid. [19] Anne Boleyn is executed. [30] Henry VIII marries Jane Seymour in the Queen's Chapel, Whitehall, only eleven days after his previous wife's execution.
Jul [22] The Duke of Richmond, the King's illegitimate son, dies aged 27.
Oct [1] The Pilgrimage of Grace begins at Louth; as a result of this rebellion against religious innovations 216 people are hanged.

1537 Robert Aske, the leader of the Yorkshire rebels in the Pilgrimage of Grace, is executed at York for treason. More

Carthusian monks are executed. Coverdale's Bible is given a royal licence by Henry VIII.

Jan [1] James V of Scotland marries Madeleine, the daughter of Francis I of France.

May [19] James V returns to Scotland.

Jul [7] Madeleine dies.

Oct [12] Edward VI is born at Hampton Court Palace. [24] His mother, Queen Jane Seymour, dies.

1538 James V of Scotland marries Mary of Guise. The surrender of the friaries. Thomas Becket's shrine at Canterbury is destroyed during an orgy of anti-papal iconoclasm.

Sep [5] Cromwell's Injunctions to the Clergy, instructing them to keep parish registers of weddings, baptisms and burials.

1539 Parliament passes an Act for the Dissolution of the Greater Monasteries; the remaining monasteries and abbeys are dissolved. Thomas Beche, Abbot of Colchester, Hugh Cook, Abbot of Reading, and Richard Whiting, Abbot of Glastonbury, are executed for treason. The Act of Six Articles sets out the points of Catholic doctrine that are still to be followed; instigated by Henry VIII, it is an attempt to stem the growing influence of English Protestants. Lady Glammis and her second husband Lord Lyon are accused of attempting to poison James V. Lady Glammis is burnt alive on the Castle Hill at Edinburgh; the next day her husband falls to his death from the rock while trying to escape. Their accuser, William Lyon, confesses to the King that they are innocent, but he is too late to save their lives.

Apr The 'Great Bible', in English, appears with Royal Approval.

1540 Robert Barnes, one of the first English Lutherans, is arrested and burnt for heresy at Smithfield.

Jan [1] Henry VIII meets Anne of Cleves for the first time. [6] Henry VIII marries Anne of Cleves. [25] Edmund Campion, English Jesuit and martyr, is born.

Feb   [9] The first recorded horse-race meeting in Britain takes place; it is held at the Roodeye Field, now the Roodee, at Chester.

Jul   [9] The King's marriage to Anne of Cleves is annulled and Cromwell is condemned for treason by a Bill of Attainder. [28] Thomas Cromwell is executed, largely for organizing the King's marriage to Anne of Cleves.

Aug [8] Henry VIII marries Catherine Howard.

1541 The Reformation begins in Scotland, led by John Knox. There is increasing friction between English and Scots in the Borders. James V of Scotland agrees to meet Henry VIII at York, but fails to turn up. Sir Thomas Wyatt dies. Henry VIII is elected King of Ireland and head of the Irish Church by the Irish Parliament; Wales is granted representation in the English Parliament.

Oct [18] Margaret, daughter of Henry VII, dies as the widow of James IV of Scotland.

1542 Ireland is formally declared to be a kingdom. Henry VIII's Second War with Scotland, precipitated by frequent border raids by the Scots. The Duke of Norfolk's army invades Scotland. The Battle of Solway Moss; the English army is victorious over the Scots, even though the Scots outnumber the English 3:1.

Feb   [13] Queen Catherine Howard is executed on Tower Green; two of her alleged lovers, Thomas Culpepper and Francis Dereham, have already been executed.

Mar [28] Margaret Davy is boiled alive for committing murder by poisoning. All Englishmen between the ages of 17 and 60 are required to possess bows and arrows.

Aug [24] The Scots defeat Sir Robert Bowes' troops at Hadden Rigg in the Borders.

Dec [8] Mary Stuart, later Queen of Scots, is born at Linlithgow Palace, the daughter of James V. [14] Demoralized by his crushing defeat at Solway Moss, James V of Scotland dies,

succeeded by Mary, daughter of James V by his second
marriage to Mary of Lorraine.

1543 An Act for the Advancement of True Religion is passed,
forbidding the labouring classes to read scripture. William
Byrd, composer, is born. Hans Holbein, painter, dies.
England is at war with France because of the 'secret'
Franco-Scottish alliance; Henry VIII and Charles V form an
alliance against France.

Jul The Treaties of Greenwich are signed by the English and
Scots, providing for the engagement of Mary, Queen of
Scots, to Prince Edward Tudor. [12] Henry VIII marries
Catherine Parr, his sixth wife, the widow of Lord Latimer.

Dec [11] The Scottish Parliament repudiates the Treaties of
Greenwich and renew the alliance with France.

1544 An Act of Parliament releases the King from his debts. Henry
VIII crosses to Calais to campaign with the Emperor Charles
V against France. The English invasion of Scotland; English
forces under Edward Seymour and John Dudley capture
Leith and leave Edinburgh in flames. Henry VIII secretly
promises to make Matthew, Earl of Lennox, Governor of
Scotland if Scotland is defeated. Princess Mary and Princess
Elizabeth are recognized by Parliament as heirs, after Prince
Edward, to the English throne.

1545
Feb [25] English forces are defeated by the Scots at Ancrum
Moor. Parliament meets to raise funds for the war against
Scotland. A French fleet enters the Solent; French troops
land on the Isle of Wight. Treport in Normandy is set on fire
by an English fleet under Lord Lisle. The sale of monastic
lands encourages the rise of the middle classes, but inflation
hits the poorest classes.

Jul [19] The warship *Mary Rose* suddenly heels over and sinks in
the Solent; 700 men are drowned as Henry watches from
Southsea Castle.

1546 The Peace of Ardres: Anglo-French hostilities end. The first book in Welsh is printed (*Yng Lhyvyr hwnn*). Henry VIII falls dangerously ill with syphilis and cirrhosis and nominates a Council of Regency for his heir. The population of England tops four million; thousands of people are close to starvation after a succession of poor harvests.

May [29] Cardinal Beaton is murdered.

Jul   Anne Askew is burnt at the stake at Smithfield for the heresy of attacking the Mass.

1547 The Vagrant Act; an able-bodied vagrant may be adjudged by two magistrates to anyone wanting him as a slave, branded with a 'V' and kept in slavery for two years. The miniaturist Nicholas Hilliard is born.

Jan [21] The Earl of Surrey, poet and soldier, is executed. [28] Henry VIII dies at Whitehall Palace at the age of 55. [31] Earl of Hertford becomes Lord Protector in the name of the new boy king, Edward VI.

Feb [16] Earl of Hertford is created Duke of Somerset. [25] Coronation of the nine-year-old Edward VI at Westminster Abbey.

Jul The town of St Andrews is captured by the Scottish Regent, Arran. In the war between the English and the Scots, the English seek to enforce the Marriage Treaty of 1543, which would unite the two kingdoms.

Sep [10] Battle of Pinkie; English troops under the Duke of Somerset defeat the Scottish army, capture Edinburgh, and crush resistance to Edward VI.

1548 The heresy laws in England are abolished. All craft guilds are abolished except for the London Guilds which are powerful and resist abolition.

Jun 6000 French troops land at Leith and Mary Stuart, aged six and engaged to the Dauphin, is taken to France.

Aug [13] Mary Stuart arrives in France.

Sep   [5] Catherine Parr, former queen of Henry VIII and now wife of Lord Seymour, dies in childbirth at Sudeley Castle near Cheltenham.

1549 A rebellion in Devon and Cornwall, caused by widespread dislike of Protestant reforms, is suppressed by Lord Russell.

Jun   [9] An Act of Uniformity, authorizing the first English Book of Common Prayer, compiled by Thomas Cranmer.

Jul   [12] Kett's Rebellion in Norfolk is prompted by economic grievances – antipathy towards the enclosure movement in particular. The rebels capture Norwich and set up a commonwealth on Mousehold Heath; they are later routed by the Earl of Warwick's troops at the Battle of Dussindale, and the leaders hanged. Thomas, Lord Seymour of Sudeley, brother of Protector Somerset, is executed for treason.

Oct   [10] The Duke of Somerset is deprived of office as Lord Protector and imprisoned in the Tower; his fall from power is due to failures in the Scottish war, the execution of his own brother for treason, and his generally overbearing conduct. The Earl of Warwick rules England as Protector.

1550 The Duke of Somerset is released from the Tower, but plots to regain his former authority. The Duke of Northumberland, formerly Earl of Warwick, fears Somerset's influence and causes him to be arrested and condemned to death for treason.

1551 Thomas Cranmer's 42 Articles, the basis of Anglican Protestantism, are published. The first civil divorce is granted on the grounds of adultery. The theodolite is invented by Leonard Digges. Stephen Gardiner, Bishop of Winchester, is deposed. Miles Coverdale becomes Bishop of Exeter.

1552 Second Act of Uniformity, authorizing the Second Protestant Prayer Book of Edward VI, which dismantles the Mass. Christ's Hospital in London is founded by Edward VI. Books of geography and astronomy are burnt in England because of fears that they may be used for magic. The poet Edmund Spenser is born.

Jan   Edward Seymour, Duke of Somerset, is executed.

1553 Sir Hugh Willoughby and Richard Chancellor try to find the North-East Passage to Asia. Willoughby discovers Novaya Zemlya and later dies on the Kola Peninsula. Chancellor reaches Archangel and journeys overland to Moscow, where negotiations lead to the founding of the Muscovy Company. Thomas Cromwell becomes Lord Chancellor.

May [21] Lady Jane Grey marries Lord Guildford Dudley, son of the Duke of Northumberland.

Jul [6] Edward VI dies of tuberculosis at Greenwich. [9] Lady Jane Grey is proclaimed Queen by the Duke of Northumberland, who had earlier persuaded the dying King to will the throne to her. Northumberland fails to secure Mary, the rightful heir, because the army will not support him; Mary escapes to East Anglia and then returns to London with her supporters. As she arrives in London, she is acclaimed as Queen by the people. [19] Lady Jane Grey is deposed, succeeded by Mary I. The Royal Supremacy is retained by Mary, but by an Act of Repeal many other Acts are revoked, such as the 1549 and 1552 Acts of Uniformity; the Mass, holy-days and celibate clergy are all revived. Miles Coverdale is deprived of his bishopric.

Aug [22] Northumberland is executed.

1554 The Corn Law of 1436 is re-enacted by the English Parliament in a vain effort to relieve serious food shortages.

Jan Wyatt's Rebellion; Sir Thomas Wyatt raises a rebel army of 4000 in Kent, in opposition to Queen Mary's impending marriage. Wyatt surrenders on the outskirts of London, is arrested and executed. Princess Elizabeth is suspected of complicity in Wyatt's Rebellion and sent to the Tower.

Feb [12] Lady Jane Grey, who was Queen of England for only nine days, is executed on Tower Green for high treason.

Jul   [25] Mary I marries Philip King of Naples and Jerusalem (who is to become King Philip II of Spain in Jan 1556); the English Parliament will not allow Philip to be crowned King of England. A reconciliation is negotiated between England and the Pope, and the Pope once again becomes head of the English Church. John Knox flees to Geneva.

Nov   A Second Act of Repeal removes all anti-papal measures passed since 1529.

1555 The persecution of Protestants begins in Britain. A Commission headed by Bishop Gardiner opens at Southwark for the trial of heretics: transubstantiation and the Pope's supremacy are the key issues. Mary appoints a committee to consider the re-foundation of certain religious houses, and monasteries at Greenwich, Smithfield, Sheen, Syon and Kings Langley are reopened. Princess Elizabeth is released from the Tower. The Muscovy Company is founded. Famine sweeps Britain.

Feb   [9] John Hooper, Bishop of Gloucester, is burned at the stake in Gloucester for heresy, under the newly-revived laws.

Oct   [16] Hugh Latimer, Bishop of Worcester, and Nicholas Ridley, Bishop of London, are burned at the stake for heresy outside the town ditch in Oxford.

Nov   Bishop Gardiner dies.

Dec   [11] Archbishop Cranmer is deprived of his office. John Knox returns to Scotland. Polydore Vergil, scholar, dies.

1556 Richard Chancellor dies when his ship is wrecked off Scotland. Stephen Borough tries to find the North-East Passage, and reaches the Kara Sea. The writer Nicholas Udall dies. The Benedictine house at Westminster is re-founded.

Mar   [21] Thomas Cranmer, the first Protestant Archbishop of Canterbury (in 1533), is burned at the stake at Oxford, condemned both as traitor and heretic. [22] Reginald Pole becomes Archbishop of Canterbury after his predecessor's execution.

Jul   Knox leaves Scotland for Geneva.

1557 Philip II visits England and persuades Mary to declare war on France.

Jul   [16] Anne of Cleves, the fourth wife of Henry VIII, dies in retirement in Lewes.

Aug   [10] Battle of St Quentin; English and Spanish armies are victorious over the French. An English whale fishery is established at Spitzbergen. The explorer Sebastian Cabot dies. The first English play to be censored, *The Sack-Full of Newes*, is put on at Aldgate in London and promptly suppressed. The composer William Morley is born.

1558 Thomas Gresham, the English financier, proposes reforms in currency based on the assumption, 'Gresham's Law', that bad money drives good money out of circulation.

Jan   [7] Calais is lost to the French; this is regarded in England as a national disaster.

Apr   The last of the Scottish Protestant martyrs, Walter Milne, is burned to death. [24] Mary Stuart marries the Dauphin, later Francis II of France.

Sep   [1] Protestant riot in Edinburgh.

Nov   [17] Mary I dies at St James's Palace, succeeded by Elizabeth I, her half-sister. Elizabeth keeps Mary's council, adding Sir William Cecil, later Lord Burghley; Sir Francis Walsingham is her private secretary. [18] Cardinal Pole dies. After the accession of Elizabeth, English Protestants begin to return from Switzerland, as more favourable conditions for them prevail in England.

1559 Elizabeth suppresses the re-founded religious houses. A Royal Injunction is issued, to the effect that a Bible must be available in every church. Act of Supremacy; Elizabeth I becomes Supreme Governor of the English Church. Act of Uniformity; this orders the use of the 1552 Prayer Book, leading to a religious settlement in England. Mary, Queen of Scots, assumes the title Queen of England and

Scotland when her husband Francis II succeeds to the French throne.

Jan [15] Coronation of Elizabeth I.

Apr [2] Treaty of Cateau-Cambrésis between France and England; Calais is to be ceded to England in eight years' time.

May John Knox preaches an inflammatory sermon at Perth, inciting the Protestant lords to rise in rebellion; they capture Edinburgh and sack religious houses.

Jun [10] The Queen Regent of Scotland dies.

Dec [17] Matthew Parker becomes Archbishop of Canterbury.

1560 Eric XIV succeeds to the Swedish throne and courts Elizabeth I, unsuccessfully. The Church of Scotland is founded. Westminster School is founded. Puritanism begins in England. Elizabeth I orders the subjugation of Shane O'Neill, who has become the most powerful man in Ireland. Mary, Queen of Scots', claim to the English throne is repudiated; Francis II of France dies and Mary is widowed.

Jan Treaty of Berwick, between Elizabeth I and the Scottish reformers. French troops are besieged at Leith.

Jul [6] Treaty of Edinburgh between England, France and Scotland; French troops are to be withdrawn from Scotland and France's interference in Scottish affairs is to end.

1561 John Knox's *Book of Discipline* establishes a church constitution in Scotland. St Paul's Cathedral in London suffers serious fire damage.

Jan [22] Francis Bacon is born at York House in the Strand.

Aug [19] Mary, Queen of Scots, returns to Scotland.

1562 John Hawkins, a naval commander, takes 300 African slaves from a Portuguese slave ship bound for Brazil; this is the beginning of British participation in the slave trade. Milled coins are introduced for the first time in England. The Earl of Tyrone leads two unsuccessful rebellions in Ireland. The first conservatory in Britain is built by William Cecil to protect his sub-tropical plants from the English weather. Treaty of Hampton Court, signed by Elizabeth I and Louis I de Bourbon, the Huguenot leader; it calls for English troops to occupy Dieppe and Le Havre.

Jan   [6] Shane O'Neill appears in London to make submission to Queen Elizabeth.

1563 English soldiers at Le Havre catch the plague and bring it back to England, where it kills 20,000 people in London alone. The 39 Articles of Anglican belief define the Elizabethan Church Settlement. The Statute of Apprentices empowers Justices of the Peace to determine wage levels. The composer William Byrd becomes organist at Lincoln Cathedral. The composers John Bull and John Dowland are born.

1564 The Peace of Troyes ends the war between England and France; England renounces its claim to Calais in exchange for a substantial payment. An English trading centre is established at Emden. Elizabeth I involves herself in the slave trade by lending John Hawkins a ship in return for a share of the profits.

Feb   [6] The poet and dramatist Christopher Marlowe is born at Canterbury.

Apr   [23] William Shakespeare is born.

1565 The Royal College of Physicians in London is officially permitted to carry out human dissections. The Royal Exchange in London is founded. Tobacco and sweet potatoes are introduced into Britain. The manufacture of pencils begins in England.

Jul   [29] Mary, Queen of Scots, marries her cousin Lord Darnley at her private chapel in Holyroodhouse. [30] Heralds proclaim Darnley as Henry, King of Scots, but without Parliament's agreement.

1566 Archbishop Parker's 'Advertisements' demand religious conformity. David Rizzio, Italian private secretary to Mary,

Queen of Scots, is murdered in Holyroodhouse on the orders of her husband, Lord Darnley.

Jun [19] James VI of Scotland is born in Edinburgh, the son of Henry Stewart, Lord Darnley, and Mary, Queen of Scots.

1567 Rugby School is founded by Laurence Sheriff. The writer Thomas Nashe is born.

Jan Thomas Campion, physician, composer and poet, is born.

Feb [10] Lord Darnley, second husband of Mary, Queen of Scots, is murdered in the early hours of the morning at a house near Edinburgh called Kirk o' Field. There is an explosion, which wrecks the house, but Darnley's corpse is found some distance away; he has apparently been strangled while trying to escape. Lord Bothwell, the probable murderer, pretends to abduct Mary.

May [15] Mary, Queen of Scots, marries Bothwell.

Jun [15] Mary surrenders at Carberry Hill. [16] Mary is imprisoned at Loch Leven Castle. [24] Mary, Queen of Scots, is deposed, abdicating under pressure in favour of her son, James VI. The Earl of Moray is named Regent.

1568 John Hawkins is defeated and his slave-trading voyages come to an end. Adventurers from Devon attempt to settle in Munster, Ireland. Twenty years of conflict between Catholic and Protestant Churches begin. Elizabeth I's tutor, Roger Ascham, dies.

May [2] Mary, Queen of Scots, escapes from Loch Leven. [13] Mary and her supporters lose the Battle of Langside. [16] Mary sails across the Solway Firth to England. [19] Mary is captured and imprisoned at Carlisle Castle. [28] Mary receives Sir Francis Knollys and Lord Scrope and urges her right of access to Queen Elizabeth.

Jun [8] Elizabeth I writes to Mary, assuring her safety and saying that it would be one of her 'highest worldly pleasures' to receive her, once she was acquitted of the crime of her husband's murder.

1569 A public lottery is held in London to help pay for repairs to the port. The Revolt of the Desmonds in Ireland. Miles Coverdale, translator of the Bible, dies. Rebellion in England of the Northern (Catholic) Earls, led by the Earls of Northumberland and Westmorland in an abortive attempt to restore Catholic worship and release Mary, Queen of Scots, from captivity. They ransack Durham Cathedral, but flee to Scotland when faced with Elizabeth's army.

1570 Thomas Cartwright, Professor of Divinity at Cambridge, compares the Elizabethan Church unfavourably with the early Church, and is subsequently dismissed.

Jan [23] The Earl of Moray, the Scottish Regent, is assassinated by the Hamiltons, resulting in a civil war with Mary's supporters. [27] The Earl of Lennox is proclaimed Regent.

Feb Queen Elizabeth is anathametized and declared deposed by Pope Pius V. As a result, Catholics come under suspicion as possible traitors.

1571 Harrow School and Jesus College, Oxford, are founded. Roberto di Ridolfi, a Florentine, plots with Philip II, the Duke of Alva and the Pope to marry Mary, Queen of Scots, to the Duke of Norfolk, depose Queen Elizabeth and restore Catholicism to England. The plot is exposed; the Duke of Norfolk and the Earl of Westmorland are later executed.

Jan [23] The Royal Exchange in London is opened as a bankers' meeting house.

Apr [7] The Archbishop of St Andrews is hanged for complicity in the Earl of Moray's murder.

Sep [4] The Scottish Regent, the Earl of Lennox, dies, succeeded by the Earl of Mar.

1572 The Society of Antiquaries in London is founded. The Duke of Norfolk and Earl of Northumberland are executed for treason. Lord Burghley becomes Lord High Treasurer.

Jun [11] The poet and dramatist Ben Jonson is born at
      Westminster.
Oct The Scottish Regent, the Earl of Mar, dies.
Nov [24] The Earl of Morton is elected Scottish Regent; John Knox
      dies.

1573 The composer Christopher Tye dies; the composer John
      Wilbye is born. John Donne, poet, is born. The Revolt of the
      Desmonds in Ireland is crushed. Fighting in Scotland ends
      with the Pacification of Perth. Edinburgh Castle later
      surrenders to an English army, finally freeing Elizabeth I
      from all threats from Scotland; support for Mary in Scotland
      collapses. Sir Francis Drake captures a huge shipment of
      Spanish silver in Panama.

Jul [15] The architect Inigo Jones is born in London.

1575 Parliament guarantees freedom from arrest to its members
      and their servants. Elizabeth I grants Thomas Tallis and
      William Byrd a music-publishing monopoly.

Mar [5] William Oughtred, mathematician and inventor of the
      slide rule, is born at Eton.
May [17] Archbishop Parker dies.
Jul [7] English troops are defeated by Scots in a skirmish at
      Redswire in the Borders.

1576 Peter Wentworth, a Puritan MP, alleges that the Queen is
      curbing free speech in the Commons, and is sent to prison
      for saying so. The Theatre in Shoreditch is the first
      purpose-built theatre in Britain. Martin Frobisher discovers
      Frobisher Bay in Canada.

Feb [15] Edmund Grindal becomes Archbishop of Canterbury.
Dec The Queen instructs Grindal to suppress all prophesyings,
      but he refuses to comply on the grounds that this will
      exclude Puritans from the Church; he offers to resign.

1577 At the 'Black Assize' in Oxford, all those in court, including
      the judge and jury, die of typhus carried by the prisoners. Sir

Thomas Gresham establishes by will the first British institute for teaching science, which is later to become the Royal Society. London's second playhouse, The Curtain, opens in Finsbury.

Jun   Archbishop Grindal is suspended for continuing to oppose the Queen on the matter of prophesyings.

Dec   [13] Francis Drake begins his voyage round the world in the *Golden Hind*, embarking from Plymouth.

1578 Sir Humphrey Gilbert is granted a patent to settle North America.

Mar   [12] James VI of Scotland assumes personal rule when the Regent, the Earl of Morton, resigns.

Apr   [1] William Harvey, discoverer of the circulation of the blood, is born at Folkestone.

1579 The English Eastland Company is chartered to trade with Scandinavia and the Baltic States. The first Englishman to settle in India, Father Thomas Stephens, settles in Goa. The Duke of Anjou lands in England to propose marriage to Queen Elizabeth. There is a new outbreak of the Desmond revolt in Ireland; Munster is laid waste by the fighting.

Jun   [17] Francis Drake claims 'Nova Albion' (California) in the name of Queen Elizabeth, according to a brass plaque discovered near the Golden Gate Bridge.

1580 New building in London is prohibited to prevent the city from growing any larger.

Apr   [6] An earth tremor kills two people in London and damages Old St Paul's Cathedral. In the summer a Jesuit mission in England is begun by Edmund Campion and Robert Parsons.

Sep   [26] Drake and his crew return to Plymouth in the *Golden Hind* at the end of the world voyage.

1581 In England, fears spread that a Jesuit invasion is imminent. Converts to Roman Catholicism in Britain are subject by law to the penalties for high treason. Edmund Campion's *Decem*

Rationes is secretly printed at Stonor Park in Oxfordshire. The *Ark Royal* is built for Sir Walter Raleigh, as *Ark Raleigh*, and then sold to the Queen as a flagship. Sedan chairs come into general use in Britain.

Jan [4] Archbishop Ussher is born.

Apr [4] Francis Drake is knighted on the *Golden Hind* at Deptford.

Jun [2] The Earl of Morton is executed for his part in Lord Darnley's murder.

Dec Edmund Campion is executed.

1582 Sir Humphrey Gilbert's expedition reaches Newfoundland. 30,000 people die in Munster, mainly of starvation. Edinburgh University is founded. London's first waterworks are installed, pumping water to private houses for the first time.

Aug [22] The Raid of Ruthven; James VI of Scotland is kidnapped by Protestant nobles to separate him from the influence of his Catholic favourites.

Nov [27] William Shakespeare marries Anne Hathaway at the age of 18.

1583 Sir Walter Raleigh goes to Virginia. Gerald Earl of Desmond dies; the Plantation (or colonization) of Munster begins. The composer Orlando Gibbons is born. Francis Throckmorton leads a conspiracy to overthrow Queen Elizabeth and free Mary Stuart; Throckmorton's plot is discovered and he is executed.

Jun [27] James VI escapes from his abducters and hides in St Andrews.

Jul [6] Archbishop Grindal dies.

Sep [9] Sir Humphrey Gilbert, the explorer, is drowned during his voyage home; his ship, *The Squirrel*, sinks off the Azores drowning all on board. [23] John Whitgift becomes Archbishop of Canterbury.

1584 Walter Raleigh founds a colony on Roanoke Island and is knighted for his services. With Parliamentary approval, an

Association of noblemen is formed to 'pursue to the death
anyone plotting against the Queen': it is even signed by
Mary.

May [4] The Earl of Gowrie, one of the instigators of the Raid of
Ruthven, is beheaded at Stirling.

1585 The English intervene in the Spanish-Dutch War: Drake
attacks Spanish ports and English ships in other Spanish
ports are confiscated. John Davis discovers the Davis Strait
between Greenland and Canada. William Shakespeare leaves
Stratford for London. The composer Thomas Tallis dies. John
Schorne's bones are removed to an unknown place from his
tomb in St George's Chapel, Windsor. Dr William Parry is
tried for alleged treason and subsequently executed. James
VI signs a peace pact with England.

Nov Secretary Fenton visits Munster and devises a scheme to
repopulate the province.

1586 The Virginia settlers choose to return to England with Drake
rather than stay in America. In York, Margaret Clitheroe is
pressed to death for hiding priests. The Babington Plot to kill
the Queen is uncovered by Sir Francis Walsingham; Francis
Babington and his fellow conspirators are executed. Mary
Stuart is clearly implicated in the plot, but her sentence is
postponed. Thomas Cavendish leaves Plymouth to sail
round the world, becoming the second British commander to
do so. John Ford, playwright, is born in Devon.

Jul [28] The first potatoes arrive in Britain, brought from
Colombia to Plymouth by Sir Thomas Harriot.

Sep [22] Battle of Zutphen; Anglo-Dutch victory.

Oct Sir Philip Sidney dies of battle wounds after the Battle of
Zutphen.

1587 Sir Francis Drake makes further raids on Spanish shipping.

Feb [8] Mary, Queen of Scots, is executed at Fotheringhay Castle
after nearly 19 years in prison. She is executed for her

implication in the Babington Plot to overthrow Queen
Elizabeth and restore Roman Catholicism in England.

Apr   [18] John Foxe, author of *The Book of Martyrs*, dies.

1588 31 Catholic priests are executed during the year. Robert
Dudley, Earl of Leicester, dies. Timothy Bright publishes the
first shorthand manual, *An Arte of Shorte, Swifte and Secrete
Writing by Character*.

May   [19] The Catholic invasion fleet, the Spanish Armada, sets
sail from Lisbon.

Jul   [29] The Spanish Armada is defeated by an English fleet
under Howard and Drake, off Plymouth. The defeat of the
Armada opens the world to English trade and colonization.

1589 The stocking frame, the first knitting machine, is invented by
William Lee. John Harington invents, designs and instals the
world's first flushing water closet at his house at Kelston near
Bath; he calls it 'Ajax'. A Commission is appointed to
examine the progress of the Munster colonization project.

Apr   The Portugal Expedition; Drake fails in an attempt to capture
Lisbon with 150 ships and 18,000 men.

Aug   [20] James VI of Scotland marries Anne of Denmark.

1590

Apr   [6] Sir Francis Walsingham, diplomat and creator of Elizabeth
I's secret service, dies.

May   [1] James VI of Scotland returns to Leith.

1591 Trinity College, Dublin, is founded. The composer Thomas
Whythorne dies. Sir Christopher Hatton, Lord Chancellor
and favourite of the Queen, dies. Sir Richard Grenville, the
naval commander, is killed when his ship, the *Revenge*, is
sunk by a large Spanish squadron in a battle off the Azores.

1592 Queen Elizabeth visits Kelston, tries the 'Ajax' flushing
lavatory, likes it and orders one for herself. John Davis, the
English explorer, discovers the Falkland Islands. Sir John
Burrows captures the Portuguese galleon *Madre de Dios* with

its £800,000 cargo. Plague in London kills 15,000 people. John Jenkins, composer, is born.

Feb [7] The Earl of Moray is murdered by the Earl of Huntly.

1593 London's theatres close for a year because of the plague. Admiral Sir Richard Hawkins recommends drinking orange and lemon juice as a way of preventing scurvy in the Navy. George Herbert, writer, is born.

May [30] Christopher Marlowe, poet and playwright, is murdered in mysterious circumstances in a pub brawl at Deptford; he is 29.

Aug [9] Izaak Walton, author, is born at Stafford.

1594 The first of five consecutive bad harvests starts an economic recession. The Scottish Highlanders under the Earl of Argyl are defeated by the Earl of Huntly. Hugh O'Neill, Earl of Tyrone, leads a rising in Ulster, appealing to Spain for help. Martin Frobisher is killed while helping an Anglo-French force to recapture the port of Brest from the Spanish. The London theatres re-open.

Feb [19] Henry, son of James VI of Scotland, is born.

1595 Raleigh explores 300 miles of the Orinoco with four ships and 100 men, in his search for El Dorado. Attempts by Sir John Norris, commander of the English forces in Ireland, fail to stamp out the Tyrone revolt. The University of Cambridge is divided over the issue of predestination; the Queen intervenes, calling a halt to the discussion. Londoners riot for bread. The bow is finally abandoned by the English army as a weapon of war.

Aug Expedition to the West Indies; Richard Hawkins and Francis Drake leave on their last voyage to the Spanish Main. The expedition is a failure and both Drake and Hawkins die during the voyage.

1596 The Pacification of Ireland is signed, but the Earl of Tyrone refuses to abide by it. Cadiz is sacked by the English; the

Spanish capture Calais. Tomatoes are introduced into Britain, where they are grown initially as ornamental plants. Bartholomew Steere and 20 others are executed in Oxford for planning a rebellion.

Jan [28] Sir Francis Drake dies of dysentery on board his ship and is buried at sea.

1597 A second Armada leaves for Britain, but is scattered by storms. Hammocks are authorized by the Admiralty for use on Royal Naval vessels. Sentences of transportation for criminals are prescribed by Act of Parliament. Several Acts are passed which try to deal with problems of poverty and social distress: the Act against the Decay of Towns and Houses, the Act for the Maintenance of Husbandry and Tillage, the Act for the Relief of the Poor.

Sep Nine people are reported to have died 'for want in the streets' in Newcastle.

Oct 16 more die in the streets in Newcastle.

1598 The Poor Law Act: Parliament provides for the founding of workhouses and the punishment of beggars. Parliament votes to levy increased taxation to pay for the Spanish War. William Cecil, Lord Burghley, dies. The Bodleian Library at Oxford is founded by Sir Thomas Bodley.

Aug [14] Battle of the Yellow Ford; English forces are defeated.

Sep Francis Bacon is arrested for debt.

1599 The Earl of Tyrone leads a rebellion against English rule. Robert Devereux, Earl of Essex, is appointed Lord Lieutenant in Ireland. The Globe Theatre is opened in Southwark; it is owned by the actors themselves.

Mar [22] Sir Anthony van Dyck, Court painter to Charles I, is born at Antwerp.

Apr [25] Oliver Cromwell is born at Huntingdon, the son of Robert Cromwell and Elizabeth Steward.

| Sep | [8] Essex signs a truce with the Irish rebel leader, the Earl of Tyrone, after being defeated at Arklow. [28] Essex returns to England without leave. |
| Nov | Essex is arrested and banished. |

1600

1600	The Earl of Essex is tried for his actions in Ireland and deprived of his offices. Will Kemp morris-dances all the way from London to Norwich. William Gilbert discovers the earth's magnetism. The Queen grants a charter establishing the East India Company.
Jan	The Earl of Tyrone and his men invade Munster; Mountjoy succeeds Essex as Deputy.
Aug	[5] Gowrie and Ruthven conspire to murder James VI; both are killed.

| 1601 | Monopolies are abolished. The Poor Law Act: a codification of all the previous Tudor Poor Laws. Elizabeth's 'Golden Speech' to Parliament, in which she reviews England's achievements during her reign. Two fleets from Spain arrive to help the Irish in their rebellion against English rule. The writer Thomas Nashe dies. |
| Feb | [8] The Earl of Essex's Rebellion. [25] The Earl of Essex is executed. |

| 1602 | English forces under the command of Lord Mountjoy capture an invading Spanish army in Ireland. The Jesuits are ordered to leave England. The composer Thomas Morley dies; the composer William Lawes is born. |

1603	
Mar	[24] Elizabeth I dies at Richmond Palace aged 69. [31] Accession of James VI of Scotland as James I of England, uniting the kingdoms of England and Scotland.
Apr	[5] King James leaves Scotland for England. [28] Elizabeth I's funeral in Westminster Abbey.

May [7] James enters London.
Jul [25] Coronation of James I. Sir Walter Raleigh is suspected of
leading a plot (the Main Plot) to dethrone James I; he is tried
for treason and imprisoned in the Tower. Plague becomes
widespread in Britain. Puritans present the Millenary
Petition to James I, objecting to pluralities, non-residence
and non-preaching ministers. Cobham's Plot to dethrone
James I and place Arabella Stuart on the throne results in
Cobham's imprisonment.

1604 Treaty of London: Peace between Britain and Spain. A
commercial treaty with France is signed.

Jan [14] The Hampton Court Conference meets to discuss Church
reforms, based on the Millenary Petition. James I disappoints
the Puritans and fails to resolve religious conflicts, but the
conference does lead to the production of the Authorized
Version of the Bible.
Feb [29] Archbishop Whitgift dies.
Dec [10] Richard Bancroft becomes Archbishop of Canterbury.

1605 The first railway in Britain is constructed, a pit-head track
built by Sir Francis Willoughby at Wollaton in
Nottinghamshire. The Butchers' and Shipwrights'
Companies are incorporated in London.

Nov [5] The Gunpowder Plot. Failing to gain religious toleration
from James, Catholics plan to destroy King and Parliament;
the plot fails when 36 barrels of gunpowder are discovered in
the cellars of the Houses of Parliament. This is the last major
Catholic conspiracy. Some of the conspirators, including
Robert Catesby, are killed at Holbeach House; others,
including Guy Fawkes, are captured and tortured.

1606 Impositions (taxes) are levied at English ports as part of the
Royal Prerogative. The Virginia Company is formed and
granted a Royal Charter: 120 colonists set off for Virginia. Sir
William Davenant, writer, is born.

Jan   [31] Guy Fawkes and his fellow-conspirators are executed by being hanged, drawn and quartered.

Apr   [12] The Union Jack is adopted as the English flag.

1607 King James's plan to unite the kingdoms of England and Scotland fails; the English Parliament rejects the proposed union. Nevertheless, the courts confirm the common citizenship of English and Scottish subjects born after James's accession to the English throne.

May   [13] Virginia is re-colonized; Jamestown is founded by Captain John Smith.

1608 The first municipal library is opened in Norwich: it contains mainly theological books. The Royal Blackheath Golf Club is founded in London. John Dee, Queen Elizabeth I's astrologer, dies in extreme poverty.

Dec   [9] The poet John Milton is born at Cheapside in London.

1609 Rebellion of the Northern Earls in Ireland; beginning of the Planting of Ulster by Scots and English Protestants. James I encourages the colonization of North America. A regular financial grant to the King is discussed in Parliament but not agreed. James I appoints Justices of the Peace to prevent feuding in the Scottish Border country.

1610 Arabella Stuart, Pretender to the throne, is imprisoned in the Tower for marrying William Seymour, Earl of Hertford. The Great Contract between King and Commons is drafted by the younger Cecil; the King offers to give up some of his feudal rights in return for an annual allowance of £200,000, but the Commons reject the proposal. Henry, the King's son, is created Prince of Wales and Earl of Chester. Archbishop Bancroft dies.

1611 Colonization of Ulster by English and Scottish colonists; the confiscated estates of rebel lords are shared out among the immigrants. The Authorized Version of the Bible appears, probably the only great literary work ever to have been produced by a committee. The Order of Baronets is instituted by James I to raise money. James I dissolves Parliament for the first time.

Apr [9] George Abbot becomes Archbishop of Canterbury.

1612 Robert Cecil, Lord Salisbury, dies. Robert Carr, Viscount Rochester, becomes the King's chief minister in his place. A flag is flown at half mast to signify a death for the first time, as a tribute to the master of the *Heartsease*, who dies while searching for the North-West Passage. The two last people to be burnt for heresy are Bartholomew Legate and Richard Wightman of Lichfield.

Jan [17] Thomas Fairfax, commander of the Parliamentary army in the Civil War, is born.

Nov [6] Prince Henry, James's promising elder son, dies.

1613 Sir Thomas Overbury, poet and courtier, is sent the Tower for disrespect to the King. He has circulated a poem entitled *A Wife*, which is interpreted as an attack on Lady Essex, whom the King's favourite Robert Carr wished to marry. Overbury dies slowly, poisoned with copper sulphate by Lady Essex's agents.

1614 George Villiers is introduced to James I in an attempt to win the King away from Robert Carr. The scandal surrounding Sir Thomas Overbury's death is made public. Carr and Lady Essex are disgraced and her agents are hanged. The first logarithm tables are published by John Napier.

Apr– Second Parliament of James I; its 300 new members include
Jun John Pym, Thomas Wentworth and John Eliot.

Jun [7] James I dissolves the 'Addled' Parliament, which has disputed non-stop with the King over impositions and produced no legislation. For seven years after this James I calls no Parliament.

1615 A monopoly for the export of British cloth is granted to the Merchant Adventurers. Firewood becomes increasingly scarce and expensive; cheap coal becomes a popular substitute for the first time. Coin-in-the-slot vending machines for loose tobacco are introduced into taverns. Lady Arabella Stuart dies in the Tower.

Aug [28] The singer and composer John Baldwin dies.

1616 James I begins selling peerages to raise money. Raleigh is released from the Tower on parole to search for El Dorado. Charles is created Prince of Wales. William Baffin discovers and names Baffin Bay while searching for the North-West Passage. The dramatist Francis Beaumont dies.

Apr [23] William Shakespeare dies.

Nov [23] Richard Hakluyt dies.

1617 Francis Bacon is made Keeper of the Great Seal of England. James I travels to Scotland to meet the Scottish Parliament. One-way streets for traffic control are introduced in London by an Act of Common Council. George Villiers, the King's new favourite, is created Earl of Buckingham. Thomas Weelkes, composer, is dismissed as choirmaster at Chichester for persistent drunkenness.

Apr [4] The mathematician John Napier dies.

1618 Francis Bacon is created Lord Chancellor. Suffolk is dismissed. A dredger is invented by Captain John Gilbert. Sir Peter Lely, painter, is born.

Oct [29] Sir Walter Raleigh, explorer, adventurer and courtier, is executed at Whitehall, ostensibly for treason, but in fact for attacking Spaniards in South America. The Banqueting House, Whitehall, destroyed by fire (rebuilt 1619-22).

1619 Dulwich College is founded.

Jan [7] Nicholas Hilliard, the miniature portrait painter, dies.

1620 Negotiations are under way with Spain to arrange a marriage between Prince Charles and the Infanta Maria. The Duke of Buckingham digs at the centre of Stonehenge.

Feb   Thomas Campion, writer, dies.
Sep   [16] The Pilgrim Fathers sail in the *Mayflower* under Captain
       Myles Standish.
Oct   [31] John Evelyn, diarist, is born.
Dec   [21] The Pilgrim Fathers land at Plymouth, Massachusetts
       and settle in New England.

1621   There is friction between the House of Commons and James I
       over the proposed marriage of Charles, Prince of Wales, to
       the Spanish Infanta. This leads to a declaration (December) of
       Parliamentary rights by the Commons called 'the Great
       Protestation'. Robert Cromwell, the first son of Oliver
       Cromwell, is born. John Donne becomes Dean of St Paul's
       and begins to compose his famous sermons. The poet Henry
       Vaughan is born.

Jan   Third Parliament of James I.
Mar   [31] The poet Andrew Marvell is born.
May   [3] Bacon is charged with accepting bribes for granting
       monopoly patents. impeached, fined £40,000 and banned
       from Parliament and Court; the King later pardons him and
       remits the fine.
Jun   [2] The first issue of the British newspaper, *The Corante*, is
       published.

1622   Prince Charles and Buckingham set off in secret for Spain to
       woo the King of Spain's daughter. Oliver Cromwell, second
       son of Oliver Cromwell, is born. The Archbishop of
       Canterbury, George Abbot, accidentally kills a gamekeeper;
       a commission of enquiry into the incident cannot agree on a
       conclusion, so he remains in office. Enraged by the Great
       Protestation, James I dissolves Parliament. John Pym, Sir
       Edward Cole, John Selden and the Earl of Southampton are
       arrested for criticizing the King's policy. William Oughtred
       invents the slide rule.

1623   Prince Charles and Buckingham arrive in Madrid in disguise,
       but the Infanta does not like Charles and the King of Spain

expects him to become a Catholic. The port of Gloucester is founded. A patents law comes into force, protecting inventors. The historian William Camden and the composer William Byrd die.

Oct   Prince Charles returns to England, rebuffed and angry. George Villiers becomes the Duke of Buckingham.

Nov   Thomas Weelkes, composer, dies.

1624 James I's Fourth Parliament (February-March). In spite of its anger, Parliament refuses to declare war on Spain; nevertheless, supplies are voted for increased defence. Monopolies are declared illegal. The English are driven out of the Spice Islands by the Dutch. The Dutch settle in New Amsterdam (later to become New York). An Anglo-French Treaty is signed, providing for Prince Charles's marriage to Henrietta Maria, daughter of Henry IV of France. The first working submarine, built by the Dutch physicist Cornelius Drebbel, travels underwater in the River Thames for two hours, propelled by 12 oarsmen. Lionel Cranfield, the Lord Treasurer, is impeached for bribery and dismissed.

1625 England, Denmark and France form an alliance against the Hapsburgs. An Anglo-Dutch alliance against Spain is formed by the Treaty of Southampton. John Fletcher, dramatist, dies.

Mar   [27] James I dies at Theobalds Park, Cheshunt, succeeded by his son Charles I. Mytens is appointed Court painter.

May   [1] Charles I marries, by proxy, the 16-year-old Henrietta Maria, sister of Louis XIII of France.

Jun   [5] Orlando Gibbons, composer, dies suddenly while waiting to officiate at Charles I's marriage service. The Black Death kills 41,000 people in London alone; Charles I's First Parliament adjourns to Oxford for safety. Parliament grants additional funds to continue the war with Spain. A tobacco tax is levied.

1626

Feb Charles I's Second Parliament is convened. Buckingham is
-Jun impeached; Sir John Eliot leads the attack, denouncing
Buckingham as 'the canker in the King's treasure'. Digges
and Eliot are sent to the Tower for conducting the
impeachment, and the Commons refuse to continue with
business until Digges and Eliot are released. Charles obliges,
but dissolves the Parliament. Charles offers knighthoods for
sale, to raise funds independently of Parliament. The
composer John Dowland dies.

Mar [12] John Aubrey, antiquary, is born.

Apr [9] Francis Bacon, philosopher and statesman, dies in
London as Lord Verulam.

Oct [4] Richard Cromwell is born, the third son of Oliver
Cromwell.

1627 England declares war on France, largely because of a
personality clash between Buckingham and Richelieu.
Charles sends the Duke of Buckingham with a fleet in an
abortive attempt to help the French Huguenots defend La
Rochelle. Robert Boyle, scientist, is born.

Jul [2] Thomas Middleton, dramatist, dies.

1628 John Bunyan, writer, is born. Harvey publishes his work on
the circulation of blood.

Jan [20] Henry, fourth son of Oliver Cromwell, is born.

Mar [12] John Bull, composer and organist, dies. Oliver Cromwell
enters Charles I's Third Parliament. A Petition of Right (Pym
and Wentworth) requests that no-one should be compelled to
pay a loan, benevolence or tax without Parliament's consent
and that no subject should be imprisoned without cause
shown: the King accepts these proposals.

Jul [5] Michael Cavendish, composer, dies.

Aug [23] The Duke of Buckingham is murdered; Wentworth
deserts the popular party and becomes the King's chief
adviser.

1629 Rubens, now in England, is knighted. The colony of
Massachusetts is founded in America. Charles I meets
opposition in the House of Commons; resolutions by Sir
John Eliot are read criticizing illegal taxation and royal
intolerance.

Mar [5] Charles has Eliot and eight other members arrested and
begins Personal Rule, advised by Laud and Wentworth. [10]
Parliament is dissolved for 11 years. Charles raises money by
various means, including fines imposed by the Star Chamber
and sales of monopolies.

Nov Eliot dies in the Tower.

1630 Large-scale emigration to Massachusetts begins. The English
gentry is forced to contribute large sums to the Crown by an
extortionate method called Distraint of Knighthood. Sash
windows are used for the first time, installed by Inigo Jones
at Raynham Hall in Norfolk.

May [29] Charles II is born at St James's Palace.

1631 The British settlement of St Kitts marks the start of
colonization in the Leeward Islands. William Oughtred
introduces the multiplication sign (x).

Mar [31] The poet John Donne dies.
Aug [9] John Dryden, poet, is born at Aldwincle in
Northamptonshire.
Nov [4] Mary, daughter of Charles I, is born.

1632 Anthony van Dyck is appointed Court painter to Charles I.
Sir Francis Windebank becomes Secretary of State. The
colonies of Maryland and Antigua are founded. George
Herbert, writer, dies.

Aug [29] John Locke, philosopher, is born.
Oct [20] Sir Christopher Wren, architect, is born.

1633 William Prynne's book *Historio-mastix*, denouncing the
theatre, is the first book to be publicly burnt by the
hangman; Prynne himself is sentenced to lose his ears. A

sawmill powered by wind is built in London. Bananas appear in British shops for the first time, in the window of Thomas Johnson in London. Charles I is crowned in Edinburgh.

Feb [23] Samuel Pepys, diarist, is born in Fleet Street.
Jul Thomas Wentworth, Earl of Strafford, takes up his post as Lord Deputy of Ireland; he proceeds to subdue Ireland ruthlessly.
Aug [4] Archbishop Abbot dies.
Sep [19] William Laud becomes Archbishop of Canterbury.
Oct [14] James II is born at St James's Palace, the son of Charles I and Henrietta Maria.

1634 Charles I attempts during the next three years to raise taxes without Parliament. Ship Money is introduced, a tax on seaports and maritime counties, ostensibly to raise a fleet for defence. Covent Garden Market is opened in London. Milton's masque *Comus* is performed at Ludlow Castle. Sir Julius Vermuyden, the Dutch engineer, drains the Fens.

1635 Ship Money is now exacted from inland towns too. Charles I makes Archbishop Spottiswoode Chancellor of Scotland. A public postal service between London and Edinburgh is established; the rates are 2d-8d. A speed limit of 3 mph is imposed on hackney coaches in London. The colony of Rhode Island is founded in America.

Jul [18] Robert Hooke, physicist, is born.

1636 The colony of Connecticut is founded in America. William Juxon, Bishop of London, is appointed Lord High Treasurer. William Gascoigne invents the micrometer.

1637 Ship Money is declared by the legislature to be a legal form of tax. John Hampden refuses to pay Ship Money, but judgement is given against him. On Laud's advice, Charles tries to force the English Liturgy onto the Scottish Church. The Scots resist by organizing Four Tables or committees to oppose the measure.

1638 The Solemn League and Covenant is widely signed in
Scotland as a show of solidarity in defence of the reformed
religion; Charles threatens to impose his will on Scotland by
force. The Covenanters form an army under Alexander
Leslie. Torture is abolished in Britain.

Nov A general assembly at Glasgow abolishes episcopacy in
Scotland and gives final form to the Scottish Kirk.

1639 Charles moves against the Scots to force them to reinstate the
bishops they evicted last year. The Covenanters rise up
against the alleged introduction of 'Popery'. Charles charges
them with seeking to overturn royal power. The Covenanters
capture Edinburgh, Stirling and Dumbarton; the First
Bishops' War.

May Robert Cromwell, eldest son of Oliver Cromwell, dies aged
18.

Jun Charles I comes to terms with the Scots, signing the
Pacification of Berwick. The transit of Venus is
accurately predicted and observed by Jeremiah
Horrocks.

Jul [8] Henry, son of Charles I, is born.

1640 Charles I makes Thomas Wentworth Earl of Strafford and
chief adviser. William Wycherley and Thomas Shadwell,
dramatists, are born. The first stagecoach lines are opened,
with coaching houses at regular intervals.

Jan [25] Robert Burton, clergyman, scholar and author, dies.
Apr Charles I summons his Fourth or Short Parliament.
Aug The Second Bishops' War; Scottish forces cross the Tweed
and enter Newcastle and Durham. [28] English forces are
defeated by the Scots at Newburn.

Oct [26] Treaty of Ripon; Charles I agrees to pay the Scottish
army £850 a day until a permanent settlement can be
reached. Charles summons a Great Council of Peers at York
but, fearful of acting independently of the Commons, it
recommends calling another Parliament.

Nov Giles Farnaby, composer, dies. [3] The Fifth or Long
Parliament begins. Royal prerogatives are abolished;
Strafford and Laud are impeached; Leyton, Prynne and other
victims of the Star Chamber are released.

1641 The first cotton factories are opened in Manchester. Mary,
Charles I's daughter, marries William II, Prince of Orange.
Thomas Dekker, the prolific dramatist, dies.

Mar The trial of the King's minister, Thomas Wentworth, Earl of
Strafford.

May [12] Execution of Strafford. [15] Triennial Act; every
Parliament is to be dissolved after three years and only
dissolved with its own consent.

Jul The Courts of the Star Chamber and High Commission are
abolished.

Oct Thousands of Protestant settlers in Ulster die in the
rebellion. The Marquis of Montrose plots the seizure of the
Earl of Argyle, the Presbyterian leader. The Montrose
plot seems to implicate Charles I himself, who
virtually surrenders control to Argyle and the
Presbyterians.

Dec [9] Sir Anthony van Dyck, Flemish Court painter to Charles
I, dies at his studio in Blackfriars.

1642 Thomas Shadwell, writer, is born near Grantham. Income tax
and property tax are introduced.

Jan [3] Charles I orders the impeachment of five members of
Parliament for treasonable correspondence with the Scots
during the recent troubles; the Commons refuse to order the
arrests. [4] Charles I enters the Commons Chamber in person
in an attempt to arrest the Five Members (Hollis, Hampden,
Strode, Haselrigg and Pym), but fails because they are in
hiding. The Commons follow the Five Members to the
Guildhall, where they are secure in the protection of the
citizens of London. [10] Charles I withdraws from London.
The Commons, emboldened, prepare Bills excluding bishops

from the House of Lords and giving Parliament control of the
army.

Mar   Charles I, now in York, refuses to give assent to the Bills.

Jun   Parliament makes a final appeal to the King to assent to the
Militia Bill, but he refuses.

Jul   Parliament appoints a committee of public safety and puts
Essex in charge of an army of 24,000; King and Parliament
prepare for war. The theatres close, and remain closed until
1660.

Aug   [22] Charles I raises his standard at Nottingham, opening the
military phase of the Great Rebellion; the outbreak of the
English Civil War.

Oct   [23] In the First Campaign, the first general engagement is
the Battle of Edgehill, which has no clear outcome.

Nov   [12] Charles I marches on London, but is beaten back at
Turnham Green.

Dec   [25] Isaac Newton, scientist, is born.

1643   In the Second Campaign of the Civil War, the King's armies
prosper. Royalist victories include the Battles of Chalgrove
Field, Atherton Moor and Roundway Down, and the sacking
of Bristol by Prince Rupert. Parliamentary victories include
Bradford, Gainsborough, Grantham and Winceby. The
English Parliament agrees to the Solemn League and
Covenant, securing the services of the Scottish army. Scots
Covenanters invade England on the Parliamentary side.

Apr   [27] Skirmish at Reading in Essex.

Jun   [18] Skirmish at Chalgrove Field, in which Hampden is
mortally wounded.

Jul   [25] Prince Rupert captures Bristol.

Sep   Essex's Parliamentary troops relieve Gloucester. [20] The
First Battle of Newbury is indecisive.

1644   Isaac Fuller's now-lost altarpiece is described by John
Evelyn as 'too full of nakeds for a chapel'. John Milton
opposes censorship. The 'Clubmen' risings of armed

neutrals become a threat to both sides in the Third
Campaign of the Civil War. The Queen flees to France.
The Self-Denying Ordinance is passed by the Commons;
this removes all MPs except Cromwell from Military
commands.

Jan Charles I calls a Royalist Parliament at Oxford. [25] Royalists
are defeated at the Battle of Nantwich.

Feb [15] Parliamentarians form a joint committee of the two
kingdoms of England and Scotland.

Mar Oliver, Cromwell's second son, dies aged 22.

Apr Fairfax's Parliamentary troops besiege York.

Jul [1] Prince Rupert raises the siege of York. [2] Battle of
Marston Moor; Parliament wins the decisive battle of the
Civil War.

Aug Montrose enters Scotland in disguise and raises the Highland
clans in support of Charles I.

Sep [1] Battle of Tippamuir; Royalist Highlanders defeat the
Covenanters.

Oct [14] William Penn, the founder of Pennsylvania, is born. [27]
The Second Battle of Newbury is indecisive; after it, Charles
escapes to Oxford.

1645 The composer William Lawes dies. Wallpaper is used for the
first time as a cheap substitute for tapestry.

Jan [10] William Laud, Archbishop of Canterbury from 1633, is
beheaded on Tower Hill for treason; he is not replaced until
1660.

Feb [2] Battle of Inverlochy: Royalist Highlanders are victorious
over Covenanters.

Apr [3] The Self-Denying Ordinance is passed by the House of
Lords, with the intention of removing faint-hearted generals
from their posts. All MPs except Cromwell are required to
resign their commissions within 40 days. Fairfax supersedes
Essex as captain-general.

May [1] Battle of Auldcarn; Royalists defeat Covenanters.

Jun   [14] Battle of Naseby; the main Royalist army is crushed,
       effectively terminating the war. [18] The Royalist town of
       Leicester falls to Parliamentarian troops.
Jul   [2] Battle of Alford; Royalists defeat Covenanters. [23]
       Bridgewater, another Royalist town, falls to the
       Parliamentarians.
Sep   [13] Battle of Philiphaugh; Montrose's army supporting
       Charles in Scotland is destroyed by General Leslie's troops.
       Montrose escapes to the Continent.

1646 Jeremiah Rich, the first shorthand teacher, starts shorthand
       classes in London.
May   [5] Charles I surrenders to the Scots at Newark, bringing the
       military phase of the Civil War to an end.
Jul   The King is presented with Parliament's Newcastle
       Propositions, demanding that he relinquish control of the
       army to Parliament for 20 years and agree to religious
       reforms favouring Protestants. Charles cannot accept
       them and makes an abortive attempt to escape from
       captivity.
Aug   [19] The astronomer John Flamsteed is born.

1647 Parliament votes to disband most of the army, but the army
       refuses to comply. Radical movements criticize Parliamentary
       tyranny. The writer, the Earl of Rochester, and the composer,
       Pelham Humfrey, are born.
Jan   [30] At Newcastle, the Scots agree to hand Charles I over to
       the English Parliament for £400,000.
Jun   [4] At Holmby House in Northamptonshire, Charles I is
       seized by the army. On the same day, Cromwell flees from
       Parliament to rejoin the army at Triptow Heath. [10] From St
       Albans, the army submits to Parliament a 'humble
       representation', asking for the exclusion of 11 members of
       whom it disapproves; about 100 MPs flee to the army.
Aug   [6] The army enters London, forcing Parliament to take back
       the members who left in June.

Oct	The Agreement of the People, the Leveller constitution, is debated in the Army Council at Putney.
Nov	[11] Charles I flees from Hampton Court to the Isle of Wight; he is once again detained and imprisoned at Carisbrooke Castle. He signs a secret treaty with the Scots, who promise to restore him by force.
Dec	[24] Parliament presents the King with four Bills to sign, one giving Parliament control of the army for 20 years, one requiring all declarations against Parliament to be recalled, one excluding all the Peers created by Charles from sitting in the House of Lords, one allowing the two Houses to adjourn at their own pleasure.

1648	The Levellers, a Puritan group, demand an egalitarian and republican society.
Jan	[15] Parliament renounces allegiance to the King and votes to have no further communication with him. The Scots now join Charles I in a Second Civil War.
Mar	The army returns to London, pressing for the King to be brought to trial; the King is brought from Hurst Castle to Whitehall.
Aug	[17-20] Battle of Preston; a Scottish army under the Duke of Hamilton invades England in support of Charles I, but is beaten back by Cromwell.
Dec	[1] Charles is once again seized by the army. [6-7] Pride's Purge; Colonel Pride forcibly excludes 96 Presbyterian members from Parliament, which is known from this time on as the Rump Parliament, consisting of only 60 members. [13] The Rump decides to discontinue the reopened negotiations with the King and instead bring him to trial.

1649	The Royal Navy takes delivery of its first frigate, the *Constant Warwick*. John Aubrey draws attention for the first time to the megalithic monument at Avebury.
Jan	[20] An Army Council draws up a temporary Instrument of Government. [20-27] Trial of Charles I: no defence witnesses

are called. [30] Charles I is executed on a scaffold outside the Banqueting House of Whitehall Palace; the executioner is Richard Brandon.

Feb [5] The Scots proclaim Charles II King in Edinburgh; the Irish under Ormond also rise in Charles II's favour. [9] Charles I's funeral and burial in the Garter Chapel at St George's, Windsor.

Mar [16] The monarchy and the House of Lords are abolished. Parliament sets up a Commonwealth run by a Council of State with Bradshaw as President and Milton as Latin Secretary. The Levellers claim their 'Agreement of People' as the basis for a new constitution; they are defeated at Burford and their leaders arrested and executed.

Apr [9] The Duke of Monmouth, son of Charles II and Lucy Walter, is born at Rotterdam.

Sep [12] The storming of Drogheda by Ireton's army marks the conclusion of the reconquest of Ireland.

1650

Feb [2] Nell Gwyn, barmaid, actress and mistress of Charles II, is born. The Marquis of Montrose returns to Scotland.

Apr [27] Battle of Corbiesdale; Montrose is defeated and captured.

May [14] Parliament votes in favour of the death penalty for adultery, but the law is never implemented. [21] Montrose is executed at Edinburgh. [26] The Duke of Marlborough is born at Ashe in Devon as John Churchill.

Jun [24] Charles II lands in Scotland, takes the covenant and is proclaimed King.

Sep [3] Battle of Dunbar; Cromwell's army invades Scotland and succeeds in defeating a Scottish army twice its size.

Oct George Fox, in court on a charge of preaching illegally, urges the judge, Gervase Bennet, to 'tremble at the word of the Lord'; the judge replies that the only quaker in the court is Fox himself, and the nickname sticks.

Nov [4] William III is born at The Hague, the posthumous son of William II of Orange and Mary Stuart, daughter of Charles I.

1651 The first edition of *Mercurius Scoticus*, the first Scottish newspaper, appears. All courts in Britain now begin recording their proceedings in English.

Jan [1] Charles II is crowned King of Scotland at Scone Palace. Afterwards, Charles marches south into England.

Aug [2] Cromwell's army takes Perth.

Sep [3] Battle of Worcester; Charles II's supporters are defeated and Charles makes his escape to France.

Oct [9] First Navigation Act; aimed at the growing Dutch threat, this measure gives British shipping a monopoly of foreign trade and also helps to precipitate an Anglo-Dutch War.

1652 The first tea reaches Britain: a small amount is found on a captured Dutch ship and brought home. A Perpetuation Bill is introduced in an attempt to make all existing MPs members for life. The writer Nahum Tate is born.

Feb Act of Indemnity and Oblivion; this deals with the return of confiscated Royalist estates in an attempt to reconcile Royalists.

Mar [3] Thomas Otway, dramatist, is born. [29] 'Black Monday': a total eclipse of the sun causes widespread apprehension and disturbance.

May Battle of the Downs; the English fleet scores a victory over the Dutch before war is formally declared.

Jun [21] The architect Inigo Jones dies.

Jul [8] The First Anglo-Dutch War begins.

Aug Act of Settlement for Ireland.

1653 Thomas Durfey, writer, is born.

Feb [18] In the Anglo-Dutch War, an English fleet under Blake and Monk defeats a Dutch fleet under Van Trump off Portland.

Apr [20] Cromwell dissolves the Rump Parliament and becomes head of state, setting up a council of 10 members and a nominated Parliament of 140 members.

Jul   The 'Bare-Bones Parliament' meets. [31] Battle of the Texel;
       the English under Monk are victorious, and Admiral Van
       Trump is killed in action.
Dec   [12] Cromwellian MPs resign their powers to Cromwell. [16]
       Cromwell sets up a Protectorate with a Council of State and
       himself as Lord Protector.

1654 Surveyors are empowered by an Act of Parliament to assess
       the inhabitants of each parish, hire labour and carts, and
       mend the highways; this leads to rapid improvements in the
       roads and the speed of travel. A treaty of commerce between
       England and Sweden is signed. The formal Union of Ireland
       and Scotland with England and Wales is arranged, with free
       trade and representation at Westminster. The First
       Protectorate Parliament meets, including MPs from the three
       kingdoms.
Apr   [5] The Treaty of Westminster ends the First Anglo-Dutch
       War.
Sep   [3] The Republican party headed by Vane opposes
       Cromwell in Parliament, calling into question the
       legality of 'the Instrument' and the pre-eminence of
       Cromwell himself. [12] Cromwell orders an exclusion of
       members.

1655 Under Cromwell's 'Western Design', the Caribbean is to
       become an arena for British ambition. Charles II is expelled
       from France following an Anglo-French treaty directed
       against Spain.
Jan   Parliament votes that the office of Protector should be
       elective not hereditary. [22] Cromwell turns to the idea of
       military rule, dissolving Parliament. Major-generals are
       appointed to supervise the eleven military districts of
       England.
Mar   A Royalist insurrection in the West Country (Colonel
-May   John Penruddock's Rising) is a complete failure, ending in
       Penruddock's execution.

1656 Letters posted in London are delivered in Winchester the next day. *The Siege of Rhodes*, the first English opera, is produced, with words by William Davenant and music by Locke, Lawes, Crooke, Colman and Hudson.

Mar [21] James Ussher, retired Archbishop of Armagh, dies at Reigate.

May An English expedition led by Penn and Venables to capture Jamaica causes Spain to declare war on Britain.
[30] The regiment of Grenadier Guards is founded.

Sep [9] Blake captures Spanish treasure ships off Cadiz.
[17] The Second Protectorate Parliament meets.

1657 Cromwell founds Durham University.

Jan Sindercombe's Plot to assassinate Cromwell is discovered.

Mar Parliament's 'Humble Petition and Advice' offers Cromwell the title 'King' and the right to name his successor.

May [8] Cromwell rejects the title 'King', but elects to nominate the members of his own House of Lords.

Jun [3] William Harvey, physician and anatomist, dies.

Aug [7] Robert Blake, one of the greatest naval commanders, dies as his ship sails into Plymouth.

1658 Cromwell's Third and Last Protectorate Parliament assembles in its reconstructed form, with a second house of 60 members, although only one of these actually takes his seat. Cromwell dissolves this Parliament after only 16 days, ruling for the rest of his life without Parliament. France joins Britain against Spain.

Jun [4] Allied Anglo-French troops defeat a Spanish force at the Dunes and capture Dunkirk.

Sep [3] Cromwell dies of pneumonia in Whitehall. He is succeeded as Protector by his son Richard. Cromwell is buried in Westminster Abbey, his effigy wearing a crown and holding an orb and sceptre.

1659 Henry Purcell, composer, is born.

Jan [27] Richard Cromwell's Parliament meets; a new dispute between Parliament and army quickly develops.

Feb [16] The first cheque known to have been drawn on a British bank is written today.

Apr [22] Richard Cromwell dissolves his Protectorate Parliament.

May [7] The Rump Parliament is restored. [24] The Rump induces Richard Cromwell to abdicate as Protector.

Oct The Rump is expelled by the army and a military committee of safety is appointed; another military dictatorship seems imminent.

Dec [26] Reaction against military coups results in a restoration of the Rump Parliament.

1660 The war with Spain ends. Robert Boyle invents the air pump.

Jan [1] Samuel Pepys begins his diary.

Feb [3] General Monk arrives in London from Scotland and assumes control of the Government. [21] Monk re-establishes the Long Parliament.

Mar [16] The Long Parliament finally dissolves itself. [28] George I is born at Osnabruck Castle in Hanover.

Apr [4] Charles II issues the Declaration of Breda, promising a lawful Parliamentary settlement, a general pardon to all except those named by Parliament (the regicide judges), and a measure of religious liberty. [25] Monk summons a Convention Parliament to consider the Declaration.

May [1] The Convention Parliament resolves to restore the monarchy with limited powers and invites Charles II to return. [8] The formal restoration of the monarchy in England, when Charles II is proclaimed King. [25] Charles II returns to England. [29] Charles enters London amid great rejoicing: it is his thirtieth birthday. Ten regicides are executed. The bodies of Cromwell,

Bradshaw and Ireton are dragged from Westminster Abbey, hanged at Tyburn and buried beneath the gallows. The theatres reopen. An actress plays Desdemona in *Othello*: the first appearance of an actress in the English theatre. The Royal Society is founded.

Jun [30] William Oughtred, mathematician, dies.

Oct [2] The army is disbanded except for about 5,000 men.

Dec [24] Mary, Charles I's daughter and wife of William II of Orange, dies. [29] The Convention Parliament is disbanded.

1661 The architect Nicholas Hawksmoor and the novelist Daniel Defoe are born. Matthew Locke is appointed Court composer by Charles II. The first London playhouse with a proscenium arch, Lincoln's Inn Fields Theatre, opens with *Hamlet*.

Apr [16] Charles Montagu, founder of the Bank of England, is born. [19] Postmarks are introduced by the Post Office. [23] Coronation of Charles II.

May [1] The tallest and longest-standing maypole in England is erected in the Strand to a fanfare of trumpets and drums: it is 130 feet high. [8] Charles II's First Parliament, the 'Cavalier Parliament', meets. It establishes the Anglican Church and enacts a series of repressive measures that will later be known as the Clarendon Code. All Acts of Cromwell's Parliaments are annulled. According to the Treason Act it is now treason merely to plan rebellion: no open act is required.

1662 Tea-drinking is introduced to Court by the Queen. Britain sells Dunkirk to France for £400,000. Quakers Act: severe penalties are imposed on Quakers meeting for worship. Licensing Act: new books on theology are to be vetted by the Church. The Act of Settlement authorizes Justices to send any newcomer who might become a charge on the rates back to his last address.

1663 The first theatre in Drury Lane is built. Turnpike tolls are levied for the first time. The first gold guinea is minted. Sheerness Royal Naval Dockyard is established. Samuel Pepys begins to use one of the newly-invented fountain pens to write his diary. A Hearth Tax is introduced. It becomes apparent that the Clarendon Code is restricting religious freedom.

Feb [24] John Milton marries for the third time.

Aug [31] Gilbert Sheldon becomes Archbishop of Canterbury.

1664 The colony of New Jersey is founded in America. The British Government protests to the Dutch that the island of Pulo Run has still not been handed over: calls for war with Holland are restrained by Charles II, who fears the cost.

Jan Sir John Vanbrugh, architect and dramatist, is born.

May The Conventicle Act discriminates against nonconformists by forbidding meetings of more than five people for worship unless they are Anglican.

1665 Isaac Newton conceives the idea of gravitation after watching an apple fall in his garden. Robert Hooke discovers living cells in plants. Christopher Wren meets the architect Bernini in Paris.

Feb [6] Queen Anne is born at St James's Palace: she is the second daughter of the Duke of York by his first wife, Anne Hyde.

Mar The Second Dutch War begins after a Swedish ship carrying ships' masts to England is captured by the Dutch.

Jun [3] The Duke of York defeats a Dutch fleet off Lowestoft; the Dutch Admiral Opdam is killed in the action and 16 of his ships are sunk. [7] The Great Plague is first reported in London: it is an exceptionally hot day. 70,000 people are to die by October. Plague forces the Cavalier Parliament to meet for its fifth session in Oxford.

Oct The Five Mile Act drives ejected dissenting clergymen from the towns.

Nov [16] The *London Gazette* is first published.

1666 Isaac Newton propounds integral calculus.

Jan France declares war on Britain.

Jul [25] Off the North Foreland, a British fleet under Albemarle is defeated by De Ruyter and De Witt. Growing debts and the Dutch blockade of Newcastle colliers cause Charles II and Clarendon to open negotiations for peace, using Sweden as negotiator.

Sep [2] The Great Fire of London breaks out in Pudding Lane in the bakehouse of Thomas Farriner. The splendid medieval St Paul's Cathedral and a large area of central London are burnt. [6] The Great Fire burns itself out. Pratt, May and Wren are appointed to rebuild the city of London.

Nov [28] A revolt of Scottish Covenanters is ruthlessly crushed in the Battle of Pentland Hills.

Dec The Great Plague comes to an end.

1667 Robert Hooke proposes systematic weather recording, marking the start of meteorology.

Jun A Dutch fleet under De Ruyter enters the Medway estuary and tows away the British flagship, the *Royal Charles*, and sinks six other ships. The incident produces near-panic throughout the country.

Jul [21] The Second Anglo-Dutch War ends with the Treaty of Breda. Britain gives up her claim to Pulo Run, but retains New Amsterdam.

Aug The Lord Chancellor, Clarendon, falls from power, a scapegoat for the Cavalier Parliament's many unpopular measures. Parliament begins the process of impeachment, so Clarendon leaves for France. Parliament sentences him to

perpetual banishment. The Cabal Ministry, a kind of
Cabinet, is formed (Clifford, Arlington, Buckingham, Ashley
and Lauderdale).

Nov   [30] The satirist Jonathan Swift is born in Dublin.

1668 Isaac Newton builds the first reflecting telescope. The East
India Company takes control of Bombay.

Jan   [13] A Triple Alliance (Britain, Holland and Sweden) is
formed to check the power of Louis XIV.

Apr   [7] Sir William Davenant, writer, dies. [13] John Dryden is
appointed first Poet Laureate.

1669 The Yeomen Warders of the Tower of London are nicknamed
'Beefeaters' because of their reputation for eating large daily
rations of beef.

May   [31] Samuel Pepys' diary comes to an end.

1670 The colonies of North and South Carolina are founded in
America. The rebuilding of London's churches begins, under
Christopher Wren's direction; 87 destroyed churches are to
be replaced, in due course, with 51. James Fitzjames, natural
son of James Duke of York, is born.

Feb   [10] The dramatist William Congreve is born.
Jun   [1] The two Treaties of Dover (one secret, one public)
between Charles II and Louis XIV. Charles II secretly agrees
to declare his conversion to Catholicism and subsequently to
restore it to Britain, in return for two ports on the mouth of
the River Scheldt. Charles II does not announce his
conversion, to Louis' annoyance, although the Duke of York
does.

1671 John Evelyn discovers the woodcarver Grinling Gibbons and
introduces him to Charles II and Christopher Wren. Sir
Henry Morgan, sometime buccaneer, is appointed Deputy
Governor of Jamaica by Charles II.

Mar   [31] Anne Hyde, Duchess of York, dies.

May [9] Captain Thomas Blood, disguised as a clergyman, attempts to steal the Crown Jewels from the Tower of London.

Nov [12] Thomas Fairfax, general and leader of the Parliamentary army in the Civil War, dies.

1672 Newton reads his new theory about light and colours to the Royal Society. The composer William Young dies.

Mar Charles II issues his Declaration of Indulgence, permitting freedom of worship and assuming the right to cancel all penal legislation against both Protestants and Catholics. [17] The Third Anglo-Dutch War begins, because Charles II is bound under the secret provisions of the Treaty of Dover to support Louis XIV.

May [28] A naval battle between English and Dutch fleets in Southwold Bay is indecisive.

1673 The Dutch successfully fend off an Anglo-French attempt to invade Holland. Christopher Wren is knighted. Dentists fit the first metal dental fillings. The Earl of Clarendon dies in exile, lonely and ill-rewarded.

Feb The Test Act deprives Catholics and nonconformists of public office; two members of the Cabal are forced to resign as a result.

Mar [23] Henry Cromwell, fourth son of Oliver Cromwell, dies aged 45.

Nov [21] James Duke of York marries Maria d'Este of Modena.

Dec The Cabal ministry disintegrates under Parliamentary opposition. Louis XIV sends Charles £500,000 to stop him making a separate peace with the Dutch, to no avail.

1674 The composer Pelham Humfrey dies. The painter Godfrey Kneller settles in Britain. There is agitation throughout Britain to exclude the Duke of York from the succession because of his known Catholic leanings and his new Catholic wife.

Feb [19] The Treaty of Westminster ends the Third Dutch War;
the Dutch agree to pay an indemnity of £180,000 and to
salute British ships from Cape Finisterre to Norway. New
Amsterdam becomes British by formal treaty and is renamed
New York.

Nov [8] The poet John Milton dies at Chalfont St Giles,
Buckinghamshire.

1675 John Ogilby's *Britannia* is published: this is the first road
book based on an actual survey of the British road system.
Charles II receives a bribe of 500,000 crowns from Louis XIV,
enabling him to prorogue Parliament for 15 months.
Corpuscular theory of light (Isaac Newton).

Jun [21] Work on Sir Christopher Wren's new St Paul's Cathedral
begins. Foundation stone laid.

Aug [10] The Royal Observatory at Greenwich is founded.

1676 Robert Hooke devises the universal joint to help manoeuvre
astronomical instruments. William Sherwin develops a
fast-dyeing process for calico. Observance of the Sabbath
Day gains legal protection. Thomas Tompion is appointed
clockmaker for the new Royal Observatory. An influenza
epidemic sweeps across Britain.

Aug [26] Sir Robert Walpole, the first British Prime Minister, is
born at Houghton Hall in Norfolk.

1677 Edmund Halley observes the transit of Venus.

Nov [4] In London, William III marries his 15-year-old cousin
Princess Mary, eldest daughter of James Duke of York and
Anne Hyde.

1678 The poet Andrew Marvell and the composer John Jenkins
die. The composer William Croft is born. Charles II bows to
pressure of public opinion, by concluding an alliance with
the Dutch against the French. There are eclipses of the sun
and moon, and the Devil is reputedly sighted in Scotland; a
credulous and hysterical mood grips the country.

Jan   [27] William Sancroft becomes Archbishop of Canterbury.

Aug   The 'Popish Plot' concocted by Israel Tonge and Titus Oates
        is whipped up by Danby, the Lord High Treasurer. Tonge
        reveals that in April Catholic conspirators plotted to kill the
        King. Some 35 Catholics are executed as a result of this
        fraud.

Nov   A Disabling Act disqualifies Catholics from sitting in
        Parliament, the Duke of York excepted: this act is not to be
        repealed until 1829. [21] Lord Chief Justice Scroggs brutally
        condemns a Catholic banker, William Staley, to death for
        'speaking treason'.

Dec   Danby is impeached on a charge of criminal correspondence
        with France and dismissed from office.

1679   Robert Hooke's law of elasticity.

Jan   [24] The Cavalier Parliament is dissolved.

Mar   [6] The Third Parliament of Charles II begins. Danby's
        impeachment peters out, but he remains in the Tower. The
        Scottish Convenanters rebel against the repressive measures
        of Lauderdale.

May   [3] Archbishop Sharpe is pulled from his coach near St
        Andrews and murdered. [22] Samuel Pepys is committed to
        the Tower on a charge of treason. [27] The Habeas Corpus
        Act defines the procedure for ensuring speedy trials: when
        asked, judges must issue a writ ordering a gaoler to bring a
        prisoner before a court and show why he or she has been
        imprisoned.

Jun   [1] Battle of Drumclog: Claverhouse is defeated by
        Covenanters led by Balfour. [22] Battle of Bothwell Bridge;
        the Scottish Covenanters are suppressed by the Duke of
        Monmouth's troops. The Bill of Exclusion, designed to
        exclude James Duke of York from the line of succession, is
        drafted.

1680   Lord Shaftesbury organizes nationwide petitions to exclude
        the Duke of York from the succession; the petitioners become

known as Whigs and their opponents, the Abhorrers, become the Tories. The Penny Post is instituted in London. The colony of New Hampshire is founded in America. The writer the Earl of Rochester dies. Henry Purcell is appointed organist at Westminster Abbey. The Cameronians, a group of Scottish field-preachers, renounce their allegiance to Charles II, for which their leaders, Cameron and Cargill, are killed.

Mar   Pepys is released from the Tower.
May   [27] The Third Parliament of Charles II is dissolved.
Aug   [24] Captain Blood, the Irish adventurer, dies.
Sep   [25] Samuel Butler dies.
Oct   [21] The Fourth Parliament of Charles II begins.
Nov   [30] The painter Sir Peter Lely dies.

1681   The colony of Pennsylvania is founded. The Test Act, designed to repress Presbyterians, causes 80 bishops to resign. Oliver Plunket, Archbishop of Armagh, is put to death at Tyburn (Plunket is canonized in 1975). Lord Shaftesbury is prosecuted for treason, but a grand jury rejects the charge; Shaftesbury nevertheless leaves for Holland.

Mar   [21] Charles II's Fifth or Oxford Parliament. Charles II rejects the Exclusion Bill when it is introduced and dissolves Parliament; he offers to install William III of Orange as a regent for James as a compromise and begins to rule without Parliament.
Dec   The trial and condemnation of Argyle, who leaves the country.

1682   Edmund Halley, the Astronomer Royal, observes a bright comet, checks his records and realizes that it has returned every 76 years – and that it was this same comet that was seen shortly before the Battle of Hastings; it has become known as Halley's Comet. Elias Ashmole founds a museum in Oxford. French Protestants are excluded from employment in the Civil Service and the King's Household.

Nov [21] George (later George I) marries Sophia Dorothea, the daughter of George Duke of Luneburg-Celle.

1683 Newton explains the connection between tides and gravitation. The last wild boar in Britain is killed. The Rye House Plot, a Whig plot to assassinate Charles II, is discovered. Two of the leaders of the conspiracy, Lord William Russell and Algernon Sydney, are executed: another, Essex, commits suicide; Monmouth, the King's natural son, is pardoned.

Jun [6] The first museum in Britain, the Ashmolean Museum in Oxford, is opened to the public by its owner, Elias Ashmole.

Jul [28] Anne, daughter of James Duke of York, marries Prince George of Denmark.

Oct There is a rain of small toads on the village of Acle in Norfolk. [30] George II, the only son of George I, is born at Hanover.

Dec [15] Izaak Walton, author of *The Compleat Angler*, dies at Winchester aged 90.

1684 Robert Hooke invents the heliograph. The first attempt is made to light the streets of London. The Duke of Monmouth, who, as well as being the illegitimate son of Charles II, is the exclusionist candidate for the throne, is banished to Holland in the aftermath of the Rye House Plot. The Duke of York is restored to his former offices.

1685 Titus Oates is found guilty of perjury and sentenced to life imprisonment. Dangerfield, another of the informers in the Popish Plot, is flogged to death; it is the last time this cruel and unusual type of punishment is given in Britain.

Feb [2] Charles II has an apoplectic fit. [6] Charles II dies, succeeded by his brother as James II of England and VII of Scotland. [23] George Frederick Handel is born at Halle.

May [19] The Parliament of James II opens. Danby is released from the Tower.

Jun Argyle lands in Scotland, but cannot raise the support of the Covenanters. [30] Argyle is captured and executed. Monmouth lands at Lyme Regis and is proclaimed King at Taunton.

Jul [6] Battle of Sedgemoor, the last formal battle to be fought on English soil; Monmouth's Protestant rebellion is crushed. [15] The Duke of Monmouth is beheaded with five axe-strokes on Tower Hill: Jack Ketch bungles another execution. Judge Jeffreys conducts the 'Bloody Assizes', sentencing 320 of Monmouth's supporters to death and 840 to be sold into slavery. Jeffreys is later appointed Lord Chancellor.

1686 Edmund Halley draws the first meteorological map, using it to explain monsoon and trade winds. The writer Allan Ramsay is born. James II challenges the validity of the Test Act; the test case of Sir Edward Hales results in the readmission of Catholics into the army. James II visits St Winifrid's Well at Shrewsbury, a holy well which his wife has had restored.

1687 James II expels the Fellows of Magdalen College, Oxford, because they will not appoint a Catholic, Dr Parker, as their President. James II creates his natural son, James Fitzjames, Duke of Berwick. Admiral Herbert is dismissed and a Catholic, Admiral Strickland, is given command of the fleet. Laws of gravitation and motion – Isaac Newton.

Apr [1] James II's Declaration of Liberty of Conscience; although professing toleration for all religions, this measure favours Catholics.

Nov [13] Nell Gwyn, who had two sons by Charles II, dies in London at the age of 37.

1688
Apr James II's Second Declaration of Liberty of Conscience, which is to be read out in churches. Seven bishops including

Archbishop Sancroft petition the King to be excused from
reading the Declaration.

May [21] The poet Alexander Pope is born.

Jun [10] The 'Glorious Revolution' begins when a son, James
Stuart (the Old Pretender), is born to James II, opening up
the prospect of a succession of Catholic Kings. [29-30] The
Seven Bishops are tried and acquitted.

Jul [7] Whig and Tory leaders invite the King's son-in-law,
William III of Orange, to save Britain from Catholicism. In
alarm, James reinstates the Fellows of Magdalen College.

Sep [30] William of Orange accepts the invitation.

Nov [5] William of Orange lands at Torbay.

Dec [10] The Queen and the baby Prince James are sent to France.
[11] James II drops the Great Seal into the Thames and
attempts to escape. He is stopped at Sheerness and brought
back to London, but his reign is legally over and an
interregnum begins. [19] William enters London. [22] James
finally succeeds in escaping to France. [24] The Lords in
London assume executive functions for the duration of the
interregnum.

1689

Jan [22-27] The Convention Parliament is summoned on the
advice of the House of Lords. [28] The Commons declare that
James II has tried to subvert the constitution and can be
considered to have abdicated. Although the Lords disagree
on the use of the word 'abdicate', there is agreement
between the two Houses that the Crown should be offered to
Mary and the regency to William. William rejects this offer.

Feb [13] Parliament offers the Crown to William and Mary
jointly. A Declaration accompanies Parliament's new offer;
making or suspending laws without Parliament's consent is
illegal; it is lawful to petition the sovereign; maintaining an
army without Parliament's consent is illegal; election of MPs
must be free; Parliament should meet frequently. [22] The
Convention Parliament is transformed into a regular
Parliament.

Mar A Scottish Convention Parliament orders the proclamation of William and Mary as sovereigns. [14] James lands in Ireland with a few followers. [24] James enters Dublin. Tyrconnel raises a rebellion in James's favour. The Protestants in the north of Ireland declare for William, taking refuge in Derry.

Apr [11] William III and Mary II become joint sovereigns of Great Britain, Mary exercising the royal power during William's absences abroad. They are crowned by the Bishop of London, because the Archbishop of Canterbury refuses to do it. [16] Mrs Aphra Behn, the writer, dies. [18] Judge Jeffreys dies in the Tower. [20] Derry is besieged by a Catholic army led by James. [24] Toleration Act, establishing permanent freedom of worship.

May [7] War breaks out with France. In Scotland, Claverhouse (Viscount Dundee) raises his standard in support of James among the Highlanders.

Jul [24] Anne (later Queen Anne) gives birth to a son, William. [27] Battle of Killicrankie; Dundee defeats the Whig General Mackay but is himself killed in the battle. The Highland revolt peters out.

Dec [16] Bill of Rights, a Parliamentary enactment of the earlier Declaration of Rights, summarizing the liberties established by the 'Glorious Revolution', and asserting that no Catholic may become sovereign.

1690 There are fears of a French invasion.

Feb [1] Archbishop Sancroft is deprived of his office.

Jun [30] Battle of Beachy Head; the French are victorious over Anglo-Dutch forces under Herbert. The English Admiral Lord Torrington is court-martialled and acquitted, but dismissed the service. William goes to Ireland.

Jul [1] Battle of the Boyne; at Oldbridge near Drogheda William's army defeats James II's army. James flees to Waterford and then to France.

Aug James's supporters, led by Sarsfield, still resist in Limerick.

1691 A new East India Company is established. William III subdues the south of Ireland and the Irish rebels retreat west of the Shannon.

Jan   [13] George Fox, founder of the Society of Friends, the 'Quakers', dies in London.

May   [31] John Tillotson becomes Archbishop of Canterbury.

Jul   [12] Battle of Aughrim: Sarsfield and the French St Ruth are defeated by William's forces under Ginkel.

Oct   [3] Limerick is besieged and taken by William; James II's Irish and French supporters surrender on conditions (the Treaty of Limerick) which are later not fulfilled by the Irish Parliament, which is predominantly Protestant. William nevertheless makes the agreement in good faith and returns to England. William calls on all the Scottish Highland chiefs to take the oath of allegiance before the end of the year; Ian MacDonald of Glencoe fails to do so. Lloyd's Coffee House becomes an office for maritime insurance.

Dec   [30] Robert Boyle, scientist, dies.

1692 The writer Thomas Shadwell dies.

Jan   [6] Ian MacDonald takes the oath of allegiance, but knowledge of this is suppressed by William's agent, the Master of Stair.

Feb   [13] Massacre of Glencoe. The MacDonalds are treacherously massacred by the Campbells, their traditional enemies. Sir John Dalrymple wishes to make an example of the MacDonalds and orders the Campbells to kill every member of the MacDonald clan under the age of 70. Dalrymple is later forced to resign. Louis XIV and James II contemplate an invasion of England, amassing a fleet at Brest and an army of 30,000 in Normandy.

May   [19] Battle of the Cap de la Hogue; a large French fleet is destroyed by a British fleet under Russell.

Jun   [28] Louisa Maria Theresa, daughter of James II, is born.

1693

Jan   Britain's National Debt begins when William III borrows £1 million at 10% to pay for the war with France. William's forces are defeated at Landen.

1694   The composers Henry Carey and Joseph Gibbs are born. The tax on salt is doubled. The Royal Navy bombards Le Havre, Dieppe and Dunkirk, but is repulsed at Brest. This last failure is blamed on John Churchill, who supports James II and who may have betrayed military secrets to France. Greenwich Hospital is founded by Queen Mary. The Licensing Act runs out, which frees the press from censorship.

Jul   [27] The Bank of England is founded by Montagu, the Chancellor of the Exchequer, to carry out all the monetary business of the Government and to obtain interest on the Government's money.

Dec   [22] Triennial Act, requiring a new Parliament to be elected every third year. [28] Mary II dies of smallpox; after this William III reigns alone.

1695   British troops recapture Namur. The composer Maurice Greene is born. The poet Henry Vaughan dies. Isaac Newton becomes master of the Mint. The first public drinking fountain in Britain is built in Hammersmith by Sir Samuel Morland.

Jan   [16] Thomas Tenison becomes Archbishop of Canterbury.

Nov   [1] The Bank of Scotland is founded. [21] The composer Henry Purcell dies of tuberculosis in London at the age of 36. [22] William III's Third Parliament begins.

1696   Henry Winstanley begins work on the first Eddystone Lighthouse. The Assassination Plot to murder the King near Turnham Green is discovered; Sir George Barclay and Sir John Fenwick are among the conspirators. The Second Treason Act; this entitles the accused to have a copy of the indictment and a list of the jurors a few days before the trial; it also entitles the accused to have the aid of counsel. The

Habeas Corpus Act is suspended in the aftermath of the Assassination Plot. The Board of Trade is founded. The Window Tax is introduced; this influences domestic architecture for at least 50 years.

1697 Whitehall Palace is burnt down. The Royal African Company has its trading monopoly withdrawn by Parliament. Sir John Fenwick is tried for high treason. One of the two witnesses required by the Second Treason Act absconds, so the trial ends. Nevertheless, a Bill of Attainder is passed against Fenwick enabling his execution.

Jun   John Aubrey, antiquary, dies.

Sep   [20] Treaty of Ryswyck between William III and Louis XIV; William is internationally acknowledged as the King of England and Anne as his successor.

Nov   [10] The painter William Hogarth is born at Smithfield, London.

Dec   [2] The consecration and formal reopening of the rebuilt St Paul's Cathedral.

1698 Newton calculates the speed of sound. Thomas Savery patents his heat-operated vacuum pump for emptying tin and coal mines of water, but it is not strong enough to cope. The slave trade across the Atlantic from Africa is officially sanctioned for British merchants by Parliament. The London Stock Exchange is founded. White's Club opens in London, with the opening of Mrs White's chocolate house: it soon becomes the headquarters of the Tory Party.

Dec   [6] The Fourth Parliament of William III opens.

1699 With Admiralty backing, William Dampier explores the west coast of Australia in the *Roebuck*. The Darien scheme; some Scots colonists attempt to found a settlement on the Isthmus of Darien with the idea of trading with both East and West Indies. The scheme fails for lack of support and opposition from the East India Company. Billingsgate Market opens in London. William III becomes increasingly unpopular because

of his grants of English land to his Dutch favourites and
several blatantly anti-Catholic measures.

Feb   Disbanding Act; this reduces the army to 7000 men.
May   Shrewsbury, Montagu and Russell resign their offices.

1700

1700 William Dampier explores New Guinea.

May   [1] John Dryden, Poet Laureate for over 20 years, dies in
London.
Jul   [30] William Duke of Gloucester dies aged 11. He is the only
surviving child of (Queen) Anne; as a result the succession to
the throne passes to the Electress Sophia of Hanover.

1701 Britain, Holland, Savoy and the Emperor Leopold form a
Grand Alliance. Jethro Tull invents the first practical seed
drill at about this time. Henry Playford, the music publisher,
opens a series of weekly concerts in Oxford.

Feb   [6] William III's Fifth Parliament begins.
May   [8] 'Captain' William Kidd, the pirate, is tried at the Old
Bailey. [23] Kidd is hanged at Execution Dock; he is hanged
three times, because the rope breaks twice.
Jun   [12] The Act of Settlement settles the royal succession on the
Protestant descendants of Sophia of Hanover.
Sep   [17] Ex-King James II dies after a stroke at St Germain in
France; his son James Edward (the Old Pretender) is
proclaimed King of Great Britain and Ireland by Louis XIV.
Dec   [30] William III's Sixth Parliament begins. Attainder of James
Edward, the 'pretender' Prince of Wales.

1702 The colony of Delaware is founded in America.

Mar   [8] William III dies after falling from his horse at Hampton
Court. Anne, his sister-in-law, succeeds. A combined
Whig-Tory Ministry takes the Government, under Churchill
and Godolphin. [11] The first English daily newspaper, the

Daily Courant, is published by E. Mallet. [23] Coronation of Queen Anne. Lord Cornbury, governor-general of America, opens the New York Assembly on the Queen's behalf – dressed as the Queen, which causes great consternation. The Queen is under the influence of her favourite, Sarah Churchill. Her husband, John Churchill, becomes captain-general of England's land forces. In a successful campaign, he captures Kaiserworth, Venloo and Liege; as a reward he is created Duke of Marlborough.

Oct   Sir George Rooke, commanding an English fleet, is repulsed at Cadiz but captures a Spanish treasure fleet in Vigo Bay. The Queen gives her approval to horse-racing and sweepstakes. [20] First Parliament of Queen Anne begins.

1703   Marlborough's troops capture Bonn, Huy, Limoges and Guelders. England is devastated by a hurricane-force storm; the Eddystone lighthouse is completely destroyed.

Mar   [3] The scientist Robert Hooke dies.

May   [26] Samuel Pepys dies at Clapham.

Jun   [17] The evangelist John Wesley is born at Epworth.

Jul   Daniel Defoe is sentenced to a fine, the pillory and imprisonment for libelling the Church; he is wreathed with flowers in the pillory, but then sent to Newgate prison.

Dec   [27] The Methuen or Port Wine Treaty is signed by England and Portugal; this gives preference to the import of Portuguese wines into England: in return, English woollen goods are admitted into Portugal.

1704   After a quarrel, Alexander Selkirk, first mate on a ship in the Pacific, is put ashore on the uninhabited island of Juan Fernandez, at his own request. Selkirk is to be marooned for four years before being rescued. Jeremiah Clarke becomes the Chapel Royal organist. Beau Nash becomes master of ceremonies at Bath.

Jul   [24] Capture of Gibraltar from the Spanish by Admiral Sir George Rooke and Sir Cloudesley Shovel.

Aug   Defoe is released from prison. [13] Battle of Blenheim; a
      major Anglo-Austrian victory under Marlborough and Prince
      Eugene against French and Bavarian armies.

1705 Edmund Halley correctly predicts the return of the comet
      that now bears his name. Isaac Newton is knighted.

Jul   [13] Titus Oates, the conspirator who fabricated a Catholic
      plot to assassinate Charles II, dies.

Aug   [22] George (later George II) marries Caroline, daughter of
      John Margrave of Brandenburg-Anspach.

Oct   [4] Lord Peterborough captures Barcelona.

1706 The merchant Thomas Twining opens Tom's Coffee House in
      London and starts a major tea importing business. Work
      begins on the second Eddystone Lighthouse. Parliament
      creates the first Turnpike Trust, empowering local gentry to
      take over a certain length of road from the parish, and to
      improve and maintain it by charging tolls. The Earl of
      Galway and the Allies enter Madrid.

Feb   [27] John Evelyn, diarist for the last 65 years of his life, dies at
      Wotton near Dorking.

May   [23] Battle of Ramillies, near Louvain in Belgium; the
      Spanish and French are defeated by allied British, Dutch and
      Danish armies under Marlborough. The Spanish Empire in
      Europe is dismantled.

Nov   [17] Sophia Dorothea, daughter of George I, marries Prince
      Frederick William of Prussia.

1707

Jan   [20] Frederick, eldest son of George II, is born.

Apr   George Farquhar, dramatist, dies. [22] The novelist Henry
      Fielding is born at Sharpham Park, Glastonbury.

May   [1] Act for the Union of England and Scotland. The English
      and Scottish Parliaments are united at Westminster; Scotland
      is to send 16 elective peers to the House of Lords and 45
      members to the Commons. The Union Jack (Crosses of St
      George and St Andrew) is adopted as the national flag. The

two countries are nevertheless to retain their own independent legal systems and Churches.

Oct [23] The First Parliament of Great Britain begins; in reality, it is the Second Parliament of Queen Anne revived by proclamation. From this time on, parliaments cease to be numbered officially by reigns.

Dec [1] The composer Jeremiah Clarke commits suicide. [18] The evangelist and hymn writer Charles Wesley is born at Epworth in Lincolnshire.

1708 Lord Cornbury, the transvestite governor-general of America, is finally recalled to England in debt. Thomas Newcomen patents his steam engine for pumping water out of mines; although this is effective, it is expensive to run because it uses a lot of fuel. New figures of Gog and Magog at the London Guildhall replace those destroyed in the Great Fire. New and old East India Companies are amalgamated as the United East India Company, becoming the most influential power on the coasts of India.

Mar The Old Pretender, James Edward, lands in Scotland from France in a short and unsuccessful attempt to regain the British throne for the Stuarts. The French fleet sent to assist him is beaten by Admiral Byng. Robert Walpole is appointed Secretary of War.

Jul [11] Battle of Oudenarde in west Belgium; the Duke of Marlborough's troops are victorious over the French led by Vendome. Marlborough also captures Lille after a four-month siege.

Nov [15] William Pitt the Elder is born at Westminster.

1709 Alexander Selkirk is rescued from his desert island; his story forms the basis of Defoe's *Robinson Crusoe*. High-quality and low-cost iron is produced by Abraham Darby, an iron worker at Coalbrookdale in Shropshire; the iron ore is smelted with coke and moulded in sand. The new process leads to the mass production of iron. Francis Hawksbee makes the first

accurate observation of capillary action in glass tubes.
Postage rates are regulated by mileage.

1710 The composer William Boyce is born. Handel comes to
Britain; in London he writes *Rinaldo* in 14 days. A Tory
government under Harley and St John replaces the
Whig-Tory government, reducing British involvement in the
European war.

Feb– Impeachment of Dr Henry Sacheverell, a hot-headed political
Mar preacher who attacked the Whigs. Sacheverell is found
guilty, sentenced to abstain from preaching for three years
and his sermon to be burnt by the public hangman; there is
great public support for Sacheverell and a strong Tory
reaction generally to the impeachment.

Mar [12] Thomas Arne, composer of 'Rule Britannia', is born in
London.

1711 The tuning fork is invented by John Shore, trumpeter at the
Chapel Royal. Sir Godfrey Kneller founds the Academy of
Painting in St Martins Lane, London. Lord Cornbury is made
a Privy Councillor. The South Sea Company is incorporated
by Parliament. Occasional Conformity Act; this stops the
practice by which dissenters qualify for state office by taking
the Anglican Communion on rare occasions. Landed
Property Qualifications Act; this measure is an attempt by
landowners to exclude merchants, financiers and
industrialists from Parliament. It is not successfully enforced
but not repealed until 1866.

Mar [1] *The Spectator* is first published, succeeding *The Tatler* as the
great British review.

Aug [7] The first Royal Ascot horse-race meeting takes place,
attended by Queen Anne.

1712 Thomas Newcomen develops the first piston-operated
steam-engine at Tipton. The last witch trial and execution for
witchcraft take place in England. Rob Roy becomes an outlaw
after the chief of the Macgregor clan evicts him from his

lands for debt. Robert Walpole is expelled from the Commons and sent to the Tower on charges of corruption and bribery while in the Navy Office.

Jul [12] Richard Cromwell, sometime Lord Protector, dies at the age of 86.

1713 The tall north-west flanking stone of the Cove at Avebury is taken down and destroyed. Robert Brydges, friend of Charles II, drowns in a lake while trying to save his dog. Roger Cotes produces a revised edition of Newton's *Principia*. The South Sea Company takes over the whole of the National Debt at 8% interest. Lord Bolingbroke plots for the accession of the Old Pretender. Spain gives Britain the exclusive right to supply the Spanish colonies with slaves for the next 30 years.

Apr [11] Treaty of Utrecht; this establishes the terms of peace with Louis XIV's France: Gibraltar and Minorca are formally ceded to Britain. [22] Daniel Defoe is prosecuted for libel, imprisoned and immediately pardoned.

Nov [24] The writer and cleric Laurence Sterne is born at Clonmel in Tipperary. The painter Allan Ramsay is born.

1714 The Board of Longitude offers a prize of £20,000 for the discovery of a North-West Passage to the Far East. The Schism Act aims at restoring the Church's educational monopoly and destroying nonconformist schools.

Feb [16] The Fifth Parliament of Queen Anne, the Fourth of Great Britain, opens.

Aug [1] Queen Anne dies; the German Prince George Louis of Hanover succeeds as George I under the 1701 Act of Settlement: he speaks no English. A Whig Ministry is formed under Townsend, Stanhope and Walpole.

Sep [18] George I lands in England. [27] George I's son (later George II) is created Prince of Wales.

Dec William Congreve is appointed Secretary for Jamaica.

1715 Robert Walpole becomes Chancellor of the Exchequer. Nicholas Rowe is appointed Poet Laureate. Andrew Becker invents the first practical diving suit and demonstrates it in the Thames. The Riot Act is passed.

Mar [17] A new Parliament meets, with a large Whig majority. It impeaches Oxford (Harley), Bolingbroke (St John) and Ormond for surrendering British honour and interests under the terms of the Treaty of Utrecht. Ormond and Bolingbroke manage to escape to France, but Oxford is caught and sent to the Tower.

Nov A Jacobite Rising (the '15') is suppressed at Preston and Sheriffmuir. Some Jacobite supporters are able to escape to France, others are captured and executed, Derwentwater and Kenmure among them. The Rebellion, organized by the Earl of Mar, aims at overthrowing the Hanoverian succession and installing the 'Old Pretender'.

Dec [14] Archbishop Tenison dies. [22] James Stuart, the 'Old Pretender', lands at Peterhead but is forced to return to France straight away with the Earl of Mar.

1716 The first central-heating system in Britain, a hot water system in a greenhouse, is installed by Swedish engineer Martin Triewald. Mineral waters are discovered at Cheltenham, and the town is soon transformed into a popular spa. Nicholas Hawksmoor, one of the two architects to the Commission for Fifty New Churches, begins work on St Mary Woolnoth, considered by some to be his finest church. The Royal Regiment of Artillery is founded. The Septennial Act prolongs the life of a Parliament from three to seven years: this is a response to the unsettled political situation. Treaty of Westminster; Britain and Austria become allies in a mutual defence pact. Britain signs a similar treaty with France.

Jan [16] William Wake becomes Archbishop of Canterbury. The Jacobite troops are dispersed.

Feb [24] The leaders of the Jacobite rising captured at Preston are executed. The Pretender himself escapes.

Dec   [26] Thomas Gray, poet, is born in London.

1717 The Strand maypole is taken down to be used by Sir Isaac Newton as a support for his new telescope. The composer Handel stays at Canons in Edgware, the seat of the Duke of Chandos. The value of the golden guinea is fixed at 21 shillings.

Jan   [4] A Triple Alliance is concluded between Britain, France and Holland to uphold the Treaty of Utrecht; the Old Pretender has to leave France. Robert Walpole resigns and Lord Stanhope becomes First Lord of the Treasury.

Feb   [19] The actor David Garrick is born at Hereford.

Mar   [8] Abraham Darby, the first ironmaster to use coke to smelt iron, dies at Worcester.

Jun   [24] The first Freemasons' Lodge is inaugurated, in London.

1718 Thomas Lombe patents a machine to make thrown silk. A machine-gun is patented by lawyer James Puckle. The Society of Antiquaries is founded. Lord Stanhope becomes Secretary of State. Lady Mary Wortley Montagu introduces inoculation against smallpox.

Jan   The Occasional Conformity and Schism Acts are repealed.

Jul   [30] William Penn, the English Quaker leader and founder of the American state of Pennsylvania, dies.

Aug   [2] A Quadruple Alliance is formed by England, France, Holland and Austria against Spain, after Spain seizes Sicily and raises the spectre of another European war. Admiral Byng is sent with a fleet to defend Sicily. In a sea battle off Cape Passaro, he completely destroys the Spanish fleet.

Nov   [22] Edward Teach, the English pirate known as 'Blackbeard', is killed off the coast of North Carolina.

1719 Spanish troops invading Scotland in support of the Jacobites are defeated at Glenshiel. The Peerage Bill, aimed at restricting the House of Lords, is rejected by the Commons.

Jun   [17] Joseph Addison, the writer, dies at Holland House, London.

Dec [31] John Flamsteed, the first Astronomer Royal, for whom Charles II built the Greenwich Royal Observatory, dies, his catalogue of stars for ships' navigators still incomplete after 40 years of work.

1720 Handel becomes director of the Royal Academy of Music in London. Ralph Allen of Bath is granted a monopoly of the country (non-London) posts; he establishes a postal system using post-boys on horseback. Walpole and Townsend are recalled to office, Townsend as President of the Privy Council.

Jan The 'South Sea Bubble' bursts; many investors are ruined after speculating in the stock of the South Sea Company. The Quadruple Alliance makes peace with Spain.

1721 The compensator pendulum for clocks is invented by George Graham. The directors of the collapsed South Sea Company are prosecuted. The writer Tobias Smollett is born.

Apr [3] Sir Robert Walpole becomes the first British Prime Minister; he is also First Lord of the Treasury and Chancellor of the Exchequer. Walpole's policy of maintaining a permanent National Debt brings prosperity. [15] William Augustus, son of George II, is born.

Aug [3] The woodcarver Grinling Gibbons dies.

1722 The Atterbury Plot: Francis Atterbury, Bishop of Rochester and a leading Jacobite, is arrested for alleged conspiracy in a plot to seize the King, the Tower and the Bank of England in order to restore the Old Pretender. The Habeas Corpus Act is suspended. Workhouse Test Act, for the care and housing of the needy.

Jun [16] The Duke of Marlborough, Britain's most successful military commander, dies at Windsor.

1723 The young William Stukeley and his patron Lord Winchelsea dance a minuet on top of one of the Stonehenge trilithons. Wood's Halfpence; Wood, an English ironmaster, is given a

patent by Walpole to issue copper coinage in Ireland.
Dean Swift of Dublin writes against the coinage, stirring
up popular feeling in Ireland to the extent that Walpole has
to withdraw it. Francis Atterbury is sentenced to
banishment for life for his part in the plot to overthrow
the King. Treaty of Charlotteburg between Britain and
Prussia; George I's grandson will eventually marry a
Prussian princess and Prince Frederick of Prussia will
marry the Prince of Wales' daughter. Walpole reduces the
duty on tea.

Feb [22] Mary, daughter of George II, is born. [25] Sir
Christopher Wren dies in London at the age of 91. [26] The
prolific playwright Thomas Durfey dies.

Jun [5] Adam Smith, economist and philosopher, is born at
Kirkcaldy.

Jul [16] The painter Sir Joshua Reynolds is born near Plymouth,
Devon.

1724 The Three Choirs Festival is founded. Longman's, one of the
oldest surviving publishing house in Britain, is founded. The
Sanctuary, a megalithic monument near Avebury, is
destroyed by farmers. John Carteret, the King's favourite, is
sent to Ireland as Lord Lieutenant, clearing the way for his
cabinet rivals, Walpole and Townsend.

Jun [8] The civil engineer John Smeaton is born.

Aug [24] The painter George Stubbs is born at Liverpool.

Nov [16] Jack Sheppard, the notorious highwayman, is hanged at
Tyburn.

Dec [12] Admiral Samuel Hood is born at Thorncombe in Devon.

1725 Guy's hospital is founded. Lord Bolingbroke is given
permission to return to England and take possession of his
estates. George I revives the Military Order of the Bath.
Stereotyping invented by William Ged.

Sep [3] Treaty of Hanover between Britain, France and Prussia.
[29] Robert Clive, soldier and administrator, is born.

1726 Stephen Hales, a clergyman and physicist, measures blood-pressure for the first time. John Harrison, a clockmaker, invents the gridiron pendulum. Handel becomes a British citizen. Lloyd's List, a record of shipping data and news, is published for the first time in London. General George Wade builds 250 miles of military road in Scotland. The first circulating library in Britain is established in Edinburgh by Allan Ramsay. War breaks out between Britain and Spain. The writer Charles Burney is born. William Augustus, George II's son, is created Duke of Cumberland.

Mar   [7] The writer and musician Charles Burney is born. [8] Admiral Richard Howe is born. [26] Sir John Vanbrugh, dramatist and architect of Blenheim Palace, dies of a quinsy in London.

1727 The first railway bridge, the Tanfield Arch, is built by Ralph Wood over a colliery railway at Cawsey Dell. William Kent publishes Inigo Jones' architectural designs. War between Britain and Spain over Gibraltar begins. Britain for the first time employs mercenaries from Hesse to fight in battle. The composer William Croft dies. First Indemnity Act for Nonconformists.

Jan   [2] General James Wolfe is born at Westerham.

Mar   [20] Sir Isaac Newton dies in London.

May   [14] Thomas Gainsborough, painter, is baptized at Sudbury, Suffolk.

Jun   [11] George I dies of apoplexy on his way to Hanover, in the room where he was born at the castle at Osnabruck. He is succeeded by his 44-year-old son, George II.

Oct   [11] Coronation of George II. [17] John Wilkes, the political agitator, is born at Clerkenwell. Sir Spencer Compton is briefly appointed Prime Minister by George II, but he is so incompetent that Walpole is quickly recalled.

1728 The architect and designer Robert Adam is born. Colley Cibber becomes manager of Drury Lane Theatre. The Siege

of Gibraltar is lifted by Spain after 14 months. The
Anglo-Spanish War ends with the Convention of Prado.
Publication of Parliamentary debates is declared to be a
breach of privilege. The governor of the Fleet Prison,
Thomas Bainbridge, is accused of brutality to the inmates
and a Parliamentary inquiry into his conduct is opened.

Jan [29] The first performance of *The Beggar's Opera*.
Oct [28] The explorer Captain James Cook is born at Marton,
Yorkshire.
Nov [10] The poet, novelist and dramatist Oliver Goldsmith is
born.

1729 James Bradley, the astronomer, detects stellar aberrations,
the apparent shift in position of stars caused by the Earth's
movement; this is the first definitive confirmation of
Copernicus' theory that the Earth revolves around the sun.
The Methodist movement begins in Oxford. The dramatist
William Congreve dies.

Jan [12] The statesman Edmund Burke is born in Dublin.
Aug [5] Thomas Newcomen, who invented the first steam-engine
in 1705, dies.
Nov [9] Treaty of Seville between Britain and Spain; by this treaty,
Britain retains Gibraltar.
Dec Samuel Johnson leaves Pembroke College, Oxford after only
one year.

1730 The mathematician John Hadley invents the reflecting
quadrant. The Serpentine is created in Hyde Park.

May [15] Townsend resigns from the Government after a quarrel
with Walpole, and becomes an agricultural pioneer, devising
a four-crop rotation system.
Jul [12] Josiah Wedgwood is born at Burslem, Staffordshire.

1731 The first lightship, *The Nore*, is anchored in the Thames
estuary. George Lillo writes the first serious play in which
the leading characters are not all from the upper classes. 10

Downing Street becomes the Prime Minister's official residence. Captain Jenkins of the English ship *Rebecca* loses an ear in a skirmish with Spanish coastguards; this incident is to be used in eight years' time as a pretext for war with Spain.

Mar [16] Treaty of Vienna, between Britain, Spain, Austria and Holland; the Ostend East India Company, Britain's main colonial trading rival in cotton and spices, is dissolved.

Apr [26] The novelist and author of *Robinson Crusoe*, Daniel Defoe, dies.

Oct [10] Henry Cavendish, the discoverer of hydrogen, is born at Nice.

Nov [15] The poet William Cowper is born at Berkhamsted.

1732 The Academy of Ancient Music is founded in London. A threshing machine is invented by Michael Menzies. The first sedative, the 'Dover sedative powder', is invented by Captain Thomas Dover. The colony of Georgia is founded: the last of the 'Thirteen Colonies' which make up English East Coast America.

Apr [13] The Tory Prime Minister Lord North is born.

Jun [10] Handel's masque *Acis and Galatea* is performed in public for the first time at the King's Theatre, London.

Dec [4] The poet and playwright John Gay dies. [6] Warren Hastings, the first Governor-General of India, is born. [7] Covent Garden Opera House is opened. [23] Sir Richard Arkwright, inventor of mechanical spinning processes in the cotton industry, is born at Preston, the last of 13 children.

1733 John Kay invents the flying shuttle, the first of the great textile inventions. Britain prohibits trade between her American and West Indian colonies by the Molasses Act; this measure leads to widespread smuggling. Walpole's attempt to introduce excise duty instead of 'customs' levied at ports only (on wine and tobacco) brings great unrest. The Tories are too weak to overthrow Walpole, but the Excise Bill is withdrawn.

Mar [13] Joseph Priestley, the scientist who later discovers oxygen, is born at Leeds.

1734 A Trade Treaty between Britain and Russia is signed. The Dilettanti Society is founded in London, to encourage travel for the collection of classical antiquities. George II's daughter Marie Anne marries the Prince of Orange-Nassau. James Fitzjames, the Duke of Berwick, dies; he was the illegitimate son of James II.

1735 William Pitt becomes MP for Old Sarum, a 'rotten borough' with so few constituents that election is in the gift of the landowner. John Harrison invents the ship's chronometer.

Jul [9] Samuel Johnson marries Mrs Porter.
Sep [14] Robert Haikes, founder of the Sunday School system, is born.

1736 The tenor voice first displaces the castrato in a leading operatic role when John Beard sings at Covent Garden. The witchcraft statutes are repealed in England. John and Charles Wesley return from Georgia and begin their evangelical mission in England. George Whitefield, their collaborator, is ordained. The architect Nicholas Hawksmoor dies. The Porteous Riots take place in Edinburgh when a smuggler is hanged for theft. Captain Porteous orders his Town Guard to fire on the rioting mob. He is found guilty of murder, reprieved and finally lynched on a barber's pole in Grassmarket.

Jan [19] The engineer and inventor James Watt is born at Greenock.
Feb [19] The first performance, at Covent Garden, of *Alexander's Feast*, with words by Dryden and music by Handel.

1737 The portrait painter Joseph Nolleken is born in Soho. Queen Caroline dies, weakening Walpole's authority, which relied partly on favour at Court. Frederick Prince of Wales quarrels with his father, siding with the anti-Walpole faction. The opposition party supported by the Prince of Wales calls itself 'The Patriots'. The Licensing Act subjects all plays to censorship by the Lord Chamberlain.

Jan   [24] Archbishop Wake dies. [29] The political thinker Thomas Paine is born at Thetford.

Feb   [28] John Potter, Bishop of Oxford, becomes Archbishop of Canterbury.

Mar   Samuel Johnson goes to London, taking one of his pupils, David Garrick, with him.

Apr   [27] Edward Gibbon, historian, is born at Putney.

1738   The first spinning-machines are patented in England, although invented by a Swiss physicist, Lewis Paul. The House of Lords is invaded by a bevy of peeresses, led by the Duchess of Queensberry, in the middle of a debate.

May   [24] George III is born in lodgings at St James's Square in London.

Nov   [15] Sir William Herschel, astronomer and discoverer of the planet Uranus in 1781, is born at Hanover.

1739   John Wesley begins his life-long crusade as an open-air preacher. Walpole gives in to the demand for war with Spain, although he personally opposes it; the War of Jenkins' Ear begins, partly because of the right claimed and exercised by the Spanish of searching all British vessels while at sea, and partly also because of the resulting acts of violence done to British sailors by the Spanish.

Apr   [7] Dick Turpin, the notorious highwayman, is hanged at York for murder, cattle-stealing, smuggling and holding up stage-coaches.

Nov   [22] Admiral Vernon captures the Spanish base of Porto Bello.

1740   Benjamin Huntsman invents the crucible method of making steel from scrap iron. Admiral Edward Vernon issues the naval rum ration diluted with water; he is known as 'Old Grog' because of his grogram coat, and the weakened tot also becomes known as 'grog'. Vernon and Wentworth make an unsuccessful attack on Cartagena. David Garrick becomes manager of Drury Lane Theatre.

May   [8] George II's daughter Mary marries Frederick, who later is to become Landgrave of Hesse-Cassel.

Oct   [29] James Boswell, diarist and biographer, is born at Edinburgh.

Nov   [4] The hymn writer Augustus Toplady is born at Farnham.

1741 David Garrick makes his first appearance on the London stage, in *Richard III*. The Royal Military Academy at Woolwich is founded. Walpole is attacked by his critics, but an attempt to have him dismissed fails. Highways Act, to improve the roads.

Feb   [21] The agricultural pioneer Jethro Tull dies near Hungerford.

1742 Cotton factories are set up in Birmingham and Northampton. Britain forms an alliance with Prussia. Support for Austria in the War of Austrian Succession and opposition to the war with Spain lead to the fall of Walpole.

Feb   [26] Walpole is succeeded by John Lord Carteret as Prime Minister.

Apr   [13] The first performance of Handel's *Messiah* in Dublin: the climax of Handel's popularity.

1743 The composer Henry Carey dies.

Apr   [24] Edmund Cartwright, inventor of the power loom, is born at Marnham.

Jun   [16] Battle of Dettingen, the last battle in which a British monarch commands an army on the field of battle; George II defeats the French.

Aug [16] Jack Broughton, the champion pugilist, assembles the earliest code of boxing rules for the prize-ring. [27] The Whig Henry Pelham becomes Prime Minister.

Oct [27] George II's daughter Louisa marries Prince Frederick, later King of Denmark.

1744 George Anson arrives back in Britain after a successful four-year circumnavigation of the world. In retaliation for Dettingen, the French send a fleet led by Charles Edward, the Old Pretender's son, to invade Britain; a storm scatters the fleet. The words and music of the first stanza and the original second stanza of the National Anthem first appear in print. Robert Clive arrives in Madras as an employee of the East India Company. War between Britain and France continues intermittently in Europe, India, North America and the West Indies from now until 1815. In a Cabinet reshuffle, John Carteret, who is accused of favouring Hanoverian against British interests, loses his position as Secretary of State; he is replaced by Henry Pelham.

May [30] The poet Alexander Pope dies at Twickenham.

1745 The agriculturalist Robert Bakewell produces the Leicester breed of sheep, with twice the amount of meat compared with earlier breeds. The composer Charles Dibden is born.

Mar [18] Sir Robert Walpole, Prime Minister from 1721 to 1742, dies in London.

May [11] Battle of Fontenoy; the British army under the Duke of Cumberland is defeated by the French under Marshal Saxe.

Jul [25] The Young Pretender, Charles Edward, lands in Scotland.

Aug [19] Intent on claiming the throne, Prince Charles Edward raises his father's standard at Glenfinnan.

Sep [11] 2,000 Jacobites enter Edinburgh. [21] Battle of Prestonpans; Bonnie Prince Charlie's Jacobite army gains a victory over English forces led by Sir John Cope. Charles leads his army into England, vainly hoping for popular

English support and decides to return to Scotland. [28] The first known performance of the National Anthem, 'God Save the King', at Drury Lane Theatre.

Oct [19] The satirist Jonathan Swift dies aged 77.

Dec [18] Jacobite victory at Penrith.

1746 John Roebuck invents a process for manufacturing sulphuric acid, used to bleach textiles, on an industrial scale. Canaletto arrives in London. Pelham resigns his ministry when George II refuses to accept William Pitt; he eventually forces the King's hand, returning to office with Pitt as Paymaster of the Forces.

Jan [17] Battle of Falkirk; Charles defeats General Hawley's troops.

Apr [16] Battle of Culloden; the Jacobites are finally annihilated by a Hanoverian force under the Duke of Cumberland, and attempts by the Stuarts to regain the British throne are ended. Culloden is the last battle fought on Scottish soil. Now a fugitive, Charles roams the Scottish Highlands during the summer. The Highlanders are disarmed and forbidden to wear their tartans; the hereditary jurisdiction of the Highland chiefs over their clans is abolished.

Sep [20] Prince Charles Edward escapes capture by dressing as a girl and sailing to France on the French ship *L'Heureux*.

1747 Under David Garrick's management, audiences are removed from the stage of the Drury Lane Theatre and the orchestra is brought down from the gallery. James Bradley discovers that the Earth's axis is variable. Simon Fraser, Lord Lovat, is beheaded for supporting the Jacobite rising. A Carriage Tax is imposed by Parliament. Horace Walpole acquires a villa (Strawberry Hill) at Twickenham; with his striking alterations, it is to become the stimulus for the Gothic revival in domestic architecture. The Duke of Cumberland's forces are defeated by a French army at Lauffeld. Britain, Holland and Russia sign the Convention of St Petersburg.

Oct [10] John Potter, Archbishop of Canterbury, dies.
Nov [10] The Fourth Parliament of George II opens. [24] Thomas
     Herring, Archbishop of York, becomes Archbishop of
     Canterbury.

1748 John Palmer of Bath persuades the Government to accept the
     idea of a Mail-Coach service, protected against highwaymen
     by armed guards. Treaty of Aix-la-Chapelle.
Feb [15] Jeremy Bentham is born.
Nov [25] The hymn writer Isaac Watts dies.

1749 There are serious riots at Bedminster, Bristol, against
     turnpike tolls. Consolidation Act, authorizing the
     reorganization of the Royal Navy.
Jan [24] The Whig statesman and orator Charles James Fox is
     born in London.
Apr [27] Handel's *Music for the Royal Fireworks* is first performed in
     Green Park, London.
May [17] Edward Jenner, vaccination pioneer, is born at Berkeley
     vicarage.

1750 In India, Robert Clive captures and defends Arcot. Jonas
     Hanway is the first *man* to use an umbrella in public; he
     suffers jeers and catcalls in the streets of London. Britain
     surrenders the Asiento, a monopoly of selling black slaves to
     the Spanish colonies, for £100,000. The interest on the
     National Debt is reduced to 3%; from this time on, the Bank
     of England assumes responsibility for the debt. The bounty
     on whales is increased to £2 a ton to encourage greater
     participation in the whaling industry. Iron Act; this is
     designed to prevent American colonists from manufacturing
     their own iron products. One of the stones (Stone 14) at
     Stonehenge falls over.
Mar [2] Earth tremor in London.
Apr [2] Earth tremor in Warrington.
Aug [23] Earth tremor at Spalding.

Sep [26] Lord Collingwood, Nelson's second-in-command at Trafalgar, is born at Newcastle. [30] Earth tremor at Northampton.

1751 Clive holds Arcot against the French with a force of only 500; by doing so, he establishes British control over southern India.

Mar [20] The Prince of Wales, Frederick Lewis, dies after being hit by a cricket ball; he had lived in a state of perpetual enmity towards his parents after being dismissed from Court in 1737.

Oct [30] The dramatist Richard Brinsley Sheridan is born in Dublin.

1752 Robert Clive relieves the siege of Trichinopoly. Government by a regular cabinet comprising the heads of the main administrative departments is adopted.

Jan [1] Officially 'New Year's Day' for the first time; until now the year officially began on March 25.

Jun [13] The novelist and diarist Frances (Fanny) Burney is born at King's Lynn.

Sep [14] Britain belatedly adopts the Gregorian calendar introduced by Pope Gregory XIII in 1582. The Gregorian calendar is adopted by the British Parliament at the instigation of Lord Chesterfield. The changeover results in a loss adjustment of 11 days, losing the 11 days September 3-13 inclusive. There is widespread protest from people who innocently believe that their lives have been shortened: 'Give us back our eleven days!'

Nov [20] The poet Thomas Chatterton is born.

1753 James Lind, a Scottish doctor, advocates the use of citrus fruits as a cure for scurvy. The Jewish Naturalization Act faces so much opposition that it is repealed. A Land Tax of two shillings in the pound is imposed throughout England and Wales. The Marriage Act is introduced by the Earl of Hardwicke, with the intention of putting an end to clandestine marriages solemnized without a licence; it states that banns of marriage must be published in the parish church where the parties live for three successive Sundays, and that no licence should be granted to a minor. The Broad Wheels Act fixes nine inches as the minimum width for wheels except for those of light vehicles. The intention of this act is to reduce damage to road surfaces; in fact, instead of causing ruts, broad wheels grind the whole road surface to powder.

Jan [11] Sir Hans Sloane dies. The British Museum is begun with the Government purchase of Sloane's collection of antiquities.

Sep [10] John Soane, architect of the Bank of England, is born.

Dec [3] Samuel Crompton, inventor of the spinning mule which substituted machinery for hand work in the cotton industry, is born at Firwood near Bolton.

1754 The first iron rolling-mill is established at Fareham. The Scottish chemist Joseph Black discovers carbonic gas. Henry Pelham dies and is succeeded by Thomas Pelham, Duke of Newcastle, as Prime Minister.

Jan [28] In a letter to a friend written after reading a fairy-tale, Horace Walpole coins the word 'serendipity' to describe the Three Princes of Serendip's happy knack of making discoveries entirely by accident.

Aug [5] James Gibbs, the architect who designed St Martin-in-the-Fields, dies. [21] William Murdock, who will invent coal-gas lighting in 1792, is born at Auchinleck.

Sep [9] William Bligh, Captain of the *Bounty*, is born at Plymouth.

Oct [8] The author Henry Fielding dies.

1755 Joseph Black demonstrates the difference between lime and magnesium. Henry Fox, originally Pitt's ally but later his rival, is manoeuvred into the Cabinet by the Duke of Newcastle, becoming Secretary of State and leader of the House of Commons; he succeeds in having Pitt dismissed from the Pay Office. The composer Maurice Green dies. The artist John Flaxman is born.

1756 Joseph Black discovers carbon dioxide. General Braddock is sent by the British Government to assist American colonists against the French; he is defeated and killed at Fort Duquesne. Britain and Prussia become allies; Britain declares war on France. The Seven Years War begins; Britain becomes involved because she is competing with France for colonies in India and America. Highland regiments serve for the first time in this war. Minorca is taken from the British by a large French fleet; Admiral John Byng is sent to the rescue, but he withdraws to Gibraltar. Outcry at the loss of Minorca and inept handling of the war leads to the fall of Newcastle's ministry.

Jun [20] The Black Hole of Calcutta; the suffocation of many British subjects imprisoned by Surarjak Dowlah, the Nawab of Bengal, in the tiny guardroom at Fort William: only 23 survive out of 146 people imprisoned overnight. Clive is sent from Madras to punish the Nawab; he retakes Calcutta and forces the Nawab to sign a peace treaty.

Nov [16] Newcastle is succeeded by William Cavendish, Duke of Devonshire, as First Lord of the Treasury. William Pitt is Secretary of State and quickly becomes the main influence in the British Government.

1757 The Duke of Cumberland's forces are defeated in two engagements at Hastenbeck and Klosterseven.

Mar [13] Archbishop Herring dies. [14] Admiral John Byng is shot by firing squad on the quarter deck of the *Monarque*, after being court-martialled for failing to relieve the island of Minorca.

Apr [29] Matthew Hutton, Archbishop of York, becomes Archbishop of Canterbury.

Jun [22] Captain George Vancouver, explorer of the Pacific coast of North America, is born at King's Lynn. [23] Battle of

Plassey in Bengal; Clive conquers the Indian forces, securing Bengal for Britain and laying the foundations of the British Empire in India.

Jul   [2] The Duke of Newcastle becomes First Lord of the Treasury and Prime Minister again; Pitt continues as Secretary of State.

Aug   [9] Thomas Telford, engineer of roads, canals and bridges, is born at Westerkirk.

Nov   [28] The poet, artist and visionary William Blake is born in London.

Dec   [11] The organist and composer Charles Wesley is born. [12] Colley Cibber dies.

1758 Jedediah Strutt invents a ribbing machine for manufacturing stockings. The first blast furnace is installed by John Wilkinson, an ironmaster at Bilston. John Bird invents the sextant. Fort Duquesne is taken from the French by a mixed force of Americans and Scots under Generals Washington and Forbes; they rename the captured town 'Pittsburgh'. The Duke of Cumberland is recalled after several defeats and replaced as commander of British-Hanoverian forces by Duke Ferdinand of Brunswick.

Mar   [13] The return of Halley's Comet, as predicted by Edmund Halley in 1682. [19] Archbishop Hutton dies.

Apr   [21] Thomas Secker, Bishop of Oxford, becomes Archbishop of Canterbury.

Sep   [29] Horatio Nelson is born at Burnham Thorpe rectory, Norfolk.

1759 James Brindley designs the Worsley–Manchester Canal; this is the first true dead-water canal and marks the beginning of a new form of transport in Britain. General Wolfe is appointed by Pitt to take command of the British army in Canada and drive the French out. It is the 'Year of Victories' or Annus Mirabilis for Britain, with victories at Quebec, Minden, Lagos and Quiberon Bay. Horace Walpole says, 'one is forced to ask every morning what victory there is for fear of missing one'.

Jan [12] Anne, daughter of George II and wife of Prince William IV of Orange, dies. [15] The British Museum at Montague House in Bloomsbury is opened to the public. [25] The poet Robert Burns is born at Alloway, Ayrshire.

Apr [14] The death of Handel at the age of 74.

May [28] William Pitt the Younger is born at Hayes.

Jul [23] Work begins on the building of HMS *Victory* at Chatham.

Aug [24] William Wilberforce, campaigner against slavery, is born at Hull.

Sep [13] General Wolfe dies in battle on the Plains of Abraham near Quebec, defeating the French forces under Montcalm. [14] Montcalm dies from his wounds. [18] The British capture Quebec from the French, virtually ensuring British supremacy in Canada.

Nov [20] Naval Battle of Quiberon Bay; Admiral Hawke's first fleet destroys the French invasion fleet under Admiral Conflans.

1760 Josiah Wedgwood establishes his pottery works at Etruria in Staffordshire. Dr Johnson writes his final weekly piece for the Idler column of the *Universal Chronicle*. Thomas Braidwood of Edinburgh opens the first school specially for the deaf and dumb. The Botanical Gardens at Kew are opened. Portsmouth Dockyard is burnt out. In India, Colonel Eyre Coote's troops defeat the French at Wandewash and take Madras; this marks the end of French power in India.

May [5] The hangman's drop is used for the first time at Tyburn for the execution of Earl Ferrers.

Oct [25] George II dies suddenly, at 8 a.m., aged 76. He is succeeded by his grandson, George III.

1761 The British capture Belle Isle and Dominica. In India, Pondicherry is captured from the French. The German painter Johann Zoffany settles in England.

Jun [7] John Rennie, civil engineer, is born.

Jul [4] Samuel Richardson, novelist, dies. [17] The Bridgewater Canal (Worsley-Manchester) is opened.

Sep [8] George III marries Charlotte, daughter of Charles Duke of Mecklenburg-Strelitz. [22] Coronation of George III.

Oct [5] Fall of William Pitt. Pitt fears the close alliance of France and Spain under the Family Compact and wants to declare war on Spain; he is not supported by his colleagues, and resigns. Newcastle is Prime Minister in the new Cabinet.

1762 John Nash, architect, dandy and leader of fashion, is born. Cast iron is converted into malleable iron at the Carron Ironworks in Scotland.

Jan Britain declares war on Spain, capturing Havana, Manila, Martinique, St Lucia, St Vincent, Grenada. British forces under General Burgoyne drive the Spanish out of Portugal.

May [26] The Duke of Newcastle is succeeded as Prime Minister by the King's friend John Stewart, Earl of Bute.

Aug [12] King George IV is born at St James's Palace. [19] The new prince is created Prince of Wales.

1763 The painter George Morland is born. The scientific instrument maker at Glasgow University, James Watt, is given a model of the Newcomen engine to repair ; it sets him thinking about ways of devising a more efficient steam-engine. Pontiac's conspiracy; the Red Indian attempt to destroy British power in America fails.

Feb [10] Treaty of Paris, between Britain, France and Spain, by which Canada is ceded to Britain, along with Cape Breton, Nova Scotia, Minorca, Tobago, St Vincent, Grenada, Dominica, Senegal and Florida; the British make great colonial gains by this treaty.

Mar [9] William Cobbett, political journalist, is born at Farnham.

Apr [16] The Earl of Bute is forced to resign; he is succeeded as Prime Minister by Charles Grenville. [23] John Wilkes, a radical MP, is expelled from the House of Commons and outlawed for writing scurrilous articles attacking both King and Government in his newspaper, the *North Briton*. He is later released on grounds of Parliamentary privilege.

Aug [16] Frederick, the second son of George III, is born.

1764 Numbered houses appear for the first time in London. James Hargreaves invents the spinning-jenny. Sugar Act; Britain hopes to recover revenue from the American colonies, but this arouses much local opposition. Tension increases between the American colonists and the British Government, because of the British assumption that colonies exist for the benefit of the founding country. Mozart meets Carl Philipp Emanuel Bach in London.

Jul [9] The authoress Ann Radcliffe is born.
Oct [26] The painter William Hogarth dies in London.

1765 The steam-engine with separate condenser is invented by James Watt. Nelson's flagship, HMS *Victory*, is launched at Chatham. Robert Clive reforms the Indian administration; the British rule Bengal and Bihar, maintaining a puppet Mogul emperor. Regency Bill; this is drawn up by Grenville's ministry as a result of the King's worsening mental condition. The Queen's name is deliberately omitted from the list of regents, and this so angers the King that Grenville is forced to resign.

Jul [13] Grenville is succeeded as Prime Minister by the Marquis of Rockingham. The American Stamp Act, the taxation of legal documents as a way of getting the colonies to help pay for the troops maintained for their protection, angers the American colonists.

Jul [27] William Augustus, Duke of Cumberland, son of George II, dies.

1766 Henry Cavendish discovers hydrogen, making the development of the balloon possible. John Byron takes the Falklands for Britain, unaware that de Bougainville has already claimed the islands for France.

Jan   David Hume brings Rousseau to England. [1] James Stuart, son of James II, dies in Rome.

Feb   [17] The economist Thomas Malthus is born. [24] The composer Samuel Wesley is born. Rockingham repeals the Stamp Act, but the Declaratory Act reaffirms the right of the British Parliament to tax the colonies. George III dismisses Rockingham and Pitt is created Earl of Chatham.

Jul   [30] Pitt becomes Prime Minister, but illness prevents him from attending the House so the Government is controlled by the Duke of Grafton.

Sep   [6] John Dalton, chemist and physician, is born at Eaglesfield. [29] Charlotte, daughter of George III, is born.

Dec   [5] Christie's, the London auctioneers, hold their first sale. [29] Charles Macintosh, inventor of waterproof fabrics, is born in Glasgow.

1767   Robert Clive leaves India for England for the last time, leaving disorder behind him. Revenue Act; the Chancellor of the Exchequer, Charles Townshend, taxes American imports of tea, glass, paper and lead to help pay for the defence and government of the American colonies. Townshend dies and is succeeded by Lord North as Chancellor of the Exchequer.

Nov   [2] George III's fourth son, Edward, is born.

Dec   The Duke of Grafton becomes Prime Minister.

1768   William Brodie of Edinburgh begins his long career in crime, copying some bank keys and stealing £800; he escapes suspicion by being a pillar of the establishment. Richard Arkwright invents the water frame, a water-powered machine for spinning cotton into strong thread. Lord Shelburne resigns from the Cabinet in protest against Townshend's taxes on American imports. John Wilkes is elected MP for Middlesex; he then waives his Parliamentary privilege and is sentenced to two years' imprisonment and fined £1000 for his offences of 1763. The St George's Fields Riots; a mob tries to rescue John Wilkes.

Mar [18] Laurence Sterne, writer and cleric, dies in poverty in London.

May [10] George III's Second Parliament opens. [25] Beginning of Captain Cook's first voyage of exploration.

Aug [3] Archbishop Secker dies.

Oct [14] The Duke of Grafton becomes Prime Minister.

Nov [8] George III's daughter Augusta is born.

Dec [10] The Royal Academy of Arts is founded, with Sir Joshua Reynolds as its first President. [22] The landscape painter John Crome is born at Norwich.

1769 James Watt's steam-engine is patented. Watt forms a partnership with John Roebuck, founder of the Carron Iron Works; they build a full-sized trial engine – which does not work. Richard Arkwright builds a spinning mill, using the newly invented water frame, a water-powered spinning machine. Venetian blinds are patented in London by Edward Bevan. The 'Letters of Junius', anonymous attacks on the Duke of Grafton, Lord Mansfield and other members of the Government, begin to appear in the *Daily Advertiser*; no one ever discovers who wrote them, but the author is believed to be Sir Philip Francis. The portrait painter Thomas Lawrence is born.

Apr [29] The Duke of Wellington is born in Dublin.

Jun [18] Lord Castlereagh is born, also in Ireland.

Oct [7] Captain Cook reaches New Zealand.

1770 The Falklands Islands Crisis; the conflict between Spanish and British interests in the islands is resolved by French intervention – for the time being. The Duke of Grafton faces increasing opposition from the colonies and from sympathizers with John Wilkes; his ministry is finally overthrown by George III and Lord North.

Jan [28] Lord North, Earl of Guildford, becomes Prime Minister. To conciliate the American colonists, North abolishes all the import duties except the one on tea; this is retained in order to establish the British right to tax Americans.

Mar [5] Boston massacre; British troops fire into a crowd, killing five; the incident leads to the War of Independence. [11] William Huskisson, Tory politician, is born.

Apr [7] William Wordsworth is born at Cockermouth, Cumberland. [11] George Canning, Tory Prime Minister, is born. [24] Thomas Chatterton leaves Bristol for London. [28] Captain James Cook discovers the east coast of Australia, claiming it for Britain; he lands at Botany Bay.

May [22] George III's daughter Elizabeth is born.

Aug [23] The poet Thomas Chatterton commits suicide.

Nov [14] James Bruce discovers the source of the Blue Nile, Lake Tana.

1771 Spain cedes the uninhabited Falkland Islands to Britain. Captain Cook returns home after his first Pacific expedition. The Secret Debates Dispute; the Commons attempt to arrest a printer, Brass Crosby, for publishing reports of their debates. The City authorities support Crosby and a quarrel ensues between the Commons and the Aldermen. The Commons finally agree to allow debates to be reported.

Apr [13] Richard Trevithick, designer of steam-engines, is born at Illogan near Redruth.

May [14] Robert Owen, industrialist and social reformer, is born at Newtown in Wales.

Jun [5] George III's son Ernest Augustus is born.

Jul [30] The poet Thomas Gray dies.

Aug [15] The novelist Sir Walter Scott is born in Edinburgh.

Sep [10] Mungo Park, surgeon and West African explorer, is born at Foulshiels near Selkirk. [17] Tobias Smollett, the novelist, dies at Leghorn in Italy.

1772 Daniel Rutherford discovers nitrogen. Warren Hastings becomes Governor of Bengal. Captain James Cook leaves on his second voyage of exploration. Royal Marriage Act, preventing undesirable marriages of descendants of George II.

Apr [19] The economist David Ricardo is born.

Sep [30] James Brindley, who built the Bridgewater, Grand Trunk and Manchester Canals, dies at Turnhurst in Staffordshire.

Oct [21] The poet Samuel Taylor Coleridge is born at Ottery St Mary, Devon.

1773 Warren Hastings prepares for his campaign against the Mahrathas by forming an alliance with the state of Oudh. Clive defends his former conduct in India in the House of Commons. Act for the Regulation of India, introduced by Lord North to give the Crown direct control over the East India Company; the administration of Bengal is vested in the Governor-General, Warren Hastings. Samuel Johnson goes on a tour of Scotland with Boswell. Josiah Wedgwood sets up a new pottery at Etruria.

Jan [17] Captain Cook's *Resolution* becomes the first ship ever to cross the Antarctic Circle. [27] George III's son Augustus is born.

Dec [16] The Boston Tea Party, promoted by protest against Britain taxation. A group of radical colonists disguised as Indians board British ships and empty their cargoes of tea into the sea. The British Government declares the port of Boston closed and takes away the colony's charter.

1774 Joseph Priestley discovers oxygen. John Wilkinson, ironmaster, patents a cannon-borer that will allow accurate boring of cylinders for steam-engines. John Wilkes is elected Lord Mayor of London. American colonists regard the closure of Boston intolerable. Congress at Philadelphia, at which the American Declaration of Independence is set out. The importation of goods is prohibited.

Feb [24] George III's son Adolphus is born.

Apr [4] Oliver Goldsmith dies in London.

Aug [12] The Poet Laureate Robert Southey is born at Bristol.

Nov [22] Robert Clive, soldier and administrator, commits suicide.

1775 Watt and Boulton work in partnership at the Soho
Engineering Works, Birmingham. Alexander Cummings
takes out a patent for the flushing water closet similar to
Harington's 'Ajax' of 1589. In India, the British gain control
of Ghazipur (part of the Ganges valley). Pitt's Bill to
conciliate the American colonists is rejected.

Jan [17] First performance of Sheridan's *The Rivals* at Covent
Garden.

Feb [10] Charles Lamb, essayist, is born.

Apr [23] The painter Joseph Mallord William Turner is born at
Covent Garden. The American War of Independence begins,
10 miles from Boston, with skirmishes at Lexington and
Concord. In the Battle of Lexington British troops are
defeated by a group of American settlers led by George
Washington.

May Representatives from all the American colonies meet at the
Philadelphia Congress and set up an army under George
Washington's leadership. The Duke of Grafton resigns
because he opposes the war; the Earl of Dartmouth replaces
him as Lord Privy Seal.

Aug [6] The Irish nationalist leader Daniel O'Connell is born.

Dec [16] The novelist Jane Austen is born at Steventon in
Hampshire, the seventh of the Rector's eight children.

1776 Britains recruits 29,000 Hessian mercenaries for the American
War. A submarine is used unsuccessfully against British
ships in New York Harbour; it is the first time a submarine is
used in warfare. British troops under General Howe are
forced to leave Boston. For the first time a motion is put
before the Commons to abolish slavery in Britain and the
British colonies; it is proposed by David Hartley.

Mar [24] John Harrison, watchmaker and inventor of the
chronometer, dies.

Apr [25] George III's daughter Mary is born.

Jun [11] The artist John Constable is born.
Jul [4] American Congress draws up and passes the Declaration
     of Independence. [11] Captain Cook sails from Plymouth in
     the *Resolution*, accompanied by the *Discovery*, on his third
     and last expedition.

1777 The Habeas Corpus Act is suspended. Tailors in Birmingham
     form a co-operative workshop, to provide work for men on
     strike. Battle of Saratoga; General Burgoyne is hemmed in by
     American troops and forced to surrender to the Americans
     under General Horatio Gates.

Jan [3] Battle of Princeton: Washington defeats British forces
     under Lord Cornwallis.
Sep [11] Battle of Brandywine Creek; British troops under
     General Howe defeat George Washington, but fail to follow
     up this major success.
Nov [3] George III's daughter Sophia is born.

1778 France and Holland form a military alliance with the
     American colonists. In retaliation, Britain declares war on
     France. Dominica is captured by the French for use as a naval
     base; the British counter-action is to capture St Lucia from the
     the French. In India, Warren Hastings captures
     Chandernagore from the French and Sir Hector Munro
     captures Pondicherry. Lord North's plan for conciliating the
     Americans, the Reconciliation Bill, is rejected. Roman
     Catholic Relief Act; this relaxation of the penal laws against
     Catholics reflects the Government's confidence.

Mar [5] The composer Thomas Arne dies.
Apr [22] James Hargreaves, who invented the spinning-jenny,
     dies at Nottingham.
May [11] William Pitt the Elder, Earl of Chatham, dies at
     Hayes.
Jun [7] George 'Beau' Brummell, leader of fashion, is born in
     London.
Aug [14] Augustus Toplady, author of the hymn 'Rock of Ages',
     dies.

Dec [17] Sir Humphry Davy, scientist and inventor, is born at Penzance.

1779 Spain joins France and declares war on Britain; the great Franco-Spanish siege of Gibraltar begins. The British capture Senegal. French forces capture St Vincent and Grenada. The Irish raise a Protestant Volunteer Movement, 40,000 strong, to defend Ireland in the event of a French invasion; Britain ends restrictions on Irish trade. Samuel Crompton invents the spinning-mule, introducing an era of mass production in the British textile industry.

Jan [20] The actor and theatre manager David Garrick dies.

Feb [7] The composer William Boyce dies. [14] Captain Cook is stabbed to death by natives at Kealakekua Bay in the Hawaiian Islands.

Mar [15] Lord Melbourne, Prime Minister, is born in London as William Lamb.

Sep [23] John Paul Jones on the *Bonhomme Richard* defeats the British ship *Serapis* in an engagement off Flamborough Head.

1780 A petitioning movement begins in Yorkshire, spreading across the whole country; the complaint is that taxes are too high and the Government is wasting money. Britain declares war on Holland because of Holland's support for the American colonists. Russia, Sweden and Denmark enter an alliance, the Armed Neutrality, to prevent the British from exercising their old 'right' of searching vessels at sea. The Irish MP Henry Grattan demands Home Rule for Ireland; Lord North grants Ireland the right to trade freely with the colonies, but this small concession does not satisfy the Irish.

Jan [16] Battle of Cape St Vincent; Admiral Rodney destroys all but four ships of the Spanish fleet and succeeds in temporarily lifting the siege of Gibraltar.

Mar [26] The first Sunday newspaper, the *British Gazette and Sunday Monitor*, appears.

May [4] The first Derby (three-year-olds over a distance of 1½
miles) is run at Epsom; it is won by 'Diomed'. [21] Elizabeth
Fry, the prison reformer, is born at Norwich.

Jun [2] The Lord George Gordon Riots break out in London:
anti-Catholic demonstrations.

1781 Dr James Graham, an eccentric Edinburgh physician, offers
childless London couples the chance to solve their problems
by spending a night on his 'Celestial Bed' at £500 a time;
these and other bizarre treatments become a craze in
Fashionable London. Warren Hastings deposes the Rajah of
Benares for refusing to contribute to war expenses. The first
noticeable effects of the Industrial Revolution are felt, with
the sudden growth of the cotton industry. A British plan to
seize the Cape of Good Hope is thwarted by the French.
William Pitt the Younger enters Parliament.

Mar [13] Sir William Herschel discovers the planet Uranus; at first
he names it Georgium Sidus, in honour of George III.

Jun [8] George Stephenson, the builder of the 'Rocket', is born at
Wylam-on-Tyne.

Sep [5] Battle of Chesapeake Bay, between French and British
fleets off the Atlantic coast of America.

Oct [19] Lord Cornwallis surrenders with 7000 men to General
Washington at Yorktown in Virginia, marking the end of the
fighting in the American War of Independence.

1782 James Watt invents the double-acting rotary steam-engine,
a much more powerful engine than his earlier invention.
Josiah Wedgwood becomes the first manufacturer to
install a steam-engine in his factory. The painter Richard
Wilson dies. Grenville travels to Paris to negotiate for peace
in the American War of Independence with Benjamin
Franklin and the Count of Vergennes. Henry Grattan
makes his Irish Declaration of Rights, demanding
legislative freedom for Ireland. Fox introduces the Repeal
of Ireland Bill which grants Ireland legislative independence
and removes the power of British Parliaments to control Irish

Parliaments. Lord North wants to end the American War as soon as possible, is opposed by George III, and resigns.

Mar [27] The Whig Marquis of Rockingham becomes Prime Minister again.

Jul [4] Rockingham dies and is succeeded by the Whig William Petty, Earl of Shelburne (Marquis of Lansdowne).

Aug [29] HMS *Royal George*, a 100-ton battleship, sinks at anchor at Spithead; over 900 lives are lost as the ship turns turtle, including that of Admiral Kempenfelt.

Nov [30] Preliminary Treaty of Paris; the United States (i.e. the Anglo-American colonies), Great Britain, France, Spain and Holland recognize the independence of the 13 United States; Britain is to surrender Tobago and Senegal to France.

1783

Feb [6] Lancelot 'Capability' Brown, the landscape gardener, dies.

Apr [2] Lord Shelburne resigns after being censured over the peace preliminaries with America and is succeeded as Prime Minister by William Bentinck, Duke of Portland. [26] After the death of Archbishop Frederick Cornwallis, John Moore, Bishop of Bangor, becomes Archbishop of Canterbury.

May [22] William Sturgeon, inventor of the first working electromagnet, is born at Whittington.

Jun [17] Samuel Johnson is paralyzed by a stroke.

Sep [3] Treaty of Versailles; American independence is formally recognized. Britain is to pay a war indemnity of £10 million. The Treaty also provides for Britain ceding Tobago, St Lucia, Senegal, Pondicherry and Chandernagore to France in exchange for Grenada, Dominica, St Vincent, Nevis, Montserrat, St Kitts and the Gambia; Britain is to relinquish Florida and Minorca to Spain in exchange for Providence, the Bahamas and Gibraltar.

Dec [7] William Pitt the Younger becomes Britain's youngest Prime Minister at the age of 24.

1784 Shrapnel, invented by Lt Henry Shrapnel, is first tested at Stirling. Warren Hastings makes an effective peace with the Mahrathas; Margalore, a strategic shipbuilding base, is ceded to Britain. Pitt reduces the duties on tea and spirits.

Aug [2] The first specially constructed Royal Mail coach runs, from Bristol to London. [13] East India Act; the company is placed under a Board of Control to manage its revenues and administration.

Oct [20] Lord Palmerston is born at Westminster, as Henry Temple.

Dec [13] Dr Samuel Johnson, writer and lexicographer, dies.

1785 Edmund Cartwright invents the power loom, which mechanizes weaving, and paves the way to mass production in the textile industry. The English Channel is successfully crossed by balloon for the first time. Jean-Pierre Blanchard and Dr John Jeffries, his American backer, launch from Dover but begin to lose height prematurely six miles from the French coast. They jettison everything, including their clothes, in order to make landfall in France. James Hutton's *Theory of the Earth* lays the foundation of modern geology and geomorphology; it is based on a uniformitarian view of earth processes and proposes a very great age for the earth. Learning of Pitt's East India Act, Warren Hastings resigns and returns to Britain. Supported by Fox, Pitt proposes a scheme for parliamentary reform, but it is rejected by the Commons.

Aug [15] Thomas de Quincey, the writer, is born.

Oct [18] The essayist Thomas Love Peacock is born.

1786 An economic boom begins, based on the growth of the coal-mining and cotton industries; industrial towns begin to grow rapidly in the Midlands and North of England, and in the Scottish Lowlands. Charles Cornwallis becomes Governor-General of India. The Rajah of Kedah cedes

Penang to Britain. Anglo-French commercial treaty; duty is reduced on English clothes, cotton and iron goods, and on French soap, wines and olive oil. William Brodie's criminal career comes to an end with an abortive raid on the headquarters of the Scottish Customs and Excise; Brodie escapes to Amsterdam, but is extradited to stand trial in Edinburgh.

Oct [31] George II's daughter Amelia dies.

1787 The Association for the Abolition of the Slave Trade is founded, mainly by the Quakers. Warren Hastings is impeached for alleged irregularities during his administration in India; the attack on him is led by Burke, Fox and Philip Francis.

1788 Sierra Leone becomes a British refuge settlement for black waifs and ex-slaves. Andrew Meikle patents the threshing machine he has invented. George III shows signs of insanity; the Commons debate the possibility of a regency, but the King recovers. The seven-year-long trial of Warren Hastings begins; there are 22 charges of cruelty, oppression and robbery towards the princes of India. The composer Joseph Gibbs dies.

Jan [22] George Gordon, Lord Byron, is born in London.
[26] The first consignment of English convicts arrives at Botany Bay; the founding of the penal colony there marks the beginning of the colonization of Australia. [31] Prince Charles Edward, the Young Pretender and leader of the Jacobite Rebellion aimed at deposing George II, dies in Rome.

Feb [5] Sir Robert Peel is born at Bury in Lancashire, the son of a cotton millionaire.

Mar [29] The evangelist Charles Wesley dies.

Aug [2] The painter Thomas Gainsborough dies.

Sep [30] Lord Raglan, the Field Marshal responsible for the disastrous Charge of the Light Brigade, is born at Badminton.

Oct [1] William Brodie is hanged at Edinburgh; his career inspires Robert Louis Stevenson to write *The Strange Case of Dr Jekyll and Mr Hyde*.

1789 The Scottish explorer Sir Alexander Mackenzie discovers the River Mackenzie in North America (named for him).

Apr [28] The mutiny on the *Bounty*, in the Friendly Islands; Captain Bligh and 17 others are set adrift in an open boat, eventually reaching Timor.

Mar [20] William, George III's third son, is created Duke of Clarence.

Jul [14] The outbreak of the French Revolution sends shock waves through Britain. Coleridge, at 16, writes his first truly original poem, *The Fall of the Bastille*.

1790 Crompton's Mule, until now a cottage spinning machine, is harnessed to water power for the first time by William Kelly, the manager of the New Lanark Mills; the machine's use spreads very rapidly. A stone coffin containing a boy's skeleton is discovered at Lincoln, beneath the shrine of Little St Hugh. Turner exhibits his first watercolour at the Royal Academy. Sir Joshua Reynolds delivers the last of his 'Discourses on Art'. James Watt applies his flyball governor to regulate the speed of a steam-engine. An election returns Pitt's Government with an increased majority.

Jan [30] The first purpose-built lifeboat, called *The Original*, is launched at South Shields.

Mar [5] Flora Macdonald, the Jacobite heroine who helped Prince Charles Edward to escape from the island of Benbecula, dies.

Jul [11] William Wordsworth and his friend Robert Jones set off on their walking tour of France and Switzerland. [17] The economist Adam Smith dies in Edinburgh.

1791 Indiarubber cloth is patented by Samuel Peel. Joseph Priestley's house in Birmingham is burnt down by a mob in protest at his support for the French Revolution. The Royal

Navy is expanded because of Russian hostility in the Black Sea. In Ireland, the Society of United Irishmen is formed; its aim is to persuade the French to invade Ireland, throw off English rule and set up a republic. William Wilberforce proposes a Parliamentary motion for the abolition of slavery; the motion is carried.

Mar [2] John Wesley, evangelist and founder of the Methodist Movement, dies in London aged 87.

Sep [22] The chemist and physicist Michael Faraday is born at Newington Butts.

Nov [26] The poet Wordsworth sails from Brighton for France, where he is to visit the National Assembly in Paris.

Dec [4] The Sunday newspaper *The Observer* is published for the first time.

1792 Coal gas is used for the first time for lighting. The London Corresponding Society is founded by artisans to campaign for electoral reform.

Feb [23] Sir Joshua Reynolds, the first President of the Royal Academy, dies in London; he is succeeded as President by Benjamin West.

Mar [3] The architect and designer Robert Adam dies.
[7] The astronomer Sir John Herschel is born at Slough.

May [24] Admiral Lord Rodney dies at Hanover Square in London.

Jul [10] The novelist Frederick Marryat is born.

Aug [3] Sir Richard Arkwright, inventor of the mechanical spinning process, dies. [4] The poet Percy Bysshe Shelley is born at Warnham. [5] Lord North, Tory Prime Minister 1770-82, dies.

Oct [28] John Smeaton, designer of the third Eddystone Lighthouse, dies.

Nov [19] A Decree published by the French Convention offers help 'to all those nations who desire to overthrow their kings'; this is seen as provocative.

1793

Feb   [1] The French Republic declares war on Britain. The Government takes action against agitation by drafting the Traitorous Correspondence Bill. Exchequer bills are issued by Pitt to help finance the war with France. The British economy enters a depression.

Apr   [15] The first Bank of England £5 notes are issued.

Nov   [1] Lord George Gordon, the anti-Catholic agitator and leader of the 'Gordon Riots' in 1780, dies in Newgate Prison.

1794 Haydn visits London for the second time. The Habeas Corpus Act is suspended.

Jan   [16] The historian Edward Gibbon dies.

May   The trial of Hardy, Horn Tooke and Thelwall on charges of high treason begins.

Jun   The poet Coleridge leaves Cambridge without taking a degree. [1] Battle of Brest, the 'Glorious First of June'; Lord Howe gains a resounding victory over the French fleet.

Nov   Jay's Treaty between Britain and the United States.

Dec   Hardy, Horn Tooke and Thelwall are acquitted.

1795 The Speenhamland system of outdoor relief is adopted, making up wages to equal the cost of subsistence. Holland joins France, so Britain is forced to declare war on Holland. The British take Ceylon (Sri Lanka) from the Dutch. The Cape of Good Hope is also captured by the British. Mungo Park explores the upper reaches of the Gambia river and the Niger. Joseph Bramah invents the hydraulic press. Warren Hastings is acquitted after a trial lasting seven years.

Jan   Raisley Calvert dies, leaving Wordsworth £900 – enough to enable him to write. [3] Josiah Wedgwood, the creator of blue jasper ware, dies.

Apr   [8] George (later George IV) marries Caroline, daughter of Charles Duke of Brunswick-Wolfenbuttel.

May [19] James Boswell, biographer of Dr Johnson, dies. [23] Sir Charles Barry, co-architect of the Palace of Westminster, is born.

Jun [13] Thomas Arnold, educationalist, is born at Cowes.

Dec [3] Sir Rowland Hill, pioneer in postal services, is born at Kidderminster. [4] The historian Thomas Carlyle is born at Ecclefechan.

1796 A 27-year-old engineer, William Smith, proves from his own fieldwork that the geological succession is the same throughout England and Wales, an important concept which opens the prospect of devising a history of the Earth. The violin is introduced into India by the British; Indian musicians absorb the new instrument into their own music. Through Swiss mediators, Pitt initiates secret but unsuccessful negotiations with France.

Jan [7] The Prince of Wales' daughter Charlotte is born.

Apr [2] The first and only performance of *Vortigern and Rowena* at the Drury Lane Theatre; this 'long-lost play by Shakespeare' is a hoax, written by the 17-year-old William Henry Ireland.

May [14] Edward Jenner successfully proves the vaccination theory, laying the foundations for modern immunology and leading directly to the eradication of smallpox in Britain.

Sep [17] Opening of Parliament.

Dec An attempted invasion of Ireland by the French under General Hoche fails when the French fleet is scattered by a storm.

1797 The top hat is worn in public for the first time, by James Hetherington in London, drawing a huge disorderly crowd. Hetherington is arrested and charged with causing a breach of the peace, having 'appeared on the public highway wearing a tall structure of shining lustre and calculated to disturb timid people'.

Jan [3] One of the Stonehenge trilithons (stones 57 and 58) falls down, causing an earth tremor felt half a mile away.

Feb [12] The last invasion of Britain; 1400 French troops under the command of the Irish-American General Tate land in Dyfed; they later surrender to British soldiers. [14] Battle of Cape St Vincent; British forces under Admiral Sir John Jervis and Commodore Nelson defeat the Spanish fleet. [26] £1 notes are first issued by the Bank of England, and the first copper pennies are minted.

Apr [15] Sailors mutiny at Spithead off Portsmouth.

May [18] George III's daughter Charlotte marries Prince Frederick of Wurtemberg. [23] The Nore Mutiny, led by Richard Parker, against bad food and inadequate pay begins.

Jun [5] Coleridge walks to Racedown Lodge in Dorset to meet the Wordsworths for the first time. He characteristically jumps over a gate and runs down through a field of corn to meet Dorothy; it is the beginning of an important creative relationship. [30] The collapse of the Nore Mutiny.

Jul [9] The politician and writer Edmund Burke dies.

Aug [11] A secret Home Office report records that Coleridge and the Wordsworths are suspected of being enemy agents because of their strange behaviour, wandering about the countryside with camp-stools and making detailed observations about the landscape. [30] Mary Shelley, author of *Frankenstein*, is born.

Oct Coleridge writes *Kubla Khan* at Ash Farm near Culbone. [11] Battle of Camperdown off the Dutch coast; the British under Admiral Duncan are victorious over a Dutch fleet challenging Britain's naval supremacy.

Dec [26] John Wilkes, radical politician and agitator for the freedom of the press, dies.

1798 Henry Cavendish, chemist and physicist, determines the mean density of the Earth. The Romantic movement begins with the publication of *Lyrical Ballads* by Wordsworth and Coleridge. The vault and coffin of Henry VI come to light in St George's Chapel, Windsor. Lord Stanhope constructs the first printing press with an iron frame. Pitt increases the tax on newspapers. Richard Wellesley, elder brother of the Duke of Wellington, becomes Governor-General of India. A Second Coalition against France is formed by an Anglo-Russian Alliance.

Mar   [23] Coleridge completes *The Rime of the Ancient Mariner* and takes it to show Wordsworth.

Jun   [21] In the Irish Rebellion, stimulated by the spread of republicanism, the rebels are defeated at Vinegar Hill near Wexford by General Lake's troops.

Aug   [1] Battle of the Nile: Nelson destroys 11 out of 13 French battleships which have convoyed Napoleon to Egypt, thus effectively trapping the French army in the Middle East.

1799   A peace offer by France is rejected by Britain and Austria. The Duke of York, commanding the British army in Holland, ignominiously surrenders to the French at Alkmaar. The British assume control of the Carnatic (southern India) after Tipu Sahib, the last ruler of Mysore, is killed in battle. The rebellion of the United Irishmen is suppressed. Combination Laws make trade unions illegal.

Jan   [9] William Pitt the Younger introduces income tax, at two shillings in the pound on incomes over £200, to raise money for the war with France.

Apr   [24] George III's sons Edward and Ernest are created Dukes of Kent and Cumberland.

May   [23] The poet Thomas Hood is born.

Aug   [5] Admiral Richard Howe dies.

Dec   [27] William and Dorothy Wordsworth move to Dove Cottage in the Lake District.

1800

1800   Sir William Herschel discovers infra-red rays in sunlight. The Royal College of Surgeons is founded in London. The Armed Neutrality of the North; an alliance between Russia,

Denmark, Sweden and Prussia to counter the British right of search on the high seas, and to keep the British out of the Baltic. Malta is captured by the British. Henry Maudslay invents the lathe.

Feb [11] The pioneer photographer William Fox Talbot is born at Evershot.

Apr [4] 'Galloping Dick' the highwayman is hanged at Aylesbury.
[25] The poet William Cowper dies at East Dereham.

May [15] James Hatfield attempts to assassinate George III at the theatre in Drury Lane.

1801 William Cunnington excavates the Boles long barrow at Heytesbury and finds a large block of bluestone in it, showing that bluestones were being imported from Wales well before the building of Stonehenge. Health and Morals of Apprentices Act; this forbids children under nine from working and restricts the working day of older children to 12 hours in the daytime only.

Jan [1] Act of Union of Great Britain and Ireland becomes effective. The name of the newly-constituted state is to be the United Kingdom. Ireland is to send four spiritual lords, 28 temporal peers elected for life from the Irish peerage, and 100 Commons MPs to Westminster. The Churches are to be united into one Protestant Episcopal Church.

Feb [3] Pitt proposes to include concessions to Catholics in the plans for the Union: the King objects, and Pitt resigns after 17 years in office. [21] Cardinal Newman is born.

Mar [17] Pitt is succeeded as Prime Minister by the Tory Henry Addington, Viscount Sidmouth.

Apr [2] Battle of Copenhagen; Nelson, who is second in command on board the *Elephant*, puts a telescope to his blind eye and in consequence does not see Admiral Hyde Parker's signal to break off the naval engagement. The Danish fleet is destroyed and the Northern League against Britain is shattered. [28] Lord Shaftesbury, one of the great

Victorian social reformers, is born in London as Anthony Cooper.

Jun [29] The results of Britain's first-ever census are published.

Aug [3] Sir Joseph Paxton, architect of the Crystal Palace, is born at Milton Bryant near Woburn.

Nov [27] George III's sons Augustus and Adolphus are created Dukes of Sussex and Cambridge.

Dec . [24] Richard Trevithick's steam carriage, the first steam-powered vehicle to run on British roads, is given its first outing in spite of outspoken warnings from James Watt that the high pressure involved will cause the boiler to explode.
[27] Trevithick takes some friends out to a pub in his steam carriage, leaving the boiler fire burning, and emerges from the pub to find the carriage a smoking wreck.

1802 Madame Tussaud arrives in Britain with her waxworks collection. Thomas Telford begins building roads in the Scottish Highlands. It is proposed for the first time to link Britain and France with a Channel Tunnel; the French engineer Albert Mathieu visualizes horse-drawn coaches passing through a candle-lit tunnel. Wars in the Deccan lead to the supremacy of the British East India Company in India. Ceylon becomes a Crown colony.

Feb [6] Sir Charles Wheatstone, pioneer of telegraphy, is born at Gloucester.

Mar [7] The painter Sir Edwin Landseer is born in London. [27] Peace of Amiens, between Britain and France; Britain returns most of the gains made during the Revolutionary Wars, except for Ceylon and Trinidad: Malta is returned to the Knights of St John.

Sep [28] William Cunnington digs at the centre of Stonehenge.

Nov [15] The portrait artist George Romney dies at Kendal.

1803 John Dalton, physicist and chemist, introduces the atomic theory. John Horrocks of Stockport installs the first power looms made wholly of metal; this is a decisive development in the mechanization of the textile industry. John Crome founds the Norwich Society. The philosopher Arthur Schopenhauer arrives as a very young boy to attend Nelson House School, Wimbledon; the experience turns him against Christianity for life. Britain refuses to evacuate Malta until Napoleon gives up Piedmont, Piacenza and parts of Switzerland. Napoleon assembles a huge fleet at Boulogne and an army of 150,000 at Dunkirk in preparation for the invasion of Britain. British forces capture Tobago and St Lucia from France. Robert Emmet's rebellion in Ireland is encouraged by Napoleon; Lord Kilwarden is murdered in Dublin.

Mar [3] The Duke of Bridgewater, pioneer of the canal network, dies.

May [16] Britain is again at war with France. [25] Lord Lytton is born.

1804 William Wollaston isolates palladium from platinum. Richard Trevithick builds the first steam train to haul a load successfully. Urged on by Napoleon (now Emperor), Spain declares war on Britain.

Feb [6] Joseph Priestley, discoverer of oxygen, dies at Northumberland in Pennsylvania.

Apr [30] Shrapnel is used in warfare for the first time, by the British against the Dutch in Surinam.

Mar [10] Lord Sidmouth resigns and is succeeded by the Tory William Pitt as Prime Minister.

Jun [3] Richard Cobden, economist and politician, is born at Heyshott.

Dec [21] Benjamin Disraeli is born in Theobald's Road, London.

1805 The painter Samuel Palmer is born. Richard Wellesley is recalled from India and briefly replaced by Lord Cornwallis as Governor-General.

Feb [4] The writer Harrison Ainsworth is born. [5] The *Earl of Abergavenny*, a large and well-known East Indiaman, is wrecked in a gale off Portland Bill. The poet Wordsworth's brother, Captain John Wordsworth, is drowned along with 300 others; the sinking is felt to be a national disaster. [21] After the death of Archbishop John Moore, Charles Sutton, Bishop of Norwich, becomes Archbishop of Canterbury.

Jun [4] The first 'Trooping the Colour' ceremony takes place, at Horse Guards Parade in London.

Oct Lord Byron goes to Cambridge. [21] Battle of Trafalgar: Nelson's great victory over a joint French-Spanish fleet off the coast of Portugal. Nelson himself is killed in the action.

Dec [2] Battle of Austerlitz; Napoleon's victory stuns Pitt.

1806 Rear-Admiral Sir Francis Beaufort designs the wind strength scale named after him.

Jan [9] The funeral and burial of Lord Nelson at St Paul's Cathedral. [23] William Pitt the Younger, Tory statesman and twice Prime Minister, dies at Putney.

Feb [11] William Lord Grenville succeeds as Prime Minister, leading a Whig Coalition Government.

Mar [6] Elizabeth Barrett Browning, poetess and wife of Robert Browning, is born at Coxhoe Hall, Durham.

Apr [9] The engineer Isambard Kingdom Brunel is born at Portsmouth.

Jul [10] The painter George Stubbs dies aged 81.

Sep [13] Charles James Fox, the Foreign Secretary, dies at Chiswick.

Oct [7] Ralph Wedgwood, the inventor of carbon paper, secures a patent for his invention. [22] Thomas Sheraton, furniture designer and cabinet-maker, dies. Food prices rise and the textile industry declines as a result of Napoleon's 'Continental System', which is in effect an economic blockade.

1807 At the extravagant Gothic Revival masterpiece of Fonthill Abbey in Wiltshire (designed by James Wyatt), the 270 feet high central tower collapses. The Geological Society of London is founded. Lord Byron has his first volume of poetry, *Hours of Idleness*, published while he is still an undergraduate. Gas lighting is first introduced in London; by 1820, much of the city will be gas lit. The Slave trade is abolished throughout the British Empire. Grenville rejects Catholic Emancipation, and his 'Ministry of All the Talents' falls as a result.

Mar [31] Grenville is succeeded as Prime Minister by the Tory Duke of Portland.

1808 The French occupy Spain; there is a Spanish rising. The Peninsular War begins.

Aug [21] British troops under Wellington defeat the French.
Sep   William Cunnington excavates the Bush Barrow near Stonehenge and finds a spectacularly rich burial of an Early Bronze Age chief; Sir Richard Colt-Hoare misses the dig because he has a migraine. [19] Covent Garden Theatre burns down.
Nov [22] The pioneer travel agent Thomas Cook is born at Melbourne in Derbyshire.

1809 Humphry Davy invents the arc lamp. Lord Chatham, William Pitt's elder brother, commands the Walcheren Expedition, which fails to capture Antwerp. George Canning, the Foreign Secretary, tries to remove Lord Castlereagh from the War Office because of the Walcheren fiasco; they fight a duel over it and Canning is wounded.

Jan [16] Battle of Corunna; Sir John Moore is killed in action.
Feb [12] Charles Darwin is born at Shrewsbury.
Mar [31] The scholar and poet Edward Fitzgerald is born.
Jun [8] Thomas Paine, radical political activist and author of *Rights of Man*, dies in poverty in New York.

Jul [28] Battle of Talavera in the Peninsular War comes to an end; Wellesley is victorious over Soult. Wellesley is rewarded with the title Duke of Wellington.

Aug [6]·Alfred Tennyson, poet, is born at Somersby rectory, Lincolnshire. [18] Matthew Boulton, James Watt's partner, dies in Soho.

Oct [4] The Duke of Portland resigns owing to ill health; the Tory Spencer Perceval becomes Prime Minister.

Dec [29] William Ewart Gladstone, four times Prime Minister, is born at Liverpool.

1810 John Metcalfe, known as 'Blind Jack of Knaresborough', dies. In spite of his disability he has constructed 180 miles of turnpike road, mostly in Lancashire and Yorkshire, doing the survey work himself by tapping his way across the moors with a stick; he pioneered side drains along the road edges and the cambered surface. George III loses his sanity entirely and remains insane until his death. William Cobbett is sent to prison for libel. Wellington forces a large French army into retreat at Torres Vedras near Lisbon. Guadeloupe, the last remaining French colony in the West Indies, is captured by the British.

Feb [9] Robert Coates makes his stage début as Romeo in Bath. His performance is so appalling that he becomes a cult figure overnight; he goes on to be a major success in London. [24] Henry Cavendish, who discovered the properties of hydrogen and other gases, dies.

Apr [24] William Cunnington leaves a bottle of port under the Slaughter Stone at Stonehenge.

Sep [29] The novelist Elizabeth Gaskell is born in Chelsea.

1811 The Prince Regent gives a lavish banquet at Carlton House. Along the length of the main table, 200 feet, runs an artificial stream flowing from a silver fountain at its head. The Prince presides from a plume-backed throne beneath a crown and an illuminated 'GR' cipher. Sir Samuel Romilly contrasts 'the great expense of this entertainment' with 'the misery of the starving weavers of Lancashire and Glasgow'. There are outbreaks of Luddite riots and machine breaking in Nottinghamshire and Yorkshire; unemployed weavers fear the impact of mechanization on their livelihood. Two new music publishing houses are founded in London – Novello and Chappell.

Feb [5] George III is formally declared insane; the Prince of Wales becomes Prince Regent, ruling in his father's place.

Mar [25] The poet Shelley is sent down from Oxford for publishing *The Necessity of Atheism*.

Apr [5] Robert Raikes, founder of the Sunday School movement, dies at Gloucester.

Jul [18] The novelist William Makepeace Thackeray is born in Calcutta.

Nov [16] The radical politician John Bright is born at Rochdale.

Dec [14] Byron sees Kemble on the London stage for the first time, and thinks his acting 'glorious'.

1812 The food-canning process is invented by Bryan Donkin of London. The Elgin marbles are brought from Athens to Britain. The year of the waltz: the Continent-wide craze for the new dance reaches Britain. The first meat cannery in Britain is set up at Bermondsey, but the technology is not yet perfected: the cans have to be opened with a hammer and chisel.

Jan [8] Two more regiments are called out to control the Luddite rising, which breaks out at various places during the year.

Feb [7] The novelist Charles Dickens is born at Portsmouth. [27] Lord Byron's maiden speech in the House of Lords is well received; he opposes Lord Liverpool's Frame-Breaking Bill, which seeks to make frame-breaking a capital offence, advising against the hasty introduction of a 'death bill'. Byron becomes a celebrity during the year, following the publication of *Childe Harold*, which achieves unprecedented popularity.

May [10] The Duchess of Devonshire writes: 'Byron continues to
be the great attraction at all parties and suppers . . . He is
going back to Naxos, and then the husbands may sleep in
peace. I should not be surprised if Caro William (Lady
Caroline Lamb) were to go with him'. [11] Spencer Perceval,
the Tory Prime Minister, is assassinated in the Lobby of the
House of Commons by an insane merchant called Francis
Bellingham. Lord Liverpool becomes Prime Minister. [12]
The eccentric poet and artist Edward Lear is born at
Highgate.

Oct [12] Annabella Milbanke wisely declines Byron's proposal of
marriage.

1813 The architect James Wyatt is killed when a coach he is
travelling in overturns near Marlborough. Robert Southey
is appointed Poet Laureate. The Royal Philharmonic Society
is founded in London. The last gold guinea coins are
minted. The East India Company's monopoly is abolished
in India. Parliament abandons the Catholic Relief Bill.
Brewster's law (polarization of light) – Sir David
Brewster.

Jan [4] Isaac Pitman, pioneer of phonetic shorthand, is born in
Trowbridge. [19] Sir Henry Bessemer, inventor of a method
for converting iron into steel, is born at Charlton.

Feb [3] The writer Leigh Hunt begins two years in prison (Surrey
Gaol) for describing the Prince Regent as 'a corpulent man of
50, a violator of his word, a libertine over head and ears in
disgrace, a despiser of domestic ties, the companion of
gamblers and demireps, a man who has just closed half a
century without one single claim on the gratitude of his
country'.

Mar [19] The explorer and missionary David Livingstone is born
at Blantyre.

Jun [21] Wellington defeats the French at Vitoria.

Oct [16-19] The Fourth Coalition (Britain, Russia, Prussia,
Sweden, Austria) closes in on Napoleon, forcing him back to

Leipzig where he is heavily defeated in the 'Battle of the Nations'.

Dec [29] Alexander Parkes, the chemist who will later invent celluloid, is born at Birmingham.

1814 George Stephenson builds his first steam locomotive.

Jan [14] Britain makes peace with Denmark, restoring all conquests except Heligoland.

Mar [9] Treaties of Chaumont, between the Allies, arranged by Lord Castlereagh who has hurried to France to prevent the premature break-up of the Coalition. The treaties provide for continuing the struggle against Napoleon and guard against separate peace agreements. [10] Battle of Laon; the Allied forces defeat Napoleon. [12] Wellington captures Bordeaux. [31] The Allies' victorious entry into Paris; Napoleon is declared deposed in his absence by the French Senate.

Apr [10] Soult's army is finally defeated by Wellington at Toulouse. [11] Napoleon abdicates. [12] The writer and composer Charles Burney dies. Byron sees Edmund Kean play Hamlet. [20] Louis XVIII, returning to France to claim his throne, makes a triumphal entry into London. The French King has to be lifted out of his carriage to greet the Prince Regent, who is dressed incongruously as a field-marshal.

May [30] First Peace of Paris, settled mainly by Castlereagh and Metternich; France is to renounce all claims to Germany, Italy, Holland, Switzerland and Malta, but to keep her 1792 borders.

Jun [6] The King of Prussia and Emperor of Russia arrive in London, to scenes of great popular excitement and acclaim. [8] The novelist Charles Reade is born. [22] The first cricket match is played at the Lord's Ground in London. [27] The King of Prussia and Emperor of Russia leave London for home.

Jul [1] The Watier's Masquerade for 1700 guests at Burlington House, held in honour of Wellington's return to England.

Byron dresses as a monk, and Lady Caroline Lamb wears green pantaloons; Colonel Armstrong, the Duke of York's aide-de-camp, dresses up as an old lady, fanning himself and cracking outrageous jokes to 'admirers'. [19] Matthew Flinders, the explorer who surveyed and charted the coasts of Australia, dies at the age of 40.

Sep   The Congress of Vienna begins (and lasts until June 1815): a conference to negotiate the Resettlement of Europe.

1815 Sir Humphry Davy invents the miners' safety lamp. William Smith produces the first geological map of England and Wales. The quadrille is danced for the first time in Britain. Corn Law; imports of foreign grain are virtually banned from Britain until home-grown grain reaches a minimum price of 80 shillings a quarter, after which imports will be allowed in duty free. One effect of this measure is to cause even greater hardship to the working class by increasing the price of bread. John Loudon McAdam improves roads by the use of crushed stone and tarmac.

Jan   [2] Lord Byron marries Annabella Milbanke, after two refusals; on their wedding night he wakes up shouting, 'Good God! I am surely in Hell!' [15] Emma Hamilton, Nelson's mistress, dies in poverty in Calais.

Feb   [3] Leigh Hunt is released from prison. [26] Napoleon escapes from Elba.

Apr   [7] Byron meets Sir Walter Scott for the first time; Byron gives Scott a silver urn from Greece and Scott gives him a Turkish dagger. [24] The novelist Anthony Trollope is born.

Jun   [18] Battle of Waterloo; in spite of Ney's great cavalry charges, Napoleon's army and political career are ruined: a great victory for Blücher and Wellington. To celebrate Waterloo, Southey and Wordsworth throw a party on the summit of Skiddaw, light a bonfire, roll lighted tar barrels down the mountain, and sing 'God Save The King'. [22] Napoleon's second abdication.

Nov [20] Second Peace of Paris; this time France is restricted to her 1790 frontiers, all looted art treasures are to be returned, 700 million francs war indemnity are to be paid, and an Allied army of occupation is to be installed: France is to lose that part of Savoy that she had been allowed to keep in the First Peace. The Quadruple Alliance, between Britain, Austria, Prussia and Russia, is renewed. [24] Grace Darling, heroine of the famous 1838 North Sea rescue, is born at Bamburgh.

1816 Lord Elgin sells the Elgin marbles to the British Museum. British forces defeat the King of Kandy; Ceylon becomes a British colony. Poverty and distress lead to rising numbers of people emigrating to North America. Britain enters an economic depression following the end of the Napoleonic Wars, contrary to popular expectation; dislocated and impoverished markets in Europe are unable to absorb the stockpiles of British manufactured goods. Thousands of people employed in industry are consequently thrown out of work. Unemployment is swelled further by the demobilization of 400,000 men in the armed services. George Canning joins the Cabinet as President of the Board of Control for India.

Jan [15] Lady Byron leaves her husband, although apparently not because of his affair with his sister Augusta.

Mar The 10% income tax is abolished in an attempt to alleviate distress, but the benefits of this measure are offset by adding duties to many products, and this raises prices. [25] Byron is, as he requested, given first refusal on Napoleon's coronation robes by the French, but he does not take up this offer.

Apr [13] William Sterndale Bennett, composer, is born at Sheffield. [21] The novelist Charlotte Brontë is born at Thornton, Yorkshire. [25] Byron sails from Dover into self-imposed exile in Italy.

May [2] The Prince Regent's daughter Charlotte marries Prince Leopold of Saxe-Coburg-Saalfeld.
Jun [27] Admiral Samuel Hood dies at Bath aged 91.
Dec [2] The Spa Fields Riot; a crowd gathers to hear an address on Parliamentary reform, and turns violent. [30] The poet Shelley marries Mary Wollstonecroft after his first wife's suicide.

1817 In Derbyshire, workers riot in protest at low pay and unemployment. The Habeas Corpus Act is suspended after a secret report to Parliament about an imminent rebellion. The economic slump results in the Blanketeers' March and other disturbances. Shots are fired in an attempt to assassinate the Prince Regent after he opens Parliament. The painter George Frederick Watts is born. The Third Mahratha War begins in India, an Indian rebellion against British rule. The kaleidoscope is invented by Sir David Brewster.

Mar Coercion Acts; these repressive measures suspend the Habeas Corpus Act, extend the 1798 act against seditious meetings, extend to include the Prince Regent in all the safeguards against treason that have hitherto only secured the monarch, and provide for the punishment of all attempts to undermine the loyalty of soldiers and sailors.
Jul [5] The first sovereigns are issued. [18] The novelist Jane Austen dies in lodgings in College Street, Winchester.
Nov [6] The Prince Regent's daughter, Princess Charlotte, dies.

1818 The first iron ship is built on the Clyde: the lighter *Vulcan*. The British East India Company effectively controls India. Java is given back to the Dutch.
Jul [11] William Duke of Clarence marries Adelaide, daughter of George Duke of Saxe-Meiningen. [30] The novelist Emily Brontë is born at Thornton, Yorkshire.
Dec [24] The physicist James Joule is born at Salford.

1819 Britain acquires Singapore through the East India Company; it is administrated by Sir Stamford Raffles. The Factory Act is

passed after a campaign by Robert Owen. The 'Six Acts' limit
the scope of political meetings, to curb the spread of rioting.
The steamship *Savannah* arrives at Liverpool, having crossed
the Atlantic mainly under steam power. The painter William
Frith is born.

Feb [8] The writer, artist and critic John Ruskin is born at
Dulwich.

Mar [11] Sir Henry Tate, the philanthropist whose money and
pictures are to be the foundation of the Tate Gallery,
London, is born at Chorley.

Apr [11] Sir Charles Hallé, pianist, conductor and founder of the
Hallé Orchestra, is born in Germany.

May [24] Queen Victoria is born at Kensington Palace; she
is the daughter of Edward Duke of Kent and Mary
the daughter of Francis Duke of Saxe-Coburg-
Saalfeld.

Jun [5] John Adams, astronomer and co-discoverer of the
planet Neptune, is born near Launceston. [12] The
clergyman and author Charles Kingsley is born at Hone
vicarage.

Aug [16] A radical Parliamentary reform meeting at St Peter's
Fields, Manchester, is dispersed by the army; 11 people are
killed. The incident is widely referred to as the 'Peterloo'
massacre and becomes a symbol of goverment repression.
[19] James Watt, inventor of the modern steam engine, dies
near Birmingham at the age of 83. [26] Prince Albert is born
at Rosenau in Bavaria.

Nov [22] The novelist George Eliot is born near Nuneaton as
Marian Evans.

Dec The 'Six Acts'; these increase the penalties for seditious libel,
impose a newspaper stamp duty on all periodicals containing
news (a blow aimed at the radical press), limit the scope of
public meetings, forbid training in the use of weaponry, and
empower magistrates to search for and seize arms. The Six
Acts greatly increase the Cabinet's unpopularity and increase
unrest.

1820

Jan [17] The novelist Anne Brontë (known as Acton Bell) is born at Thornton, Yorkshire. [23] George III's son, Edward Duke of Kent, dies. [29] George III dies aged 81, the longest-lived and longest-reigning King of England. The Prince Regent accedes to the throne as George IV. His long-separated wife Caroline returns from the Continent to claim her position as Queen; she is warmly received by the public, who see her as grossly wronged by her husband. George IV nevertheless induces his Cabinet to begin divorce proceedings.

Feb [23] The Cato Street Conspiracy, a plot to assassinate the entire Cabinet with explosives and set up a provisional government, is discovered; the conspiracy is led by Arthur Thistlewood. The Cato Street Conspiracy leads to renewed fears of radicalism and deals a severe blow to the cause of moderate reform.

Mar [30] Anna Sewell, author of *Black Beauty*, is born at Great Yarmouth.

Apr [10] The first British settlers arrive in South Africa, landing at Algoa Bay.

May [12] The hospital reformer Florence Nightingale is born in Florence.

Jun [19] Sir Joseph Banks, the botanist who accompanied Captain Cook, dies.

Jul [5] Introduction of the Bill of Pains and Penalties, designed to deprive the Queen of her royal title and dissolve the royal marriage. Canning resigns from Lord Liverpool's Cabinet over the treatment of Queen Caroline.

Sep John Keats, dying of tuberculosis, sails to Italy.

Nov [10] The Bill of Pains and Penalties is dropped by the Government when it sees that it will be heavily defeated in the Commons. The royal marriage fiasco results in a serious decline in the Cabinet's prestige.

1821 Sir Charles Wheatstone demonstrates that sound reproduction is possible. Famine in Ireland begins, lasting two years. The London Co-operative Wholesale Society is founded. Shortly before her death, Queen Caroline is granted an annuity of £50,000. Work begins on the building of the Stockton-Darlington Railway.

Feb [23] The poet John Keats dies in Rome, aged only 25.

Mar [19] The explorer and writer Sir Richard Burton is born at Torquay.

Jul [19] Coronation of George IV in Westminster Abbey.

Oct [4] The bridge designer John Rennie dies. [11] George Williams, founder of the YMCA in 1844, is born at Dulverton.

1822 Congress of Verona; the congress system breaks down with Britain's refusal to intervene against revolution. The Royal Academy of Music in London is founded.

Feb [16] Sir Francis Galton, pioneer in eugenics, is born in Birmingham.

Jul [8] The poet Shelley is accidentally drowned off Leghorn in Italy while sailing in his boat *Ariel*.

Aug [12] Lord Castlereagh commits suicide; George Canning replaces him as Foreign Secretary. [25] The astronomer Sir William Herschel dies.

Oct [20] The author Thomas Hughes is born at Uffington.

Dec [24] The poet and critic Matthew Arnold is born near Staines.

1823 Michael Faraday succeeds in liquefying chlorine. Charles Babbage invents a rudimentary calculator. Von Beuth, the Prussian Minister of Commerce, travels in Britain and is impressed by the size and modern construction methods of British factories; many are eight and nine storeys high with thin walls, iron columns and iron beams. The death penalty is abolished for over 100 different crimes. Robert Peel initiates a pioneering prison reform act. Charles Macintosh invents waterproof fabric. The portrait sculptor Joseph Nollekens dies.

Jan [3] Robert Whitehead, inventor of the naval torpedo, is born
at Bolton-Le-Moors. [26] Edward Jenner, pioneer in
vaccination, dies at Berkeley.
Feb [7] The writer Ann Radcliffe dies.
Sep [11] The economist David Ricardo dies.
Oct [30] Edmund Cartwright, inventor of the power loom, dies at
Hastings aged 80.
Nov [25] Brighton's Chain Pier is opened.

1824 The painters Constable and Bonington exhibit their work at
the so-called 'English Salon' in Paris. The Anglo-Burmese
Wars begin, after Burmese aggression; Britain moves towards
the annexation of Burma. After a campaign led by Francis
Place and Joseph Hume, the Combination Acts which have
forbidden trade unions are repealed.
Jan [8] The writer Wilkie Collins is born in London.
Feb [10] Samuel Plimsoll is born at Bristol.
Mar [4] The Royal Naval Lifeboat Institution is founded by Sir
William Hillary.
Apr [19] Lord Byron dies at sunset of marsh fever at Missolonghi
during the Greeks' struggle for independence: he is 36.
Jun [26] The physicist and mathematician Lord Kelvin is born in
Belfast as William Thomson.
Oct [21] Portland cement is patented by Joseph Aspdin of
Wakefield.

1825 Michael Faraday isolates benzene. Horse-drawn buses
appear in London. An act to regulate cotton mills and
factories is passed; children under 16 are not allowed to work
more than 12 hours a day. The electromagnet is invented by
William Sturgeon.
May [4] Thomas Huxley is born.
Jun [24] W. H. Smith, the founder of the book-selling chain, is
born in London.
Sep [27] The steam locomotive 'Active' pulls the first train 27
miles along the Stockton-Darlington railway line, starting

from Shildon: this is the first railway to carry goods and passengers.

1826 The Royal Zoological Society is founded in London by Sir Stamford Raffles. The Burmese War ends with the Treaty of Yandabu. Sir Walter Scott is financially ruined by the collapse of his publisher, Ballantyne & Co.

Jul [5] Sir Stamford Raffles, founder of Singapore, dies in London.

1827 John Walker, a chemist at Stockton-on-Tees, sells his first box of friction matches; unfortunately, he does not bother to take out a patent on his invention. Richard Bright first describes the disease that bears his name. The Treaty of London is signed by Britain, France and Russia to protect the Greeks from Turkish tyranny. A combined British, Russian and French fleet under Admiral Codrington destroys a Turkish-Egyptian fleet in Navarino Bay.

Jan [5]Frederick Duke of York, George III's second son, dies.

Apr [2] The painter William Holman Hunt is born. [5] Joseph Lister, surgeon and pioneer of antiseptics, is born. [10] Lord Liverpool resigns as Prime Minister after suffering a stroke. [30] The Tory George Canning succeeds as Prime Minister.

May [18] William Corder murders Maria Marten in the Red Barn at Corder Farm, Polstead: her body is not discovered for a year.

Jun [26] Samuel Crompton, inventor of the spinning-mule in 1779, dies at Bolton.

Jul [16] The potter Josiah Spode dies.

Aug [8] George Canning, Prime Minister for only three months, dies at Chiswick. [31] Viscount Goderich (Earl of Ripon) succeeds Canning as Prime Minister.

1828 The London Protocol is concluded by Britain, France and Russia, recognizing Greek independence. University and King's Colleges, London, are founded. James Nielson first uses a blast furnace. The Australian interior is explored by Charles Sturt.

Jan [22] Lord Goderich resigns as Prime Minister; he is succeeded by the Duke of Wellington.

Feb [12] The poet and novelist George Meredith is born at Portsmouth.

Apr [27] Regent's Park in London is opened.

May [9] The Test Act is repealed. [12] The poet and painter Dante Gabriel Rossetti is born in London as Gabriel Charles Dante.

Jul [15] A new Corn Law is passed; imports of foreign grain are allowed with duties on a sliding scale, varying with the current price of British corn. [21] Archbishop Sutton dies.

Aug [15] William Howley, Bishop of London, becomes Archbishop of Canterbury.

Oct [31] Sir Joseph Swan, inventor (independently of Edison) of the electric lamp, is born at Sunderland.

1829 Thomas Graham, a Scottish chemist, formulates his law on the diffusion of gases. Suttee, the Indian practice of sacrificing a widow on her husband's funeral pyre, is declared illegal in British India. The Irish leader Daniel O'Connell MP begins to agitate for repeal of the Act of Union. The Earl of Surrey becomes the first Catholic MP, representing Horsham. The composer Felix Mendelssohn visits the Hebrides.

Apr [10] William Booth, founder of the Salvation Army, is born at Nottingham.

May [29] Sir Humphry Davy, inventor of the miners' safety lamp in 1815, dies in Geneva.

Jun [8] Sir John Millais, painter, is born at Southampton. [10] The first Oxford and Cambridge University boat race takes place; Oxford wins easily. [19] Sir Robert Peel founds the London Metropolitan Police Force.

Jul [4] The first regular scheduled bus service in Britain is introduced in London by George Shillibeer.

Oct [6] Trials begin at Rainhill near Liverpool for a locomotive for use on the Liverpool and Manchester Railway. The five entrants are 'Rocket', 'Cycloped', 'Sans Pareil',

'Perseverance', 'Novelty'; Stephenson's 'Rocket' is the
winner.

1830 The first major cholera epidemic strikes Britain. The British
East India company takes Mysore.

Jun [26] George IV dies, succeeded by his brother as William IV.

Sep [15] The politician William Huskisson is knocked down and
killed by Stephenson's 'Rocket' at Parkside; the accident
happens when he is attending the opening of the Liverpool
and Manchester Railway, the first railway in the world to be
built for passenger traffic as well as for freight. It marks the
beginning of the railway age.

Nov [16] The Duke of Wellington resigns as Prime Minister. He is
succeeded by the Whig Earl Grey, whose liberal Cabinet is
determined to make Parliamentary reforms.

Dec [5] The poetess Christina Rossetti is born.

1831 The Captain Swing riots; rebellion in rural areas of England
against the mechanization of agriculture and low pay for
farm labourers. Britain and France guarantee the
independence of Belgium. Michael Faraday discovers
electro-magnetic induction (previously discovered by Joseph
Henry but not published).

Feb [27] Captain John Briscoe discovers the continent of
Antarctica.

Mar [22] The First Reform Bill is introduced by Lord John Russell
and rejected by the Lords.

Apr [19] Lord Grey dissolves Parliament, going to the country
with the Reform Bill as the main issue. The election result is a
Whig triumph.

Jun [1] James Ross finds the North Magnetic Pole and plants a
Union Jack there.

Aug [7] Dean Farrar, writer of school stories, is born in
Bombay.

Sep [8] Coronation of William IV. [21] The Second Reform Bill is
passed in the Commons.

Oct [8] The Second Reform Bill is rejected by the Lords. Agitation for reform in the country now turns violent; troops kill or maim 100 people and civil war is narrowly averted.

Dec [27] The Admiralty survey ship *HMS Beagle*, with Charles Darwin on board, sets out from Plymouth on its famous five-year scientific voyage round the world; its findings are to have profound effects on scientific thought.

1832 A cholera epidemic kills thousands of people in Britain. William Ewart Gladstone enters politics. The Irish Reform Act is passed.

Jan [27] Lewis Carroll (Charles Lutwidge Dodgson) is born at Daresbury.

Mar [23] The Third Reform Bill is passed by the Commons. The Lords demand amendments, which leads to renewed popular agitation. Grey advises the King to create enough liberal peers to pass the measure; William IV refuses, and Grey and his Cabinet resign. Wellington is unable to form an alternative ministry. William IV is forced to recall Grey and promise to appoint the new peers if they are needed.

Jun [4] The threat of a changed composition of the House of Lords is sufficient to force the more reactionary Lords to withdraw, allowing the passage of the Bill. [6] Jeremy Bentham dies.

Sep [21] Sir Walter Scott dies at Abbotsford. [30] Field Marshal Lord Roberts is born at Cawnpore in India.

1833 The Tithe War continues in Ireland; the predominantly Catholic Irish resent the enforced payment of tithes to support the Protestant Church, and resort to violence. Britain's sovereignty over the Falkland Islands is proclaimed. The East India Company is granted a renewal of its charter, with the proviso that its monopoly of trade with China and India will end. The first Education Grant of £20,000 for elementary education is passed. The painter and designer Sir Edward Burne-Jones is born. The 'Oxford Movement' in the

Anglican Church begins: it involves a belief in a 'catholic', i.e. undivided, Church.

Jan [28] General Gordon is born at Woolwich.

Apr Coercion Bill; this gives the Lord Lieutenant of Ireland unlimited powers to supress public meetings. [22] Richard Trevithick, pioneer of steam railway locomotives, dies at Dartford.

Jul [29] William Wilberforce, who played a large part in the abolition of slavery, dies.

Aug [2] Irish Church Temporalities Bill; this attempt to reduce the burden of tithes outrages O'Connell and his followers. [23] Slavery is abolished in the British colonies, and compensation totalling £20 million is provided for slave-owners.
[29] Factory Act; the first measure of its kind, applied only to the textile industry, but it is the forerunner of a whole string of reforms; it forbids the employment of children under the age of nine, and children under 13 are to have two hours of schooling a day.

Sep [15] Tennyson's close friend Arthur Hallam dies suddenly in Vienna at the age of 22.

1834 Michael Faraday discovers electrical self-induction. The colony of Victoria is founded in Australia. The artist James Whistler is born.

Jan Robert Owen sets up the Grand National Consolidated Trades Union, with the aim of organizing a general strike for an eight-hour working day. This results in a Government clamp-down.

Mar [6] The novelist and artist George du Maurier is born. [17] Kate Greenaway, illustrator of children's books, is born. [18] Six Dorset farm workers, the Tolpuddle Martyrs, are sentenced to transportation to Australia for swearing an oath to join a trade union; they formed a lodge of the Grand National. [24] The artist, publisher, writer and designer William Morris is born.

Apr [22] The Quadruple Alliance (Britain, France, Spain and
Portugal) is formed to protect Spain and Portugal.
Jul [2] Grey resigns as Prime Minister, succeeded by Lord
Melbourne. [25] The poet Coleridge dies.
Aug [14] The New Poor Law (Poor Law Amendment Act)
provides workhouses for the destitute; it also takes Poor Law
administration away from the old parish authorities and
gives it to elected Boards.
Sep [2] Thomas Telford, engineer, 'the Colossus of Roads', dies.
Oct [16] The Palace of Westminster is burnt down; firemen
manage to save Westminster Hall and St Stephen's Chapel.
Nov [15] Lord Melbourne resigns as Prime Minister; he is
succeeded by Sir Robert Peel.
Dec [23] The Hansom cab is patented by the architect Joseph
Hansom. Thomas Malthus, the economist, dies. [27] Charles
Lamb, essayist and friend of Coleridge and Wordsworth,
dies.

1835 British trade with China increases as the East India
Company's monopoly ends. 4000 Boers begin the Great Trek
in South Africa to find new territory free from British rule.
English becomes the official government language in India.
The abolition of slavery in the colonies leads to increases in
the prices of products. An early computer is invented by
Charles Babbage.
Jan In the General Election, Sir Robert Peel sets out his
conception of a new kind of liberal Conservatism in the
'Tamworth Manifesto'; it embodies an acceptance of the 1832
Reform Act and a readiness to proceed with a programme of
moderate reforms.
Apr [18] The Whig Lord Melbourne becomes Prime Minister
again.
May [13] John Nash, architect of Regent's Park and Brighton
Pavilion, dies on the Isle of Wight. [16] Felicia Hemans, the
poetess who wrote *The boy stood on the burning deck*, dies in
Dublin. [30] The poet Alfred Austin is born.

Jun [18] William Cobbett, journalist and reformer, dies near Guildford.
Nov [21] The poet James Hogg dies.
Dec [4] The novelist and satirist Samuel Butler is born.

1836 The Tithe Commutation Act orders that tithes should be paid in cash, not in kind. Parliament provides for the systematic registration of births, marriages and deaths. The Chartist Movement starts, when a Working-men's Association in London sets out its programme for Parliamentary reform in a People's Charter, in effect a petition addressed to Parliament. The Charter demands manhood suffrage, vote by ballot, the abolition of the property qualification for MPs, payment of MPs, equal electoral districts, and annual Parliaments. The working class is rapidly won over to the People's Charter by missionary speakers who tour the country addressing huge public meetings. Screw propeller invented by Sir Francis Smith.

Mar [2] The first point-to-point meeting is held, at the Madresfield Estate by the Worcester Hunt.
May [17] Sir Norman Lockyer, discoverer of helium, is born.

1837 Isaac Pitman invents his system of shorthand. Charles Wheatstone and William Cooke invent the first electric telegraph. Disraeli makes his maiden speech in the House of Commons. The composer Samuel Wesley dies.

Jan [20] Sir John Soane, architect, dies in London. [23] John Field, composer and inventor of the nocturne, dies.
Mar [31] The painter John Constable dies.
Apr [5] The poet Algernon Swinburne is born. [20] Robert Southey writes to Charlotte Brontë, telling her that 'Literature cannot be the business of a woman's life, and it ought not to be'.
Jun [20] William IV dies at Windsor, succeeded by Queen Victoria. Hanover now becomes separated from Britain because female succession is forbidden by Salic Law; Ernest

Augustus, Duke of Cumberland and son of George III, succeeds as King of Hanover.

Jul   [1] Registration of births, marriages and deaths begins in Britain. [13] Queen Victoria adopts Buckingham Palace as the official royal residence. [19] Brunel's 'Great Western' is launched at Bristol. [20] Euston Railway Station, the first in London, is opened.

1838   The Chartist Movement grows, especially in the North. War breaks out between the British and the Afghans; the First Afghan War results from British attempts to curb Russian influence. The National Gallery opens.

Feb   The first reported attack by Spring-Heeled Jack, who is apparently a sadist wearing a hideous mask and metal claws; he brutally assaults a girl called Jane Alsop in Bow. [6] The actor Sir Henry Irving is born in Somerset as John Henry Brodribb.

Apr   [8] Regular steamship services between Britain and America start; Brunel's *Great Western* leaves Bristol for New York on her maiden voyage under Captain James Hosken. [22] The *Sirius* reaches Sandy Hook, New York, becoming the first ship to cross the Atlantic entirely under steam power (left Queenstown on April 4).

Jun   [28] Coronation of Queen Victoria. [31] Poor Law Bill introduced, designed to extend to Ireland the provisions of the New Poor Law.

Sep   [7] The *Forfarshire* is wrecked near the Farne Islands off the Northumberland coast; Grace Darling rescues the crew.

1839   William Fox Talbot invents photography (simultaneously with the French Daguerre). Kirkpatrick MacMillan of Dumfries invents the first true bicycle. The Peninsula and Oriental Line begins a regular steamship service between Britain and Egypt, to meet East India Company ships coming from the east. The Treaty of London establishes the independence of Belgium.

Feb The first National Convention of Chartists is held in London.
[26] The first official Grand National Steeplechase is run at
Aintree; it is won by Jem Mason on 'Lottery'.

Apr [9] The Jamaica problem surfaces in British politics. The
liberation of slaves creates great difficulties for the planters,
who have treated the slaves with brutality. In view of the
disorder, Melbourne feels obliged to suspend the Jamaica
Constitution for five years, but feels that his own position
has become untenable.

May [7] Melbourne resigns. [13] The Charter is presented to
Parliament, but it is rejected.

Jun [12] Wordsworth receives an honorary doctorate at Oxford.
[14] The first Henley Regatta takes place.

Jul There are Chartist riots in Birmingham.

Oct [25] The first national railway timetable, *Bradshaw's Railway
Companion*, is published.

Nov [3] The Opium War with China breaks out. [4] There is a
Chartist riot at Newport, South Wales; the crowd is fired on
by constables and 20 people are killed. John Frost, the
Chartist leader, is sentenced to transportation.

1840 Sir William Grove invents the incandescent electric light. The
Botanical Gardens at Kew are opened. The Afghan War ends
with the Afghans surrendering. Treaty of London; Britain,
Russia, Prussia and Austria agree to limit Egyptian
expansion. Municipal Act; this confers the right to vote on all
persons paying at least £10 rent a year.

Jan [6] Fanny Burney, novelist, diarist and friend of Dr Johnson,
dies. [10] The Penny Post is instituted.

Feb [5] John Boyd Dunlop, vet and patentee of the pneumatic
bicycle tyre, is born at Dreghorn. [10] Queen Victoria marries
Prince Albert of Saxe-Coburg-Gotha; both are aged 20.

Mar [30] Beau Brummell, the Regency dandy, dies at Caen in a
pauper lunatic asylum.

Apr [27] Edward Whymper, mountaineer and the first person to
climb the Matterhorn, is born in London.

May [6] The first adhesive postage stamps (Penny Black and
Twopence Blue) are introduced; the first stamp on the first
sheet of Penny Blacks is stuck on a letter to George
Waterman of Thame, Oxfordshire. [21] New Zealand is
declared a British Colony.

Jun [2] The novelist Thomas Hardy is born at Bockhampton. [6]
John Stainer, composer, is born. [10] Edward Oxford, a
servant in a pub, fires two shots at Queen Victoria and Prince
Albert as they travel up Constitution Hill in an open carriage:
both shots miss. Oxford is sent to a mental hospital, then
exiled.

Jul [4] Samuel Cunard founds the Cunard Steamship Company,
and his first vessel, the *Britannia*, sails on her maiden voyage
from Liverpool to Halifax, Nova Scotia.

Sep [22] George III's daughter Augusta dies.

Nov [21] The first of Queen Victoria's children, Victoria, is born.

1841 The Straits Convention; Russia, Britain, France and Austria
agree to close the Dardanelles and Bosporus to foreign
shipping. The Second Afghan War begins after Afghans
massacre British soldiers. Sir James Clark Ross discovers
some of the coastline of Antarctica. The British
Pharmaceutical Society is founded.

Jan [26] Britain acquires Hong Kong. [28] Sir Henry Stanley,
journalist and explorer, is born at Denbigh as John
Rowlands.

Aug [28] Lord Melbourne resigns as Prime Minister. [30] The Tory
Robert Peel becomes Prime Minister again.

Nov [9] Edward VII, second child and eldest son of Queen
Victoria, is born at St James's Palace.

Dec [4] Edward is created Prince of Wales.

1842 The first railway telegraph system, between Paddington and
Slough, comes into service. The Treaty of Nanking ends the
Opium Wars and opens Chinese ports to British trade. British
forces surrender at Kabul, and are wiped out during their
retreat to India. Mudie's lending library opens in London.

James Nasmyth invents the steam hammer. Lord Ashley's Mines Act prohibits the employment of child or female labour underground. Peel abolishes the prohibition on meat and cattle imports.

Apr [12] – May [12] The Second National Convention of Chartists; a second petition to Parliament is rejected on May 3.

May [13] Sir Arthur Sullivan, composer of operettas, is born at Lambeth. [30] John Francis attempts to assassinate the Queen as she drives down Constitution Hill with Prince Albert.

Jun [12] Thomas Arnold, educationalist and reformer, dies aged 46. [13] Queen Victoria's first train journey, from Slough to Paddington.

Sep [20] Sir James Dewar, inventor of the vacuum flask, is born at Kincardine-on-Forth.

Oct [20] Grace Darling, who saved the crew of the *Forfarshire*, dies.

Nov [12] The physicist Lord Rayleigh is born at Witham near Maldon.

1843 In Ireland, Daniel O'Connell persistently demands the repeal of the Union, and his Young Ireland Party causes unrest; O'Connell and his co-agitators are arrested and the situation quietens. Maori revolts against the British break out in New Zealand. The first workers' Co-operative Society is formed: the Pioneers of Rochdale.

Mar [21] Robert Southey, Poet Laureate since 1813, dies at Keswick. [25] The Thames Tunnel, linking Wapping and Rotherhithe, is formally opened; it is later turned into a tube tunnel.

Apr [6] William Wordsworth is appointed Poet Laureate. [15] Henry James, American novelist, is born in New York. [21] Augustus, Duke of Clarence dies. [25] The royal yacht *Victoria and Albert* is launched at Pembroke. Queen Victoria's daughter Alice is born.

Jun [21] The Royal College of Surgeons is founded.
Jul [19] Brunel's *Great Britain*, the first all-metal liner, is launched
at Wapping by Prince Albert. [25] Charles Macintosh, the
chemist who patented waterproof fabric in 1823, dies in
Glasgow.
Oct [1] The *News of the World* begins publication.
Nov [3-4] The 17-foot statue of Lord Nelson is hauled up in two
pieces to the top of the column in Trafalgar Square. [21]
Vulcanized rubber is patented by Thomas Hancock.

1844 Potato famine in Ireland. Railway mania grips the country;
massive speculation and investment lead to the building of
5000 miles of track this year and the next. Bank Charter Act;
Peel gives the Bank of England a monopoly on printing
money, but separates banking and note-issuing into two
separate departments.

May [3] The theatre impresario Richard D'Oyly Carte is born.
Jul [22] Revd William Spooner, originator of spoonerisms, is
born. [27] John Dalton, chemist and physicist, dies.
Aug [6] Queen Victoria's son Alfred is born.
Oct [23] Robert Bridges, Poet Laureate, is born at Walmer.
Dec [21] The Rochdale Pioneers open the first co-operative shop,
at Toad Lane.

1845 Potato famine in Ireland continues. The world's largest
telescope is built in Ireland by the Earl of Rosse, an amateur
astronomer; it allows a view, for the first time, of galaxies
beyond our own. Peel's 'Free Trade' Budget repeals all
export duties and many import duties. The Maori rebellion in
New Zealand continues. The Anglo-Sikh Wars in northern
India result in Britain annexing the Punjab.

Feb [7] The Portland Vase, a unique dark blue carved Roman
glass vessel, is smashed by a madman with a stone; it is
afterwards restored.
Mar [11] Self-raising flour is patented by Henry Jones of Bristol.
May [3] The poet Thomas Hood dies after a long illness.

Jun [17] Richard Barham, author of the *Ingoldsby Legends*, dies.
Jul [4] Thomas Barnardo, founder of homes for destitute
     children, is born in Dublin. [26] The *Great Britain*, Brunel's
     only surviving ship, leaves Liverpool on her maiden voyage
     to New York.
Oct [12] The social worker and prison reformer Elizabeth Fry
     dies.
Dec [10] The first pneumatic tyres are patented by Scottish
     engineer Robert Thomson.

1846 The continuing famine in Ireland results in mass emigration
     to the United States. Defeated by the British, the Sikhs settle
     for peace under the Treaty of Lahore. Louis Napoleon
     escapes from the fortress where he has been confined and
     reaches London. Mendelssohn's *Elijah* is first performed at
     the Birmingham Festival.

May [15] Customs Law; this measure abolishes duty on all live
     animals and nearly every kind of meat, and reduces the
     duties on other foods.
Jun [6] Repeal of the Corn Laws; the import duty on corn is fixed
     at one shilling a quarter from 1849 onwards, and there is to
     be a small protective duty on corn between now and 1849.
     [27] Charles Parnell, Irish politician, is born at Avondale in
     County Wicklow. [29] Peel's government is overthrown by a
     revolt led by Disraeli, who objects to a new coercion Bill for
     Ireland. [30] The Whig Lord John Russell becomes Prime
     Minister.

1847 Famine and the resulting distress continue in Ireland; mass
     emigration also continues. Factory Act; women and young
     people 13-18 are prohibited from working more than 10
     hours a day. British Museum opens. Dr James Simpson first
     uses chloroform as an anaesthetic.

Jan [14] Wilson Carlile, founder of the Church Army, is born at
     Buxton.
Feb [27] The actress Ellen Terry is born at Coventry.

Mar [3] The inventor of the telephone, Alexander Graham Bell, is born in Edinburgh.

May [7] Lord Rosebery, Prime Minister, is born. [15] The Irish political leader Daniel O'Connell dies at Genoa.

Jun [11] Sir John Franklin, the Arctic explorer, dies in Canada attempting to discover the North-West Passage.

1848 Huge Chartist meeting on Kennington Common. The Pre-Raphaelite Brotherhood is founded. The Second Sikh War begins. The Public Health Act rules that every new house must have a 'water closet, privy or ash pit'.

Feb [11] Archbishop Howley dies. [27] The composer Sir Hubert Parry is born at Bournemouth.

Mar [10] John Sumner, Bishop of Chester, becomes Archbishop of Canterbury. [18] Queen Victoria's daughter Louise is born.

Apr [22] The surviving members of the crew of the Franklin expedition abandon ship. According to later Innuit reports, 'they fell down and died as they walked'; they are probably the victims of lead poisoning.

Jul [18] The cricketer W. G. Grace is born at Downend near Bristol. [25] Arthur Balfour, the Conservative Prime Minister, is born in East Lothian.

Aug [6] The officers and crew of HMS *Daedalus* see a huge sea monster in the Atlantic; the incident is reported by Captain Peter McQuhae to the Admiralty in October. [9] The author Frederick Marryat dies at Langham in Norfolk. [12] George Stephenson, the engineer who built the first modern railway in 1825, dies at Tapton.

Nov [1] W. H. Smith's first railway bookstall opens, at Euston Station in London. [24] Lord Melbourne, twice Prime Minister, dies near Welwyn.

Dec [19] The novelist and poet Emily Brontë dies aged 30.

1849 The Sikhs surrender at Rawalpindi after being defeated by British troops. Thomas Macaulay begins, never to finish, his *History of England*. Disraeli becomes leader of the Conservative Party. The Navigation Acts are repealed. William Sterndale Bennett forms the London Bach Society.

Feb [13] Lord Randolph Churchill, politician, is born at Blenheim Palace.

May [19] William Hamilton attempts to assassinate Queen Victoria. [28] The novelist and poet Anne Brontë dies at Scarborough aged 29.

Dec An anti-semitic crowd in Athens burns the house of a British subject, Don Pacifico, who has a large claim against the Greek government. Lord Palmerston sends a squadron to Piraeus to force a settlement of the claim on Don Pacifico's behalf; the Greeks will not comply. [2] Queen Adelaide, widow of William IV, dies. [12] Sir Marc Isambard Brunel, builder of the Thames Tunnel, dies aged 80.

1850 The first issue of *The Germ*, the Pre-Raphaelite Brotherhood magazine, is published. The railway from London to Edinburgh is completed. Southwark Roman Catholic Cathedral becomes the first Catholic cathedral since the Reformation; the fabric of the building was completed in 1848, as St George's Church, and it becomes a cathedral with the restoration of the Catholic hierarchy.

Jan The British squadron at Piraeus lays an embargo on all Greek ships in the harbour.

Apr [6] Madame Tussaud, founder of the wax museum, dies aged 90. [23] Wordsworth dies of pleurisy at midday at Rydal Mount, Grasmere. [26] The Greek government complies with Palmerston's demands.

May [1] Queen Victoria's son Arthur is born.

Jun [24] Lord Kitchener is born near Ballylongford in Ireland. [29] Lord Palmerston's 'civis Romanus sum' speech stirs feelings of patriotic pride and nationalism.

Jul [2] Sir Robert Peel dies in London as a result of a horse riding accident. [8] Adolphus Duke of Cambridge, one of George III's sons, dies.

Nov   [13] The writer Robert Louis Stevenson is born in Edinburgh.
       [19] Alfred Lord Tennyson is appointed Poet Laureate, a post he will hold until his death in 1892.

Dec   [4] William Sturgeon, who devised the first electro-magnet, dies at Prestwich.

1851   Following the Don Pacifico affair, the Queen, aided by her husband, Prince Albert, and Baron Stockmar, draws up a memorandum demanding that she be kept fully informed at all times and that once she has approved a measure it should not be altered. Queen Victoria is increasingly irritated by Palmerston's indiscretions and his high-handed behaviour in office.

Feb   Ecclesiastical Titles Bill; this forbids priests and bishops of the Roman Catholic Church from assuming titles taken from any place in the United Kingdom. The law remains a dead letter and is eventually repealed in 1871. [1] Mary Shelley, author of *Frankenstein*, dies.

Mar   [29] Marble Arch is moved from Buckingham Palace to its present site.

May   [1] The Great Exhibition at the Crystal Palace in Hyde Park, the first world fair, is opened by Queen Victoria.

Sep   [19] William Lever, soap-maker and philanthropist, later Viscount Leverhulme, is born at Bolton.

Oct   [15] The Great Exhibition ends.

Nov   [13] The telegraph service between London and Paris is opened. [18] The Duke of Cumberland, a son of George III and also King of Hanover, dies.

Dec   [2] Palmerston expresses approval at Louis Napoleon's *coup d'état*, but without referring back to the Queen.
       [5] The Cabinet, in accordance with the Queen's memorandum, carries on as if the French coup had not occurred. [19] The Queen dismisses Palmerston for his discourtesy. The painter J. M. W. Turner dies in a lodging in Chelsea, under the assumed name of Booth.

1852 Lord Kelvin and W. Rankine invent refrigeration. British forces subdue Burma. Britain recognizes the independence of the Transvaal. Hector Berlioz visits London.

Feb [14] The first patient, Eliza Armstrong, is admitted to the Children's Hospital in Great Ormond Street, London. [20] Lord John Russell's Government is defeated on a militia bill. [23] Lord John Russell resigns. [27] The Tory Earl of Derby becomes Prime Minister.

Sep [12] Herbert Asquith, Liberal Prime Minister, is born at Morley. [14] The Duke of Wellington dies at Walmer Castle aged 83. Augustus Pugin, co-designer of the Houses of Parliament, dies at Ramsgate. [30] The composer Charles Stanford is born.

Oct [2] Sir William Ramsay, discoverer of inert gases, is born in Glasgow.

Nov [18] Funeral of the Duke of Wellington in St Paul's Cathedral.

Dec [19] Earl of Derby resigns as Prime Minister. [28] A Coalition Ministry led by Lord Aberdeen begins.

1853 The Queen uses chloroform to help her through the birth of her seventh child, Leopold, on April 7; this establishes chloroform as the favoured anaesthetic in Britain.

Jul [5] The colonial administrator Cecil Rhodes is born at Bishop's Stortford.

1854 The Chartist movement comes to an end. Edwin Chadwick is forcibly retired because he has come to be regarded as a nuisance in his campaign for healthier living conditions. The Northcote-Trevelyan Report introduces reforms in the Civil Service. The Offices of Colonial Secretary and Secretary for War are separated. Sir John Elder invents the compound marine steam-engine.

Mar [28] The Crimean War begins when Britain and France declare war on Russia.

Jun [13] Sir Charles Parsons, engineer and inventor, is born. [21] A 20-year-old Irishman, Charles Lucas, throws an unexploded Russian bomb over the side of HMS *Hecla* in the Baltic. He is posthumously awarded the first Victoria Cross.

Aug [8] The Vienna Four Points, agreed by Britain and France; the conditions of peace are to be the guarantees of the preservation of Serbia, free passage through the mouths of the Danube, a revision of the Straits Convention, and abandonment of Russia's claims to a protectorate over the Sultan's Christian subjects. Russia rejects these terms.

Sep [14] Allied French and British troops land in the Crimea. [20] Battle of Alma.

Oct [16] Oscar Wilde is born in Dublin. [17] The Allies begin bombing Sebastopol; it is the beginning of a long siege. [25] The Charge of the Light Brigade, led by Lord Cardigan, takes place in the Battle of Balaklava.

Nov [5] Battle of Inkerman: French and British forces are victorious over the Russians. [13] John Peel, the famous hunting squire, dies at Caldbeck in Cumbria.

Dec [2] Austria forms a defensive and offensive alliance with Britain and France.

1855 David Livingstone discovers the Victoria Falls on the Zambezi. Alexander Parkes patents the first synthetic plastic, later named celluloid. Florence Nightingale initiates nursing reforms during the Crimean War. The Crystal Palace concerts begin. Richard Wagner conducts in London. The Bessemer converter is invented by Sir Henry Bessemer. Robert Bunsen invents the Bunsen burner.

Jan [20] Lord Aberdeen resigns as Prime Minister.

Feb [6] The Whig/Liberal Lord Palmerston becomes Prime Minister. [9] Mysterious hoof-prints appear overnight in the snow in Devon; a two-legged hoofed creature appears to have trekked 100 miles over fields, walls and roof-tops; no satisfactory explanation is available.

Mar [2] Tsar Nicholas I dies; his successor Alexander is more disposed to make peace with the Allies, but negotiations break down. [31] Charlotte Brontë, author of *Jane Eyre*, dies.

May [24] The dramatist Sir Arthur Wing Pinero is born.

Jun [28] Lord Raglan, Commander of the Expeditionary Force in the Crimean War, dies. [29] The first issue of the *Daily Telegraph* is published.

Sep [11] The Russians abandon Sebastopol to the Allies, blowing up their forts as they go.

1856 Natal and Tasmania become self-governing British colonies. Lord Dalhousie, Governor-General of India, dethrones the King of Oudh because of his tyranny and annexes his kingdom. The Arrow War breaks out; Britain and France ally against China when a ship flying the British flag, the *Arrow*, is boarded by the Chinese and the crew arrested. 'Big Ben', the clock-tower bell of the Houses of Parliament, is cast at Whitechapel. William Perkin creates mauve, the first artificial dye: it soon appears on textiles.

Jan [29] The Victoria Cross, Britain's highest military decoration, is instituted by Queen Victoria.

Feb [1] Russia agrees to preliminary peace conditions at Vienna.

Mar [5] The second Covent Garden Theatre burns down. [30] The Crimean War ends with the Treaty of Paris: Britain, France and Austria guarantee the independence of Turkey and the Black Sea is declared neutral.

Jun [22] Rider Haggard, the novelist, is born at Bradenham Hall in Norfolk.

Jul [26] George Bernard Shaw, the dramatist and critic, is born in Dublin.

Aug [15] Keir Hardie, the Labour leader, is born in Lanarkshire.

Dec [18] Sir J. J. Thomson, discoverer of the electron, is born near Manchester. [23] The geologist and author Hugh Miller commits suicide.

1857 The Peace of Paris ends the Anglo-Persian War; the Shah recognizes the independence of Afghanistan. A Chinese fleet is destroyed by the Royal Navy; British and French troops take Canton. Charles Hallé founds the Hallé Orchestra in Manchester. Prince Albert is created Prince Consort. The

Matrimonial Causes Act establishes divorce courts in England and Wales.

Jan   [30] The naval uniform for ratings in the Royal Navy is authorized.

Feb   [22] Lord Baden-Powell, founder of the Boy Scout movement, is born in London.

Apr   [14] Queen Victoria's daughter Beatrice is born. [30] Mary Duchess of Gloucester, daughter of George III, dies.

May   [10] The Indian Mutiny begins. Discontented sepoys mutiny, capture the prison at Meerut and march on Delhi.

Jun   The Siege of Delhi begins, leading eventually to the banishment of Bahadur Shah and the end of the Mogul Empire. [2] The composer Edward Elgar is born at Broadheath. [26] The first investiture ceremony of VCs is held, in Hyde Park.

Jul   [15] Massacre at Cawnpore; a three-week siege at Cawnpore comes to an end when the garrison is offered a safe conduct by the sepoys. All the men are killed as they come out and the women and children are thrown in prison. [17] Havelock arrives at Lucknow, butchering the mutineers in retaliation for the Cawnpore massacre.

Sep   [25] First Relief of Lucknow by Havelock.

Nov   [3] The first attempt to launch the *Great Eastern* is abandoned when a spinning winch handle kills a workman. [16] The final Relief of Lucknow by Campbell.

Dec   [3] The novelist Joseph Conrad is born in Poland.

1858   Queen Victoria is proclaimed Sovereign of India. Sir Richard Burton and John Speke discover Lake Tanganyika. The property qualification for MPs is removed. The composer Dame Ethel Smyth is born.

Jan   [31] The *Great Eastern*, 692 feet long, is finally launched at Millwall after three months delay.

May   [15] The present Royal Opera House at Covent Garden (the third) is opened.

Jul   [14] The suffragette Emmeline Pankhurst is born at
       Manchester.
Aug   [2] Government of India Act; the British Government takes
       complete control over India, the East India Company losing
       its political powers. [3] Lake Victoria is discovered by John
       Speke. [5] The first transatlantic cable is completed (laid by
       USS *Niagara* and HMS *Agamemnon*) and opened by Queen
       Victoria and President Buchanan exchanging pleasantries.
       [19] The novelist Edith Nesbit is born.
Sep   [16] Andrew Bonar Law, Conservative Prime Minister, is
       born in Canada.
Nov   [17] The social reformer Robert Owen dies aged 87.

1859 The folk-song collector Cecil Sharp is born.
Feb   [9] John Lewis, working in a timber yard at Mountain Ash in
       Glamorgan, is hit by a rainstorm of falling fish. [21] George
       Lansbury, the Labour Party leader, is born near Lowestoft.
Mar   [8] Kenneth Grahame, author of *The Wind in the Willows*, is
       born in Edinburgh.
May   [2] Jerome K. Jerome, author, is born at Walsall. [22] The
       novelist Sir Arthur Conan Doyle is born in Edinburgh. [31]
       'Big Ben' first begins to tell the time.
Jun   [12] Lord Derby's ministry is defeated on Disraeli's Reform
       Bill; Derby resigns. [18] Lord Palmerston becomes Prime
       Minister again.
Sep   [15] Isambard Kingdom Brunel, engineer and innovator, dies
       at Westminster.

1860 British and French troops enter Peking, ending the
       Anglo-Chinese War . The Second Maori War begins in New
       Zealand. The first modern Eisteddfod is held. The painters
       Walter Sickert and Wilson Steer are born. Robert Burke and
       William Wills cross Australia from south to north (1860-61).
       Joseph Lister introduces antiseptic surgery.

Jan   [23] A Commercial Treaty (the Cobden-Chevalier Treaty) is
       concluded with France.

May [9] The playwright and novelist J. M. Barrie is born at
Kirriemuir. [12] Sir Charles Barry, co-architect of the new
Palace of Westminster, dies.
Jun [17] The *Great Eastern* begins its first transatlantic voyage.
Jul [13] The last naval execution at the yard-arm takes place
today, aboard HMS *Leven* in the River Yangtse; the victim is
Marine Private John Dalliger.
Aug [30] The first tramway in Britain opens, at Birkenhead.
Oct [17] The first professional golf tournament takes place, at
Prestwick in Scotland; it is won by Willie Parks.
Dec [29] The first sea-going ironclad warship, HMS *Warrior*, is
launched.

1861 A British colony is founded in Nigeria, the first true British
colony in Africa. The firm of Morris, Marshall, Faulkner &
Co is founded as an association of 'fine art workmen'. Daily
weather forecasts begin. The Post Office Savings Bank is
established. The Royal Academy of Music is founded in
London. The singer Dame Nellie Melba is born. Frederick
Walton invents Linoleum.

Apr [22] Viscount Allenby, army commander, is born at
Brackenhurst.
Jun [19] Earl Haig, army commander, is born in Edinburgh. [30]
Elizabeth Barrett Browning dies in Florence.
Dec [14] Prince Albert dies of typhoid at Windsor Castle.

1862 Britain recognizes Zanzibar's independence. The Companies
Act introduces limited liability companies. A cotton famine
brings starvation and disaster to Lancashire mill-workers.

Jan [29] The composer Frederick Delius is born at Bradford.
Feb [11] Elizabeth Siddall dies; Dante Gabriel Rossetti, her
husband, buries his unpublished manuscript poems in her
coffin. [17] Edward German (Jones), composer, is born at
Whitchurch in Shropshire.
Jul [1] Princess Alice marries Prince Louis of Hesse-Darmstadt.
Sep [6] John Sumner, Archbishop of Canterbury, dies.

Nov [26] Charles Longley, Archbishop of York, becomes Archbishop of Canterbury.

1863 Henry Clifton Sorby discovers the microstructure of steel; this leads to the development of metallurgy. Sir Lawrence Alma-Tadema visits Pompeii and begins painting archaeological subjects.

Jan [10] The first section of the London Underground is opened to passengers by Mr Gladstone: the Metropolitan Railway Line from Paddington to Farringdon Street. [17] David Lloyd George is born at Manchester.

Feb [9] Anthony Hope, author of *The Prisoner of Zenda*, is born in London. [21] A new Post Office mailbag service begins, using pneumatic conveyors underneath London's streets.

Mar [10] The Prince of Wales marries Princess Alexandra of Denmark in St George's Chapel, Windsor. [27] Sir Henry Royce, car manufacturer, is born at Alwalton.

May [27] Broadmoor Asylum for the criminally insane is established at Crowthorne in Berkshire.

Oct [16] Sir Austen Chamberlain, politician, is born in Birmingham.

Nov [21] Sir Arthur Quiller-Couch, writer, is born.

Dec [24] William Makepeace Thackeray, novelist, dies.

1864 Octavia Hill begins her work reforming housing in the London slums. James Clerk Maxwell proposes the electromagnetic theory of light.

Jan [8] The Prince of Wales's son Albert is born. [11] Charing Cross railway station is formally opened.

Apr [28] Britain makes the Ionian Islands over to Greece.

Jun [9] Charles Dickens is involved in a train crash at Staplehurst in Kent; he has to return to his wrecked carriage to retrieve the manuscript of part of *Our Mutual Friend*.

Sep [15] The explorer John Speke dies in a shooting accident.

Dec [25] The first Christmas Day dip in the Serpentine.

1865 Joseph Lister pioneers antiseptic surgery, applying carbolic acid to wounds. The Second Maori War ends.

Feb [28] Sir Wilfrid Grenfell, medical missionary, is born.

Apr [2] Richard Cobden dies.

Jun [3] George V is born at Marlborough House in London, son of Edward Prince of Wales and Princess Alexandra. [8] Sir Joseph Paxton, architect, landscape gardener and designer of the Crystal Palace, dies. [13] William Butler Yeats, poet, is born at Sandymount near Dublin.

Jul The *Great Eastern* leaves Ireland to lay a new cable across the Atlantic. [2] William Booth founds the Salvation Army with a revival meeting in Whitechapel. [5] The world's first speed limit is imposed in Britain, under the Locomotives and Highways Act, nicknamed the 'Red Flag Act'. [13] Edward Whymper becomes the first person to climb the Matterhorn. [15] Lord Northcliffe, newspaper proprietor, is born near Dublin. [25] Dr James Barry, a retired army surgeon, dies in London aged 73; the post-mortem reveals that he was a woman and had, moreover, probably borne a child.

Oct [18] Lord Palmerston, the Prime Minister, dies at Brocket Hall, Welwyn. [29] Lord John Russell succeeds him as Prime Minister; Gladstone becomes Leader of the House.

Nov [12] The novelist Elizabeth Gaskell dies near Alton.

Dec [4] Edith Cavell, nurse and war heroine, is born at Swardeston. [30] Rudyard Kipling, story and verse writer, is born in Bombay.

1866 Thomas Barnardo opens his first home for destitute children. A cholera epidemic ravages Britain. The Sanitary Act empowers local authorities to take action in cases of nuisance caused by smoke.

Feb [24] Sir Arthur Pearson, newspaper owner, is born at Wookey.

Mar [29] John Keble, the clergyman who inspired the Oxford Movement, dies at Hursley.

May [24] Queen Victoria's son Albert is created Duke of Edinburgh.

Jun [28] Lord John Russell is succeeded by the Conservative Earl of Derby as Prime Minister.

Jul [5] Queen Victoria's daughter Princess Helena marries Prince Christian of Schleswig-Holstein. [28] Beatrix Potter, author and illustrator of children's books, is born in South Kensington.

Aug [6] The hymn writer John Neale dies at East Grinstead.

Sep [21] The author H. G. Wells is born in Bromley, Kent.

Oct [12] Ramsay MacDonald, the Labour Prime Minister, is born at Lossiemouth.

1867 George Grove and Arthur Sullivan visit Vienna and discover the music for Schubert's *Rosamunde*. Disraeli says, 'we do not, however, live - and I trust it will never be the fate of this country to live - under a democracy'. The London Conference guarantees the neutrality of Luxembourg. The British North America Act establishes the status of Canada as a British dominion; at this time Russia sells Alaska to the United States.

Jan [31] The completed Nelson's Column, with its statue and four lions, is unveiled in Trafalgar Square, London.

Feb [20] The Prince of Wales' daughter Louise is born.

Apr [18] Sir Robert Smirke, the architect who designed the façade of the British Museum, dies.

May [20] The foundation stone of the Royal Albert Hall is laid. [26] Queen Mary, the wife of George V, is born in Kensington Palace.

Jun [17] Joseph Lister performs the first operation under antiseptic conditions on his own sister, at Glasgow Infirmary.

Jul [1] Canada becomes a British dominion. [14] Alfred Nobel first demonstrates dynamite at Merstham Quarry, Redhill. [24] The author E. F. Benson is born.

Aug [3] Stanley Baldwin, Prime Minister, is born at Bewdley. [14] The novelist and playwright John Galsworthy is born in

Surrey. [15] Second Parliamentary Reform Bill; this measure
introduces household suffrage to all house-holders paying
rates and to lodgers who pay at least £10 a year in rent. [25]
Michael Faraday, scientist and inventor, dies at Hampton
Court.

1868 The Third Maori War begins in New Zealand. Sir Charles
Napier makes a dash across Abyssinia to rescue British
captives. The Trades Union Congress is founded. Sir William
Ramsay discovers helium.

Feb   [27] Lord Derby resigns as Prime Minister due to ill health.
       [29] The Conservative Benjamin Disraeli becomes Prime
       Minister.
Mar   [28] The Earl of Cardigan, who led the disastrous cavalry
       charge at the Battle of Balaklava in 1854, dies.
Apr   [10] The film actor George Arliss is born in London as George
       Andrews.
May   [26] The last public execution in Britain takes place outside
       Newgate Prison; Michael Barrett, the hanged man, had
       murdered 12 people with a bomb.
Jun   [2] The first Trades Union Congress opens in
       Manchester.
Jul   [6] The Prince of Wales' daughter Victoria is born.
Aug   [7] The composer Granville Bantock is born.
Oct   [21] Sir Ernest Swinton, one of the inventors of the military
       tank, is born in India.
Nov   Disraeli is defeated in a General Election.
Dec   [9] W. E. Gladstone (Liberal) becomes Prime Minister for the
       first time.

1869 A College for Women, afterwards called Girton College, is
founded at Cambridge. Mahatma Gandhi is born. The
science of eugenics is founded by the explorer and scientist
Sir Francis Galton. Gladstone becomes committed to
disestablishing the Anglican Church in Ireland, where the
nationalist movement is gaining in strength.

Mar [3] Sir Henry Wood, conductor and founder of the Promenade Concerts, is born in London. [18] Neville Chamberlain, Conservative Prime Minister, is born in Birmingham. [29] The architect Edwin Lutyens is born in London.

Jul [26] The Irish Episcopal Church is to be disestablished as from January 1, 1871.

Oct Elizabeth Siddal's coffin is dug up and opened so that Dante Gabriel Rossetti, who has changed his mind about the poems interred there, can retrieve them.

Nov [16] The opening of the Suez Canal revolutionizes communication between Britain and India. [26] The Prince of Wales' daughter Maud is born.

1870 The painters Monet and Pissarro take refuge in England; Tissot and Alma-Tadema also come to England. Married Women's Property Act; this measure extends the rights of women to property in marriage.

Feb [12] The music hall singer Marie Lloyd is born as Matilda Wood.

Apr [4] Peace Preservation Act; the Government increases its powers of repression to meet agrarian outrages, particularly in Ireland but also in England.

Jun [9] Charles Dickens dies at Godshill near Rochester.

Jul [27] The writer Hilaire Belloc is born at St Cloud near Paris.

Aug [9] Education Act; this provides for compulsory primary education in Britain, with the option of two types of school, voluntary (i.e. independent) and board (i.e. local authority) schools.

Oct [1] The postcard is officially introduced, together with a halfpenny postage stamp. [24] The aurora borealis, the northern lights, is seen in southern England; it appears in a rare arch shape.

1871 Britain annexes the diamond mines at Kimberley in South Africa. The first catering services are provided on British trains.

Jan [17] David Earl Beatty, the First World War admiral, is born at Nantwich. [26] The Rugby Football Union is founded.

Mar [21] Princess Louise marries John Marquis of Lorne, later Duke of Argyll. [27] The first Rugby International is played at Edinburgh: Scotland defeats England.

May [11] Sir John Herschel, astronomer and pioneer of celestial photography, dies. [29] Today, Whit Monday, is Britain's first Bank Holiday.

Jun University Tests Act; this measure allows students at Oxford and Cambridge to gain degrees and fellowships without subscribing to any religious tests or requirements. [29] Trades Unions are legalized.

Nov [2] Systematic photographing of convicted prisoners begins. [10] Stanley meets Livingstone at Ujiji on the shore of Lake Tanganyika; Livingstone is not aware that he is 'lost'.

Dec [14] George Hudson, the 'Railway King', dies.

1872 The expedition of HMS *Challenger* to study marine life and physiography in the Atlantic, Pacific and Indian Oceans; this marks the foundation of the science of oceanography. Lord Kelvin invents a machine for taking depth soundings at sea; this makes possible the detailed mapping of seabed features and opens the way to the discovery of the Mid-Atlantic Ridge. The Earl of Mayo, Viceroy of India, is assassinated. The National Agricultural Labourers' Union is founded by Joseph Arch, with the aim of getting better working conditions and pay for farm workers. Third Class passengers are now carried on all trains. The Ballot Act introduces the secret ballot in Britain. Scottish Education Act.

Mar [16] The first English FA Cup Final takes place; Wanderers (ex-public school and university men) beat the Royal

Engineers 1-0 at the Oval. [31] Arthur Griffith, President of the Irish Free State, is born.

May [18] The mathematician and philosopher Bertrand Russell is born. [31] The illustrator and humorist Heath Robinson is born.

Jul [12] Lord Birkenhead, Conservative politician and law reformer, is born as Frederick Smith.

Aug [24] The writer and caricaturist Max Beerbohm is born.

Sep [25] The theatrical impresario and producer C. B. Cochran is born at Lindfield.

Oct [12] The composer Ralph Vaughan Williams is born at Down Ampney.

1873 The Second Ashanti War breaks out in West Africa, in what is now Ghana. Refrigeration goes into industrial production. The first sleeping cars are provided on trains.

Jan [9] Napoleon III dies in exile at Chislehurst.

Feb The Irish Universities Bill, which seeks to unite Irish colleges into a single university open to Protestants and Catholics alike, is defeated in Parliament; Gladstone resigns. Disraeli is not prepared to take office with a minority administration, so Gladstone returns as Prime Minister. Judicature Act; Gladstone introduces major reforms to the law courts, consolidating the three common law courts into one supreme court of judicature, to consist of two main divisions: the High Court of Justice (Queen's Bench; Chancery; Probate, Divorce and Admiralty) and the Court of Appeal. [7] The journalist and author Sheridan Lefanu dies.

Mar [13] The Scottish Football Association is formed.

Apr [25] Walter de la Mare, poet and novelist, is born at Charlton.

May [1] David Livingstone, the explorer and missionary, is found dead at Chitambo, kneeling in prayer by his bed. [9] Howard Carter, the discoverer of Tutankhamun's tomb, is born at Swaffham.

Oct [1] Sir Edwin Landseer, painter, dies in London.

1874 The Second Ashanti War ends. The Gold Coast (later to be called Ghana) becomes a British colony. Fiji is annexed by Britain. The Prince of Wales visits France. Agricultural workers strike for higher pay in eastern England.

Jan [25] The writer William Somerset Maugham is born in Paris.
Feb [15] The explorer Sir Ernest Shackleton is born at Kilkee in County Clare. [20] Benjamin Disraeli succeeds Gladstone as Prime Minister. [23] The game of lawn tennis is patented by Major Walter Wingfield under the extraordinary name of 'Sphairistike'.
Apr [18] David Livingstone is buried in Westminster Abbey.
May [24] Prince Arthur is created Duke of Connaught. [29] G. K. Chesterton, writer, is born at Kensington.
Sep [21] The composer Gustav Holst is born at Cheltenham as Gustavus von Holst.
Nov [30] Sir Winston Churchill is born at Blenheim Palace, Oxfordshire.

1875 The agricultural depression deepens; the plight of the agricultural workers worsens, with significantly lower pay than the average factory worker. Peaceful picketing is allowed by legislation, and trade disputes are freed from charges of conspiracy. The Public Health Act codifies sanitary laws. The Artisans' Dwellings Act is designed to combat slum housing.

Jan [23] The writer Charles Kingsley dies in London.
Apr [1] *The Times* becomes the first newspaper to publish a daily weather chart. The thriller writer Edgar Wallace is born at Greenwich.
Aug [15] Samuel Coleridge-Taylor, composer, is born. [25] Captain Matthew Webb becomes the first to swim the English Channel; he takes 22 hours, using the breaststroke. [26] The politician and novelist John Buchan is born at Perth.
Nov [25] On his own initiative, Disraeli negotiates and buys a decisive portion of the Suez Canal shares, gaining a

controlling interest for Britain; Parliament afterwards gratefully ratifies his action.

1876 The telephone is invented by Scottish-born Alexander Graham Bell. The art critic John Ruskin makes an outspoken denunciation of Whistler's *The Falling Rocket*; as a result, Whistler brings a libel action against Ruskin. Massacres of Christians in Turkish-occupied Bulgaria provoke anti-Turkish reaction in Britain. The Purcell Society is formed. The painter Gwen John is born. The Merchant Shipping Act is designed to prevent overloading and the use of unseaworthy vessels; this important measure results from the efforts of Samuel Plimsoll, 'the sailor's friend'.

Jan [**29**] The composer Havergal Brian is born.

Mar [**25**] The first Scotland v. Wales football international is played at Glasgow: Scotland wins.

Apr Royal Titles Bill. This measure declaring the Queen Empress of India flatters the Queen and proves to be very popular in India. Opposition to the new title as 'un-English' is met by the promise that it will not be used in Britain.

Aug Disraeli is created Earl of Beaconsfield. Charles Stanford and Hubert Parry see the first production of Wagner's 'Ring' cycle at Bayreuth.

1877 The Transvaal is annexed to the British Empire. The first shipment of frozen meat from Argentina reaches Britain, a landmark in international trade. Sir Henry Stanley traces the River Congo (Zaire).

Jan [**1**] Queen Victoria is declared Empress of India.

Mar [**15**] The first cricket Test Match takes place, when Australia play England at Melbourne - and win. [**24**] The only dead-heat in the history of the Oxford-Cambridge Boat Race takes place.

May Richard Wagner is in London to conduct six concerts of his music at the Royal Albert Hall. He stays in Bayswater, and

meets Browning, George Eliot, Queen Victoria and the
Prince of Wales.

Jun   [24] The Ambulance Association, later to become St John's
Ambulance Brigade, is formed.

Jul   [19] The first men's Wimbledon tennis final takes place: it is
won by Spencer Gore.

Sep   [17] The pioneer of photography, William Fox Talbot, dies at
Lacock Abbey, Wiltshire.

Oct   [10] Lord Nuffield, the car manufacturer, is born.

Nov   [13] There is a demonstration by socialist marchers, including
Annie Besant, in Trafalgar Square; there are violent clashes
with mounted police and guardsmen.

1878 H. J. Lawson invents the modern safety bicycle. Joseph
Swan demonstrates the first reliable filament electric lamp.
David Edward Hughes invents the microphone.
Eadweard Muybridge begins to publish his famous multiple
exposure photographs of people and animals in motion.
John Ruskin loses the libel action brought against him by
Whistler, who is awarded damages of one farthing. The
Criminal Investigation Department of Scotland Yard is
established. Lord Derby resigns as Foreign Minister and is
succeeded by Lord Salisbury. Factory and Workshop Act.
The Second Afghan War begins; Britain tries to secure her
position in India by stopping Russian expansion into
Afghanistan.

Jan   [4] The painter Augustus John is born at Tenby. [14] The
newly-invented telephone is demonstrated to Queen Victoria
at Osborne House. [23] The composer Rutland Boughton is
born at Aylesbury.

Apr   [25] The author Anna Sewell dies.

Jun   [1] The Poet Laureate John Masefield is born at Ledbury.

Jul   [12] Turkey cedes Cyprus to Britain.

Sep   [12] 'Cleopatra's Needle', an ancient Egyptian obelisk in red
granite and made originally for Thothmes III in 1460 BC, is
re-erected on the Thames Embankment.

Oct [14] The first football match played under floodlights takes place at Sheffield.

1879 The Zulu War; Britain declares war on Cetewayo, the Zulu leader. The British are defeated at Isandhlwana, but win at Ulundi and succeed in capturing Cetewayo. The frontier between India and Afghanistan is fixed by the Treaty of Gandamak. Charles Parnell mobilizes the Irish nationalists and aims to reform the Irish Land Law. The severe agricultural depression in Britain continues. The painter Matthew Smith is born.

Jan [1] The novelist E. M. Forster is born in London. [18] The first England v. Wales football international is played at the Oval: England win. [22] Battle of Rorke's Drift; a handful of British soldiers under Lieutenants Chard and Bromhead heroically and successfully resist a huge Zulu army.
Feb [26] The composer John Ireland is born.
Apr [29] The conductor Sir Thomas Beecham is born at St Helens.
May [19] Lady Astor, the first woman to sit in the House of Commons, is born in Virginia. [25] The newspaper proprietor Lord Beaverbrook is born in Canada as Max Aitken.
Aug [27] Sir Rowland Hill, the pioneer of the postal service, dies.
Sep [18] Blackpool's first annual illumination begins.
Dec [4] The Irish composer Hamilton Harty is born. [28] The Tay Bridge disaster; the railway bridge designed by Thomas Bouch collapses, carrying the Edinburgh-Dundee train and its passengers down into the Firth of Tay. About 90 people are killed. [30] The first performance of *The Pirates of Penzance* takes place at Torquay.

1880 The Second Afghan War ends. The Transvaal is declared a republic. Parliament ends the confusion over time conflicts resulting from each town using 'sun' time, by ordering the whole country to set its clocks by Greenwich Mean Time. Relief of Distress Act for Ireland.

Jan [15] The first telephone directory is published by the London
     Telephone company: it contains 255 entries.
Feb [2] The first frozen meat arrives in Britain from Australia
     aboard the SS *Strathleven*.
Apr [23] Disraeli is succeeded as Prime Minister by Gladstone
     (Gladstone's second ministry). Charles Bradlaugh, a
     newly-elected MP, refuses to take the oath on the grounds
     that he is an atheist; he asks to affirm instead, but this is not
     accepted.
Sep [6] The first cricket Test Match to be played in Britain takes
     place between England and Australia at the Oval.
     [13] The first Employers' Liability Act provides
     compensation for workers for injuries that are not their
     own fault. [22] The suffragette Christabel Pankhurst is
     born.
Nov [10] The sculptor Jacob Epstein is born in New York.
Dec [22] The novelist George Eliot dies at Chelsea.

1881 At Folkestone, work on the Channel Tunnel begins but stops
     again after only 879 yards. A Smoke Abatement Committee
     is formed in reaction to the increasing nuisance from factory
     chimneys in British towns and cities. The Affirmation Bill,
     designed to allow Charles Bradlaugh to take his seat in the
     Commons, is defeated for the first time. The Land Act is
     designed to meet Irish demands for fair rents and fixity of
     tenure, but it proves unpopular with both landlords and
     tenants. Flogging is abolished in the army and Navy. The
     Savoy Theatre in London is opened. The painter Samuel
     Palmer dies. British troops are defeated by Boers at Majuba;
     the independence of the Transvaal is recognized at the Treaty
     of Pretoria.

Jan [1] Postal orders are issued for the first time.
Feb [5] The historian Thomas Carlyle dies at 5 Cheyne Row,
     Chelsea.
Mar [9] Ernest Bevin, Labour politician, is born at
     Winsford.

Apr   [19] Benjamin Disraeli dies; the date becomes known as 'Primrose Day' from his liking for the flower.

May   [24] Queen Victoria's son Prince Leopold is created Duke of Albany. [28] There is a very severe thunderstorm at Worcester, with a heavy fall of hailstones and periwinkles.

Jul   [26] The writer George Borrow dies.

Aug   [6] Sir Alexander Fleming, discoverer of penicillin, is born.

Oct   [13] Parnell and others are sent to Kilmainham Gaol for inciting Irishmen to intimidate tenants who are trying to take legitimate advantage of the Land Act. [14] Fishing disaster at Eyemouth in south-east Scotland; 189 haddock fishermen die in a storm after being lured out to the fishing grounds by fair weather in the morning. [15] The writer P. G. Wodehouse is born at Guildford, Surrey.

1882 British forces bombard Alexandria; the French withdraw and Egypt becomes a British colony. Queen Victoria gives Epping Forest to the nation. The Primrose League is founded. Wagner's 'Ring', in the Leipzig production, is given for the first time in Britain at Her Majesty's Theatre in London under the baton of Anton Seidl. The painter Wyndham Lewis is born.

Jan   [18] A. A. Milne, creator of 'Winnie the Pooh', is born at St John's Wood. [25] The novelist Virginia Woolf is born in London.

Feb   [2] James Joyce, writer, is born in Dublin. [15] The first shipment of frozen meat from New Zealand arrives in Britain aboard SS *Dunedin*. [25] The first Wales-Ireland football international takes place at Wrexham: Wales win.

Mar   [2] R. MacLean makes an attempt to assassinate Queen Victoria at Windsor. [4] The first electric tramcars are seen in London.

Apr   [19] Charles Darwin dies. [24] Lord Dowding, responsible for victory in the Battle of Britain, is born at Moffat.

May [2] Charles Parnell is released when he agrees in the 'Kilmainham Treaty' to stop 'boycotting'. [6] Lord Frederick Cavendish, Irish Secretary, and Thomas Burke, Under-Secretary, are murdered in Phoenix Park by Fenians; Parnell dissociates himself from the killings.

Jul Prevention of Crimes Act; limited to three years, this measure suspends trial by jury and gives the police unlimited powers of search. Irish extremists resort to a campaign of terrorism.

Sep [14] British troops occupy Cairo.

Oct [14] Eamon de Valera, Prime Minister and President of the Irish Republic, is born in New York. [24] The actress Sybil Thorndike is born at Gainsborough.

Dec [1] Archbishop Tait dies. [6] The novelist Anthony Trollope dies in London. [16] The cricketer Jack Hobbs is born at Cambridge.

1883 Sir Joseph Swan produces the first synthetic fibre. Britain occupies Egypt. British forces begin evacuating the Sudan. The Royal College of Music is opened under the direction of George Grove. The Corrupt and Illegal Practices Act limits spending by political parties and individuals in general elections. The Affirmation Bill is defeated in Parliament a second time.

Jan [3] Clement Attlee, Labour Prime Minister, is born at Putney. [17] Compton Mackenzie, writer, is born at West Hartlepool as Edward Compton.

Mar [3] Edward Benson, Bishop of Truro, becomes Archbishop of Canterbury. [14] The social and political philosopher, Karl Marx, dies in London.

Jun [14] The poet Edward Fitzgerald dies in Suffolk.

Aug [1] Parcel post is introduced. [27] The eruption of Krakatoa between Sumatra and Java causes spectacular red sunsets in Britain for several weeks.

Sep [18] Lord Berners, composer, painter and writer, is born.

Oct [4] The Boys' Brigade is founded in Glasgow by Sir William Smith.

Nov [8] The composer Arnold Bax is born.

1884 Sir Charles Parsons devises his steam turbine, which revolutionizes steam engineering. Friese-Green invents the cine camera. There is a rising against the British in the Sudan, led by a charismatic leader, the Mahdi. General Gordon is sent to Khartoum to rescue the Egyptian garrison; Gordon himself is trapped and besieged at Khartoum, and an expedition headed by Wolseley is sent to rescue Gordon. The Greenwich Meridian is adopted internationally as the prime meridian, from which longitude is to be measured. The Fabian Society is formed.

Jan [28] The first Ireland v. Scotland football international takes place at Belfast: Scotland win.

Mar [13] Sir Hugh Walpole, novelist, is born at Auckland, New Zealand. [28] Leopold, Duke of Albany dies. [30] Sean O'Casey, playwright, is born.

Apr [5] John Wisden, cricketer and compiler of Wisden record books, dies in London. [11] The novelist Charles Reade dies.

Apr [22] An earthquake in the Colchester area kills four people.

Jun [14] The singer John McCormack is born at Athlone.

Dec The Franchise Act (or Third Parliamentary Reform Act) opens the franchise to almost all adult males, although domestic servants, bachelors living with their parents, and those of no fixed address are not to be given the vote. This measure adds two million voters, four times the number added in 1832.

1885 The Third Anglo-Burmese War; Burma is formally annexed by Britain. Bechuanaland in southern Africa becomes a British colony. The first public labour exchanges are established. The office of Secretary of State for Scotland is created. Sir James Dewar invents the vacuum flask.

Jan [26] The Mahdi takes Khartoum; General Gordon is killed by a spear flung by a Muslim soldier.

Mar [11] Sir Malcolm Campbell, racing driver, is born at
Chislehurst. [26] The composer Julius Harrison is born. The
first cremation in Britain in modern times takes place at
Woking Crematorium.
Jun [9] Gladstone resigns after a hostile amendment to his
budget. [24] The Conservative Robert Cecil, Lord Salisbury,
becomes Prime Minister.
Jul [12] The composer George Butterworth is born.
Aug The Ashbourne Act provides a £5 million fund for
low-interest loans to Irish tenants, enabling them to buy their
holdings.
Sep [11] The poet and novelist D. H. Lawrence is born at
Eastwood.
Dec Gladstone is converted to the idea of Home Rule for
Ireland.

1886 Upper Burma is annexed by Britain. Kenya becomes a British
colony. Gold is discovered in the Transvaal. The Severn
Tunnel is opened.
Jan Charles Bradlaugh takes the oath and his seat as an MP.
[1] Edwin Bartlett dies, apparently poisoned with
chloroform; his wife Adelaide is later acquitted of his murder,
but under grave suspicion. She disappears after the trial. [20]
The Mersey Railway Tunnel is formally opened by the Prince
of Wales.
Feb [1] Lord Salisbury resigns. [12] Gladstone becomes Prime
Minister for the third time.
Mar [10] The first Cruft's Dog Show is held in London.
Apr The first Home Rule Bill is introduced.
Jul The Home Rule Bill is defeated in the Commons, leading to a
call for a General Election. [23] Sir Arthur Brown, the aviator
who will co-pilot the first transatlantic flight, is born in
Glasgow. [26] Gladstone is succeeded as Prime Minister by
the Conservative Lord Salisbury, after the failure of the
Home Rule Bill.
Aug [22] The composer Eric Coates is born.

Nov [8] Fred Archer, the champion jockey, shoots himself at his house in Newmarket at the age of 29.

1887 Zululand is annexed by Britain. Baluchistan is united with India.

Jan [1] Queen Victoria is proclaimed Empress of India in Delhi. [22] Sir Joseph Whitworth, the engineer who standardized screw threads, dies at Monte Carlo.
Jun [21] Queen Victoria's Jubilee celebrations.
Aug [3] The poet Rupert Brooke is born at Rugby. [14] The writer Richard Jefferies dies.
Sep [26] Barnes Wallis, inventor and designer of aircraft and specialized bombs, is born.
Nov [1] The artist L. S. Lowry is born at Rusholme. [17] Viscount Montgomery, army commander in the Second World War, is born in Kensington. [23] Boris Karloff, the film actor, is born at Dulwich as William Pratt.

1888 North Borneo, Brunei and Sarawak are established as British protectorates. John Boyd Dunlop invents an improved pneumatic tyre with a rubber outer casing and an air-filled inner tube inflated through a valve: the first modern inflatable tyre. The *Great Eastern* is broken up on Merseyside. The Miners' Federation of Great Britain is founded, a landmark in the development of trade-unionism. The Local Government Act sets up County Councils. The Affirmation Act is finally established, thanks to the efforts of Charles Bradlaugh; it removes the last remaining religious disability for membership of the House of Commons.

Jan [3] The politician Herbert Morrison is born at Lambeth.
Feb [8] Dame Edith Evans, actress, is born in London.
Mar [22] The English Football League is formed.
Apr [15] The writer Matthew Arnold dies suddenly at Liverpool.
May [31] Naval Defence Act, designed to meet the growing sea-power of France and Russia.

Aug   [7] A Whitechapel prostitute, Martha Tabram, is murdered
       with 29 stab wounds; no one is arrested for the crime. [13]
       John Logie Baird, inventor of television, is born at
       Helensburgh. [15] T. E. Lawrence (of Arabia) is born at
       Tremadoc. [31] Mary Ann Nicholls is murdered at
       Whitechapel by Jack the Ripper.
Sep   [8] Annie Chapman is murdered by Jack the Ripper. [26] The
       poet T. S. Eliot is born at St Louis in Missouri. [29]The
       Central News Agency receives the 'Dear Boss' letter from
       Jack the Ripper (first use of the name); during the following
       night prostitutes Elizabeth Stride and Catherine Eddowes are
       murdered. There is widespread panic in the East End of
       London.
Nov   [9] Mary Kelly, the last of Jack the Ripper's victims, is
       murdered.
Dec   [23] The film magnate J. Arthur Rank is born at Hull.
       [31] The body of Montague Druitt, a prominent suspect
       in the Ripper murder inquiry, is found floating in the
       Thames.

1889 Sir Frederick Abel invents cordite. The London County
       Council is formed. The Board of Agriculture is created. The
       Socialist battle song, 'The Red Flag', is written in London
       following the dock strike. The painter Paul Nash is born.
Mar   [27] John Bright, the reformer who worked with Richard
       Cobden for the repeal of the Corn Laws, dies.
Apr   [8] The conductor Sir Adrian Boult is born at Chester. [16]
       Charlie Chaplin is born at Kennington in London. [24] The
       Labour politician Sir Stafford Cripps is born.
Jul   [4] The police are alerted to the use of 19 Cleveland Street,
       London as a homosexual brothel; the names of several
       aristocrats, including that of Lord Arthur Somerset, are
       drawn into the scandal.
Aug   [7] Florence Maybrick is condemned to death for poisoning
       her husband; the sentence is later commuted to life
       imprisonment. [15] The London dock strike begins.

Sep [16] The dock strike ends. [23] The novelist Wilkie Collins dies in London.
Oct [11] James Joule, who established the first law of thermodynamics, dies.
Nov [10] The character actor Claude Rains is born in London.
Dec [12] The poet Robert Browning dies in Venice.

1890 The United States overtakes Britain in steel production. The City and South London Line is the first deep underground railway line in London. Free elementary (i.e. primary) education is established. Charles Parnell is cited in a divorce case and forced to resign. The painter David Bomberg is born. The publication of Sir James Frazer's *The Golden Bough* is a landmark in the development of anthropology and psychology.

Feb [25] The pianist Dame Myra Hess is born in London.
Mar [4] The Forth Bridge, the longest bridge (so far) in Britain, is opened by the Prince of Wales.
May [7] James Nasmyth, inventor of the first steam hammer, dies. [17] The first comic paper, *Comic Cuts*, is published. [24] The Prince of Wales' son Albert is created Duke of Clarence.
Jun [16] Stan Laurel, comedian, is born at Ulverston as Arthur Stanley Jefferson.
Jul [21] Battersea Bridge is opened by Lord Rosebery.
Aug [11] Cardinal Newman, leader of the Oxford Movement, dies at Edgbaston aged 89.
Sep [15] Agatha Christie, crime writer, is born. [24] The writer and MP A. P. Herbert is born.
Oct [1] The entertainer Stanley Holloway is born in London. [20] Sir Richard Burton, explorer and writer, dies; his wife Isabel builds a bonfire of his unpublished manuscripts, some 28 complete works including his private journal, thus destroying a large body of scholarship.

1891 Joseph Chamberlain becomes leader of the Liberal Unionists in the Commons. The Liberal Party advocates Irish Home Rule, the disestablishment of the Welsh Church, 3-year Parliaments, and reform of the House of Lords. The Public Health (London) Act seeks to control factory chimney emissions in the capital. Oscar Wilde's *Picture of Dorian Gray* typifies the brilliant decadence of the 1890s. The painter Stanley Spencer is born.

Feb [9] Film star Ronald Colman is born at Richmond, Surrey.

Aug [2] The composer Sir Arthur Bliss is born.

Oct [6] Charles Stewart Parnell, Irish politician, dies at Brighton. W. H. Smith, the newsagent and bookseller, dies. [8] The first street collection for charity takes place in Manchester, for Lifeboat Day. [20] Sir James Chadwick, discoverer of the neutron, is born in Manchester.

1892 Charles Cross and E. Bevan produce viscose, which leads to the manufacture of rayon. The socialist leader Keir Hardie becomes the first Labour MP.

Jan [14] The eldest son of the Prince of Wales, Albert Duke of Clarence, dies.

Apr [13] Sir Arthur Harris, wartime bomber commander, is born. [19] Producer-Director Herbert Wilcox is born in Cork, Ireland.

May Oscar Wilde falls in love with Lord Alfred Douglas. [11] The actress Margaret Rutherford is born. [23] Broad gauge railway tracks are finally abandoned in Britain. [24] The second son of the Prince of Wales, George, is created Duke of York.

Jul [18] The pioneer travel agent Thomas Cook dies.

Oct [6] Lord Tennyson, Poet Laureate for the last 42 years, dies at Aldworth in Surrey.

Nov [6] The aviator Sir John Alcock is born at Manchester.

1893 Natal is granted self-government. The Imperial Institute in South Kensington is founded. The Liverpool Overhead Railway is opened, the first such railway to run on electricity from its inception. The painter Ivon Hitchens is born.

Jan The Independent Labour Party is formed under the chairmanship of Keir Hardie.

Feb [4] The first stretch of the Liverpool Overhead Railway (Alexandra Dock to Herculaneum Dock) is opened by Lord Salisbury. [13] The second Home Rule Bill is introduced.

Apr [24] Film actor Leslie Howard is born in London.

Jun [13] Dorothy Sayers, academic and writer of detective novels, is born at Oxford. [22] HMS *Victoria*, the Royal Navy's flagship, is rammed and sunk by HMS *Camperdown* as a result of a misunderstood order.

Jul [6] George V marries Princess Mary of Teck.

Sep [1] The second Home Rule Bill passes its third Commons reading. [8] The Home Rule Bill is rejected by the Lords. [16] The film producer Sir Alexander Korda is born in Hungary.

Oct [28] The Royal Navy's first destroyer, HMS *Havoc*, goes on its trials.

1894 Uganda becomes a British protectorate. Aubrey Beardsley becomes art editor of *The Yellow Book*. Argon is discovered by Sir William Ramsay and Baron Rayleigh.

Jan [1] The Manchester Ship Canal is opened to traffic.

Feb [10] Harold Macmillan, Lord Stockton, Conservative Prime Minister, is born in London.

Mar [3] Gladstone resigns after splitting his party over Irish Home Rule; he is succeeded by Lord Rosebery as Prime Minister.

May [6] The aviator Sir Alan Cobham is born.

Jun [23] Edward VIII is born at Richmond. There is a pit disaster at Cilfynydd in South Wales with the loss of 286 lives. [30] Tower Bridge is officially opened.

Aug [2] Death duties are introduced.

Sep [13] The author J. B. Priestley is born at Bradford. [28] The first branch of Marks and Spencer (Penny Bazaar) opens at

Cheetham Hill in Manchester. [30] The composer Peter
Warlock is born as Philip Heseltine.

Dec   [3] Robert Louis Stevenson, author of *Treasure Island*, dies on
the island of Samoa in the Pacific.

1895 Uganda becomes a British colony. The National Trust is
founded; the first property to be taken into care is the Clergy
House, Alfriston. Work begins on Westminster (Roman
Catholic) Cathedral, designed by John Bentley; it is the last
great building in Britain to be constructed in brick without
steel reinforcement.

Jan   [24] The Conservative Party leader Randolph Churchill dies.

Mar   [15] Bridget Clary, aged 27, is burned to death for witchcraft
at Battyradhen in County Tipperary.

Apr   [26] Oscar Wilde's first trial opens. [29] The conductor Sir
Malcolm Sargent is born.

May [15] Joseph Whitaker, the publisher who founded *Whitaker's
Almanack*, dies. [24] The first stage knighthood is awarded, to
Henry Irving. [25] Oscar Wilde's second trial ends; he is
sentenced to two years' hard labour.

Jun   [25] The Liberal Lord Rosebery resigns, to be succeeded by
the Conservative Lord Salisbury as Prime Minister (third
ministry).

Oct   [6] The Promenade Concerts are founded by Sir Henry
Wood. [15] The first motor show takes place, at the
Agricultural Show Ground at Tunbridge Wells.

Dec   [1] The writer Henry Williamson is born. [14] George VI, the
second son of George V, is born at Sandringham in Norfolk.
[29] The Jameson Raid into the Boer colony of Transvaal in
support of the Uitlanders, the European settlers; Sir Leander
Starr Jameson's attack on the Boers is unsuccessful.

1896 William Ramsay discovers helium. Cecil Rhodes relinquishes
the premiership of Cape Colony. Anglo-Egyptian forces
under General Kitchener begin the reconquest of the Sudan.
Tsar Nicholas II visits London.

Jan [3] The Kruger Telegram; Kaiser Wilhelm of Germany
sends a telegram to President Kruger of the Transvaal
congratulating him on defeating the British raiders led by
Jameson in his 'Raid'. This leads to an outburst of
indignation and anti-German feeling in Britain.
[19] Sir Michael Balcon, film producer, is born in
Birmingham.

Mar [22] Thomas Hughes, author of *Tom Brown's Schooldays*,
dies.

May [4] The *Daily Mail* is founded by Lord Northcliffe.

Jun [19] Bessie Wallis Warfield, later Duchess of Windsor, is born
in Pennsylvania.

Jul [19] The novelist A. J. Cronin is born at Cardross.

Aug [13] Sir John Millais, painter, dies.

Oct [3] The artist, designer and craftsman William Morris dies.
[11] Archbishop Benson dies while staying with Gladstone at
Hawarden.

Nov [16] Sir Oswald Mosley, leader of the Fascist movement in
Britain, is born.

Dec [22] Frederick Temple, Bishop of London, becomes
Archbishop of Canterbury.

1897 Sir J. J. Thomson discovers the electron. Ronald Ross
demonstrates that malaria is transmitted by the
mosquito. The first all-corridor train runs from London to
Glasgow.

Jan [8] The novelist Dennis Wheatley is born. [12] Sir Isaac
Pitman dies in Somerset.

Mar [17] Bob Fitzsimmons becomes the only British-born
boxer ever to win the world heavyweight boxing
title.

Apr [25] George V's daughter Mary is born.

May [19] Oscar Wilde is released from Pentonville Prison.
[22] The Blackwall Tunnel under the Thames is officially
opened by the Prince of Wales. [27] Sir John Cockcroft,
nuclear physicist, is born.

Jun   [12] Sir Anthony Eden, Lord Avon, the Conservative Prime Minister, is born at Bishop Auckland. Leon Goossens, oboist, is born in Liverpool.

Jun   [22] Queen Victoria's Diamond Jubilee celebrations coincide with the peak of Britain's imperialist ambitions.

Aug   [10] The Automobile Club of Great Britain, later to become the R.A.C., is founded. [11] Enid Blyton, writer of children's books, is born at Dulwich.

Sep   [10] George Smith, a London taxi-driver, is convicted of drunken driving; he is the first motorist to be so convicted.

Nov   [15] The Labour Party leader Aneurin Bevan is born at Tredegar.

1898   The Folksong Society is formed. The painter Sir Edward Burne-Jones dies. John P. Holland invents the submarine.

Jan   [9] The entertainer Gracie Fields is born at Rochdale. [14] Lewis Carroll dies at Guildford.

May   [19] William Ewart Gladstone, four times Prime Minister, dies at Hawarden Castle in North Wales aged 88.

Jun   [9] Hong Kong's New Territories are leased by Britain from China for 99 years.

Jul   [30] The sculptor Henry Moore is born at Castleford.

Aug   [13] Alfred Hitchcock, film producer, is born at Leytonstone.

Sep   [2] Battle of Omdurman; Kitchener's Anglo-Egyptian forces defeat the Khalifa's army, winning back the Sudan for Egypt. [19] Kitchener reaches Fashoda and finds the French under Major Marchand in occupation. [24] Sir Howard Florey, pioneer of penicillin production, is born in Australia.

1899   The Coal Smoke Abatement Society is founded. Rutherford identifies alpha and beta rays. The Board of Education and the London Borough Councils are created.

Jan   [19] The Anglo-Egyptian Convention establishes what becomes known as Anglo-Egyptian Sudan.

Mar [5] The composer Patrick Hadley is born. [21] A Convention
     between Britain and France confirms that France is excluded
     from the Sudan and Egypt.
Jul [1] Charles Laughton, actor, is born.
Aug [27] The novelist C. S. Forester is born in Cairo.
Sep [29] Billy Butlin, the holiday camp owner, is born in South
     Africa.
Oct [10] The Boer War begins between the British and the
     republics of the Orange Free State and the Transvaal.
Nov [2] The Siege of Ladysmith in west Natal begins; British
     troops are surrounded by Transvaal forces. [24] Wingate's
     forces pursue and kill the Khalifa in the Sudan.
Dec [2] The conductor Sir John Barbirolli is born in London. [5]
     Sir Henry Tate, philanthropist and founder of the Tate
     Gallery, dies aged 80. [10] Sir Noel Coward, actor,
     playwright, songwriter, is born at Teddington.

1900

1900 The Dunlop Rubber Company produces its first pneumatic
     motor tyre. Sir Patrick Manson identifies the anopheles
     mosquito as the carrier of malaria. The British Labour Party is
     founded by combining the Independent Labour Party, the
     Fabian Society and the Trade Unions.
Jan [3] The new royal yacht *Victoria and Albert* capsizes as it
     embarks. [6] General White repels an attack by the Boers on
     Ladysmith. [9] In the influenza epidemic in London people
     are dying at the rate of 50 a day. [10] Field Marshal Lord
     Roberts arrives in Cape Town to take command of the British
     forces in South Africa. [20] The artist and writer John Ruskin
     dies at Coniston. The novelist R. D. Blackmore also dies. [24]
     Battle of Spion Kop; Sir Redvers Buller's troops are repulsed
     with severe losses. [28] The composer Michael Head is born.
Feb [12] A meeting at Mile End to protest against the Boer
     War ends in uproar. [15] The Relief of Kimberley.

The Hippodrome Theatre in Charing Cross Road opens. [28] Relief of Ladysmith by Sir Redvers Buller's troops.

Mar [8] Queen Victoria makes a rare visit to London, greeted by an enthusiastic welcome from the public. [23] Sir Arthur Evans begins his historic dig at Knossos. [31] George V's son Henry is created Duke of Gloucester.

Apr [4] The Prince of Wales escapes unhurt when a boy fires a gun at him twice in Brussels, apparently in protest at the Boer War.

May [17] Relief of Mafeking after a Boer siege lasting 217 days. 26,000 women and children die in concentration camps set up by the British for Boer civilians. [22] The age limit for boys working in coal mines is raised from 12 to 13.

Jun [25] Earl Louis Mountbatten is born at Frogmore, Isle of Wight.

Jul [22] 11 people die when the *Campania* runs down a smaller vessel in the Thames estuary.

Aug [4] Queen Elizabeth, the Queen Mother, is born in Hertfordshire as Lady Elizabeth Bowes Lyon.

Sep [1] General Roberts annexes the Boer republic of Transvaal. [2] There are demonstrations in Dublin against British rule. [3] There is an outbreak of bubonic plague in Glasgow. [9] James Hilton, author of *Lost Horizon*, is born at Leigh in Lancashire.

Oct [3] Sir Edward Elgar's *Dream of Gerontius* is first performed at Birmingham.

Nov [22] The composer Sir Arthur Sullivan dies. [30] Oscar Wilde dies in poverty in Paris as Sebastian Melmoth.

Dec [11] Lord Roberts leaves South Africa to return to England. [22] The composer Alan Bush is born. [30] 50 people die as gales sweep across Britain. [31] At Stonehenge, Stone 22 and its lintel fall down.

1901 J. Langley demonstrates the effect of adrenalin in speeding up the heart rate. The composer Edmund Rubbra is born. The vacuum cleaner invented by Cecil Booth.

Jan	[1] The six states and two territories are federated to form the Commonwealth of Australia. [8] 12 retailers are prosecuted for selling beer containing arsenic. [22] Queen Victoria dies at Osborne House aged 81, the longest reigning monarch and longest lived of all British monarchs. [27] Edward VII, the new King, makes his nephew the Kaiser a Field Marshal in the British army.
Feb	[2] Queen Victoria's funeral. [15] Edward VII resigns as Grand Master of Freemasons.
Mar	[23] Reports that Boers are starving in British concentration camps begin to leak out.
Apr	[3] Richard D'Oyly Carte, impresario responsible for staging the Gilbert and Sullivan operettas, dies. [4] The liner *Celtic* is launched at Belfast. [21] Lillie Langtry opens as Marie Antoinette in *A Royal Necklace* at the Imperial Theatre. [30] The game of ping pong is created by James Gibb.
May	[13] Lord Salisbury speaks out against the idea of Irish Home Rule. [15] The Admiralty decides to build three huge battleships. [16] Britain's first diesel submarine, *D1*, is launched at Barrow.
Jun	[17] David Lloyd George denounces the high death rate among Boer women and children in the prison camps in South Africa. [26] The liner *Lusitania* is wrecked off Newfoundland: 350 are rescued.
Jul	[9] The novelist Barbara Cartland is born. [22] The British Congress on Tuberculosis begins.
Aug	[1] The Commons vote an extra £12 million for naval and war budgets.
Sep	[15] The yachtsman Sir Francis Chichester is born at Barnstaple. [18] A torpedo boat sinks at Grimsby, drowning 59 people. [26] An outbreak of smallpox begins to spread.
Oct	[2] The first Royal Navy submarine, *Holland I*, is launched at Barrow. [6] Sir Henry Irving and Ellen Terry leave for a US tour. [25] Joseph Chamberlain gives an anti-German speech and defends the Boer camps.

Nov [6] Kate Greenaway, illustrator, dies. [9] Edward VII's eldest
surviving son George is created Prince of Wales. [12] 200
people are killed in gales. [15] The death rate in refugee
camps for Boer families continues to rise, partly due to a
measles epidemic; charges of neglect and brutality are
rejected by an official report.

Dec [12] The first transatlantic wireless (radio) signal, the letter S,
is sent from Poldhu in Cornwall and received by Marconi at
St John's in Newfoundland. [18] Lloyd George is forced to
leave a pro-Boer meeting as a riot breaks out.

1902 Ernest Rutherford proposes the disintegration theory to
explain radioactivity. Sinn Fein (Ourselves Alone) is founded
by the Irish republican Arthur Griffith to
promote the cause of Home Rule for Ireland. Sir Ronald
Ross is awarded the Nobel Prize for Physiology and
Medicine.

Jan [28] The census shows that London's population has reached
6.5 million. [30] Anglo-Japanese Alliance formed. [31] The
number of smallpox victims in London rises to 2273.

Feb [13] The Government refuses to allow a German committee
to visit the South African concentration camps. [14] In a
speech, Lord Rosebery declares that he will never give
Ireland its independence.

Mar [26] Cecil Rhodes dies. [28] The actress Dame Flora Robson is
born. [29] The composer Sir William Walton is born at
Oldham.

Apr [1] The treadmill is abolished in prisons. [20] The actor Sir
Donald Wolfit is born at Newark-on-Trent.

May [24] Empire Day is celebrated for the first time. [29] Lord
Rosebery opens the London School of Economics. [31] The
Treaty of Vereeniging ends the Boer War; the Transvaal and
Orange Free State accept British sovereignty and Britain
provides £3 million to repair war damage.

Jun [10] Ellen Terry and Beerbohm Tree open in *The Merry Wives
of Windsor* at His Majesty's Theatre. [18] The novelist Samuel

Butler dies. [23] Edward VII founds the Order of Merit. [30] Lillie Langtry marries the MP Ian Malcolm.

Jul [7] Joseph Chamberlain is involved in a hansom cab accident: he suffers a deep head wound. [12] The Conservative Arthur Balfour becomes Prime Minister. Lord Kitchener returns to London from South Africa: he is given a triumphal welcome.

Aug [9] Coronation of Edward VII, which has been delayed six weeks by the King's appendicitis operation.

Sep [13] The first conviction on fingerprint evidence is secured by the Metropolitan Police, in a case against Harry Jackson. [19] Stanley Spencer makes a 30 mile flight in an airship of his own design.

Oct [16] The first Borstal Institution opens, at Borstal near Rochester.

Nov [8] The Kaiser arrives in London in an attempt to improve Anglo-German relations.

Dec [9] The Conservative politician R. A. Butler is born in India. [19] The actor Sir Ralph Richardson is born at Cheltenham. [20] George VI, son of George V, is born. [22] Archbishop Temple dies.

1903 Letchworth, the first garden city, is begun, to designs by Parker and Unwin.

Jan [10] The sculptor Barbara Hepworth is born at Wakefield. [27] 51 people die in a fire at a mental hospital at Colney Hatch.

Feb [6] Randall Davidson, Bishop of Winchester, becomes Archbishop of Canterbury. [21] It rains 'blood' in southern England; the rain is coloured by dust from the Sahara. [24] A British field force marches on the 'Mad' Mullah from Obbiah on the Indian Ocean.

Mar [22] Dean Farrar, clergyman and author of *Eric, or Little by Little*, dies. [29] A regular news service begins between New York and London using Marconi's wireless.

Apr [23] The Government reveals that the Boer and Boxer Wars cost one-third of the United Kingdom's annual budget.

May	[1] Edward VII arrives in Paris on a goodwill visit. [5] Foreign Secretary Lord Lansdowne declares that the Persian Gulf is the western frontier of India. [12] The actor Wilfrid Hyde White and the composer Sir Lennox Berkeley are born. [29] The comedian Bob Hope is born at Eltham as Leslie Townes Hope.
Jun	[18] 16 people die in an explosion at Woolwich Arsenal. [25] The novelist George Orwell is born at Motihari in Bengal as Eric Blair. [29] The Government protests to Belgium about atrocities in the Congo.
Jul	[1] The aviator Amy Johnson is born at Hull. [2] Sir Alec Douglas-Home, Conservative Prime Minister, is born. King Olav V of Norway is born at Sandringham. [3] Britain and Japan demand that Russia evacuates Manchuria. [7] The current birth rate, if continued, will result in a population standstill in 18 years. [20] The Government announces that larger numbers of troops will be sent to India.
Aug	[22] Lord Salisbury, Prime Minister four times, dies. [24] The painter Graham Sutherland is born. [25] A Royal Commission into the Boer War criticizes poor campaign planning and reveals that 100,000 British lives were lost.
Sep	[1] Imports of sugar from Denmark, Russia and Argentina are banned as part of an imperial preference policy. [8] The TUC opposes the Government's tariff policy. [10] A great storm in southern England causes widespread damage.
Oct	[5] Austen Chamberlain becomes Chancellor in a reshuffle following Joseph Chamberlain's resignation. [10] Mrs Pankhurst founds the Woman's Social and Political Union, to continue her campaign for votes for women with more extreme action. [12] The shipbuilders Cammell and Laird are to amalgamate. [23] HMS *Victory* is rammed by a modern battleship causing severe damage. [28] The novelist Evelyn Waugh is born.
Nov	[20] The New Zealand government approves the UK preferential trade agreement.

Dec [8] The philosopher Herbert Spencer dies. [15] The
     Australian government approves the preferential trade
     agreement.

1904 The governments of France and Britain sign the
     Anglo-French Entente ('Entente Cordiale'), ending the
     long-standing friction over territorial claims in Africa. The
     Abbey Theatre, Dublin opens. The London Symphony
     Orchestra gives its first concert. The painter George
     Frederick Watts dies. Lord Rayleigh is awarded the Nobel
     Prize for Physics and Sir William Ramsay that for Chemistry.
     Sir John Fleming devises the first electron tube (the Diode
     valve).

Jan [1] Earl Russell has the first motor vehicle registration plate in
     Britain, Al, for his Napier. [13] The composer Richard
     Addinsell is born. [14] Sir Cecil Beaton, photographer and
     designer, is born in London. [18] The film actor Cary Grant is
     born in Bristol as Archibald Leach.

Feb [1] Britain agrees with France to remain neutral in the event
     of a war between Japan and Russia. [3] John Redmond, Irish
     Nationalist, renews the call for Home Rule for Ireland. [29] It
     is revealed that the colonies would prefer metric weights and
     measures to imperial.

Mar [12] The first mainline electric train in Britain runs from
     Liverpool to Southport. [29] Edward VII opens Richmond
     Park to the public.

Apr [1] Henry Royce's firm makes its first car. [14] The first
     attempts at talking pictures are made at the Fulham
     Theatre. The actor Sir John Gielgud is born in London.
     [27] The Poet Laureate C. Day Lewis is born at
     Sligo.

May [4] Charles Rolls and Henry Royce form a car manufacturing
     company. [9] Sir Henry Morton Stanley, journalist and
     explorer, dies in London. He regretted his greeting to
     Livingstone in 1871, because he was met with 'Mr Stanley, I
     presume?' wherever he went. [26] The entertainer George

Formby is born. [30] A strike by 3000 London cab drivers begins.

Jun [9] Commons debate on the alleged Belgian atrocities in the Congo. [28] The steamship *Norge* is wrecked off Ireland: 700 Scandinavian emigrants die in the disaster.

Jul [5] Edward Elgar is knighted, following the success of the Elgar Festival at Covent Garden in March.

Aug [3] A British force under Younghusband takes Lhasa in Tibet. [4] The first Atlantic weather forecast is received by wireless. [16] The British Government protests to Russia about the sinking of neutral merchant shipping. [25] The first ocean-going turbine steamship, the *Victorian*, is launched at Belfast. [26] The author Christopher Isherwood is born.

Sep [7] Treaty with Tibet signed in Lhasa. [17] Sir Frederick Ashton, founder of the Royal Ballet, is born. [19] British pressure succeeds in making Leopold, King of the Belgians, set up a commission of inquiry into the atrocity allegations.

Oct [2] Graham Greene, novelist, is born at Berkhamsted. [10] Actress Anna Neagle is born in London as Marjorie Robertson. [22] The Russian Baltic fleet attacks and sinks two Hull trawlers on the Dogger Bank. They claim they believed they were Japanese torpedo boats, but there is widespread indignation in Britain; only French diplomatic intervention stops the Dogger Bank Incident escalating into war. [27] Royal Navy ships surround Russian ships in the North Sea.

Nov [17] The first under-water voyage of a submarine is made, crossing the Solent. [29] There is a dramatic increase in the numbers of people receiving poor relief: 800,000 in England and Wales. 250,000 are reduced to living in workhouses.

Dec [24] The Coliseum opens in London.

1905 The sculptor Jacob Epstein settles in London. The composer Alan Rawsthorne is born.

Jan [2] The composer Sir Michael Tippett is born in London. [11] Transatlantic liner tickets are costing more: it now costs £6 to cross to America third class. [25] The Cullinan Diamond, the largest ever found, is discovered in the Premier Diamond Mine; it is later presented to Edward VII. [26] Cardinal Heenan, Roman Catholic Archbishop of Westminster, is born.

Feb [11] Frenchmen land at Crystal Palace in a balloon after crossing the Channel. [17] Outbreak of typhus in East London.

Mar [1] Spending on the Navy is to treble. [10] 32 die in a pit disaster in South Wales. [15] 23 die in severe storms off Land's End. [18] The film actor Robert Donat is born in Manchester. In a Royal Command Performance of Shaw's *John Bull's Other Island*, Edward VII laughs so much he breaks his chair. [31] *The Return of Sherlock Holmes* is published by popular demand.

Apr [1] The *Victorian* arrives in Halifax, Nova Scotia at the end of her maiden voyage.

May [12] A Bill to give women the vote is 'talked out': the Bill fails.

Jun [15] The film actor James Robertson Justice is born. [26] The Automobile Association is founded.

Jul [1] The Colonial Office considers a plan to resettle Britain's surplus population in various parts of the Empire. [10] Puccini's *Madame Butterfly* is given its first UK performance at Covent Garden. [11] 124 miners die in a Glamorgan pit disaster. [12] George V's son John is born.

Aug [1] Field Marshal Lord Roberts alleges that the British armed services are worse prepared now than they were at the beginning of the Boer War.

Sep [11] Published figures show that rural lunacy is on the increase; this is attributed to the tedium of life in the country. [19] Britain and Germany hold simultaneous war manoeuvres. Thomas Barnardo, founder of children's homes, dies.

Oct [13] Sir Henry Irving dies at Bradford from a heart attack outside his hotel. [25] Lord Rosebery calls for a future Liberal government to challenge the power of the House of Lords.

Nov [7] The composer William Alwyn is born in Northampton.
     [12] Queen Alexandra launches an appeal for the
     unemployed. [14] Robert Whitehead, who invented the naval
     torpedo in 1866, dies in Berkshire. [22] The world's largest
     turbine- powered liner, the *Carmania*, leaves Liverpool on her
     maiden voyage. [26] Emlyn Williams, actor, playwright,
     screenwriter, is born.
Dec [3] British troops quell a riot at Georgetown in British
     Guyana. [5] The roof of Charing Cross Station collapses. [14]
     The trades unions call for universal suffrage, an eight-hour
     working day and old-age pensions. [23] The final heat of the
     earliest known beauty contest in Britain takes place at
     Newcastle-upon-Tyne.

1906 Sir Joseph Thomson is awarded the Nobel Prize for Physics.
Jan [22] A tram accident in Liverpool kills 30.
Feb [1] The Government drops its plan to build a faster motor
     road from London to Brighton. [7] The General Election
     results in a Liberal landslide (Liberal 399, Conservative 156,
     Labour 29) and significant gains for Labour. [8] A march of
     unemployed people from the Midlands to London meets
     with an unsympathetic reception. [10] HMS *Dreadnought* is
     launched; the revolutionary new battleship design marks the
     start of a desperate naval arms race between Britain and
     Germany.
Mar [14] Parliament approves old-age pensions in principle.
Apr [6] Sir John Betjeman, Poet Laureate, is born in London. [9]
     Hugh Gaitskell, Labour Party leader, is born. [13] The
     playwright Samuel Beckett is born. [17] The Labour Party
     calls for votes for women. [22] Delius's amanuensis Eric
     Fenby is born. [24] The Nazi collaborator William Joyce,
     'Lord Haw-Haw', is born in Brooklyn. [27] China agrees
     reluctantly to allow the British to control access to Tibet.
May [6] British soldiers kill 60 Zulus at Durban.
Jun [7] The liner *Lusitania* is launched, the largest and fastest
     passenger liner in the world. [12] Ellen Terry celebrates 50

years on the stage. 322 British ships are involved in naval exercises, making mock attacks on British ports. [23] A deputation demanding votes for women meets the Prime Minister.

Jul [3] George Sanders, film actor, is born in Russia to British parents. [7] Britain's first hot-air balloon race. [12] Ten Londoners on a day trip to Brighton are killed in a bus crash. [15] A Commons select committee proposes the introduction of school meals. [23] 1000 Zulu rebels surrender to British troops in South Africa.

Aug [8] Churchill and others protest at the excessive noise made by vehicle traffic. [9] The Boer War Commission reports that corruption and incompetence in the conduct of the war cost over £1 million. [15] Edward VII visits the Kaiser; discussions about the naval situation are fruitless.

Sep [20] The liner *Mauretania* is launched. [22] Thousands in London help in the recapture of the Life Guards' escaped mascot, a bear.

Oct [1] In sea trials, *Dreadnought* makes a record speed of 21 knots. [24] Eleven suffragettes are sent to prison after causing disturbances in Parliament.

Nov [6] Sylvia Pankhurst, a prominent suffragette, is released from prison.

Dec [15] The Piccadilly Line of the London Underground is opened. [30] The film director Carol Reed is born at Putney.

1907 Rudyard Kipling is awarded the Nobel Prize for Literature.

Feb [15] James Thompson, the laziest man in the world, is forced to get out of bed after 29 years and go for help when his 80-year-old mother becomes too ill to look after him. [27] The Central Criminal Court is opened on the site of Newgate Prison. [28] The Government is to spend less on the Navy this year, but still orders three more dreadnoughts. [21] The poet W. H. Auden is born.

Mar [8] Keir Hardie's Women's Enfranchisement Bill is defeated. [16] HMS *Indomitable*, the world's largest cruiser, is launched on the Clyde. [21] The Prime Minister opposes the Channel Tunnel Bill. [25] The Channel Tunnel Bill is defeated because of War Office opposition and lack of popular support.

May [13] The novelist Dame Daphne du Maurier is born. [22] Sir Laurence Olivier (Lord Olivier), actor, director and producer, is born at Dorking. [28] The first Isle of Man motor cycle TT Race is held.

Jun [14] The Government announces its plan to curb the power of the House of Lords.

Jul [6] The Brooklands motor racing track near Weybridge opens. [27] The dreadnought HMS *Bellerophon* is launched at Portsmouth. [29] The first Boy Scout camp begins as an experiment on Brownsea Island in Dorset.

Aug [13] The architect Sir Basil Spence is born.

Sep [10] Britain's first military airship flies successfully at Farnborough. [13] The *Lusitania* arrives in New York after a record Atlantic crossing, averaging 23 knots.

Oct [9] The Conservative politician Lord Hailsham is born as Quintin Hogg. [26] The Territorial Army is founded by the Secretary of State for War, Richard Haldane.

Nov [15] The German Kaiser is awarded an honorary degree at Oxford. [22] The liner *Mauretania* arrives in New York at the end of her maiden voyage. [27] Florence Nightingale is awarded the Order of Merit.

Dec [12] Dinizulu, the King of the Zulus, surrenders to the British; the Zulu rebellion was triggered off by the imposition of a poll tax. [17] Lord Kelvin, physicist and inventor, dies. [22] Dame Peggy Ashcroft, actress, is born at Croydon, London.

1908

Jan [12] Prices of transatlantic liner tickets fall sharply, thanks to competition between the Cunard and White Star companies. [26] The first boy scout troop is registered (First Glasgow).

Feb [11] Explorer Sir Vivian Fuchs is born in Kent. [13] Dentist Arthur Hyne is sent down for seven years for bigamy: he has five wives. [22] The actor Sir John Mills is born at Felixstowe.

Mar [5] Sir Rex Harrison, actor, is born in Liverpool as Reginald Carey. [20] Sir Michael Redgrave, actor, is born at Bristol. [21] Sir John Hare proposes a National Theatre as a memorial to Shakespeare. [25] Sir David Lean, film director, is born at Croydon.

Apr [2] HMS *Tiger* and HMS *Berwick* collide off the Isle of Wight; the *Tiger* sinks, drowning 35 men. [7] Sir Henry Campbell-Bannerman resigns due to ill health and the Liberal H. H. Asquith becomes Prime Minister, quickly introducing legislation to provide old-age pensions for those over 70. [22] Sir Henry Campbell-Bannerman, Liberal Prime Minister, dies.

May [28] Ian Fleming, novelist and creator of James Bond, is born.

Jun [10] Invalid and Old Age Pensions Act passed: non-contributory pensions for the over-70s. [21] A crowd of 200,000 in Hyde Park demonstrates for votes for women.

Jul [10] A new British torpedo is announced, with a four mile range and a speed of four knots. [16] Fire breaks out at the Moorgate tube station. [17] The first criminal appeal, against a murder conviction, is turned down at the Central Criminal Court.

Aug [6] The Admiralty announces that the battleships the Germans are building will be the most heavily armed in the world. [14] An airship blows up in London: one person is killed. [31] W. G. Grace retires from cricket, after scoring over 54,000 runs in first-class cricket.

Sep [12] Winston Churchill marries Clementine Hozier. [24] 'Pensions Day': elderly people apply for their pensions [29] Film actress Greer Garson is born in County Down, Ireland.

Oct [1] A penny post to the USA starts. [16] The first aeroplane flight in Britain takes place at Farnborough. The new harbour at Dover is opened, as part of the national defence system. [31] An indiscreet interview given by the Kaiser to the *Daily Telegraph* astonishes both British and Germans.

Nov [9] Britain's first woman mayor, Elizabeth Garrett Anderson, is elected at Aldeburgh.

1909 The first Rolls-Royce Silver Ghost is tested. The painter
William Frith dies. The painter Francis Bacon is born.

Jan [1] Old Age Pensions become payable to people aged 70
and over. [14] Churchill describes Britain as 'the best country
in the world for rich men'. [24] Film actress Ann Todd is
born.

Feb [8] The Government announces that the Navy is to have six
more dreadnoughts. [24] Colour films are shown for the first
time, in Brighton. [28] The poet Stephen Spender is born.

Mar [15] Selfridges opens in Oxford Street; it is the city's first big
department store.

Apr [5] The Aerial League of the British Empire is founded, to
promote British supremacy in the air. [9] The first closed-top
double-decker bus is introduced, at Widnes. [10] The poet
Algernon Swinburne dies.

May [15] The actor James Mason is born in Huddersfield,
Yorkshire.

Jun [13] Shackleton arrives back in Britain after his Antarctic
expedition. [26] Edward VII opens the Victoria and
Albert Museum. [29] Suffragettes are arrested in
Westminster.

Jul [27] MPs give the South African Union Bill its second
reading, but deplore the fact that it denies the black
population the right to vote.

Aug [16] The Conservative leader Arthur Balfour argues that
giving equal rights to South African blacks would
undermine white civilization. [20] Wells, Arnold
Bennett, Conrad and Thomas Hardy speak out
against the Lord Chamberlain's powers to censor stage
plays.

Sep [4] The first Boy Scout rally takes place, at Crystal Palace. [14]
The naturalist Sir Peter Scott is born. [28] It is admitted in the
Commons that some imprisoned suffragettes have been
force-fed.

Nov [5] The first Woolworths store opens in Britain. [30] The
House of Lords rejects Lloyd George's 'People's Budget' over

land value duties; this precipitates a major constitutional crisis over the roles of the two Houses. Lloyd George asks, 'should 500 men, ordinary men chosen accidentally from among the unemployed, override the judgement of millions of people who are engaged in the industry which makes the wealth of this country?'

Dec   [3] Edward VII dissolves Parliament; the taxes on beer, spirits and tobacco are lifted because no Budget has been passed.

1910 The Argentine tango becomes popular in Britain.

Jan   A General Election is fought on the issues of the Budget, the veto power of the Lords and the Home Rule Bill; the Liberals are returned. [18] The first sighting of Halley's Comet on its 1910 visit; its next appearance will be in 1986. [31] Dr Hawley Crippen poisons his wife Cora in Camden Town.

Feb   The officers of HMS *Dreadnought* are hoaxed; a quartet of Abyssinian princes piped aboard and shown round the ship turn out to be Guy Ridley, Anthony Buxton, Duncan Grant and Virginia Woolf in disguise. [1] The first 80 Labour Exchanges are opened; they are flooded by people looking for work. [20] Hurricane-force winds cause severe damage. [21] Douglas Bader, fighter pilot, is born.

Mar   [22] Nicholas Monsarrat, writer of sea stories, is born in Liverpool.

Apr   [4] The first Commons reading of a Bill to abolish the House of Lords' power of veto.

May   [6] Edward VII dies from pneumonia; he is succeeded by George V. [10] The Commons pass resolutions that the Lords may not veto a money bill and that any other measure may be passed if it has come before the Commons three times even if vetoed by the Lords twice. [20] The last broad gauge train in Britain runs from Paddington to Penzance; from now on all main lines are standard gauge. [21] Edward VII's funeral. [31] The Girl Guides are founded.

Jun   [4] Christopher Cockerell, inventor of the amphibious hovercraft, is born at Cambridge. [15] Captain Scott sets out on his ill-fated expedition to the South Pole. [22] Sir John (Lord) Hunt, leader of the successful Everest expedition, is born. [23] George V's son Edward is created Prince of Wales.

Jul   [12] Charles Rolls, aviator and co-founder of Rolls-Royce, dies in an air crash at Bournemouth. [14] Cora Crippen's remains are discovered in the cellar at her home; the police hunt for Crippen begins.

Aug   [13] Florence Nightingale dies aged 90.

Sep   [7] William Holman Hunt, painter, dies. [17] A London doctor says that if lunacy goes on increasing at its current rate the sane will be outnumbered by the insane within 40 years. [20] The huge White Star liner *Olympic*, sister-ship of the *Titanic*, is launched at Belfast. [22] Crippen is convicted of murder and condemned to death.

Nov   [8] 'Manet and the Post-Impressionists' exhibition opens in London: organized by Roger Fry, it proves to be a major influence on British painters. [11] Asquith asks George V if he will create enough peers to allow the passage of the Lords' Reform Bill. [16] Sir Edward Carson warns that Ulster (Northern Ireland) will fight the proposals for Irish Home Rule. [23] Dr Crippen is hanged at Pentonville. [28] Parliament is dissolved in preparation for the second General Election of the year.

Dec   [20] The General Election is a dead heat (Liberals 272, Conservatives 272): Asquith continues as Prime Minister. [22] The Hulton Colliery disaster: 350 miners lose their lives.

1911   Ernest Rutherford demonstrates that the atom has a nuclear structure. Charles Wilson produces the first cloud-chamber photographs of sub-atomic particles.

Jan   [1] Leon Beron, a Russian Jew, is found murdered on Clapham Common; a link with anarchists is suspected. [3] The Sidney Street Siege; three anarchists suspected of killing three policemen engage in a gun battle with 1000 soldiers and police in the East End of London. The house catches fire and two of the anarchists are burnt to death. [17] Sir Francis Galton, pioneer on heredity, dies. [30] At the Beron inquest Stinie Morrison is accused of wilful murder.

Feb [1] Edward Mylius is sentenced to one year in prison for accusing George V of polygamy. HMS *Thunderer*, the last battleship to be built on the Thames, is launched. [4] Rolls Royce adopt the 'Spirit of Ecstasy' statuette. [23] A schoolgirl in a playground in Bradford is lifted 20 feet off the ground by a freak gust of wind; she falls to the ground and is killed.

Mar [2] The Lords' Veto Bill (Parliamentary Bill) passes its second Commons reading. [9] The Government announces that five more British battleships are to be built. [15] Stinie Morrison is sentenced to death for Beron's murder.

Apr [4] The Duke of Marlborough and other former pupils bemoan the abolition of birching at Eton. [12] Morrison's sentence is commuted to life imprisonment.

May [4] The first British airship is wrecked at Aldershot. [12] The Festival of Empire opens at Crystal Palace. [15] George V and his visiting cousin the Kaiser reassert their friendship. The Parliamentary Bill is again passed by the Commons. [29] Sir William Gilbert, writer of operettas in collaboration with Sir Arthur Sullivan, dies of a heart attack in his swimming-pool. [31] The White Star liner *Titanic* is launched at the Harland and Wolff shipyard in Belfast.

Jun [10] The playwright Terence Rattigan is born. [17] Women demanding the vote march through London to a meeting at the Albert Hall. [20] Leeds introduces the first trolley-bus service in Britain. [22] Coronation of George V. Liverpool's Liver clock, 'Great George', begins telling the time.

Jul [1] The Shops Act provides a half-day holiday for shop workers. [11] Liverpool's Gladstone Dock is opened by George V. [20] The Parliamentary Bill is passed by the Lords, but with amendments unacceptable to Asquith, who threatens to create enough peers to carry the Bill in its

unaltered form. [22] George V guarantees to create the
number of Liberal peers Asquith requires.

Aug   [8] National strike of railwaymen, dockers and carters;
Manchester and other cities are brought close to famine. [10]
The Lords pass the Parliamentary Bill unamended (i.e.
Parliamentary Act). The Commons for the first time vote MPs
a salary, set at £400 a year. [18] Official Secrets Act. [23]
There are violent anti-semitic riots in Wales. [28] A
heat-wave sends the death rate up; London becomes one of
the unhealthiest cities in Europe with a death rate of 19 per
1000.

Sep   [5] The TUC condemns the use of troops in the recent strikes.
[23] Carson again rejects any possibility of Home Rule.

Oct   [6] The Labour politician Barbara Castle is born. [9] The
Navy's biggest battleship, HMS *King George V*, is launched at
Southampton.

Nov   [2] 6000 London cab drivers go on strike. [8] Arthur Balfour,
leader of the Conservative and Unionist Party, resigns.

Dec   National Insurance Act; this covers ill health and
unemployment benefits for all with incomes below £150, and
marks the beginning of the Welfare State. [12] George V is
crowned Emperor of India and founds the city of New Delhi.

1912

Jan   [1] The National Telephone Company is taken over by the
Post Office. [3] The Cabinet is reported to be divided over
votes for women. [18] Scott reaches the South Pole only to
find that Amundsen has beaten him by 35 days.

Feb   [10] Lord Lister, pioneer of antiseptic surgery, dies at Walmer
aged 84. [26] 2000 coal miners go on strike in Derbyshire.

Mar   [1] Suffragettes smash shop windows in London's West End.
[4] 96 are arrested after a suffragette raid on the House of
Commons. [5] The police raid the offices of the Women's
Social and Political Union. [7] The first non-stop aeroplane
flight from Paris to London.

Mar   [17] Lawrence Oates dies heroically during the return
journey from the South Pole with Scott: it is his 32nd

birthday. [27] The Labour Prime Minister James Callaghan is born at Portsmouth. The Coal Miners Act establishes the principle of a minimum wage. [28] The Women's Enfranchisement Bill is defeated on its second Commons reading. [29] Captain Scott dies in his tent in Antarctica.

Apr   [1] Asquith introduces the third Home Rule Bill. [9] 240,000 people demonstrate against Home Rule in Belfast. [10] Troops are called out to quell riots in Wigan. [14] The *Titanic*, steaming too fast through a sea littered with icebergs, hits one and sinks in the early hours of 15 April on her maiden voyage: 1500 lives are lost. [17] A total eclipse of the sun is seen in London. [20] Bram Stoker, author of *Dracula*, dies. [22] The contralto Kathleen Ferrier is born at Higher Walton.

May [9] The Home Rule Bill passes its second Commons reading. [29] 100,000 dockers are now out on strike in London.

Jun [12] John Seely succeeds Haldane as War Secretary. [16] Conservative politician Enoch Powell is born. [25] Asquith is attacked in the Commons over the force-feeding of imprisoned suffragettes. [28] The suffragettes start a new window-smashing campaign at Post Offices and Labour Exchanges.

Jul [3] The Board of Trade inquiry into the *Titanic* disaster finds Captain Smith guilty of negligence. [12] Second reading of the Franchise Bill, which will give all men over 21 the vote. [22] Battleships are to be withdrawn from the Mediterranean and placed on patrol in the North Sea; spending on both ships and sailors is to be increased. [23] Film actor Michael Wilding is born at Westcliff-on-Sea.

Aug [20] William Booth, founder of the Salvation Army, dies aged 83.

Sep [4] The first tube collision occurs in London: 22 are injured. [28] A week of rallies and speeches in Ulster ends with the signing of a covenant to defeat Home Rule.

Oct [12] HMS *Iron Duke*, the world's largest and most powerful battleship, is launched.

Nov [5] A British Censor of Films is appointed. [25] The writer
Francis Durbridge is born.

Dec [6] Prince Louis Battenberg and Sir John Jellicoe become First
and Second Sea Lords. [18] The discovery of Piltdown man in
Sussex is announced by Charles Dawson; that it is a hoax is
not to be discovered until 1953.

1913 Carson forms the Ulster Volunteers, a private army to
resist Home Rule by force. Atomic number invented by
Henry Mosely. The geiger counter is invented by Hans
Geiger.

Jan [1] Film censorship starts. [7] The Government introduces
proportional representation into its Home Rule proposals to
protect the interests of Protestants. [15] The first sickness,
unemployment and maternity benefits are introduced. [16]
The Home Rule Bill passes its second Commons reading.

Feb [3] Stravinsky's *Petroushka* is performed in Britain for the first
time. [5] Sylvia Pankhurst goes to prison. [10] The bodies of
Scott and his two companions are found in their tent in
Antarctica. [13] Stravinsky's *Firebird* is performed in Britain
for the first time. [19] A suffragette bomb destroys Lloyd
George's house. [24] Emmeline Pankhurst is arrested and
charged in connection with the Lloyd George bombing.

Apr [3] Emmeline Pankhurst is sentenced to three years for
inciting her supporters to place explosives at Lloyd George's
house.

May [7] A suffragette bomb is found in St Paul's. [15] The Home
Secretary bans public meetings by suffragettes. [20] The first
Chelsea Flower Show opens. [21] The world's largest liner,
the *Aquitania*, is launched on the Clyde. [25] The broadcaster
Richard Dimbleby is born.

Jun [2] Alfred Austin, Poet Laureate, dies. [4] Emily Davidson, a
suffragette, is trampled when she throws herself under the
King's horse, 'Anmer', at Tattenham Corner, Epsom. [8]
Emily Davidson dies of her injuries. [10] A misadventure
verdict is returned on Emily Davidson's death.

Jul [7] The Home Rule Bill is passed for a second time by the Commons. [8] Sylvia Pankhurst is sentenced to three months in prison. [12] The Craigavon meeting; 150,000 Ulstermen pledge to resist Home Rule by force. [15] The House of Lords rejects the Home Rule Bill a second time. [16] Robert Bridges is appointed Poet Laureate. [23] The Labour Party leader Michael Foot is born. [29] The Liberal Party leader Jo Grimond is born. [31] Lloyd George says that the Lords must be abolished.

Aug [14] The actor Herbert Wilson dies in hospital after he is shot on stage. [31] The astronomer Sir Bernard Lovell is born.

Sep [7] The actor-manager Sir Anthony Quayle is born.

Oct [14] 439 are killed in a pit disaster at Senghenydd in Glamorgan. [16] The world's first oil-powered battleship, HMS *Queen Elizabeth*, is launched.

Nov [5] The film and stage actress Vivien Leigh is born at Darjeeling as Vivian Hartley. [22] The composer Benjamin Britten (Lord Britten) is born at Lowestoft.

Dec [4] Emmeline Pankhurst is arrested on her return from the USA. [15] The battlecruiser HMS *Tiger* is launched on the Clyde. [18] Lord Plymouth gives money to allow the Crystal Palace to be bought for the nation.

1914 The Welsh Disestablishment Act disestablishes the Welsh Church. Sir Ernest Shackleton sets off on his epic Antarctic expedition. The poet Dylan Thomas is born. Sir Ernest Swinton invents the tank.

Jan [1] Lloyd George calls the arms build-up in Western Europe 'organized insanity'. [5] Vanessa Bell, Roger Fry and Duncan Grant open a London exhibition of their work following their break from Cubism. [7] Joseph Chamberlain decides to retire from politics. [8] Doctors at the Middlesex Hospital successfully treat cancer with radium.

Feb [2] The Cub Scouts are founded at Robertsbridge in Sussex. The first UK performance of Wagner's *Parsifal* takes place.

[4] Suffragettes burn two Scottish mansions. [10] Thomas Hardy marries Eva Dugdale.

Mar [5] The Irish Home Rule Bill is reintroduced in the Commons. [8] Sylvia Pankhurst is rearrested. [9] Asquith offers a compromise on Home Rule; electors in Ulster may vote to be excluded from an independent Ireland for six years. [10] Mary Richardson, a suffragette, damages the *Rokeby Venus* with a cleaver at the National Gallery in protest against 'the Government's destruction of Miss Pankhurst'.

Apr [2] The actor Sir Alec Guinness is born at Marylebone, London. [17] Yarmouth Pier is damaged by a suffragette bomb.

May [15] The Commons reject the idea of a Scottish Home Rule Bill. [25] The Irish Home Rule Bill passes its final Commons stage, without separate provisions for Ulster. [27] Sir Joseph Swan, inventor, dies aged 85.

Jun [4] Railway and mine workers join builders on strike: now two million British workers are on strike. [10] Sylvia Pankhurst is arrested for the eighth time. [14] A severe thunderstorm in London brings ten centimetres of rain in three hours. [23] Asquith's March 9 compromise is introduced in the Lords.

Jul [8] The Government agrees to accept the Lords' amendment to the Home Rule Bill excluding Ulster. [30] The Home Rule process is shelved in the fate of the growing European crisis.

Aug [2] The Royal Navy is mobilized after the Kaiser declares war on Russia. [3] The Government warns Germany that Britain will honour the 1839 Treaty of London guaranteeing Belgian neutrality. [4] German troops invade Belgium; Britain declares war on Germany. [17] A British Expeditionary Force of 70,000 men lands in France. [23] Battle of Mons, the first engagement between British and German forces; the British are defeated and pull back.

Sep [5-12] Battle of the Marne; the British and French armies advance. [8] Home Rule Act, to come into force at the end of the war. [15] Commons passes a suspending bill to delay the operation of the Home Rule Act for one year. [16] Trench warfare begins on the Aisne salient. [22] Three British cruisers are sunk by one U-boat; 1500 men are lost as the *Cressy*, *Aboukir* and *Hogue* sink. [23] British planes bomb Zeppelin sheds at Dusseldorf.

Oct [4] The first German bomb falls on London. [12] Start of the First Battle of Ypres (lasts until ll November). [30] Lord Fisher succeeds Prince Louis as First Sea Lord.

Nov [1] Battle of Coronel; the German cruisers *Scharnhorst* and *Gneisenau* sink the British cruisers *Monmouth* and *Good Hope*. [5] Britain declares war against Turkey; Cyprus is annexed to Britain. [14] Lord Roberts, the Boer War commander, dies while visiting troops in the field in France. [17] Lloyd George announces that income tax will double in 1915 to pay for the war, which is currently costing £1 million a day.
[26] HMS *Bulwark* blows up at Sheerness, killing 700 people.

Dec [11] The Royal Flying Corps adopts the roundel for easy aircraft identification. [16] Scarborough and Whitby are shelled from the sea; over 100 people are killed. [29] The first Zeppelin appears over the British coast.

1915 The Munitions of War Act forbids strikes in key industries without permission from the Government's arbitration body. Sir William H. Bragg and William L. Bragg are awarded the Nobel Prize for Physics.

Jan [1] The Military Cross is introduced and awarded for the first time. A German submarine sinks HMS *Formidable*. [19] The first air-raid casualties are inflicted in Britain when bombs are dropped on King's Lynn and Great Yarmouth by the German L3 Zeppelin. [24] A British squadron (HMS *Lion*, *Tiger* and *Princess Royal*) shells and sinks the *Blücher*, a huge German battlecruiser on its way to shell Yarmouth.

Feb [1] Passport photographs are required for the first time. [4] UK casualties to date total 104,000 dead. [18] The Germans begin a sea blockade of Britain. Shackleton's *Endurance* becomes stuck in pack-ice. [26] Armaments workers on the Clyde strike for more pay.

Mar [1] Britain begins to blockade Germany. [11] HMS *Bayano* is sunk off Scotland: 200 die.

Apr [7] George V offers to abstain from alcohol to encourage armaments workers to abstain, in the belief that alcohol consumption slows down production. [22] Britain launches a spring offensive at Ypres; there are heavy casualties in the Second Battle of Ypres (lasting until May 25): the Germans use chlorine gas. [23] The poet Rupert Brooke dies of blood poisoning on Skyros, on his way to the Dardanelles. [25] The first landing of British, Australian and New Zealand troops on the Gallipoli peninsula meets bitter and determined resistance from the Turks.

May [1] There is widespread resentment among workers at the new anti-alcohol measures. [3] The war is now costing Britain £2 million a day. [7] The liner *Lusitania* is sunk, torpedoed by a German submarine off the Old Head of Kinsale with a loss of 1198 lives. [9-25] Battle of Aubers Ridge (Second Battle of Artois); the French advance three miles at great cost. [22] The worst-ever train disaster in Britain: a triple collision at Quintins Hill near Gretna Green kills 227 - 200 of them Scots Guards on their way to war. The shocked and dishevelled survivors are later mistaken for German prisoners-of-war and stoned by civilians. [26] A Coalition Government is formed. [27] HM Auxiliary Ship *Irene* explodes at Sheerness: 270 die. [31] The first air raids on London take place.

Jun [6] The Kaiser promises that in future the German navy will not attack passenger vessels. [28] A German submarine sinks the passenger liner *Armenia* off Cornwall.

Jul [3] The war is now costing Britain £3 million a day. [15] 200,000 Welsh miners strike for improved wages.

Aug [19] A German submarine sinks the British liner *Arabic:* 44 are missing. [31] The Welsh miners go back to work.

Sep [18] The Kaiser gives renewed assurances that passenger vessels will not be attacked. [21] Stonehenge is sold by auction for £6,600; a Mr Chubb buys it as a present for his wife. [26] Keir Hardie, founder of the Labour Party, dies.

Oct [12] Edith Cavell, a nurse, is executed by a German firing squad for helping Allied prisoners to escape. [23] The cricketer W. G. Grace dies. [28] George V falls off his horse while inspecting troops in France, but suffers only bruises.

Nov [1] Actor Michael Denison is born. [9] British war casualties now total 510,000. [21] Shackleton's *Endurance* is crushed and sunk by pack-ice; Shackleton and his team drift on a disintegrating ice floe for the next four months.

Dec [8] Battle of the Falkland Islands; a British squadron under Admiral Sturdee defeats a German attack, sinking four out of the five German ships; Admiral von Spee and his two sons are killed in the action. [15] Sir John French is replaced as Commander of British forces on the Western Front by Sir Douglas Haig. [20] British troops withdraw from Anzac and Suvla after 25,000 men are killed and 76,000 wounded. [30] HMS *Natal* blows up and sinks in Cromarty Firth as a result of sabotage: 350 die.

1916

Jan [6] The Commons vote in favour of conscription, although the Home Secretary Sir John Simon resigns over the issue; single men are to be conscripted first. [8] The Evacuation of Gallipoli is completed. [29] Tanks are given their first trials at Hatfield.

Feb [19] National Saving Certificates go on sale. [21] Opening of the Battle of Verdun; the Germans launch a massive offensive that goes on until December, with enormous losses on both sides. [28] The novelist Henry James dies at Rye.

Mar [2] The Military Service Act, enabling conscription. [11] Sir Harold Wilson, Labour Prime Minister, is born at Huddersfield.

Apr [9] Shackleton and his crew leave the ice floe, taking to the sea in small boats. [12] Shackleton and his crew reach Elephant Island. [24] The Sinn Fein Rebellion in Ireland; Irish Nationalists seize the Post Office in Dublin and proclaim a provisional government. The Easter Rising lasts five days; 14 of the rebel leaders are later executed. Roger Casement is arrested after landing in Ireland from a German submarine. [25] The first Anzac Day commemorates the Gallipoli landings last year.

May [8] The Commons back William Willett's Daylight Saving plan to put the clocks forward one hour in summer. [10] Shackleton reaches South Georgia. [21] Daylight Saving is introduced. [31] Battle of Jutland; there are heavy British losses in this large-scale naval battle and the result is inconclusive, though the Germans afterwards retreat.

Jun [5] Lord Kitchener is drowned off the Orkney coast when HMS *Hampshire* hits a mine. [29] Sir Roger Casement is found guilty and sentenced to death in Dublin.

Jul [1] - Nov [13] Battle of the Somme; the largest and bloodiest engagement on the Western Front, in which 420,000 British soldiers are killed in a fruitless attempt to relieve the French: only 10 miles are gained from the Germans. [6] Lloyd George becomes War Secretary after Kitchener's death. [9] Edward Heath, Conservative Prime Minister, is born at Broadstairs. [23] Sir William Ramsay, chemist and discoverer of argon, helium, neon, krypton and xenon, dies at High Wycombe.

Aug [3] Sir Roger Casement, Irish Nationalist, is hanged in London for treason. [5] The composer George Butterworth is killed in action at Pozières. [30] Shackleton's crew are rescued from Elephant Island, after a remarkable Antarctic expedition.

Sep [15] Tanks designed by Sir Ernest Swinton are used in action for the first time by the British army in the Somme offensive. Margaret Lockwood, film actress, is born in Karachi, Pakistan to British parents. [28] Actor Peter Finch is born in London as William Mitchell. [29] The film actor Trevor Howard is born in Cliftonville.

Nov [24] Sir Hiram Maxim, the Anglo-American inventor of the machine-gun, dies in London.

Dec [7] A Coalition Government led by the Liberals is formed;
Lloyd George, as Prime Minister, forms a War Cabinet.

1917 Charles Barkla is awarded the Nobel Prize for Physics.

Jan [1] Britain and Germany agree to exchange all internees over
the age of 45. [25] HMS *Laurentic* hits a mine in the Atlantic:
350 die.

Feb [1] Unrestricted submarine warfare begins. [2] Bread
rationing starts. [25] The passenger liner *Laconia* is
torpedoed: 30 passengers die. The writer Anthony Burgess
is born.

Mar [8] A Government Commission on the Dardanelles
Campaign blames Kitchener in part for its failure. [11] British
troops occupy Baghdad. [20] The singer Vera Lynn is born in
London. [29] Lloyd George announces a plan to introduce a
Bill enabling married women over 30 the vote.

Apr [9-14] Battle of Arras. [14] Valerie Hobson, actress, is born in
Larne, New Zealand.

Jun [7] The British take Messines Ridge. Haig launches a new
Flanders offensive. [19] Large Commons majority in favour
of giving wives over 30 the vote. [26] The Royal Family
decide to drop German titles; the family name of Saxe-
Coburg-Gotha becomes Windsor, and Battenberg becomes
Mountbatten.

Jul [24] MPs are alarmed to discover that the war is costing
Britain £7 million a day. [31] The Third Battle of Ypres
begins.

Aug [4] Captain Noel Chavasse of the Royal Army Medical Corps,
the second of only three people ever to be awarded a bar to
the Victoria Cross, dies of his wounds. [7] There is a heated
debate in the House of Lords over the alleged sale of titles.
[20] Over 100 people die in an air raid on Sheppey and
Thanet. [30] The Labour statesman Denis Healey is born.

Oct [4] British victory on Passchendaele Ridge. [5] 'Chequers' is
given to the nation as the official residence of the Prime
Minister.

Nov   [6] Passchendaele is captured by the British. [8] The Balfour
      Declaration recognizes Palestine as 'a national home' for the
      Jews, and gives official British support to the founding of a
      Jewish state. [13] Bankers call for the decimalization of British
      currency. [26] Sir Leander Jameson, colonial administrator
      and leader of the notorious Jameson Raid into the Transvaal,
      dies.

Dec   [3] The Government refuses to recognize the Bolshevik
      regime in Russia. [17] Elizabeth Garrett Anderson, the first
      woman doctor, dies.

1918 Anti-tetanus vaccinations are used extensively among the
      troops, and the success of this treatment does a great
      deal to popularize vaccination among civilians. Britain is
      hit by a worldwide influenza epidemic; at its height, it
      causes 3000 deaths per week in London alone. Education
      Act; this fixes the school-leaving age at 14, resulting in the
      perpetuation of very large classes, many of them with over
      60 pupils.

Jan   [30] The House of Commons rejects the Lords'
      recommendation for proportional representation.

Feb   [6] Representation of the People Act, giving men over 21
      and, for the first time, women over 30 the right to vote.

Mar   [7] Bonar Law asks the Commons for another war loan of
      £600 million. [21] A German offensive against the British is
      opened on the Somme.

Apr   [1] The Royal Air Force is formed by amalgamating the Royal
      Flying Corps and Royal Naval Air Service. [9-25] Second
      German offensive on the Somme. [18] Military Service Act;
      the maximum conscription age is raised to 50, and is
      extended to include Ireland for the first time. [23] The British
      raid Zeebrugge and Ostend, with the intention of bottling up
      the two submarine bases.

May   [9] HMS *Vindictive* is sunk in Ostend harbour.

Jun   [18] The Government asks for a further war loan of £500
      million. An Allied counter-attack on the Western Front

begins. [19] General rationing begins. [20] After protests, the Government abandons Irish conscription.

Aug [8] British, Canadian and Australian troops attack the Germans near Amiens: the Germans retreat.

Sep [15] Mr C. Chubb presents Stonehenge to the nation. [26] A general Allied offensive on the Western Front begins; the Germans are fighting now only to cover their retreat.

Oct [7] The composer Sir Hubert Parry dies. [15] Britain's first oil well is sunk at Hardstoft in Derbyshire. [23] The Commons vote in favour of allowing women to become MPs.

Nov [4] The poet Wilfrid Owen is killed in action, trying to get his men across the Sambre Canal. [9] The Germans sign the Armistice. [11] The German army surrenders to Marshal Foch. [14-15] Widespread celebrations in Britain. [21] The German High Seas Fleet is handed over to the British for internment at Scapa Flow.

Dec [14] Women vote for the first time in a General Election.

1919 The Irish Republican Army is founded by Michael Collins to fight against Britain until a united Republic of Ireland is established: a long campaign of bombing and guerilla warfare begins. At St Magnus' Cathedral, Kirkwall, the bones of Saints Magnus and Rognavald are discovered secreted within the Norman piers of the Cathedral; St Magnus was murdered in 1117. The Paris Peace Conference (Britain, France, Italy, USA) discusses terms for the Treaty of Versailles. Ernest Rutherford discovers the proton.

Jan [1] 200 sailors returning home from the war drown when the *Stornoway* sinks off Scotland.

Feb [3] London tube workers strike for shorter hours.

Mar [10] The Government is reported to favour the idea of a Channel Tunnel. [29] The Kaiser threatens suicide rather than submit to a trial.

Apr [5] Eamon de Valera is elected president of Sinn Fein. [24] Edward Prince of Wales is to become a freemason.

May [12] The first post-war performance at Covent Garden (*La Bohème*). [18] The ballet dancer Dame Margot Fonteyn is born at Reigate as Margaret Hookham.

Jun [21] The German fleet (72 ships) is scuttled in Scapa Flow on the orders of Rear-Admiral von Reuter. [23] The Government's Coal Commission recommends nationalizing the coal industry. [28] The peace treaty with Germany is signed at Versailles. [30] The physicist Lord Rayleigh dies at Witham, Essex.

Jul [6] The British airship 'R34' arrives in New York from Scotland (starting July 2), becoming the first airship to cross the Atlantic. [9] The Government decides to raise the price of coal. [18] Edwin Lutyens' war memorial, the Cenotaph, is unveiled. [22] The Commons vote to ratify the terms of the Treaty of Versailles.

Aug [3-4] There are riots in Liverpool during the police strike. [29] The daily air service between London and Paris begins.

Sep [10] The TUC favours nationalizing the coal industry.

Oct [10] Teachers ask for their salaries, still at their pre-war level, to be doubled.

Nov [12] Pilots Smith and Ross set out from Hounslow on the first aeroplane flight to Australia.

Dec [1] Nancy, Lady Astor, MP for Portsmouth (Sutton), becomes the first woman to take her seat in the House of Commons. [13] Smith and Ross reach Darwin in Australia. [18] Sir John Alcock, aviator, dies of injuries received in an aeroplane accident. [23] Sex Disqualification Removal Act; the professions are now opened to women.

1920 Irish Republicans begin an assassination campaign against British soldiers; in reprisal, the Black and Tans open fire on innocent spectators at a football match. The Road Fund is established; licence money collected from motorists is to be used for road building and maintenance, although this fund is later to be 'raided' by successive Chancellors of the Exchequer. The Coal Mines Act limits the profits of private pit-owners and sets up a welfare fund for the miners. Unemployment Insurance Act; this gives financial assistance for up to 15 weeks to unemployed people who contribute regularly to the scheme.

Feb [5] The Germans refuse to hand over alleged war criminals to the Allies. The Royal Air Force College at Cranwell opens.

Mar [26] A magistrate is dragged from a train and murdered in Ireland: it is the 29th political murder in Ireland this year. [29] Sir William Robertson attains the rank of Field Marshal, and becomes the only private ever to have risen to that rank.

Apr [13] 300,000 workers strike in protests against British treatment of Sinn Fein prisoners. [14] 89 Sinn Fein hunger strikers are released from Dublin Prison.

May [30] 20 people drown in serious flooding in Lincolnshire.

Jun [4] Prince George (George VI) is created Duke of York.

Jul [1] Germany surrenders her largest airship 'L71', to Britain. [8] British troops set up roadblocks outside Dublin. [13] The LCC bans the employment of foreigners in council jobs.

Aug [3] The novelist P. D. James (Baroness James) is born.

Sep The politician Victor Grayson mysteriously disappears, never to be seen again. [5] The composer Peter Racine Fricker is born. [11] A motor-cycle speed record of 100 mph is set at Brooklands. [22] The Metropolitan 'Flying Squad' is formed.

Oct [7] The first 100 women are admitted to Oxford to take degrees. [16] The coal miners go on strike. [17] Michael Fitzgerald is the first Irish hunger striker to die. [28] Sylvia Pankhurst is sent to prison for six months after urging people to loot the docks.

Nov [10] The body of an unknown British soldier arrives in London for burial in Westminster Abbey. [11] The politician Roy Jenkins (Lord Jenkins) is born at Abersychan. [20] Actress Dulcie Gray is born. [29] The IRA kills 15 army cadets amid escalating violence.

Dec [3] Rudyard Kipling wins £2 damages from a medical firm that has used part of his poem *If* in its advertising campaign.

1921 Railways Act; over 100 lines amalgamate into four large
companies (LMS, LNER, GWR and SR) in the interests of
efficiency. The first Everest Reconnaissance Expedition is led
by Lt Col Howard-Bury. Frederick Soddy is awarded the
Nobel Prize for Chemistry.

Jan   [3] Airships 'R-36' and '37' are completed; they are capable
of carrying 50 passengers. [8] Lloyd George becomes the
first Prime Minister to occupy 'Chequers', the house given to
the nation by Lord Lee of Fareham. [20] Six policemen in
Ireland are killed by the IRA. The British submarine 'K5'
sinks in the Channel: 56 are drowned. [22] British tanks and
troops seal off parts of Dublin in an attempt to catch the
gunmen.

Feb   [16] Eight Sinn Fein supporters are shot dead in a gun battle
with British soldiers.

Mar   [11] Queen Mary becomes the first woman to be awarded an
Oxford degree. [17] Marie Stopes opens her first birth control
clinic in Holloway. [31] The jockey Sir Gordon Richards rides
'Gay Lord' at Leicester, the first of his 4870 winners.
Churchill promises that Britain will abide by the Balfour
Declaration to create a Jewish homeland in Palestine.

Apr   [3] Coal rationing becomes necessary because of the miners'
strike. [15] Railway and transport unions decide not to strike
in support of the coal miners. [27] The Allies claim £6650
million compensation from Germany for damage done
during the war; the Germans reluctantly agree, but it will put
a great strain on Germany's war-damaged economy.

Jun   [10] Prince Philip is born on Corfu. [12] Postmen stop
collecting and delivering mail on Sundays.

Jul   [12] de Valera comes to London to discuss the Irish crisis with
Lloyd George.

Aug   [14] de Valera rejects Lloyd George's offer of Dominion
status for Ireland.

Oct   [2] Robert Runcie, Archbishop of Canterbury, is born.

Oct   [21] The composer Malcolm Arnold is born. [23] John Boyd
Dunlop, inventor of the pneumatic tyre, dies.

Nov [11] The British Legion holds its first Poppy Day.

Dec [6] The Irish Free State is established by peace treaty with Britain; six of the nine counties of Ulster are given limited self-government as the province of 'Northern Ireland'. [25] Gandhi's organized mass boycott of the Prince of Wales as he arrives in Calcutta is successful.

1922 'Oxford bags' are in fashion. The Transport and General Workers Union is formed. Archibald Hill (British) and Otto Meyerhof (German) are awarded the Nobel Prize for Physiology and Medicine.

Jan There are many deaths from influenza. [5] Sir Ernest Shackleton, explorer, dies on South Georgia.

Feb [28] The British protectorate over Egypt comes to an end.

Mar [8] There are 100 mph winds along the south coast. [31] The Irish Free State Bill receives the Royal Assent today.

Apr [13] The author John Braine is born at Bradford. [16] The poet and novelist Sir Kingsley Amis is born in London.

May [11] The British radio station '2LO' is opened at Marconi House in the Strand. [29] The MP Horatio Bottomley is sentenced to seven years in prison for his Victory Bonds fraud.

Jun [12] The Mallory expedition succeeds in climbing to within 3,200 feet of the summit of Everest.

Aug [22] The Irish politician and revolutionary Michael Collins is assassinated by republican extremists in an ambush between Bandon and Macroom.

Oct [7] Marie Lloyd, the music hall entertainer, dies after collapsing on the stage of the Alhambra Theatre. As unemployment grows in the North, trade unionists and socialists in Glasgow organize the first Hunger March to London. [18] The BBC is formed. [23] Bonar Law becomes Prime Minister.

Nov [1] Radio licences costing ten shillings a year are introduced. [5] Howard Carter discovers the tomb of King Tutankhamun in Egypt. [9] Sir William Horwood, the Metropolitan Police

Commissioner, is poisoned by arsenic-filled chocolates. [25] Carter opens the inner tomb of Tutankhamun and sees 'wonderful things'.

Dec [6] Trial of Edith Thompson and Frederick Bywaters for the murder of Percy Thompson begins. [17] The last British troops leave the Irish Republic. [23] The BBC starts broadcasting a daily news programme.

1923 Sir Frederick Banting (Canadian) and John MacLeod (British) are awarded the Nobel Prize for Physiology and Medicine. W. B. Yeats receives the Nobel Prize for Literature.

Jan [1] Re-grouping of British railways according to the Railways Act. [9] Edith Evans is hanged for murder, even though she shouted 'Oh, don't' as her lover stabbed her husband; Bywaters, the lover, is hanged at the same time. The New Zealand writer Katherine Mansfield dies.

Feb [9] The playwright Brendan Behan is born in Dublin. [17] Lord Caernarvon 'officially' opens the inner tomb of Tutankhamun.

Mar [27] The astronomer and broadcaster Patrick Moore is born at Pinner. [27] Sir James Dewar, inventor, dies aged 80.

Apr [16] Stanley Baldwin's Budget cuts income tax by sixpence. [26] The Duke of York, later to become George VI, marries Lady Elizabeth Bowes-Lyon (the Queen Mother) in Westminster Abbey.

May [8] Jack Hobbs scores his one hundredth century in first class cricket. [21] Stanley Baldwin becomes Prime Minister following Bonar Law's resignation on being told he has an incurable throat cancer.

Jul [18] Matrimonial Causes Act, allowing wives to divorce adulterous husbands. [31] Housing Act, providing subsidies for house building.

Aug [29] Sir Richard Attenborough, film actor and producer, is born at Cambridge.

Sep [11] The actor Alan Badel is born at Rusholme, Manchester.

Oct [1] Britain agrees to the creation of an autonomous Southern Rhodesian (Zimbabwe) government. [4] Five men are rescued from a flooding pit at Redding near Falkirk after being trapped for ten days. [30] Andrew Bonar Law, Conservative Prime Minister, dies.

Dec [13] Lord Alfred Douglas is sentenced to six months in prison for libelling Winston Churchill. [31] The chimes of Big Ben are broadcast for the first time.

1924 Work begins on the trunk road system. Ampleforth Abbey is founded. Agricultural Wages Act; this sets up county boards to fix wage rates, but some farmers lay off workers rather than pay the higher wages.

Jan [10] Submarine 'L-34' sinks off Weymouth: all 43 on board die. [22] The first Labour Government is formed under Ramsay MacDonald, following the December 6 election.

Feb [1] The Labour Government formally recognizes the Communist regime in Russia. [5] The BBC time pips are broadcast for the first time. [16] The dock strike begins.

Mar [30] Sir Charles Stanford, composer, dies.

Apr [23] The Empire Exhibition opens at Wembley Stadium.

May [4] Sir Edward Elgar is appointed Master of the King's Musick. The author Edith Nesbit dies.

Jun [8] On the third Everest Expedition, Mallory and Irvine are lost somewhere above 8450m; it is generally believed that they did not reach the summit.

Jul [30] Eric Liddell sets a new 400m running record at the Paris Olympics.

Aug [3] The novelist Joseph Conrad dies. [8] Commercial treaty with Russia. [15] Robert Bolt, playwright and screenwriter, is born in Sale. [16] The British Government agrees to withdraw British troops from of the Ruhr.

Oct [7] The Labour Party resists a move from the Communist Party to affiliate. [29] The Conservatives win the General Election by a large majority after a press story about the

Zinoviev letter (October 25) urging British Communists to whip up revolution in Britain.

Nov [1] de Valera is sentenced to one month in prison for entering Ulster illegally. [7] The second Baldwin Ministry begins. [21] The treaties made with Russia during the previous government are repudiated.

1925 John Logie Baird invents a working television system. George Bernard Shaw is awarded the Nobel Prize for Literature.

Mar [12] Britain rejects the Geneva Protocol. [14] The poet John Wain is born. [18] Fire destroys two floors of Madame Tussaud's waxworks museum, London. [20] Lord Curzon dies.

Apr [22] The actor George Cole is born in London.

May [1] Cyprus becomes a British colony.
[7] Lord Leverhulme (William Lever), manufacturer, dies. [13] Gold Bullion Standard Act; Churchill introduces this return to the Gold Standard. [14] The novelist Sir Rider Haggard dies. The composer Tristram Cary is born. [22] General Sir John French dies. [28] The Home Secretary orders all known 'subversives' to be barred from entering the country.

Jun [13] The opening night of Noel Coward's *Hay Fever*. [11] The first murder in the air takes place, when a London gem dealer is thrown out of a plane.

Aug [7] Summer Time Act; changing clocks in the summer is made a permanent institution.

Sep [8] The comedy actor Peter Sellers is born at Southsea. [9] The TUC votes against the amalgamation of all trade unions.

Oct [6] The Archbishop of Canterbury blames low church attendance on poor preaching and outdated clergy. [13] Margaret Thatcher, Conservative Prime Minister, is born in Grantham as Margaret Roberts.

Nov [10] The actor Richard Burton is born at Pontrhydfen, Wales as Richard Jenkins. [12] The submarine 'M-1' is lost in the

Channel: all 68 men on board die. [20] Queen Alexandra, widow of Edward VII, dies.

Dec [3] The Irish boundary agreement is signed, fixing the border between Northern Ireland and the Irish Free State.

1926 The Hadow Committee's Report on Education recommends raising the school-leaving age to 15 and dividing children at the age of 11 by means of testing.

Jan [5] The first widows' pensions are paid out. [27] John Logie Baird gives the first public demonstration of television to members of the Royal Institution in his workshop in Soho. [30] The British occupation of the Rhineland ends as troops move out.

Mar [5] Four paintings by Constable are stolen from the Royal Academy. [6] The Shakespeare Memorial Theatre at Stratford is destroyed by fire. [24] The Miners' Federation refuses to accept the Royal Commission's proposals to cut wage levels and abolish the minimum wage.

Apr [6] The Northern Ireland politician Ian Paisley is born. [7] The Hon. Violet Gibson attempts to assassinate Mussolini, but the bullet only grazes his nose. [21] Queen Elizabeth II is born at 17 Bruton Street in London, the daughter of the Duke and Duchess of York.

May [1] The coal miners go on strike; the TUC calls for a General Strike in their support. [2] The trade union leader Clive Jenkins is born. [3] The General Strike begins. [8] The naturalist and broadcaster Sir David Attenborough is born. [12] The General Strike ends; the TUC backs down, saying that the Government is better prepared for a long conflict than the strikers. [20] The miners, feeling betrayed by the unions, vote to stay out on strike.

Jun [8] Dame Nellie Melba gives her farewell performance at Covent Garden.

Aug [3] London's first traffic lights come into use at Piccadilly Circus. [6] Actor Frank Finlay is born in Farnworth, Lancs. [9] Southern Railway decides to convert from steam to electric by 1928. [21] Riots break out among the striking coal miners.

Oct   [5] Most of the miners return to work. [15] There is a clash between police and striking miners near Port Talbot. [19] The Imperial Conference begins.

Nov   [2] The formation of Imperial Chemical Industries is announced. [18] The Imperial Conference ends with a declaration that Britain and her dominions are of equal political status and in no way subordinate to one another. [20] The British Empire is renamed the British Commonwealth.

Dec   [3] The novelist Agatha Christie disappears from her London home. [14] Agatha Christie is found in a Harrogate Hotel, apparently having lost her memory; she never accounts for the eleven lost days.

1927   The Unemployment Insurance Act extends the benefit period. Arthur Crompton (American) and Charles T. W. Wilson (British) are awarded the Nobel Prize for Physics.

Jan   The newly-founded British Broadcasting Corporation (formerly Company) broadcasts its first programme.

Feb   [4] Malcolm Campbell breaks the world land speed record on Pendine Sands (174 mph). [8] Sir Stanley Baker (actor) is born at Ferndale, Wales.

Mar   [29] Henry Segrave breaks the world land speed record in Florida (203 mph).

Jun   [14] Jerome K. Jerome, author of *Three Men in a Boat*, dies. [20] There is a fight between Communists and Fascists in Hyde Park. [28] Trade Disputes and Trade Union Act; this measure makes sympathy strikes and lock-outs illegal, and forbids the use of union funds for political purposes.

Jul   [6] The Church of England approves revisions to the Book of Common Prayer.

Oct   A newspaper article about the Oscar Slater case (1909) includes an interview with a witness; Ramsay MacDonald, the Prime Minister, orders Slater's release after 18 years of wrongful imprisonment. Slater receives £6000 compensation from the Scottish Office.

Nov [5] The first automatic traffic lights begin working, at the Prince Square crossroads in Wolverhampton. [8] The comedian Ken Dodd is born in Liverpool. [12] The first veteran car rally from London to Brighton takes place, sponsored by the *Daily Sketch*. [22] 200 unemployed Welsh miners march to London but fail to meet Stanley Baldwin.

Dec [25] A white Christmas.

1928 Owen Richardson is awarded the Nobel Prize for Physics.

Jan [5] The first Old Age Pensions, of ten shillings a week are drawn. [6] The Thames bursts its banks, flooding London: four drown. [11] The poet and novelist Thomas Hardy dies aged 87. [29] Earl Haig, the First World War army commander, dies.

Feb [15] Herbert Henry Asquith, Prime Minister 1908-16, dies. [22] The entertainer Bruce Forsyth is born.

Mar [4] Alan Sillitoe, writer, is born at Nottingham. [19] The Revised Book of Common Prayer is published.

May [7] The voting age for women is brought down from 30 to 21.

Jun [14] The suffragette Emmeline Pankhurst dies. [28] Sir Cyril Smith, Liberal politician, is born at Rochdale.

Jul [3] The world's first colour television pictures are tramsmitted by John Logie Baird at the Baird Studios in London. [21] The actress Ellen Terry dies aged 81.

Aug [1] The Morris Minor appears. [19] Lord Haldane, who founded the Territorial Army, dies.

Nov [12] Archbishop Davidson resigns. [22] The first £1 and 10 shilling notes come into circulation. [23] The King's illness is made public. [30] Cosmo Gordon Lang, Archbishop of York, becomes Archbishop of Canterbury.

Dec [20] A treaty is concluded with China, recognizing the Nanking government, in return for which China abolishes coast and interior duties.

1929 Local Government Act; the de-rating of farms and farm buildings is designed to help farmers. Christian Eijkman (Dutch) and Sir Frederick Hopkins (British) are awarded the Nobel Prize for Physiology and Medicine. Arthur Harden (British) and Hans von Euler-Chelpin (German/Swedish) are awarded the Nobel Prize for Chemistry.

Jan [31] The actress Jean Simmons is born in London.

Feb [4] The first 'Green Belt' area is approved near Hendon. [8] de Valera is sentenced to a month in prison for illegal entry into Northern Ireland. [12] The actress Lillie Langtry dies in Monte Carlo.

Mar [23] Roger Bannister, the first athlete to run a mile in under four minutes, is born at Harrow. [29] Jeremy Thorpe, Liberal Party leader, is born.

May [21] Lord Rosebery, Prime Minister, dies. [30] Labour wins the General Election (Labour 288, Conservatives 260).

Jun [7] Ramsay MacDonald forms Britain's second Labour Government.

Jul The police seize 12 of D. H. Lawrence's paintings on show in a Mayfair gallery, after receiving complaints about their obscenity. [31] The World Boy Scouts' Jamboree opens at Arrowe Park, Birkenhead.

Aug [6] Britain and Egypt agree a draft treaty for the evacuation of British troops from Egypt, except for the Suez Canal zone. [11] The Welsh composer Alun Hoddinott is born.

Sep [25] The comedian Ronnie Barker is born at Bedford. [28] Ramsay MacDonald begins a visit to the USA and Canada.

Oct [1] Diplomatic relations with Soviet Russia are resumed. [14] The 'R101' airship flies on its first trial from Cardington across London. [26] It is announced that all London buses will be painted red; trials with red-and-yellow proved unpopular. [28] The London Stock Exchange feels the first shock waves from the Wall Street Crash; shares fall sharply.

Nov [1] Ramsay MacDonald returns to Britain.

Dec [2] Britain's first 22 public phone boxes come into service in London. [5] 94 mph winds sweep across Britain, killing 26 people. [12] The actor and playwright John Osborne is born.

1930 Sir Frank Whittle invents the jet engine.

Jan [15] Ramsay MacDonald advocates that the world powers abolish battleships.

Feb [25] A Bill to abolish blasphemy as a legal offence is dropped.

Mar [2] The poet and novelist D. H. Lawrence dies of tuberculosis. [7] The Earl of Snowdon, ex-husband of Princess Margaret, is born as Antony Armstrong-Jones. [14] The Government Channel Tunnel Committee approves the building of a Channel Tunnel. [19] Arthur Balfour, Conservative Prime Minister 1902-5, dies aged 81.

Apr [1] Robert Bridges, Poet Laureate, dies.

May [5] Amy Johnson takes off from Croydon on her solo flight to Australia, arriving on May 24. [9] John Masefield is appointed Poet Laureate. [25] Randall Davidson, retired Archbishop of Canterbury, dies. [29] The BBC Symphony Orchestra is founded under Sir Adrian Boult.

Jun [1] Toscanini conducts at the Albert Hall. [5] The Government rejects proposals for a Channel Tunnel. [11] The luxury liner *Empress of India* is launched at Clydebank by the Prince of Wales. [13] Sir Henry Segrave is killed when his speed-boat crashes at nearly 100 mph on Lake Windermere. [30] Britain formally recognizes Iraq as an independent state.

Jul [7] Sir Arthur Conan Doyle, creator of Sherlock Holmes, dies. [17] A Labour MP seizes the mace in the House of Commons, causing uproar. [28] The airship 'R-101' starts its maiden flight across the Atlantic.

Aug [17] Ted Hughes, Poet Laureate, is born. [21] Princess Margaret is born at Glamis Castle. [29] William Spooner, the creator of spoonerisms, dies.

Sep [29] George Bernard Shaw declines the offer of a peerage. [30] The politician Lord Birkenhead dies.

Oct [5] The 'R-101' is destroyed when it crashes at Beauvais in France on its first flight to India; 48 lives are lost, including that of the Air Minister, Lord Thomson. The loss of the 'R-101' marks the end of British interest in airships. [10] The Tyne Bridge at Newcastle is opened. The playwright Harold Pinter is born.

Nov [10] Four elephants run amok in the Lord Mayor's Show, injuring 30 people.

Dec [7] Mosley's manifesto advocating a programme of public works is published. Sir Yehudi Menuhin (aged 13) plays at the Albert Hall. [15] A Commons Select Committee recommends ending the death penalty.

1931
Jan [1] Road Traffic Act comes into force; it introduces traffic police and compulsory third-party insurance for motorists. [6] The new Sadler's Wells Theatre opens in London. [20] Julia Wallace is murdered at her home in Wolverton Crescent, Anfield, Liverpool; police suspect her husband, but Herbert Wallace claims as his alibi that he was lured out of the house to meet a man called Qualtrough. [21] The Bill to raise the school-leaving age to 15 is defeated in the Commons. [26] Churchill resigns from Baldwin's shadow cabinet over Indian policy, a proposed federation with limited self-government.

Feb [2] Herbert Wallace is charged with murder. [5] Malcolm Campbell breaks the world land speed record at Daytona Sands (245 mph). [11] Sir Charles Parsons, inventor of the first practical steam turbine in 1884, dies at Kingston in Surrey. [28] Sir Oswald Mosley forms his New Party.

Mar [27] The novelist Arnold Bennett dies of typhoid; he drank water from a carafe in a Paris hotel in order to show that it was safe.

Apr [14] The first Highway Code is issued. [22] The trial of Herbert Wallace starts; he is found guilty but acquitted on appeal. The real murderer, the mysterious 'Qualtrough', who is believed to have died in in April 1980, was never brought to trial. [30] Mosley's New Party splits the Labour vote, letting in the Conservative candidate in the Ashton-under-Lyne by-election.

Jun [2] George V creates no new peers in his Birthday Honours List. [7] Violent earth tremors are felt throughout Britain.

Jul [6] The census result shows that the population of the United Kingdom (44.8 million) is almost at a standstill.

Aug [24] The Labour Government is defeated and replaced by an all-party Coalition or National Government led by Ramsay MacDonald.

Sep [7] George V decides to take a £50,000 pay cut for the duration of the economic crisis. [20] Sterling is taken off the Gold Standard; the pound falls dramatically in value from 4.86 to 3.49 dollars.

Oct [2] After two nights of rioting in Glasgow in protest against the Government's emergency measures, 49 people are arrested. [27] A second General Election results in a National Government landslide, with Ramsay MacDonald continuing as Prime Minister.

Dec [11] Statute of Westminster, recognizing the independence of the British Commonwealth.

1932 Sir James Chadwick discovers a new sub-atomic particle, the neutron. The new Shakespeare Memorial Theatre opens in Stratford-on-Avon. The London Philharmonic Orchestra is founded by Sir Thomas Beecham. Unemployment reaches 2.75 million; the Trade Unions organize the largest ever hunger march on London, protesting against the means-testing of unemployment benefits. John Galsworthy is awarded the Nobel Prize for Literature.

Jan [25] Dartmoor Prison riot; the prison governor's life is saved by a man who has been reprieved from hanging. [27] The submarine 'M2' sinks; 50 die.

Feb [4] A 10% tariff is imposed on all imports, with concessions for those from the Empire. [27] The film actress Elizabeth Taylor is born in London. [29] Protective Tariffs

Acts; these trade-restrictive measures include a new 'corn law' giving British farmers a guaranteed price for their wheat.

Mar   [31] Revd. Harold Davidson, Rector of Stiffkey, is charged with immoral behaviour with teenage girls.

Apr   [24] A mass trespass on Kinderscout to establish a public right of access results in five arrests. [26] Motor Traffic Act: drivers who kill may be found guilty of manslaughter.

May   [9] Piccadilly in London is lit by electricity for the first time. [11] After Ireland's threat to abolish the Loyal Oath to the King, the British Government warns that she may lose her tariff preference. [19] A Bill abolishing the Loyal Oath becomes law in Dublin.

Jun   [12] The Rector of Stiffkey tries to grab the Bible from a stand-in clergyman during a service.

Jul   [6] Kenneth Grahame, author of *The Wind in the Willows*, dies. [8] The Rector of Stiffkey is found guilty of disreputable association with women.

Aug   [10] The composer Alexander Goehr is born.

Oct   [1] Richard Harris, actor, is born in Limerick. [30] Ralph Reader presents the first Gang Show at the Scala Theatre, London.

Dec   [25] George V makes the first Royal Christmas Day broadcast to the Empire. [30] The London-Brighton railway line is electrified.

1933   'A London surgeon' takes, and publishes in the *Daily Mail*, the first photograph of the Loch Ness Monster; this starts an ongoing interest in the contents of the lake. Paul Dirac (British) and Erwin Schrödinger (Austrian) are awarded the Nobel Prize for Physics.

Jan   [12] The writer Compton Mackenzie is fined for revealing in *Greek Memories* the identity of British Secret Servicemen in the First World War. [18] The botanist and conservationist David Bellamy is born. [31] The novelist John Galsworthy dies.

Feb [9] The 'King and Country' debate at the Oxford Union; the motion 'that this house would in no circumstances fight for King and Country' is won.

Mar [14] The film actor Michael Caine is born (as Maurice Micklewhite). [22] The car manufacturer Sir Frederick Henry Royce dies.

May [23] Actress Joan Collins is born in London. [24] The TUC calls for a boycott of Germany to protest at Hitler's regime.

Jul [15] The musician Sir Julian Bream is born. [20] 30,000 Jews take part in a Hyde Park March to protest against Nazi anti-semitism. [23] The World Monetary and Economic Conference ends in London without any agreement. Its failure leads the British Government to extend its policy of economic nationalism; free trade is finally abandoned and people are encouraged to 'buy British'.

Aug [14] Richard Hardy complains that the English language is becoming polluted by fashions for such words as 'definitely, frightfully, absolutely, awfully and priceless'. [21] The singer Dame Janet Baker is born.

Sep [10] Forest fires accompany the long drought.

Oct [15] Mosley and his Fascist sympathizers are stoned in Manchester.

Dec [17] For this day only members of the public are allowed to walk through the newly completed Mersey Road Tunnel.

1934 The Glyndebourne Operatic Festival is founded. Schoolchildren are to be given half a pint of milk a day as part of a national policy of improving nutrition. The Government grants a subsidy to Cunard-White Star to enable the firm to complete the liner *Queen Mary*. The Unemployment Assistance Board is founded; extended benefits are to be means-tested, a very unpopular development. A speed limit of 30 mph is reintroduced in built-up areas, owing to the large number of accidents.

Jan   [16] Churchill says in a broadcast that Britain has never been so defenceless as it is now. [21]There is a large rally of the British Union of Fascists in Birmingham.

Feb   [17] Actor Alan Bates is born. [20] Anthony Eden has a friendly meeting with Hitler. [23] The composer Sir Edward Elgar dies at Worcester.

Mar   [26] Driving tests are introduced.

Apr   [27] Britain and France warn Germany not to default on war reparations payments.

May   [3] H. G. Wells stands by his earlier prediction that there will be another world war by 1940. [25] The composer Gustav Holst dies.

Jun   [10] The composer Frederick Delius dies.

Jul   [15] The composer Sir Harrison Birtwistle is born at Accrington. [18] The Mersey Road Tunnel is opened by George V.

Sep   [8] Sir Peter Maxwell Davies, composer, is born. [9] Police separate Fascists and anti-Fascists in a London march. [22] The Gresford pit disaster in North Wales; 265 miners are killed. [26] The liner *Queen Mary* is launched at John Brown's yard at Clydebank.

Oct   [10] Prince George, George V's son, is created Duke of Kent.

Nov   [30] The Flying Scotsman reaches a record speed of 97 mph.

Dec   [9] Actress Dame Judi Dench is born. [28] Actress Dame Maggie Smith is born.

1935 A prototype of the Spitfire is built. The first Penguin paperback books are produced by Allen Lane. Eric Shipton leads an expedition to survey the Everest region. Sir James Chadwick is awarded the Nobel Prize for Physics.

Feb   [26] RADAR (Radio Detection And Ranging) is first demonstrated, in secret, by Robert Watson-Watt at Daventry.

Mar   [7] Malcolm Campbell sets a new world land speed record (276 mph). [24] George Stoner murders Francis Rattenbury, his mistress's husband.

Apr   [15] Chamberlain claims that Britain has '80% recovered' from the Depression. [19] Dudley Moore, comedian, musician and composer, is born in London.

May   [4] Leicester Square tube station opens. [6] George V's Silver Jubilee prompts a national demonstration of loyalty and patriotism. [22] The RAF is to be trebled in size within two years, to make sure that the British air force equals Germany's.

Jun   [7] Stanley Baldwin succeeds Ramsay MacDonald following a General Election precipitated by MacDonald's resignation for health reasons; a Conservative-led National Government is formed. [18] Anglo-German naval agreement; Germany is to have no more than 35% of Britain's tonnage; this in turn leads to a distinct cooling in relations between Britain and France.

Aug   [2] Government of India Act; a step towards self-government.

Oct   [8] Clement Attlee becomes Labour Party leader. [20] The ex-Labour leader Arthur Henderson dies. 11 are killed in a 92 mph wind.

Nov   [20] Lord Jellicoe, Admiral of the Fleet in the First World War, dies.

1936 Sir Henry Dale (British) and Otto Loewi (German/Austrian) are awarded the Nobel Prize for Physiology and Medicine.

Jan   [11] Arthur Scargill, National Union of Mineworkers leader, is born. [18] The writer Rudyard Kipling dies. [20] George V dies at Sandringham aged 70; he is succeeded by his son as Edward VIII.

Feb   [11] Dame Laura Knight becomes the first woman to be admitted to membership of the Royal Academy.

Mar   [29] The composer Richard Rodney Bennett is born.

Apr   [30] The Government announces its plan to build 38 warships.

May   [9] Actress Glenda Jackson is born. The actor Albert Finney is born in Salford. [18] Jasmine Bligh and Elizabeth Cowell become the BBC's first women announcers. [27] The first open prison in Britain, New Hall near Wakefield, is opened. The *Queen Mary* sails on her maiden voyage.

Jun   [3] Emperor Haile Selassie arrives in London in exile. [6] Gatwick Airport opens. [11] Leslie Mitchell is to be the first television announcer. [14] The author G. K. Chesterton dies.

Jul   [14] Britain starts mass-producing gas masks. [16] George McMahon, a journalist, makes an attempt to assassinate Edward VIII. [24] The 'Speaking Clock' is introduced by the Post Office at the suggestion of Eugene Wender. [31] Education Act, raising the school-leaving age to 15.

Aug   [21] The first television broadcast from Alexandra Palace.

Sep   [30] The Pinewood Film Studios open.

Oct   [5] The Jarrow Hunger March begins. [11] There are violent clashes in the East End of London between Mosleyite Fascists and their opponents: 80 people are injured. [12] The London-Paris through-train service opens. [16] Lord Beaverbrook calls on the King in order to come to an agreement about press silence on the King's relationship with Mrs Simpson.

Nov   [11] Baldwin refuses to meet the Jarrow marchers. [18] Edward VIII visits South Wales, sees several thousands of unemployed men and says, 'something must be done'.

Dec   [10] Edward VIII abdicates after a reign of 325 days; his younger brother, the Duke of York, becomes George VI.

1937   Walter Haworth (British) and Paul Karrer (Swiss) are awarded the Nobel Prize for Chemistry. Sir George Thomson (British) and Clinton Davidson (American) are awarded the Nobel Prize for Physics.

Jan   [1] Public Order Act comes into force; the Government is determined to end the British Union of Fascists' provocative marches. [2] Anglo-Italian Mediterranean Agreement; this is intended to reduce the dangerous level of friction between Britain and Italy in the Mediterranean. [3] Britain makes a formal protest to France about the shelling of the *Blackhill* in the Bay of Biscay. [10] The Government bans volunteers from fighting in Spain, introducing a two-year prison sentence for offenders. [18] Horse-drawn traffic is banned from a large area of the West End of London.

Feb [4] The German ambassador von Ribbentrop gives George VI a Nazi salute.

Mar [16] Sir Austen Chamberlain, Conservative politician, dies.

Apr [1] London's Green Belt is proposed. [13] HMS *Ark Royal* is launched.

May [12] Coronation of George VI (the BBC's first outside television broadcast). [14] Viscount Allenby, army commander in Palestine in the First World War, dies. [28] Following Baldwin's resignation, a Coalition Government under Neville Chamberlain is formed: a Conservative-led National Government.

Jun [3] The Duke of Windsor (ex-King Edward VIII) marries Mrs Wallis Simpson at Monts in France. [19] Sir James Barrie, creator of 'Peter Pan', dies. [29] Italy and Germany oppose Anglo-French patrols round the coasts of Spain.

Jul [1] The '999' emergency telephone service comes into operation. [8] The Peel Report proposes dividing Palestine into Jewish and Arab states, but Parliament will not agree to it. [9] The painter David Hockney is born. [28] The ex-Rector of Stiffkey is mauled by a lion at Skegness.

Sep [10] The TUC votes in favour of re-armament.

Oct [10] Sir Oswald Mosley is hit by a stone and knocked unconscious at a rally in Liverpool. [14] The first Motor Show opens at Earls Court. [19] Lord Rutherford, the founder of atomic theory, dies at Cambridge. [22] The Duke and Duchess of Windsor meet Hitler in Berlin, on something approaching a state visit.

Nov [9] Ramsay MacDonald, Labour Prime Minister, dies at sea while on a cruise. [17] Lord Halifax arrives in Berlin for talks with Hitler on the Sudeten Germans; this is the first step in the appeasement policy.

Dec [29] The new Irish Constitution comes into force; the Republic is to be called Eire. [31] Actor Anthony Hopkins is born.

1938

Jan [8] Sigmund Freud arrives in London to escape persecution.

Feb [14] The British naval base at Singapore opens. [17] John Logie Baird demonstrates a prototype colour television. [20] The Foreign Secretary, Sir Anthony Eden, resigns in protest against Chamberlain's determination to try to obtain agreement with Italy without waiting for a settlement over Spain.

Mar [30] £11 million are to be spent on new RAF airfields. [31] Sir David Steel, Liberal Party leader, is born. Sir Edwin Lutyens' plan for a National Theatre is made public.

Apr [1] Britain and the US abandon the London naval treaty to allow them to build battleships. [16] Anglo-Italian Agreement; this measure, which Chamberlain has been working towards, is to come into force as soon as Italian 'volunteers' are withdrawn from Spain.

May [9] Scotland Yard announce that they are to use police dogs. [16] The Women's Voluntary Service is founded by the Marchioness of Reading.

Jun [2] Regent's Park Children's Zoo is opened by Robert and Edward Kennedy. [9] The Government signs a contract to buy 400 planes from the USA.

Jul [7] Augustus John opens a London exhibition of art banned in Germany. [15] The Government orders 1000 spitfire fighters. [28] The liner *Mauretania* is launched at Birkenhead.

Sep The German-Czechoslovakia Crisis begins. [15] Chamberlain visits Hitler at Berchtesgaden concerning Czechoslovakia. [22] Chamberlain meets Hitler again, at Godesberg. [27] The liner *Queen Elizabeth* is launched at Clydebank by the Queen Mother. [28] The British Navy is mobilized. [29] Chamberlain meets Hitler, Mussolini and Daladier at Munich; the Munich

Agreement is a guarantee to Czechoslovakia against further aggression.

Oct [4] Hitler's troops invade the Sudetenland.

Nov [2] The Anglo-Italian Agreement is ratified. [9] The British Government calls a conference on the future of Palestine.

Dec [1] A national register for war service is opened, initially on a voluntary basis, as a preliminary to war. [2] 206 German Jewish schoolchildren arrive in Britain as refugees. [21] The Government allocates £200,000 to the building of air-raid shelters.

1939 George Bernard Shaw wins an Academy Award for his screen adaptation of *Pygmalion*. The IRA begin a bombing campaign in mainland Britain; a bomb in Coventry kills five passers-by.

Jan [11] Chamberlain and Lord Haldane visit Mussolini to discuss recognition of the Franco regime. [25] Sir Stafford Cripps is expelled from the Labour Party. [28] The poet W. B. Yeats dies.

Feb [3] The police hunt for IRA extremists after bombs explode at London tube stations. [27] Britain recognizes Franco's government. Borley Rectory, reputed to be Britain's most haunted house, is burnt to the ground. [28] Hitler denounces the Anglo-German Naval Treaty and the Polish Non-Aggression Treaty.

Mar [2] Howard Carter, discoverer of Tutankhamun's tomb in 1922, dies. [17] Talks on Palestine end in failure. Chamberlain denounces Hitler. [26] The first commercial oil deposit is found in Britain at Eakring in Nottinghamshire.

Apr [5] HMS *Illustrious*, Britain's largest aircraft carrier, is launched. [6] Britain, Poland and France sign a mutual assistance pact in case of attack. [25] The Budget allocates £1.3 billion to defence. [27] Conscription of 20-21 year old men is introduced. [28] Hitler tears up the 1934 naval treaty with Britain.

May [3] British farmers are urged by the Government to plough
up pasture to increase food production. [11] Chamberlain
warns Hitler that if the Germans use force in Danzig it will
mean war. [17] George VI and Queen Elizabeth begin a short
visit to North America in an attempt to strengthen
Anglo-Saxon solidarity. [19] The TUC decides not to oppose
the Government's conscription plans. [25] An Anglo-Polish
treaty is signed in London. Actor and director Sir Ian
McKellen is born.

Jun [1] The submarine *Thetis* sinks during trials in Liverpool Bay,
with the loss of 99 lives.

Jul [10] Chamberlain reaffirms Britain's pledge to stand by
Poland.

Aug [22] Britain and France again reaffirm their pledge to Poland.
[23] The German-Soviet Pact is signed by von Ribbentrop.
[25] Movable treasures are taken to safety from London's
museums and galleries. [28] The Admiralty declares the
Baltic and Mediterranean closed to British Merchant
Shipping.

Sep [1] The German army invades Poland. The BBC radio
'Home Service' (later to become Radio 4) begins
broadcasting. [1-4] Evacuation schemes are put into action
in England and Wales; 1.2 million people are moved.
[2] Military service for all British men between ages of 18 and
41 becomes compulsory. [3] At 11 am war is declared
between Britain and Germany as from 5 pm; this marks the
beginning of the Second World War. [4] A German
submarine sinks the British liner *Athenia* off the Irish coast.
The RAF raid the entrance to the Kiel Canal and bomb
German warships. [6] First German air raid on Britain. [11]
British troops land in France. [18] HMS *Courageous* is sunk in
the Atlantic: 500 men die. [23] Sigmund Freud, the founder
of modern psychology and psychoanalysis, dies in
Hampstead aged 83.

Oct [1] 250,000 more conscripts are called up. [14] The battleship
Royal Oak is torpedoed at anchor in Scapa Flow; 810 men die.

Nov [13] The first German bombs fall on British soil, in the Shetlands.

Dec [13] Battle of the River Plate; the German warship *Admiral Graf Spee* is engaged by HMS *Exeter, Ajax* and *Achilles*. [18] The *Admiral Graf Spee* is scuttled by her crew at the mouth of Montevideo harbour.

1940 Sir Howard Florey devises an important new process that will enable the large-scale production of penicillin; clinical trials begin.

Jan [3] Unity Mitford, who tried to befriend Hitler, returns to England after her unsuccessful suicide attempt. [8] Rationing of butter, bacon and sugar is introduced.

Feb [11] The novelist John Buchan dies. [6] 299 British prisoners are rescued from the German ship *Altmark* in Norwegian waters.

Mar [11] Meat rationing starts. [12] British ships are to be fitted with a device to protect them against magnetic mines. [29] Metal strips are put into banknotes for the first time as a defence against forgery.

Apr [14] Actress Julie Christie is born. [15] British troops arrive in Norway. The politician and writer Jeffrey Archer is born.

May [2] British troops withdraw from Norway. [10] Belgium, Luxembourg and the Netherlands are invaded by German troops; British troops cross into Belgium. Neville Chamberlain resigns as Prime Minister, and a National Government is formed under the leadership of Winston Churchill. [13] Churchill gives his 'Blood, toil, tears and sweat' speech. The Dutch Queen Wilhelmina arrives in London at the beginning of her exile. [22] Emergency Powers Act. [27] The Belgian army surrenders to the Germans; British forces begin to withdraw from Belgium and northern France. Dunkirk; the British Expeditionary Force and the First French Army are cut off near Dunkirk. 335,490 men are evacuated from the beach by 299 British warships and 420 small boats under continual German attack; the withdrawal takes a week (May 17-June 4). **[31]** Mosley is interned at Brixton Prison.

Jun   **[4]** Churchill makes his famous 'We shall fight them on the beaches' speech in the Commons. Later the same day, actor Norman Shelley reads the speech on the radio, impersonating Churchill's voice. **[5]** The Government bans strikes. Hitler declares a war of total annihilation against his enemies. **[10]** Italy declares war on Britain and France. **[16]** Churchill proposes a union of France and Britain. **[17]** The troopship *Lancastria* is sunk off St Nazaire with the loss of 2500 lives.

Jul   **[1]** The Channel Islands are occupied by German troops. **[10]** The British Union of Fascists becomes a banned organization.

Aug   **[17]** The German blockade of British waters begins. **[22]** Sir Oliver Lodge, pioneer of wireless telegraphy, dies. **[25]** The RAF begins night bombing in Germany. **[30]** Sir J. J. Thomson, discoverer of the electron, dies.

Sep   **[6]** London experiences the largest air attack since the start of the war and is severely damaged. **[15]** The Battle of Britain ends with victory for Britain; the Germans lose 1,733 aircraft and the British 915. Because the Germans' air supremacy is broken they are now unable to invade Britain; it is a turning-point in the war. **[23]** The George Cross, the highest civilian award for acts of courage, is instituted.

Oct   **[9]** The musician John Lennon is born in Liverpool. Churchill is elected leader of the Conservative Party. **[10]** A German bomb destroys the high altar of St Paul's Cathedral. **[19]** Actor Michael Gambon is born.

Nov   **[9]** Neville Chamberlain, Conservative Prime Minister 1937-40, dies of cancer. **[14]** A massive German attack on Coventry destroys the cathedral. **[17]** The sculptor and engraver Eric Gill dies. **[20]** A Luftwaffe raid on Birmingham. **[29]** Air raid on Liverpool.

Dec   **[2]** Bristol is heavily bombed. Britain invades Libya. **[22]** Sir Anthony Eden becomes Foreign Secretary again. **[29]** The City of London is badly burned by incendiary bombs; the Guildhall and eight of Wren's churches are destroyed.

1941

Jan   [5] Amy Johnson dies in plane crash in the Thames Estuary; officially she has 'disappeared', but it will emerge in years to come that she has been shot down by mistake by the British. [7] British troops capture Tobruk airport. [8] Lord Baden Powell, founder of the Boy Scout movement, dies. [10] British bases on Malta are bombed. [13] The novelist James Joyce dies in Zürich.

Feb   [1] The RAF raids Tripoli. [5] The war is costing Britain £11 million a day. [7] British and Commonwealth troops take Benghazi. [18] Churchill's Government receives a unanimous vote of confidence in Parliament. [27] Jeremy (Paddy) Ashdown, leader of the Liberal Democrats, is born.

Mar   [4] The British raid the Lofoten Islands. [28] The Battle of Cape Matapan; the Italian fleet is mostly destroyed by the British off the south coast of Greece. Virginia Woolf, novelist, drowns herself in the Sussex Ouse at Rodmell.

Apr   [3] British-led troops evacuate Benghazi as Rommel advances. [7] A War Budget raises income tax to a record 50%. [27] The Germans capture Athens.

May   [2] British and Commonwealth troops complete their evacuation of Greece. [5] Haile Selassie returns to Ethiopia from exile in Britain after his country is liberated by British forces. [10] Rudolf Hess lands by parachute in Scotland. [11] In a severe bombing raid on London the Chamber of the House of Commons is destroyed. [12] The Commons meet for the first time in the House of Lords. [15] The first jet-propelled aircraft, designed by Frank Whittle, flies for the first time. [20] Crete is invaded by German troops. [24] HMS *Hood* is sunk 13 miles off the Greenland coast: only three out of the crew of 1,421 survive the disaster. [27] The German battleship *Bismarck* is sunk. British forces withdraw from Crete. [31] The first shipments of food arrive from the USA.

Jun   [2] Clothes rationing begins. [7] The RAF reveals for the first
       time that radar has been used to locate enemy bombers.
Jul   [11] Sir Arthur Evans, who excavated Knossos, dies.
Aug   [14] The Atlantic Charter; this is a joint US and UK
       declaration of peace aims. [24] Churchill promises the US aid
       if the US becomes involved in a war with Japan. [25] British
       and Russian troops enter Iran and set up a new regime that
       will be sympathetic to their interests.
Oct   [16] The composer Derek Bourgeois is born.
Nov   [6] The counter-tenor James Bowman is born. [14] The
       aircraft carrier *Ark Royal* is sunk near Gibraltar. [18] The Battle
       of Libya begins: the Eighth Army's first offensive in North
       Africa. [24] HMS *Dunedin* is torpedoed. [25] HMS *Barham* is
       sunk.
Dec   [8] The United States declares war on Japan. Britain declares
       war on German puppet regimes in Finland, Romania and
       Hungary. [9] British forces in Tobruk are relieved. [10] HMS
       Repulse and *Prince of Wales* are sunk off Malaya by Japanese
       aircraft action. [11] Germany and Italy declare war on the US.
       [25] Hong Kong surrenders to the Japanese.

1942 The painters Philip Steer and Walter Sickert die. The
       Beveridge Report on Social Insurance and Allied
       Services recommends state social insurance 'from the cradle
       to the grave', and forms the basis of post-war social
       legislation.

Jan   [19] The entertainer Michael Crawford is born at Salisbury as
       Michael Dumble-Smith. [9] The first edition of 'Desert Island
       Discs' is broadcast, with Roy Plomley in the chair.
Feb   [9] Soap is rationed. [12] The German raiders *Scharnhorst*,
       Gneisenau and *Prinz Eugen* escape through the English
       Channel. [15] The British naval base of Singapore is
       surrendered to the Japanese.
Mar   [28] Neil Kinnock, Labour Party leader, is born. The RAF
       begins its terror bombing campaign with an attack on
       Lubeck. [29] Stafford Cripps meets Gandhi in Delhi and

offers him a British plan for full Indian independence after the war. [31] Archbishop Lang retires.

Apr   [15] Malta is awarded the George Cross for heroism during German and Italian bombardments. [17] William Temple, Archbishop of York, becomes Archbishop of Canterbury. [18] Lord Mountbatten is put in charge of combined Allied operations in South-East Asia. [25] Princess Elizabeth registers for war service.

May   [7] Madagascar is invaded by British troops to forestall the Japanese. [30] Thousand-bomber raid on Cologne. Churchill and Molotov agree a 20-year mutual aid treaty.

Jun   [3] The Government announces that it will take over the coal mines. [9] The US and UK agree to pool all food and production resources in order to ensure victory. [18] Paul McCartney, musician, is born in Liverpool. [20] Tobruk is captured by the Germans.

Jul   [16] The RAF makes its first daylight raid on the Ruhr.

Aug   [6] Montgomery becomes commander of the Eighth Army. [11] HMS *Eagle*, *Manchester* and *Cairo* are lost in Malta convoy action. [12] Churchill begins a four-day visit to Moscow, to discuss with Stalin the establishment of a second front in Europe. [19] The Dieppe Raid, called 'Operation Jubilee'; there are unexpectedly heavy casualties. [25] George, Duke of Kent, is killed in action.

Sep   [6] Two Belfast policemen are shot dead by the IRA.

Oct   [2] The British cruiser *Curaçao* collides with the liner *Queen Mary* off the coast of Donegal and sinks immediately with the loss of 338 lives. [10] Following German action, in chaining 2,500 Allied prisoners after the Dieppe Raid, British camps are now chaining up German prisoners-of-war. [23] Battle of El Alamein; the Allied offensive opens in Egypt. The German Afrika Corps is only 80 miles from Alexandria; British and Commonwealth troops under Montgomery and Alexander counter-attack and break the German forces. [31] The Germans bomb Canterbury as a reprisal for the bombing of Cologne.

Nov   [4] Rommel's army is in full retreat. [7] Allied invasion of North Africa, with Eisenhower in command. [10] Churchill's 'end of the beginning' speech on the Alamein victory. [13] Tobruk is recaptured by the Allies.

1943 Mulberry harbours are constructed. Daily expenditure on the war, in Britain alone, is estimated at £14 million.

Jan   [14] The Casablanca Conference (until January 24) between Roosevelt and Churchill. [23] Allied troops recapture Tripoli. [27] After the Casablanca Conference it is announced that plans have been made for an Allied offensive in Europe that will secure the Axis powers' unconditional surrender.

Feb   [12] Lord Nuffield founds the Nuffield Foundation with a gift of £10 million.

Mar   [2] The RAF bombs Berlin. [3] 178 people are killed in an accident at the Bethnal Green air raid shelter. [6] Heavy bombing raid on Essen.

Apr   RAF bombers raid Stuttgart.

May   [3] It becomes compulsory for British women of 18-45 to do part-time work. [7] Tunis and Bizerta are captured by the Allies. [12] German resistance in Tunisia ends. Churchill visits Washington to discuss the preparation of a second front in Europe and to promise British assistance in the war against Japan. [16] The Mohne, Sorpe and Eder dams in the Ruhr are breached by the RAF, using special bouncing bombs invented by Sir Barnes Wallis. [27] The entertainer Cilla Black is born in Liverpool.

Jun   [1] The actor Leslie Howard is killed when his plane is shot down over the Bay of Biscay. [21] Sir Michael Tippett is sentenced to three months in prison at Oxted for refusing to do military service.

Jul   [10] The Allies invade Sicily. [16] A White Paper recommends raising the school-leaving age again, to 16.

Aug   [13] The Allies bomb Rome, Milan and Turin. [7] Sicily is secured by the Allied forces.

Sep [3] Allies invade the Italian mainland. [7] Italy surrenders to the Allies. [21] The Patronal Festival of St Matthew's, Northampton, organized by Canon Walter Hussey; first performance of Britten's *Rejoice in the Lamb* and Tippett's *Fanfare*. [23] The German battleship *Tirpitz* is seriously damaged and disabled.

Nov [20] Mosley is released from prison, but is to remain under house arrest. [22] The Labour Party protests against Mosley's release. [25] Bomber Harris undertakes to bomb Berlin 'until the heart of Nazi Germany ceases to beat'. [28] Churchill, Roosevelt and Stalin meet in Teheran to discuss the question of a second front against the Axis.

Dec [22] Beatrix Potter, writer of children's stories, dies. [6] The last German battleship, *Scharnhorst*, is sunk.

1944 Education Act, introduced by R. A. Butler, raises the school-leaving age to 15, in effect implementing a report of 1926.

Jan [1] The architect Sir Edwin Lutyens dies. [22] The Allies land at Anzio.

Mar [10] The Education Minister R. A. Butler lifts the ban on women teachers marrying. [11] The Prime Minister of Eire, de Valera, refuses to comply with the American request to close the German and Japanese embassies in Dublin, to prevent the possible transmission of military intelligence through their agents. Britain suspends all travel between Britain and Eire. [15] The ancient monastery at Monte Cassino in Italy is destroyed by the Allies. [19] Tippett's *A Child of Our Time* is first performed. [24] Orde Wingate is killed in a plane crash in Assam.

Apr [6] From today income tax may be paid by the PAYE scheme. [30] The first pre-fabricated houses go on show in London.

May [9] The composer Dame Ethel Smyth dies. [19] 50 Allied officers are shot after escaping from a German prison camp.

Jun [4] Allied forces enter Rome. [6] D-Day; the invasion of Europe by a huge invasion fleet crossing the English

Channel. [9] There is heavy fighting near Caen. [12] The first V-1 bomb falls on Britain.

Jul [3] The evacuation of children from London begins as a response to the V-1 bombing. [9] Caen is captured by the Allies.

Aug [12] PLUTO (Pipe-Line Under the Ocean) is operational from today, supplying petrol to the Allied forces in France; it runs southwards from Shanklin. [19] The conductor Sir Henry Wood dies at Hitchin. [23] The liberation of Paris. [31] Montgomery is made a Field Marshal.

Sep [4] Brussels and Antwerp are taken by the Allies. [8] The first V-2 bomb falls on Britain. [9] John Haigh batters Donald McSwann to death in Pimlico and dissolves his body in acid. Shortly afterwards he murders McSwann's parents; strangely, their disappearance is not noticed until Haigh confesses to their murder several years later. [13] The artist Heath Robinson dies. [17] Allied air-borne troops land near Arnhem.

Oct [5] British troops land on the mainland of Greece. [14] Athens is taken by the Allies.

Nov [12] The battleship *Tirpitz* is sunk in Tromso Fjord by Lancaster bombers. [30] The largest and last of the British battleships, HMS *Vanguard*, is launched.

1945 Sir Alexander Fleming, Sir Howard Florey and Ernst Chain are awarded the Nobel Prize for Physiology and Medicine.

Feb [2] Geoffrey Fisher, Bishop of London, becomes Archbishop of Canterbury. [4] Beginning of the Yalta Conference in Crimea between Stalin, Roosevelt and Churchill (ends February 11). [12] Yalta statement: the Allies have concerted plans for Germany's final defeat. [14] The bombing of Dresden; this is one of the most destructive and controversial bombing raids of the war in which around 100,000 civilians die in the firestorms which engulf the city.

Mar [6] Cologne is captured by the Allies. [7] Allied troops cross the Rhine by way of the Ludendorff Bridge at Remagen. [11]

The Krupps factory is destroyed. [26] David Lloyd George, Liberal Prime Minister 1916-22, dies aged 82. [27] The last V-2 bomb lands at Orpington in Kent; since September 1944 over a thousand of these 'Vengeance' weapons have been launched against Britain.

Apr [15] British troops liberate Belsen concentration camp. [23] The black-out in London comes to an end. [28] Mussolini is shot. [30] Hitler commits suicide.

May [3] Rangoon is captured by the British. [4] German troops in north-west Germany surrender. [7] The German Provisional Government under Admiral Doenitz surrenders unconditionally. [8] The end of the Second World War against Germany is officially declared.

Jun [15] Family allowances are introduced: five shillings a week per child after the first child.

Jul [26] Labour win the General Election with a majority of 173 seats; Clement Attlee, the new Prime Minister, embarks on a programme of nationalization and social reform. The UK, US and China demand that Japan surrenders unconditionally; the demand is ignored.

Aug [6] The atomic bomb is used for the first time; four square miles of Hiroshima are laid waste and over 50,000 civilians are killed. [9] A second atom bomb is dropped on Nagasaki. [14] Japan surrenders to the Allies on the one condition that the Emperor will remain head of state. The secret of radar is disclosed for the first time. [26] Following some criticism of the severity of the Dresden bombing, it is announced that Sir Arthur 'Bomber' Harris is to retire. [30] Hong Kong is reoccupied by the British.

Sep [2] Victory over Japan is celebrated in Britain, and the final end of the Second World War. [16] The singer Count John McCormack dies.

Nov [20] The Nuremberg War Trials begin.

1946 The Bank of England is nationalized, although in effect it remains substantially independent of Government. The coal industry is also nationalized; the National Coal Board is to take over all mines. The Inland Transport Act nationalizes railways, road transport, docks and harbours.

Jan   [3] William Joyce, 'Lord Haw Haw', is hanged for treason. [22] Pit owners protest at the Government's plan to nationalize the mines.

Mar   [1] The Bank of England passes to public ownership. [5] Churchill gives a speech at Fulton, Missouri in which he refers to the 'iron curtain' for the first time; it is the first public acknowledgement that the Cold War has begun. [9] The Burnden Park disaster at Bolton; 33 people are killed and 400 injured as crush-barriers give way before the FA Cup match. [22] Jordan becomes an independent kingdom, having been until now under British protection.

Apr   [2] The Royal Military Academy is established at Sandhurst, after being at Woolwich since 1741. [21] The economist Lord Keynes dies.

Jun   [1] The first television licences, costing £2, are issued. [14] The inventor of television, John Baird, dies aged 58. [17] The Allies decide not to put Hirohito on trial as a war criminal.

Jul   [13] The US House of Representatives approves a loan to Britain. [22] Bread rationing begins in Britain. The British Headquarters in Jerusalem are blown up.

Aug   [1] Peace Conference opens in Paris. [13] The writer H. G. Wells dies.

Sep   [29] The BBC's Third Programme, later to become Radio 3, begins.

Oct   [16] The death sentences on Nazi criminals convicted at Nuremberg are carried out; Goering succeeds in committing suicide just before his execution.

Nov   The National Health Service Act, guided though Parliament by the Minister of Health Aneurin Bevan, is to become operative in 1948; it institutes free diagnosis and treatment, both by general practitioners and in hospitals. [10] George VI

unveils an additional inscription on the Cenotaph –
'1939-1945'.

1947 The Edinburgh Festival is founded. The India Independence
Act is rushed through Parliament; it establishes a mainly
Hindu India and a Muslim Pakistan. The 550 private
electricity generating companies are nationalized. Sir Edward
Appleton is awarded the Nobel Prize for Physics and Sir
Robert Robinson the Nobel Prize for Chemistry.

Jan   [1] The nationalization of the coal industry becomes effective.
[8] The steel works close through lack of coal. There are food
shortages as a result of the hauliers' strike.

Feb   [2] The RAF begins evacuating Britons from Palestine. [20]
Lord Mountbatten is appointed last Viceroy of India. In
Britain, very cold weather combined with fuel shortages
threaten to damage the economy.

Mar   [6] 15 towns are cut off by deep snow. [15] The worst floods
ever recorded in Britain follow the thaw; two million sheep
are drowned.

Apr   [1] The school-leaving age is raised to 15. [24] The
Government bans the use of coal and gas until September.

Jun   [5] Beginning of 'Marshall Aid'. [22] George VI issues a
proclamation renouncing the title 'Emperor of India', in
anticipation of the statutory changes in India's status. [28]
The statue of Eros returns to Piccadilly Circus.

Aug   [10] Attlee makes a radio broadcast pleading for a
wartime-style national effort to cope with the economic
crisis. [15] The first British atomic reactor is opened at
Harwell. India becomes independent.

Sep   [30] The Government asks women to wear shorter skirts, to
save cloth.

Oct   [24] 31 people die in a train crash at Croydon. [26] Berwick
train crash: 21 die.

Nov   [14] Three people are killed in secret rocket tests in
Buckinghamshire. [19] Prince Philip is created Duke of
Edinburgh. [20] Princess Elizabeth (Elizabeth II) marries

Prince Philip, son of Prince Andrew of Greece, in
Westminster Abbey.

Dec   [14] Stanley Baldwin, Earl Baldwin of Bewdley, three times
Prime Minister, dies.

1948 London hosts the first post-war Olympic Games; 59
countries take part. The railways are nationalized; the
British Transport Commission takes control of most forms
of transport, and the four railway groups are combined to
form British Railways. Patrick M. S. Blackett is awarded
the Nobel Prize for Physics; T. S. Eliot that for
Literature.

Jan   [3] Attlee denounces the USSR's 'new imperialism'. [4]
Burma becomes independent. [30] Gandhi is assassinated in
New Delhi.

Feb   [4] Ceylon Independence Act: Ceylon (Sri Lanka) becomes a
self-governing Dominion within the Commonwealth, having
been a Crown Colony since 1802. [16] Britain warns
Argentina to keep off the Falklands, as the Argentine navy
conducts sabre-rattling exercises in the area. [28] The last
British troops leave India.

Mar [22] The composer Andrew Lloyd Webber is born.

Apr   [1] The British electricity industry is nationalized. [5] The first
European Aid shipments leave the USA.

May [14] The British mandate for Palestine ends: Jews proclaim
the new state of Israel. [29] The composer Michael Berkeley is
born.

Jun   [7] Over half of the doctors in Britain agree to join the
National Health Service.

Jul   [1] The Berlin Airlift: American, French and British zones of
Berlin are supplied by air. The first Oxfam shop opens, in
Oxford. [4] Two passenger planes collide over Middlesex,
killing 39 people. [13] It is revealed that the coal industry lost
£23 million in its first year of nationalization. [29] Bread
rationing comes to an end.

Aug [8] Twelve people die in 70 mph winds.

Sep [22] Captain Mark Phillips, later to marry Princess Anne, is born at Tewkesbury.

Oct [4] The pioneer aviator Sir Arthur Brown dies. [12] The first Morris Minor comes off the production line at Cowley, Oxford.

Nov [14] Princess Elizabeth gives birth to a son, Prince Charles Philip Arthur George. [30] Severe fog in London causes three train crashes.

Dec [21] The Republic of Ireland Bill is signed in Dublin. [31] Sir Malcolm Campbell, holder of the world land and water speed records, dies.

1949 The samba, a Brazilian dance, becomes popular this year. Three major Ealing Studios comedy films appear: *Passport to Pimlico*, *Whisky Galore* and *Kind Hearts and Coronets*. The frigate HMS *Amethyst*, trapped for 14 weeks by Communist forces in the Yangtze River, makes its escape to open sea under cover of darkness. The House of Lords' power to delay legislation is reduced to one year.

Jan [9] The comedian Tommy Handley dies. [20] Attlee sets up a Royal Commission on capital punishment. [29] The British Government recognizes Israel.

Feb [23] Sir David Lean's film *Oliver Twist* is denounced in Berlin as anti-semitic.

Mar [1] After a series of accidents, Tudor IV airliners are banned from carrying passengers. [15] Clothes rationing comes to an end. [25] Sir Laurence Olivier's film of *Hamlet* wins five Oscars.

Apr [1] The National Parks Bill is approved by Parliament. [18] Eire is now officially to be called the Republic of Ireland, and its independence from Britain is re-asserted by leaving the Commonwealth. [30] Sir Alfred Munnings, the retiring President of the Royal Academy, makes a violent attack on recent developments in art as 'silly daubs'.

May [1] The Gas Industry is nationalized. [3] A ten-power conference in London leads to the formation of the Council of

Europe. [9] Britain's first launderette opens in Bayswater.
[12] The Berlin blockade is lifted.

Jul   [1] The London Docks come to a halt as the dockers go on
strike. [12] 12,000 dockers are now out on strike. [27] The
Lords vote in favour of admitting women who are peeresses
in their own right to sit in the House of Lords. [29] The BBC
televises its first weather forecast.

Aug [10] John Haigh, the acid bath murderer, is hanged.
[19] A British European Airways DC-3 crashes in Yorkshire,
killing 24 people. [24] The North Atlantic Treaty comes into
force.

Sep [11] The milk ration is reduced to 2½ pints a week. [18] The
milk ration is reduced to 2 pints a week. The pound is
devalued by 30%.

Oct [12] Lord Boyd-Orr is awarded the Nobel Peace Prize for
his work in helping the starving Third World.

Nov [29] Parliament Act, restricting the Lords' delaying
abilities.

1950 Christopher Cockerell begins experimenting with the
hovercraft idea. Excavations at Stonehenge by Stone,
Atkinson and Piggott produce the first radiocarbon date for
the monument, which proves to be unexpectedly old (around
2200 BC for the stones). Sir Fred Hoyle proposes his theory of
the continuous creation of matter ('steady state'). Cecil Frank
Powell is awarded the Nobel Prize for Physics; Bertrand
Russell that for Literature.

Jan [6] Britain officially recognizes the Communist regime in
China. [12] The submarine *Truculent* sinks after a Thames
collision with the Swedish tanker *Divina*; 65 men die. [21]
The author George Orwell dies.

Feb [23] The General Election returns are televised for the first
time; Labour is returned, but with a reduced majority. [26]
The music hall entertainer Sir Harry Lauder dies aged 79.

Mar [12] In the Cardiff air crash (a Tudor V plane) 80 people are
killed.

Apr [4] At Liverpool, the liner *Franconia* is found to be stuffed with smuggled nylon stockings with an estimated black market value of £80,000.

May [26] Petrol rationing ends. [29] 'The Archers' radio serial, created by Godfrey Baseley, is broadcast for the first time.

Jun [30] It is revealed that the National Coal Board made a profit of £9.5 million in 1949.

Jul [7] The first Farnborough Air Display takes place. [15] Churchill warns of the danger of a Third World War. [26] The British Government decides to send troops to Korea.

Aug [15] Princess Anne is born at Clarence House, London.

Sep [6] British troops are in action in Korea. [7] Attlee rejects a request from Quintin Hogg, who has just succeeded to the title Lord Hailsham, to sit in the House of Commons as an MP. [9] Soap rationing ends. [28] The Cresswell pit disaster; fire kills 80 miners.

Oct [4] Three generations of the Bowler family attend celebrations marking the centenary of the bowler hat.

Nov [2] The dramatist and critic George Bernard Shaw dies at Ayot St Lawrence aged 94. [16] King Farouk of Egypt demands the immediate evacuation of British troops from the Suez Canal. [25] The Coronation Stone, the Stone of Destiny, is stolen from Westminster Abbey by Scottish Nationalists. [28] The Peak District is designated as Britain's first National Park.

1951 Eric Shipton leads a reconnaissance expedition to Mount Everest, climbing the Khumbu Icefall and preparing the way for the first ascent in two years' time. The first smokeless zone in Britain is established in Coventry. Sir John Cockcroft and Ernest Walton are awarded the Nobel Prize for Physics.

Jan [1] The steel industry is nationalized.

Mar [6] The actor and composer Ivor Novello dies in London. [24] The Oxford and Cambridge Boat Race has to be called off when the Oxford boat sinks.

Apr   [5] The Government approves in principle the withdrawal of British troops from the Suez Canal zone. [11] The Stone of Destiny is found at Forfar in Scotland. [13] The Stone of Destiny is returned to Westminster Abbey. [14] The politician Ernest Bevin dies. [16] The submarine *Affray* sinks in the English Channel with the loss of 75 lives. [19] The first 'Miss World' contest takes place at the Lyceum Ballroom; Miss Sweden is the winner. [29] The philosopher Ludwig Wittgenstein dies.

May   [3] The Festival of Britain is opened by George VI from the steps of St Paul's Cathedral. [25] Foreign Office officials Guy Burgess and Donald Maclean disappear; they have defected to Russia.

Jun   [7] George VI is too ill to attend, so Princess Elizabeth stands in for her sick father at the Trooping the Colour ceremony.

Aug   [15] Sir Basil Spence wins the competition to design a new Coventry Cathedral. Dartmoor is designated a National Park. [21] The composer Constant Lambert dies.

Sep   [6] 12 million gallons of petrol are lost in a big oil fire at Avonmouth. [10] There are anti-British riots in Egypt. [14] Fawley oil refinery is opened. [23] The King has an operation to remove his left lung.

Oct   [3] The first British atom bomb tests take place in the Pacific. [15] The first party Political television broadcast is given, by Lord Samuel for the Liberal Party. [19] British troops take control of key points on the Suez Canal. [21] Four British warships dock at Port Said, at the northern entrance to the Suez Canal. [22] Britain's arms exports to Egypt cease. [26] The General Election is won by the Conservatives, with Winston Churchill as Prime Minister. [31] Zebra crossings are introduced.

Nov   [5] Clement Attlee is awarded the Order of Merit. [20] The evacuation of British army families from Egypt begins.

Dec   [27] The cargo ship *Flying Enterprise* capsizes in heavy seas in the English Channel.

1952 London smog kills 4000 people. Archer Martin and Richard Synge are awarded the Nobel Prize for Chemistry.

Jan [10] The freighter *Flying Enterprise* sinks off Falmouth; her captain, Kurt Carlsen, stays on board until just minutes before she sinks, refusing offers of rescue. [25] British troops capture the police headquarters of Ismailia; 46 Egyptians are killed in this action. [31] Princess Elizabeth and Prince Philip leave London on the first stage of their Commonwealth Tour.

Feb [4] The Government offers farmers £5 an acre to plough up grassland for crops. [6] George VI dies of cancer at Sandringham aged 56. He is succeeded by his eldest daughter as Elizabeth II, although she does not know of her accession for two days. [8] The Queen hears of her accession at the Treetops Hotel in Kenya. [15] The funeral of George VI at Windsor. [21] Identity cards are abolished.

Apr [21] The Labour politician Sir Stafford Cripps dies in Switzerland.

May [5] Elizabeth II takes up residence at Buckingham Palace.

Jul [6] The last London tram runs for the last time.

Aug [16] Severe localized thunderstorms in Somerset and North Devon swell the rivers, bringing devastation to the town of Lynmouth; 31 people are killed in the Lynmouth disaster.

Sep [6] A de Havilland 110 fighter disintegrates at the Farnborough Air Show, killing 28 people.

Oct [8] The Harrow train disaster, in which 112 are killed and 200 injured.

Nov [14] Charts for pop single records are published for the first time in Britain, in the *New Musical Express*. [25] Agatha Christie's *The Mousetrap* begins its record-breaking run at the Ambassador's Theatre, London. 2000 Kikuyu are rounded up in Kenya as the Mau Mau begins an open revolt against British rule.

Dec [12] On about this date Reg Christie murders his wife Ethel, because she suspects him of other murders, and puts her body under the floor at their home, 10 Rillington Place, London.

1953 Carvings of axes are noticed for the first time at Stonehenge.

Jan [1] 'Bomber' Harris, the ex-head of Bomber Command responsible for the bombing of Dresden, is knighted. [22] BOAC grounds all its Strato-cruisers after engine faults are discovered. [25] The liner *Empress of Canada* is gutted by fire at her moorings in Liverpool. [27] 200 MPs plead for Derek Bentley's controversial death sentence to be commuted but a reprieve is refused. [28] Bentley is hanged at Wandsworth Prison. [31] The car ferry *Princess Victoria* sinks off Stranraer in a storm: 128 people drown.

Feb [3] Gale-force winds accompanying high tides cause a major flood disaster on the east coast from Lincolnshire to Kent. 283 are drowned, thousands homeless. [4] Sweet rationing ends. [16] The new aircraft carrier *Hermes* is launched at Barrow. [23] An amnesty is granted to Second World War deserters. [25] An inquest is told that the *Princess Victoria's* stern doors were not properly closed and that water was allowed to sweep onto the car deck causing the ship to develop a sudden list.

Mar [15] Tito visits Britain. [20] The actress Vivien Leigh returns to Britain suffering from a serious nervous breakdown. [24] Queen Mary, the widow of George V, dies at Marlborough House in Pall Mall. [25] A hunt for the mass murderer Christie starts after bodies are discovered in a pantry by new tenants at 10 Rillington Place in London. [26] Police reveal that they have found the body of Christie's wife. [31] Queen Mary's funeral. Christie is arrested on the Thames Embankment and charged with murdering his wife.

Apr [15] Christie is charged with the murder of three more women. [16] The Royal Yacht *Britannia* is launched by the Queen.

May [2] A BOAC Comet airliner crashes near Calcutta: all 43 on board are killed. Experts want to know why the wings came off in mid-air. [18] The bodies of Beryl Evans and her baby are exhumed as the suspicion grows that Timothy Evans, who was hanged for the crime, did not murder them. [24] The Foreign Office advises British families to leave Egypt. An attempt on the south face of Everest fails. Chris Chataway runs two miles in 8 minutes 49.6 seconds, a new record. [29] Hillary and Tensing reach the summit of Everest at 11.30 am.

Jun [1] News of the conquest of Everest reaches Britain. [2] Coronation of Elizabeth II. [11] A report on the *Princess Victoria* sinking reprimands the ship-owners. [22] The Christie trial opens at the Old Bailey: he pleads insanity. [23] Churchill suffers a severe stroke, although the news is kept from the press for four days. [25] Christie is sentenced to death. Timothy Evans' family asks for his case to be reviewed, but there is no immediate response.

Jul [1] MPs reject a Bill to suspend the death penalty for five years. [15] Christie is hanged. [16] The writer Hilaire Belloc dies. Hillary and Hunt (the Everest expedition leader) are knighted: Tensing is awarded the George Medal.

Aug [27] The de Havilland Comet II makes its first test flight.

Sep [3] Florence Horsbrugh, Education Minister, becomes the first woman cabinet minister. [23] The Royal Commission on capital punishment says that the jury should be left to decide whether or not the death penalty is imposed. [26] Sugar rationing ends after nearly 14 years.

Oct [3] The composer Sir Arnold Bax dies. [8] The singer Kathleen Ferrier dies aged 41. [14] 147 soldiers arrive at Southampton from imprisonment in North Korea. [15] Churchill is awarded the Nobel Prize for Literature. [31] 30,000 new homes have been built this month.

Nov [9] The poet Dylan Thomas dies in New York aged 39. [11] MPs approve a Bill enabling Prince Philip to become regent if the need arises. [17] Sir Arthur Bliss becomes Master of the Queen's Musick. [21] The Piltdown skull, which Charles Dawson 'planted' in Sussex in 1912, is shown to be a hoax.

Dec   [1] Harold Macmillan boasts that 301,000 new homes have
      been built during the Government's second year in office.
      [10] Churchill receives his Nobel Prize in Stockholm. [31] A
      British expedition arrives in India to search for the Yeti.

1954

Jan   [10] A Comet airliner crashes into the sea off Elba, killing 35
      people; all BOAC jets are grounded as some kind of
      structural failure is suspected.

Feb   [3] The Queen and Duke of Edinburgh arrive in Australia on
      a tour of the Commonwealth. [5] The first 'breeder' nuclear
      reactor comes into operation at Harwell. [12] An Advisory
      Committee on cancer reports that it has established a link
      between lung cancer and smoking.

Mar   [1] Parliamentary approval is given to the establishment of an
      Atomic Energy Authority. [21] The suspicion grows that
      spies Guy Burgess and Donald MacLean were helped by a
      third man; Kim Philby is recalled from Washington for
      interrogation. [25] Parliament approves the inauguration of
      commercial television; this leads to the formation of the
      Independent Television Authority, and Channels 3 and 4.

Apr   [8] Another Comet airliner falls into the sea near Stromboli:
      21 people die; this is the third Comet crash. [16] Stock car
      racing is seen for the first time in Britain at the Old Kent
      Road Stadium in London. [24] 40,000 Mau Mau suspects are
      rounded up in Kenya.

May   [6] Roger Bannister runs the first sub-four-minute mile on the
      Iffley Road track at Oxford. The Home Secretary says that
      the problem of Teddy Boys is not serious . [15] The Queen
      and Prince Philip return to Britain. [22] 180,000 people flock
      to Wembley for the last rally of Billy Graham's evangelical
      tour.

Jun   [30] An eclipse of the sun is visible throughout Britain.

Jul   [2] All food rationing comes to an end. [27] The British
      Government agrees with Colonel Nasser's request to pull
      British troops out of the Suez Canal zone. [31] The

Television Act is passed, allowing independent televison transmissions.

Aug [1] The UK Atomic Energy Authority is founded, marking the beginning of the nuclear energy industry in Britain. [4] The Independent Television Authority is set up, under the chairmanship of Sir Kenneth Clark.

Sep [3] The National Trust buys Fair Isle. [6] The 'Flying Bedstead'; Rolls Royce announces that it has developed a prototype vertical take-off plane. [14] Kidbrooke School in London, London's first new comprehensive school, is opened. [24] The Roman temple of Mithras is discovered near the Mansion House in London during redevelopment.

Oct [19] Metal fatigue, a newly identified technical problem, is blamed for the Elba Comet crash; investigators will now look at the possibility that other plane crashes may be due to metal fatigue. [29] The dockers end their month-long strike. [29] Sir Winston Churchill celebrates his 80th birthday. He is presented by both Houses of Parliament with a portrait by Graham Sutherland; he dislikes it intensely, and Lady Churchill later destroys it.

Dec [19] Viscount Stansgate (later to be known as Mr Anthony Wedgwood-Benn and eventually as Tony Benn) reveals that he wants to renounce his title. [20] The novelist James Hilton dies in California.

1955

Jan [6] The comedian Rowan Atkinson is born. [9] 400 Jamaicans arrive in London in search of work; this represents the beginning of an important demographic change in Britain, one that will have social, cultural and political reverberations. [21] Archaeologists confirm that Piltdown Man was a hoax. [23] 380 Jamaican immigrants disembark at Plymouth. [27] The premiere of Sir Michael Tippett's opera *The Midsummer Marriage*.

Feb [10] The Commons vote by a majority of 31 to retain the death penalty. [15] The Government announces its plan to build 12 nuclear power stations during the next 10 years. There is an unfounded belief that electricity generated in nuclear power stations will be much cheaper than that from coal-fired stations; problems such as safety and the disposal of radioactive waste are overlooked in these calculations. [17] The Government announces that it will proceed with the manufacture of hydrogen bombs. [18] The House of Lords rejects Lord Stansgate's request to renounce his title and pursue his political career in the Commons. [25] Britain's largest ever aircraft carrier, HMS *Ark Royal*, is completed.

Mar [4] Equal salaries for women teachers, to be reached in stages, are recommended by the Burnham Committee; this is another step towards equal rights for women. [11] Sir Alexander Fleming, the discoverer of penicillin in 1928, dies.

Apr [5] Sir Winston Churchill resigns as Prime Minister. [6] Sir Anthony Eden, later Lord Avon, succeeds as Prime Minister, with Harold Macmillan as Foreign Secretary and R. A. Butler as Chancellor of the Exchequer. [28] The trial of Ruth Ellis for murder begins. There seem to be mitigating circumstances (jealousy, extreme provocation) even though she is guilty of killing David Blakeley. Her case, coming hard on the heels of the 1953 Evans-Christie case, is influential in the abolition of the death penalty.

May [26] The Conservatives win the General Election with a majority of 59. [28] 16 Teddy Boys are arrested after a disturbance at a dance hall in Bath.

Jun [21] Ruth Ellis, found guilty of murder, is sentenced to death.

Jul [1] The dock strike ends. [4] Britain undertakes to transfer her Simonstown naval base to South Africa during the next two years. [7] A Hawker Hunter fighter crashes at the Farnborough Air Show. [13] Ruth Ellis is hanged at Holloway Prison after her appeal is refused; she claims, after her trial, that someone else put the gun into her hand, but it is too late. There is a significant level of sympathy for her in the popular press. [23] Donald Campbell breaks the world water speed record in *Bluebird* on Ullswater (202 mph).

Aug   Jeans become fashionable in Britain. [3] Duncan Sandys, Housing Minister, instructs the local authorities to set up Green Belts similar to London's around other towns and cities. The intention is to stop urban areas extending across food-producing farmland, and to stop the unsightly ribbon development of the inter-war years. Where possible, most new urban development is to be 'infilling'.

Sep   [22] The first transmission of commercial television. The first televised advertisement is for Gibbs SR toothpaste. The BBC offers as a counter-attraction the burning to death of Grace Archer, a leading character in 'The Archers' radio serial.

Oct   [1] The City of London is declared a smokeless zone. The effects of this policy are to make the air cleaner in London, reduce the frequency and seriousness of smog, and make it worthwhile to clean London's blackened public buildings. [27] Princess Margaret visits the Archbishop of Canterbury. [31] It is announced that Princess Margaret has decided not to marry Group Captain Peter Townsend after all, because of the constitutional problems involved in her marrying a divorcee.

Nov   [11] An MP withdraws the allegation that Kim Philby was the third man in the Burgess and MacLean affair. [26] British troops fight terrorists in Famagusta in Cyprus.

Dec   [7] Clement Attlee announces his retirement and is created an earl. [14] Hugh Gaitskell is elected Labour Party leader.

1956 Third Class accommodation on British Railways is redesignated Second Class. The Clean Air Act comes into force. The Sudan becomes independent. The first Aldermaston march is organized by the Campaign for Nuclear Disarmament, in protest against nuclear weapons.

Jan   [1] Sudan becomes an independent republic. [2] The Astronomer-Royal says the idea of space travel is 'bilge'. [23] The film producer Sir Alexander Korda dies in London.

[31] A. A. Milne, the creator of Winnie-the-Pooh, dies at Hartfield.

Feb [21] The Duke of Edinburgh's Award Scheme is announced.

Mar [10] Riots break out in Cyprus after the British deport Archbishop Makarios. [23] Pakistan is proclaimed an Islamic republic within the Commonwealth. The Queen lays the foundation stone of the new Coventry Cathedral.

Apr [1] The first US U-2 spy planes arrive at RAF Lakenhurst. [17] The introduction of Premium Bonds is announced by Harold Macmillan. [18] The Soviet leaders Kruschev and Bulganin arrive in Britain on an official visit. [20] Commander Lionel Crabbe, a frogman, goes missing while investigating the hull of the Soviet cruiser *Ordzhonikidze* in Portsmouth Harbour.

May [20] The writer and caricaturist Sir Max Beerbohm dies. [23] Calder Hall, the first nuclear power station in Britain and the first large-scale nuclear plant in the world, comes into operation.

Jun [13] The last British troops leave Suez. [22] The poet Walter de la Mare dies.

Jul [26] President Nasser of Egypt nationalizes the Suez Canal Company. [30] Eden tells Nasser that Egypt cannot have the Suez Canal and imposes an arms embargo on Egypt.

Aug [1-2] There are talks between UK, USA and France on the Suez problem. [8] Eden says in a broadcast about the Suez crisis that Nasser cannot be trusted. [27] The National Youth Theatre is founded. [29] There is a massive build-up of French and British forces in the Eastern Mediterranean, with the object of menacing Egypt.

Sep [9] Nasser rejects a US plan for international control over the Suez Canal. [21] A Suez Canal Conference in London ends with an agreement that a Canal Users Association should be formed.

Oct [31] An Anglo-French offensive is launched against military targets in Egypt.

Nov [1] Premium Savings Bonds go on sale for the first time. [4] Demonstrators in the streets of London call for Eden's

resignation over his handling of the Suez Crisis. [7] Eden
agrees to withdraw troops from Suez if a United Nations
force goes in instead. [16] The Egyptians block the Suez
Canal by scuttling 49 ships in it. [19] Eden is said to be
suffering from 'severe overstrain'; in fact he is
psychologically disorientated by the strength of world
reaction to his action over Suez and by the Americans' failure
to support him in the way he had understood they would.
Hungarian refugees arrive in Britain. [21] A United Nations
force takes over the Suez Canal from British and French
troops; Britain withdraws under strong pressure from the
US. [23] Eden flies to Jamaica to rest and recover.

Dec   [5] British troops begin to leave Port Said. [18] Dr John
Bodkin Adams is arrested, suspected of murdering Mrs
Morrell in November 1950 and several other elderly patients
in his care.

1957 The Rent Act (Conservative measure) abolishes rent control
and allows rents to be increased. Wyndham Lewis, 'the most
fascinating personality of our time', according to T. S. Eliot,
dies. Sir Alexander Todd is awarded the Nobel Prize for
Chemistry. Antarctica is crossed by Sir Vivian Fuchs (1957-8).

Jan   [4] Salvage crews continue to clear the Suez Canal of sunken
ships. [9] Sir Anthony Eden resigns as Prime Minister. [10]
Harold Macmillan becomes Prime Minister. [16] The Royal
Ballet is founded.

Feb   [16] Sir Leslie Hore-Belisha, Minister of Transport
responsible for introducing Belisha beacons, driving tests
and the Highway Code, dies.

Mar   [6] Ghana becomes the first British colony in Africa to achieve
independence. [8] The Suez Canal is reopened for smaller
vessels. [11] The first indications that radiation may have
genetic effects are published by the World Health
Organization.

Apr   [3] The Labour Party calls for H-bomb tests to be
abolished.

May [14] Emergency petrol rationing, prompted by the Suez crisis, comes to an end. [15] The first British hydrogen bomb is detonated over Christmas Island.

Jun [1] The first Premium Bond prize winners are drawn by computer, a random number selector called ERNIE. [9] Commander Crabbe's body is found by fishermen in Chichester Harbour. [30] The British Lion is stamped on eggs for the first time; the practice ends December 31 1968.

Jul [20] Harold Macmillan makes his 'never had it so good' speech at Bradford. [23] Picket line violence breaks out during a national bus strike.

Aug [6] It is revealed that 2000 people a week are still emigrating to the Commonwealth. [15] The dock strike spreads; 12,000 dock workers are now out on strike. [31] Malaya becomes independent.

Sep [1] The horn player Dennis Braine dies in a road accident at Hatfield. [4] The Wolfenden Report is published, recommending that homosexual acts between adults in private should be legalized.

Oct [11] Jodrell Bank telescope, the largest radio telescope in the world, comes into operation. [17] Part of the Windscale atomic plant in Cumbria is closed down following a serious fire and a radioactivity leak; this is the most serious accident in nuclear energy history so far.

Dec [4] Lewisham train crash; 92 people are killed as two trains collide in fog. [17] Dorothy Sayers, creator of Lord Peter Wimsey, dies. [19] An air service opens between London and Moscow. [25] The Queen's Christmas broadcast is televised for the first time.

1958 There are serious racial disturbances at Nottingham and Notting Hill. At Stonehenge, trilithon 57-58 is re-erected and set in concrete. Frederick Sanger is awarded the Nobel Prize for Chemistry.

Jan [20] Vivian Fuchs, leading a Commonwealth expedition, reaches the South Pole.

Feb [5] First performance of Tippett's *Second Symphony*. [6] In a plane crash at Munich airport, eight Manchester United players, three club officials and eight journalists are killed. [13] The suffragette Dame Christabel Pankhurst dies.

Mar [2] Fuchs completes his crossing of Antarctica. [6] The TUC and the Labour Party call for H-bomb tests to stop. [18] The last presentation of debutantes. [21] The London Planetarium is opened. [27] Sir David Lean's film *Bridge on the River Kwai* wins three Oscars.

Apr [4] An anti-nuclear protest march from London to Aldermaston begins. [10] A Roman mosaic is discovered at Fishbourne, the first indication that there was once a Roman palace there.

May [23] Christopher Cockerell patents his newly-invented hovercraft. [24] The Dounreay nuclear reactor begins working.

Jun [1] The Clean Air Act comes into force, banning emissions of dark smoke. [4] The first Duke of Edinburgh Awards are presented at Buckingham Palace. [9] Gatwick Airport is opened by the Queen. [16] Yellow 'no waiting' lines on roads are introduced. [20] The seven-week long London bus strike ends.

Jul [10] Parking meters are in operation for the first time, in Mayfair. [23] The first life barons and baronesses are named under the Life Peerages Act. [26] The Queen creates her son Charles Prince of Wales.

Aug [17] The Government announces plans to resume nuclear bomb testing on Christmas Island. [26] The composer Ralph Vaughan Williams dies aged 85. [30] The police clash with 500 Teddy Boys at Nottingham. [31] There is fighting in Notting Hill between white and black youths.

Sep [1] British trawlers defy the Icelandic 12-mile limit, which comes into force today. [7] British scientists successfully fire their first ballistic rocket, Black Knight, from Woomera. [8] Race riot in Notting Hill.

Oct [21] The first women peers take their seats in the House of Lords.

Nov [21] Work starts on the Forth Road Bridge, to be the longest suspension bridge in Europe.

Dec An epidemic of serious deformities in British babies is thought to be caused by the drug thalidomide. [5] The first section of motorway in Britain, the Preston by-pass section of the M6, is opened by the Prime Minister, Harold Macmillan; this is a landmark in the development of the communications network. [8] The last of four nuclear reactors at Calder Hall comes into operation.

1959 D. H. Lawrence's *Lady Chatterley's Lover* is prosecuted on an obscenity charge. Rock 'n roll music begins to dominate youth culture.

Feb [15] Archbishop Makarios arrives in London for talks on Cyprus with Macmillan. [21] Macmillan arrives in Moscow on an official visit.

Mar [17] The Government announces its scheme for a major expansion of the road network. [31] Sir Winston Churchill's home is burgled; he loses £10,000 worth of property.

May [2] The first Scottish nuclear power station opens at Chapelcross. [23] The Mermaid Theatre in the City of London opens. [24] Empire Day is renamed Commonwealth Day. [30] The first hovercraft flight takes place at Cowes.

Jun [17] The pianist Liberace wins £8,000 from the *Daily Mirror* after the Cassandra column implies that he is homosexual.

Jul [7] The Litter Act comes into force. [25] The hovercraft makes its first Channel crossing, from Dover to Calais, in just over two hours.

Aug [10] Violent storms. [16] Street Offences Act comes into force; prostitution must disappear from the streets. [19] The sculptor Jacob Epstein dies.

Sep [26] The jockey Manny Mercer is killed in an accident during a parade before a race at Ascot.

Oct [3] Post codes are used for the first time, at Norwich. [8] In the General Election the Conservatives win easily (Conservatives 365, Labour 258, Liberal 6); Macmillan remains Prime Minister. [27] London housing officials say that slum clearances and rehousing cause misery and distress to those who are moved; this is the beginning of a major reconsideration of old housing, and the destruction of Victorian and Edwardian houses slows down.

Nov [6] Two motorists are killed in the first fatal accident on the M1 motorway, which was opened this week. [14] The Dounreay fast breeder reactor goes into operation. [19] The Archbishop of Canterbury says that adultery should be a criminal offence. [20] Britain joins the European Free Trade Association (EFTA).

Dec [14] The painter Sir Stanley Spencer dies. [23] The Earl of Halifax, politician and Viceroy of India 1926-31, dies.

1960 Sir Macfarlane Burnet (Australian) and Peter Medawar (British) are awarded the Nobel Prize for Physiology and Medicine.

Jan The novelist Nevil Shute dies. [25] The composer Rutland Boughton dies. [31] The composer George Benjamin is born.

Feb [3] Macmillan makes his 'wind of change' speech at Cape Town. [17] The Government agrees to allow a US missile early warning system to be built at Fylingdales Moor. [19] Prince Andrew, Queen Elizabeth II's third child, is born at Buckingham Palace.

Mar [25] Oliver Cromwell's head, severed from his body at the Restoration in 1660, is buried at Sydney Sussex College, Cambridge.

Apr [6] Dr Richard Beeching is chosen to head the team to rationalize the rail network; this process results in the closure of a great many branch lines, with far-reaching social effects. [13] The Blue Streak missile is abandoned as a weapon.

May [6] Princess Margaret marries Antony Armstrong-Jones in Westminster Abbey.

Jun [2] Planners in London devise ways of limiting the number of new high-rise buildings. [10] The first British guided-missile destroyer, HMS *Devonshire*, is launched. The Government decides to slow down the nuclear programme.

Jul [1] Ghana becomes a republic. [6] Aneurin Bevan, the Labour Minister who introduced the National Health Service in 1948, dies.

Aug [16] British rule in Cyprus comes to an end. [22] *Beyond the Fringe*, the first and most influential satirical revue, opens at the Edinburgh Festival.

Sep [12] MOT tests on motor vehicles are introduced. [15] Traffic wardens are first seen in London. [27] The militant suffragette Sylvia Pankhurst dies.

Oct [1] Nigeria becomes independent within the Commonwealth. [9] Serious flooding in southern England. [20] 'Lady Chatterley' trial opens; Penguin Books are tried for publishing an obscene book (D. H. Lawrence's *Lady Chatterley's Lover*). [21] Britain's first nuclear-powered submarine, HMS *Dreadnought*, is launched at Barrow.

Nov [1] It is announced that US Polaris missile submarines are to have a base on the Firth of Clyde. [2] Penguin Books are acquitted of the obscenity charge. [3] Hugh Gaitskell fights off Harold Wilson's challenge to his leadership. [16] The broadcaster Gilbert Harding collapses and dies on the steps of the BBC Studios in London. [17] Anthony Wedgwood-Benn succeeds to the title Lord Stansgate on his father's death, obstructing his career in politics.

Dec [9] The first episode of the television soap 'Coronation Street' is broadcast. [31] Farthings cease to be legal tender. It is the last day of call-up for National Service; from today compulsory service in the armed forces is abolished.

1961 The Graduated Pensions Scheme is introduced, to supplement the Old Age Pension. The Factories Act consolidates the safety regulations in all industrial premises and construction sites.

Jan   [14] There are prison mutinies at Maidstone and Shrewsbury.
[20] The Queen meets Archbishop Makarios in Cyprus.

Mar The Geneva Conference (UK, USA and USSR) begins, to discuss discontinuing nuclear weapons testing. [8] Sir Thomas Beecham, conductor and founder of the London Philharmonic Orchestra, dies. The first American Polaris submarines arrive at Holy Loch. [13] The old black-and-white £5 notes cease to be legal tender. The Canadian Gordon Lonsdale and four others go on trial in London for espionage. [18] George Blake is charged with spying.

May [1] The first betting shops open as the Betting and Gaming Act comes into force. [5] The Queen and Duke of Edinburgh visit Pope John XXIII at the Vatican. [8] George Blake is given a record 42-year gaol sentence. Anthony Wedgwood-Benn is refused admission to the Commons on the grounds that he is still Viscount Stansgate. [17] The new Guildford Cathedral is consecrated. [18] It is announced that there will be new Universities at Canterbury, Colchester and Coventry. [31] South Africa becomes a republic and withdraws from the Commonwealth.

Jun [27] Dr Michael Ramsey is enthroned as Archbishop of Canterbury.

Jul   [1] The Princess of Wales is born, as Lady Diana Spencer, at Park House, Sandringham. [19] A UK-US agreement is made to establish a Missile Defence Alarm Station at Kirkbride in Cumbria. [28] The High Court decides that Lord Stansgate's election victory was invalid because he is ineligible and that his defeated opponent is the new MP.

Aug [10] The UK formally applies to join the EEC. [31] Failure of the Geneva Conference; the USSR announces the resumption of nuclear weapons testing.

Sep [5] The USA announces that it will resume underground nuclear tests. [10] 86 people are killed in a plane crash at Shannon airport. [12] Bertrand Russell, the philosopher, is imprisoned for protesting against nuclear weapons, even

though he is 89. [17] There is a large anti-nuclear bomb
demonstration in London.

Oct [3] Princess Margaret's husband, Antony Armstrong-Jones,
is created Earl of Snowdon. [4] The Labour Party Conference
votes against having Polaris bases in Britain. [10] There is a
large-scale volcanic eruption on Tristan da Cunha; as a result
its entire population is evacuated to the UK. [24] Malta gains
its independence. [31] The painter Augustus John dies at
Fordingbridge.

Dec Tanganyika becomes independent. [7] The LCC approves the
building of 300-foot-high blocks of flats in Hammersmith;
they will be the highest in Britain.

1962 Commonwealth Immigration Act; uncontrolled entry into
Britain by citizens of the Commonwealth is ended. Smog in
London kills 750 people. Francis Crick and Maurice Wilkins
(British) and James Watson (American) are awarded the
Nobel Prize for Physiology and Medicine.

Jan [22] The A6 murder trial opens; James Hanratty pleads not
guilty to murdering Michael Gregston.

Feb [11] An Essex schoolboy dances the Twist for 33 hours. [17]
Hanratty is sentenced to death after a long and controversial
trial.

Mar The Liberal Eric Lubbock wins the Orpington by-election;
this is seen as a turning-point in the fortunes of the Liberal
Party.

Apr [4] Hanratty is hanged while controversy still surrounds the
question of his guilt. [26] Britain's first satellite, Ariel, is
launched from Cape Canaveral.

May [11] Prince Charles goes to Gordonstoun. [25] The new
Coventry Cathedral is consecrated. [29] First performance of
Tippett's opera *King Priam* at Coventry. [30] First
performance of Britten's *War Requiem* at Coventry.

Jun [2] The writer Vita Sackville-West dies. [12] The composer
John Ireland dies. [15] The nuclear power station at Berkeley
comes into operation.

Jul   The Prime Minister, Harold Macmillan, asks seven senior ministers to resign and reconstructs his Cabinet with Butler as deputy Prime Minister, Brooke as Home Secretary and Maudling as Chancellor of the Exchequer. [3] The Government and the LCC accept the plan for a national theatre and opera house. [20] The historian G. M. Trevelyan dies. The world's first passenger hovercraft service opens, across the River Dee from Rhyl to Wallasey. [31] Sir Oswald Mosley tries to address a meeting of the Union Movement, but is stopped by a punch on the jaw; the meeting is part of a resurgence of right-wing extremism.

Aug   [6] Jamaica becomes independent. [31] Trinidad and Tobago become independent.

Sep   [2] There is a fierce street battle between Fascists and East Enders.

Oct   [9] Uganda becomes independent. [22] William Vassall is sent to prison for 18 years for spying for the USSR.

Nov   [24] First broadcast of the satirical television programme 'That Was the Week That Was'.

Dec   [5] A British nuclear bomb is exploded underground in Nevada. [25] Britain is snow-bound. [30] Worst snowstorms in Britain since 1881. [31] British Rail Board is set up with Dr Richard Beeching as chairman.

1963   The Crowther and Newsom Reports recommend raising the school-leaving age to 16. The Offices, Shops and Railway Premises Act sets out comprehensive safety regulations for the work-place. Controversy rages over the radical theology outlined in the Bishop of Woolwich's book *Honest to God*. One of the stones at Stonehenge (stone 23) falls down in a gale. Alan Hodgkin and Andrew Huxley (British) and Sir John Eccles (Australian) are awarded the Nobel Prize for Physiology and Medicine.

Jan   [18] Hugh Gaitskell, leader of the Labour Party since 1955, dies. [29] Britain is refused entry to the EEC.

Feb [1] Nyasaland becomes independent. [14] Harold Wilson is elected leader of the Labour Party, defeating George Brown and James Callaghan.

Mar The Beeching Report on the slimming-down of British Railways (to be renamed British Rail) is published. [5-6] First frost-free night since December 22. [15] John Profumo offers to resign from the Government. [16] Lord Beveridge dies. [17] The first of the Tristan islanders return home. [22] Profumo assures his fellow MPs that there was no 'impropriety' with Christine Keeler.

Apr [5] The Bradwell nuclear power station opens. [17] The Royal Navy's first nuclear-powered submarine, *Dreadnought*, is commissioned.

Jun [5] Profumo resigns, admitting that he lied to the House. [27] President Kennedy visits his ancestors' home in County Wexford. [31] The Peerage Act comes into force, opening the way for Lord Hailsham and Lord Stansgate to present themselves as candidates for premiership in their respective parties.

Aug [1] The Criminal Justice Act comes into force; the minimum prison age is raised to 17. [3] Dr Stephen Ward, who exposed Profumo, commits suicide. [8] The Glasgow-London mail train robbery (the 'Great Train Robbery'): armed robbers attack a train near Leighton Buzzard and steal £2.5 million. [22] Lord Nuffield dies.

Sep [17] Fylingdales missile early-warning station comes into operation. [19] The cartoonist Sir David Low dies. [20] Princess Anne goes to Benenden. [25] The Denning Report on the Profumo affair is published.

Oct [10] Macmillan announces that he will resign as Prime Minister, believing, on his doctor's advice, that he is terminally ill. [18] Macmillan is succeeded by Lord Home of the Hirsel as Prime Minister. [23] Lord Home renounces his title, becoming Sir Alec Douglas-Home.

Nov [18] The Dartford Tunnel, linking Kent and Essex under the Thames estuary, is opened. [20] Lord Hailsham renounces

his title, becoming Mr Quintin Hogg. [22] The novelist
Aldous Huxley dies.

Dec [10] Zanzibar becomes independent. [12] Kenya becomes
independent.

1964 Dorothy Crowfoot Hodgkin is awarded the Nobel Prize for
Chemistry.

Feb [6] Britain and France agree to build a Channel Tunnel. [10]
The novel *Fanny Hill* is declared obscene by a magistrate,
who orders copies of the book to be confiscated.

Mar [3] The Government announces that many railway lines will
be closed. [10] The Queen's third son, Prince Edward, is born
at Buckingham Palace. [20] The playwright Brendan Behan
dies in Dublin. [28] Radio Caroline begins transmission from
the North Sea. [30] Rival groups of Mods and Rockers fight
on the beach at Clacton.

Apr [10] Macmillan declines an earldom and the Order of the
Garter. [16] Heavy sentences are passed on 12 men found
guilty of taking part in the Great Train Robbery. [21] The
BBC's second television channel begins transmission.

May [2] Nancy, Lady Astor, the first woman to sit in the House of
Commons in 1919, dies. [18] Mods and Rockers clash at
several south coast resorts.

Jun [5] The first British space flight; the 'Blue Streak' rocket is
launched from Woomera in Australia. [9] Lord Beaverbrook,
Canadian-born newspaper owner, dies aged 85.

Jul [27] Sir Winston Churchill's last appearance in the
Commons.

Aug [12] Ian Fleming, creator of James Bond, dies. [13] The last
hangings in Britain take place, the executions of Peter Allen
(at Walton Gaol in Liverpool) and John Walby (at
Strangeways Gaol in Manchester). [21] Three women in
London are found guilty of indecency for wearing the
fashionable topless dresses.

Sep [4] The Forth Road Bridge is opened by the Queen. [6] Ian
Smith arrives in London for talks on independence for

Rhodesia [18] The playwright Sean O'Casey dies at Torquay. [21] Malta becomes independent.

Oct   [16] In the General Election there is a Labour majority of five (Labour 317, Conservatives 304, Liberals 9); Harold Wilson becomes Prime Minister, George Brown his deputy and Callaghan Chancellor of the Exchequer. [23] Northern Rhodesia becomes the Republic of Zambia. [27] Wilson warns Rhodesia that a Unilateral Declaration of Independence would be treason.

Nov   [17] The Government imposes an arms embargo on South Africa, disapproving of its apartheid policy.

Dec   The IMF lends Britain £500 million. [6] Martin Luther King preaches at St Paul's. [9] Dame Edith Sitwell dies.

1965 Redundancy Payments Act, providing graduated payments proportional to length of service. A new Rent Act (Labour measure) reintroduces rent control. A prices and wages freeze is introduced. Mary Quant invents the mini-skirt, a delight to the eye which becomes a symbol for the permissiveness of the Sixties. Dennis Gabor develops holography (an idea he conceived in 1947 and subsequently developed using laser).

Jan   [4] T.S. Eliot, poet and playwright, dies. [7] The Kray brothers are remanded in custody on a charge of demanding money with menaces. [24] Sir Winston Churchill dies aged 91, seventy years to the day after his father's death. [30] State funeral of Sir Winston Churchill.

Feb   [16] British Rail publishes its plan, based on the Beeching Report, to halve the rail network. [18] The Gambia becomes independent. [25] Dr Heenan is created a Cardinal.

Mar   [3] The remains of Roger Casement are taken from Pentonville Prison to be reburied in Dublin.

Apr   [6] The Kray brothers are cleared of running a protection racket. [23] The first long-distance footpath in Britain, the Pennine Way, is opened.

May [14] The Kennedy Memorial at Runnymede is opened.

Jul [22] Sir Alec Douglas Home resigns as Conservative Party
Leader. [24] The boxer Freddie Mills is found shot dead in his
car outside his soho club. [26] The Maldive Islands become
independent [28] Edward Heath becomes the Conservative
Party Leader. [31] Cigarette advertising on television is
banned.

Sep [21] British Petroleum discovers oil in the North Sea.

Oct [8] The Post Office Tower is opened. Edward Heath says that
if elected he will take the UK into the European Community.
[28] Parliament abolishes the death penalty for murder for an
experimental five-year period. Ian Brady and Myra Hindley
are charged with the brutal and sadistic murder of a
10-year-old girl, Lesley Ann Downey.

Nov [8] The Abolition of the Death Penalty Act and the Race
Relations Act receive the Royal Assent. [11] Ian Smith, Prime
Minster of Rhodesia, announces his country's unilateral
declaration of independence; UDI is denounced by the
British Government. [22] A belated official inquiry into
Timothy Evans' conviction for murder begins. [25] The
pianist Dame Myra Hess dies in London.

Dec [16] The novelist W. Somerset Maugham dies. [17] An oil
embargo is imposed on Rhodesia. [22] The 70 mph speed
limit is introduced for all roads not restricted to lower speeds.
The broadcaster Richard Dimbleby dies. [27] The North Sea
oil rig 'Sea Gem' collapses. [28] Westminster Abbey's 900th
anniversary is celebrated.

1966 Havergal Brian hears the first of his 32 symphonies for the
first time, at the age of 78.

Feb [17] The Government protests to South Africa about petrol
supplies to Rhodesia.

Mar [5] The Nelson Monument in Dublin is blown up.
[23] The Archbishop of Canterbury meets the Pope in Rome.
[31] In the General Election, Labour is re-elected with an
increased majority (Labour 363, Conservatives 253, Liberals
12).

Apr [2] The novelist C.S. Forester dies. [5] Shell announces an
important discovery of oil off Great Yarmouth. [10] The
novelist Evelyn Waugh dies. British forces in the Middle East
are ordered to stop ships bound for Beira with oil for
Rhodesia. [14] The South Downs are designated an Area of
Outstanding Natural Beauty. [19] The Moors Murders trial
begins. [21] The opening of Parliament is televised for the
first time. [30] The first regular cross-Channel hovercraft
service begins.

May [16] Seamen's strike begins. [26] British Guiana becomes fully
independent, changing its name to Guyana.

Jun [2] de Valera is re-elected President of the Irish Republic.

Jul [3] An anti-Vietnam War demonstration takes place in
Grosvenor Square. [30] England wins the World Cup.

Aug [4] Sir Edmund Compton becomes the first Parliamentary
Commissioner (or 'Ombudsman'). [10] George Brown
becomes Foreign Secretary. [23] The Cotswolds are
designated an Area of Outstanding Natural Beauty.[27]
Francis Chichester leaves Plymouth on his single-handed
round-the-world voyage.

Sep [8] The Severn Bridge, carrying the M4 over the Severn
estuary, is opened by the Queen. [30] Bechuanaland
becomes independent, changing its name to Botswana.

Oct [4] Basutoland becomes independent, changing its name
to Lesotho. [18] The Queen grants a free pardon to
Timothy Evans, hanged in 1950 for the murder of his
wife and daughter, and now officially admitted to be
'probably innocent'. [21] The Aberfan disaster: an unstable
slag heap slides onto a junior school killing 144 people,
including 116 children. [23] BP announces the discovery of
rich gas fields in the North Sea. [30] Barbados becomes
independent.

1967 Anthony Hewish and Jocelyn Bell discover the first pulsar, a
rotating neutron star. British troops withdraw from Aden.
The Abortion Act provides for the legal termination of

pregnancy under specified conditions. A 'sit-in' at the London School of Economics triggers a wave of similar demonstrations, though with varying motives, at other universities. Ronald Norrish, George Porter (British) and Manfred Eigen (German) are awarded the Nobel Prize for Chemistry.

Jan [4] Donald Campbell is killed on Coniston Water while attempting to break the world water speed record. [18] Jeremy Thorpe is elected leader of the Liberal Party following Jo Grimond's resignation.

Feb [8] Sir Victor Gollancz, writer and publisher, dies.

Mar [4] The first North Sea gas is pumped ashore at Easington. [18] The Liberian oil tanker *Torrey Canyon* is wrecked on the Pollard Rock off Land's End, producing a disastrous oil slick almost 300 square miles in area. [28] The *Torrey Canyon* is bombed in an attempt to set fire to the leaking oil.

May [11] Britain applies to join the EEC. [12] John Masefield, Poet Laureate since 1930, dies. [14] The Catholic Cathedral at Liverpool is consecrated. [28] Francis Chichester arrives back in Plymouth at the end of his round-the-world voyage.

Jul [1] BBC2 begins televising in colour. [7] Francis Chichester is knighted at Greenwich: the Queen uses Sir Francis Drake's sword. Actress Vivien Leigh dies in London. [14] The Decimal Currency Act provides for decimal currency in 1971. [28] The steel industry is nationalized.

Aug [2] The Dartford Tunnel is formally opened. The poet Siegfried Sassoon dies. [3] The Aberfan tribunal reports that the National Coal Board was to blame for the disaster. [27] Brian Epstein, the Beatles' manager, is found dead of an overdose of sleeping pills.

Sep [10] The Gibraltarians vote overwhelmingly in favour of remaining British. [18] The nuclear physicist Sir John Cockcroft dies. [20] The passenger liner *Queen Elizabeth 2* is launched at Clydebank. [27] The *Queen Mary* arrives at Southampton at the end of her last transatlantic voyage.

[30] Re-organization of BBC Radio; Radios 1, 2, 3 and 4 begin transmission.

Oct   [3] The conductor Sir Malcolm Sargent dies. [8] Lord Attlee, Labour Prime Minister 1945-51, dies. [9] The first driver is breathalyzed, in Somerset.

Dec   [19] France vetoes Britain's entry to the EEC. The pound is devalued; Harold Wilson makes his 'pound in your pocket' television speech.

1968 Clean Air Act.

Jan   [1] C. Day Lewis is appointed Poet Laureate. [15] 20 are killed as a hurricane strikes Scotland. [31] Mauritius becomes independent.

Feb   [17] The actor Sir Donald Wolfit dies. [21] Lord Florey, who made possible the large-scale production of penicillin, dies.

Apr   [21] Enoch Powell makes his 'River Tiber foaming with much blood' speech at Birmingham, warning of the problems that may flow from unrestricted immigration. [23] The first decimal coins in Britain (5p and 10p) are issued.

May [6] A Gallup Poll suggests that 74% of Britons support Enoch Powell's views on immigration. [16] Part of the Ronan Point tower block collapses after a gas explosion; three people are killed. Many now start to question the wisdom of building high-rise blocks: building standards too are questioned.

Jun   [8] James Earl Ray is arrested at Heathrow for the murder of Martin Luther King. [10] NHS prescription charges are reintroduced. [24] The comedian Tony Hancock commits suicide.

Aug   [3] The Countryside Act allows local authorities to designate Country Parks.

Sep   [1] The first section of the new Victoria Line is opened. [6] Swaziland becomes independent. [15] The worst floods in south-east England since 1953. [16] The two-tier postal service begins. [26] The Theatres Act comes into force, abolishing censorship. [27] The French once again veto Britain's entry into the EEC. 13 members of the cast of *Hair* face the audience naked, in celebration of the abolition of censorship.

Oct [5] Clashes between police and crowds in Londonderry mark the start of violent and long-continued disturbances in Northern Ireland. [9] The HMS *Fearless* talks on Rhodesia fail. [10] Powell warns that immigrants may 'change the character of England'. [27] Anti-Vietnam War demonstration outside the American Embassy in Grosvenor Square; there are violent clashes between mounted police and demonstrators.

Nov [15] The liner *Queen Elizabeth* ends her last passenger voyage. [28] Enid Blyton, writer of children's books, dies.

1969 The Open University is founded. The Divorce Act liberalizes the law, granting divorce on any ground showing 'irretrievable breakdown' of a marriage. The first fertilization of a human egg outside the human body is achieved by Robert Edwards at Cambridge. 'Monty Python's Flying Circus' represents a significant new departure in television comedy. Derek Barton (British) and Odd Hassel (Norwegian) are awarded the Nobel Prize for Chemistry; Samuel Beckett for Literature.

Jan The People's Democracy march from Belfast to Londonderry is broken up; this is the start of escalating unrest in Northern Ireland centring on political parades. [4] 50 people die when an airliner crashes near Gatwick.

Feb [3] The London School of Economics is closed after more student protests. [23] The first broadcast of Kenneth Clark's 'Civilization', popularizing art history.

Mar [5] Ronald and Reginald Kray are sentenced to a minimum of 30 years each for murder. [11] The author John Wyndham dies. [19] British troops land unopposed on Anguilla.

Apr [9] The British Concorde makes its maiden flight from Bristol to Fairford. [17] All women over 18 are now allowed to vote. [20] Belfast post offices and the main bus station are attacked by fire bombers. [21] It is announced that the British army is

to guard key points in Northern Ireland. [22] Robin Knox
Johnston arrives back in Falmouth after completing the first
non-stop solo circumnavigation of the world. The *QE2* starts
her first commercial voyage.

May   [1] James Chichester-Clark becomes Prime Minister of
Northern Ireland. [12] The voting age is reduced to 18.

Jun   [7] The Snape Maltings is destroyed by fire. [9] Enoch
Powell proposes voluntary repatriation of immigrants, to
storms of criticism. [16] Earl Alexander of Tunis, the army
commander who led the invasion of Italy, dies. [20]
High-grade oil is discovered in the British Sector of the
North Sea.

Jul   [1] Prince Charles is invested as Prince of Wales at
Caernarvon Castle.

Aug   [12] There is a three-day street battle in Londonderry after
the Apprentice Boys' march. [19] The British army takes over
security and policing in Northern Ireland.

Sep   [27] The author Dame Ivy Compton-Burnett dies.

Oct   [10] The Hunt Committee reports on Northern Ireland,
recommending disarming the police and disbanding the 'B
Specials'. [14] The 50p coin is issued.

Nov   [3] Work begins on the National Theatre. [11] The owners of
the *Torrey Canyon* agree to pay £1.5 million compensation
each to Britain and France. [13] Quintuplets are born to Mrs
Irene Hanson of Rayleigh, Essex.

Dec   [18] The death penalty for murder is formally abolished, at
the end of a trial period. [22] Bernadette Devlin MP is
sentenced to six months in prison for incitement to riot in
Belfast.

1970 The Equal Pay Act is an important step towards stamping out
sex discrimination. Sir Bernard Katz (British), Ulf von Euler
(Swedish) and Julius Axelrod (American) are awarded the
Nobel Prize for Physiology and Medicine.

Feb   [2] Bertrand Russell, mathematician, philosopher and peace
campaigner, dies aged 97. [11] Prince Charles takes his seat

in the House of Lords. [15] Lord Dowding, chief of Fighter Command in the Battle of Britain, dies aged 87.

Mar [2] Rhodesia is declared a republic. [12] The quarantine period for dogs and cats is extended to one year as a precaution against rabies. [16] The complete New English Bible is published; a million copies are sold on the first day.

Apr [9] The Beatles split up.

May [31] The great racehorse Arkle dies.

Jun [4] Tonga becomes independent. [7] The novelist E. M. Forster dies aged 91. [15] Sir Laurence Olivier is created a Life Peer; he is the first actor to be made a peer. [17] Decimal postage stamps go on sale for the first time. [18] The Conservatives win the General Election (Conservatives 330, Labour 287, Liberals 6); Edward Heath becomes Prime Minister, Iain MacLeod Chancellor of the Exchequer, Reginald Maudling Home Secretary. George Brown loses his seat. [23] Brunel's *Great Britain*, the world's first all-metal liner, returns to Bristol from the Falklands where it has been left as a rusting wreck since 1886. [27-8] There are violent disturbances in Belfast and Londonderry. [29] Britain makes her third application to join the EEC. Caroline Thorpe, Jeremy Thorpe's first wife, dies in a car crash.

Jul [7] Sir Allen Lane, publisher and founder of Penguin paperbacks, dies. [8] The artist Dame Laura Knight dies. [20] The Chancellor of the Exchequer Iain MacLeod dies suddenly. [29] The conductor Sir John Barbirolli dies. [30] Damages are awarded to 28 child-victims of thalidomide.

Aug [2] The army fires rubber bullets for the first time during disturbances in Belfast.

Sep [12] Concorde lands at Heathrow for the first time; there are complaints from nearby residents about the noise.

Oct [10] Fiji becomes independent. [19] BP announces the discovery of a big oilfield in the British Sector of the North Sea, 110 miles east of Aberdeen.

Nov [20] The 10 shilling note goes out of circulation. [26] More working days have been lost as a result of strikes so far this year than in any other year since 1926.

Dec [2] The Commons reject a move to retain British Summer Time in the winter months.

1971 Margaret Thatcher, as Education Minister, abolishes free milk for schoolchildren. The Family Income Supplement is introduced. Internment without trial is introduced for those suspected of being members of or giving assistance to the IRA. EMI-Scanner developed by Godfrey Hounsfield from his invention of computed tomography in 1967. Dennis Gabor is awarded the Nobel Prize for Physics.

Jan [1] The Divorce Reform Act comes into force. [2] The Ibrox football ground disaster; 66 people are crushed to death when a barrier collapses. [3] The Open University begins its television transmissions. [14] The Angry Brigade lets off time bombs outside the home of Robert Carr, Secretary of State for Employment. [15] More decimal coins are issued: 1/2p, 1p and 2p. [19] Postal workers go on strike for a 19.5% pay rise.

Feb [4] Troop reinforcements are sent to Belfast after further violence. Rolls Royce is declared bankrupt. [15] Decimal Day; the decimal currency system comes into operation. [21] 100,000 trade unionists march in London in protest against the Industrial Relations Bill. [24] The Immigration Bill is introduced; this measure will end the right of Commonwealth citizens to settle in Britain.

Mar [1] One-day strike by 1.5 million engineers against the Industrial Relations Bill. [8] The postal strike ends. [18] More troops are sent to Northern Ireland, bringing the total to 9,700. [20] Chichester-Clark resigns as Prime Minister of Northern Ireland; he is succeeded by Brian Faulkner.

Jun [14] Upper Clyde Shipbuilders are forced into liquidation; the Government refuses to help 'lame ducks'. [25] Lord Boyd-Orr dies.

Jul [7] The Government publishes its terms for entry into the EEC. [30] Workers at Upper Clyde Shipbuilders take control of the shipyard.

Aug [9] Internment without trial begins in Northern Ireland.

Sep [9] Parliament is recalled for a special debate on Northern Ireland. [27] Prime Ministers Heath, Lynch and Faulkner meet at Chequers for discussions about Northern Ireland.

Oct [4] The Labour Party Conference votes by a large majority against the proposed terms for entry into the EEC. [13] The Conservative Party Conference votes overwhelmingly in favour of the EEC entry terms. [28] The Commons vote in favour of joining the EEC on the terms presented by the Government (356 to 244); 69 Labour MPs vote with the Government. [30] An opinion poll shows that most of the British electorate oppose Britain's entry into the EEC.

Nov [16] The Compton report on Interrogation in Northern Ireland finds 'some ill-treatment but no brutality'.

Dec [11] Geoffrey Rippon agrees terms with the EEC for the protection of fishing limits after Britain's entry; these turn out not to protect the interests of British fishermen. [20] Edward Heath meets Richard Nixon in Bermuda for talks.

1972 Rodney Porter (British) and Gerald Edelman (American) are awarded the Nobel Prize for Physiology and Medicine.

Jan [9] The miners' strike begins, causing widespread powercuts and disruption to industrial production. After being converted to a floating marine university at Hong Kong, and renamed 'Seawise University', the liner *Queen Elizabeth* catches fire and sinks. [18] Britain's first plastic warship, the minehunter HMS *Wilton*, is launched at Southampton. [20] Unemployment in the UK passes the 1 million mark. [22] Britain joins the EEC; the 'Six' become the 'Ten' by the Treaty of Accession (becoming effective next Jan). [30] 'Bloody Sunday' in Londonderry; 13 protest marchers are killed by British troops opening fire on an unarmed Catholic demonstration.

Feb [9] A state of emergency is declared in the power crisis;
industry is now officially to work only three days a week to
conserve coal supplies. [15] Over l.5 million workers are laid
off at the peak of the power crisis. [22] An IRA bomb attack
on Aldershot kills five cleaning women, a gardener and a
Catholic priest. [25] The miners vote to return to work.

Mar [4] A hovercraft capsizes in the Solent, killing five people.
[20] A bomb blast in Belfast kills six and injures 47. [25]
Heath decides to impose Direct Rule on Ulster from
Westminster, suspending rule from Stormont. [29] The
Tutankhamun exhibition opens at the British Museum. [30]
Direct Rule comes into force; William Whitelaw is appointed
Secretary of State for Ireland.

Apr [11] Roy Jenkins and David Owen resign from the Labour
front bench in protest at Wilson's decision to support a call
for a referendum on Britain's membership of the EEC. [13]
There are 23 explosions in the worst day of violence in Ulster
since Direct Rule was imposed. [17] A work-to-rule begins on
British Rail in support of a pay claim. [18] The new state of
Bangladesh (formerly East Pakistan) is admitted to the
Commonwealth. [19] The Widgery Report on 'Bloody
Sunday' is published.

May [3] A Church of England synod fails to reach the required
majority in favour of a union with the Methodist Church.
[13] The work-to-rule causes a complete weekend close-down
on British Rail. [18] Bomb disposal experts parachute onto
the QE2 in mid-Atlantic following a bomb threat. The Queen
meets the Duke of Windsor in Paris. [22] Ceylon becomes the
independent republic of Sri Lanka. C. Day Lewis, Poet
Laureate since 1967, dies. [28] The Duke of Windsor, ex-King
Edward VIII, dies in Paris aged 77.

Jun [5] The funeral of the Duke of Windsor takes place at
Windsor. [11] Four people are killed and 115 injured in a
train crash at Eltham. [12] The rail dispute is settled.

Jul Reginald Maudling resigns because of his association with
the Poulson corruption case; Robert Carr replaces him as

Home Secretary. [5] 30 patients die in a fire at Coldharbour Hospital, Sherborne.

Aug President Amin orders the expulsion of 40,000 Asians from Uganda; many of them come to Britain. [26] Sir Francis Chichester dies at Plymouth. [28] Prince William of Gloucester is killed in a plane crash.

Sep [1] Iceland extends her fishing limit from 12 to 150 miles, in an attempt to exclude British and other foreign fishing. [17] The first Asians arrive in Britain from Uganda.

Oct [5] The Congregational Church (England and Wales) and the Presbyterian Church in England combine to form the United Reformed Church. [10] Sir John Betjeman is appointed Poet Laureate. [12] Students jostle and insult the Queen when she visits Stirling University.

Nov [6] The Government imposes a 3-month pay freeze. [26] The Race Relations Act comes into force; from now on employers may not discriminate on grounds of colour. [30] The Government cancels its planned £10 million loan to Uganda because of Amin's treatment of Asians. The writer Sir Compton MacKenzie dies.

Dec [30] The Tutankhamun exhibition closes; 1.6 million visitors have seen it.

1973 Brian Josephson (British), Ivar Giaever (American) and Leo Esake (Japanese) are awarded the Nobel Prize for Physics. Geoffrey Wilkinson (British) and Ernst Otto Fischer (German) receive the Nobel Prize for Chemistry.

Jan [1] Britain and the Irish Republic formally become members of the EEC. [11] The Open University awards its first 800 degrees.

Feb [1] The Common Agricultural Policy of the EEC comes into operation. [5] The first Protestant Loyalists are detained without trial in Northern Ireland. [7] Widespread violence in Northern Ireland. [22] The writer Elizabeth Bowen dies.

Mar [1] A Fine Gael and Labour Party Coalition wins the Irish
     General Election; Liam Cosgrave becomes Prime Minister. [8]
     Two bombs explode in London; one person is killed and 238
     are injured. [9] The Northern Ireland referendum shows that
     592,000 are in favour of retaining links with Britain, 6,000 for
     a union with the Irish Republic. [18] John Cartland,
     proprietor of a Brighton language school, is murdered in
     Provence; his son Jeremy is suspected, but after a lengthy
     inquiry by the French authorities he is found neither guilty
     nor innocent and released. [26] Sir Noel Coward, playwright,
     songwriter and entertainer, dies.
Apr [1] Value Added Tax is introduced in Britain.
May [18] Frigates are sent to protect British trawlers inside the
     disputed waters round Iceland. [21] A British warship chases
     an Icelandic frigate in the first Royal Naval action of the 'Cod
     War'. [31] Erskine Childers succeeds de Valera as President
     of the Irish Republic.
Jun [8] Enoch Powell hints that people should vote Labour to
     protest against Britain's membership of the EEC.
Jul [4] Riot at Long Kesh Prison in Northern Ireland. [10] The
     Bahamas become independent. [11] 122 people die in the
     Paris air crash. [18] The film actor Jack Hawkins dies. [30] 18
     miners die in a pit cage accident at Markham colliery in
     Derbyshire.
Aug [2] The Summerland fire at Douglas, Isle of Man: 50 people
     die. [20] The first of a series of IRA bomb attacks in London.
Sep [2] J.R.R. Tolkien, author of *The Lord of the Rings*, dies at
     Bournemouth. [7] Len Murray succeeds Vic Feather as TUC
     General Secretary. [10] IRA bomb explosions in London
     stations injure 13 people. [16] Tommy Herron, the
     vice-chairman of the UDA, is shot dead at Lisburn. [20] A
     bomb explodes at Chelsea barracks. [28] The poet W.H.
     Auden dies.
Oct [1] Denis Healey promises that Labour will tax the rich 'until
     the pips squeak'. [31] Three Provisional IRA leaders are freed
     from Mountjoy Prison by a hi-jacked helicopter.

Nov　[8] The Cod War between Britain and Iceland ends. [13] A state of emergency is declared as miners and power workers go on strike. [14] Princess Anne marries Captain Mark Phillips at Westminster Abbey. [25] The 200th British soldier to die in Northern Ireland is killed.

Dec　[2] In a Cabinet reshuffle, Francis Pym is made Northern Ireland Secretary, Whitelaw Employment Secretary. [5] A 50 mph speed limit is imposed to conserve fuel. [13] A three-day working week is ordered by the Government because of the coal-miners' slow-down and the Arab oil embargo. [19] Nine people die in a train crash at Ealing. [31] The three-day week begins.

1974　Sir Martin Ryle and Antony Hewish are awarded the Nobel Prize for Physics.

Jan　[1] Direct Rule in Northern Ireland ends and a new Ulster Executive takes office (but Direct Rule is resumed later in the year).

Feb　[1] The escaped Great Train Robber Ronald Biggs is arrested in Brazil. [4] 12 men are killed in an army coach explosion on the M62. [7] Grenada becomes independent. [28] The General Election result is inconclusive. Edward Heath hoped for a fresh mandate after his confrontation with the miners, but there is a narrow Labour victory (Labour 301, Conservatives 297, Liberals 14, Scottish Nationalists 7). Heath tries to form a Conservative-Liberal Coalition.

Mar　[4] Heath resigns after the Liberals reject the coalition idea; a minority Labour Government is formed by Harold Wilson. [6] The miners return to work after the Wilson Government offers a 35% pay increase. [9] Britain returns to a five-day working week. [20] An attempt is made to abduct Princess Anne in the Mall; the gunman fails but injures four people.

May　[8] The nurses begin a series of strikes in protest against their low pay. [17] Car bombs in Dublin and Monaghan kill 28 people and injure over 100. [19] A state of emergency is declared in Northern Ireland. A car bomb explodes in a car park at Heathrow.

Jun [1] An explosion at the Flixborough chemical works kills 29 people. [10] Henry, Duke of Gloucester, son of George V, dies. [17] An IRA bomb explodes at Westminster Hall.

Jul [10] The Government announces that it has chosen a British-designed reactor for the next stage of its nuclear energy programme (i.e. the 1980s). [14] IRA bombs explode in Birmingham and Manchester. [17] Bombs explode in the Tower of London. [18] The Maplin airport project, which could have combined a seaport rivalling Rotterdam, is scrapped. [24] Sir James Chadwick, physicist and discoverer of the neutron, dies. [25] The International Court of Justice at The Hague rules that the UK is not bound to observe Iceland's unilateral decision (in 1972) to extend its rights from 12 miles to 50 miles from the coast. [26] An IRA bomb explodes at Heathrow car park.

Aug [15] The collapse of the Court Line leaves many holiday-makers stranded in foreign resorts.

Sep [3] Two crew members are drowned when Edward Heath's yacht *Morning Cloud* is hit by huge waves in the Channel.

Oct [1] Britain's first McDonald's hamburger restaurant opens in South London. [5] IRA bomb explosions in two Guildford pubs kill five people. [10] In this year's second General Election, Harold Wilson hopes for a fresh mandate for his (numerically weak) Government, but it produces only a small overall majority (Labour 319, Conservatives 277, Liberals 13, Scottish Nationalists 11). [15] There is rioting in the Maze Prison. [18] A Whitehall Unit is set up to prepare for the devolution of power to Wales and Scotland.

Nov [4] Judith Ward is given 12 life sentences for causing the M62 bomb deaths. [7] Two people die in a pub bombing at Woolwich. [8] After 300 years, Covent Garden market moves out of central London to a new site at Nine Elms. Ronald Milhench is sent to prison for forging the Prime Minister's signature. [9] The composer Egon Wellesz dies. [11] Sandra

Rivett, Lady Lucan's nanny, is murdered by an intruder. Lord Lucan, widely assumed to be the murderer, drives to Newhaven and mysteriously disappears, never to be seen again although alleged 'sightings' are reported occasionally. [12] Wolfson College, Oxford is opened. [15] Donald Coggan succeeds Michael Ramsey as Archbishop of Canterbury. [21] 21 people are killed and 120 injured in two Birmingham pub bombings. The MP John Stonehouse disappears on a Miami beach; it is assumed that he has drowned.

1975 Press allegations about Jeremy Thorpe's private life become an increasing embarrassment to the Liberal Party. The Community Land Act brings development land within public control (repealed in 1979). Sex Discrimination Act.

Jan [10] Two workers at Windscale die of leukaemia. [14] Lesley Whittle, a young heiress, is abducted. [24] Dr Coggan is enthroned as Archbishop of Canterbury. [27] Five IRA bombs explode in London. [31] The Duke of Norfolk dies.

Feb [11] Margaret Thatcher becomes leader of the Conservative Party, after her successful challenge to Heath's leadership. [14] The novelist P.G. Wodehouse dies aged 93. Sir Julian Huxley dies. [28] The Moorgate tube station disaster; this is the worst underground train accident so far, in which 42 people are killed as a train travelling at speed crashes into a blind tunnel.

Mar [4] Charlie Chaplin is knighted. [7] Lesley Whittle's body is found in a drain shaft; she has been strangled with a wire noose by her kidnapper, nicknamed the Black Panther. [21] John Stonehouse, the disappearing MP, is arrested in Australia for theft, forgery and deception. [25] The QE2 becomes the largest liner to have passed through the Panama Canal. [27] Sir Arthur Bliss, composer and Master of the Queen's Musick since 1953, dies.

May [20] The sculptor Barbara Hepworth dies in a fire at her studio at St Ives in Cornwall. [27] A coach crash in Wharfedale kills 32 elderly people.

Jun [1] Snow falls in London in this month for the first time since records began. [5] The National Referendum on Britain's membership of the EEC results in 17.4 million voting 'yes' and 8.5 million voting 'no'. [11] The first oil is pumped ashore from Britain's North Sea oilfields. The prosecution in the Birmingham bomb trial concedes that the six people accused have been beaten up while in custody.

Aug [1] Britain signs the Helsinki Agreement on security and co-operation in Europe. [27] Haile Selassie, the deposed Emperor of Ethiopia, dies in exile in England. [29] Eamon de Valera, three times Prime Minister of the Irish Republic and President 1959-73, dies aged 92.

Sep [28] The Spaghetti House siege; gunmen hold seven Italians hostage in a London restaurant.

Oct [3] The Spaghetti House siege ends and the hostages are freed unharmed. [15] Iceland unilaterally extends its fishing grounds from 50 to 200 miles; this leads to a resumption of the Cod War between Britain and Iceland. [23] Professor Fairley, a leading cancer expert, is killed by a car bomb intended for Hugh Fraser MP. [30] More than 16 million elm trees have so far been destroyed by Dutch Elm Disease.

Nov [7] Cardinal Heenan, Roman Catholic Archbishop of Westminster, dies. [12] An IRA bomb explodes at Scott's Restaurant in London, killing one man. [18] Two people are killed when another bomb goes off at Waltons Restaurant in London. [25] The Government authorizes the sending of three frigates to protect British trawlers fishing in the disputed waters off Iceland. [27] Ross McWhirter, compiler of the *Guinness Book of Records*, is shot dead at his home in London by two IRA gunmen.

Dec [10] The first shots are fired in the Cod War. [11] The end of the Balcombe Street siege in London; Mr and Mrs Matthews had been held hostage in their flat by IRA terrorists since December 6.

1976 The Agricultural Rent Act abolishes 'tied' farm cottages.

Jan [2] Winds up to 105 mph cause destruction and 22 deaths. [4] Five Catholics are killed in an ambush by Protestant terrorists. [5] Ten Protestants are machine-gunned at Whitecross by Catholic terrorists, in what is seen as the worst sectarian murder since 'the troubles' began in the 1960s. [7] The frigate HMS *Andromeda* is rammed by an Icelandic gunboat. The President of the Royal Academy, Sir Thomas Monnington, dies. [12] The novelist Agatha Christie dies. [21] Concorde enters passenger service with simultaneous take-offs from London and Paris. [24] Soviet commentators refer to Margaret Thatcher as 'The Iron Lady'.

Feb [12] Workmen discover a perfectly preserved rose that was cemented into a wall at Romsey Abbey in 1120. [23] The painter L.S. Lowry dies at Glossop. [24] Britain sends a fourth gunboat to Iceland.

Mar [16] Harold Wilson resigns as Prime Minister. Norman Scott tells a court of his relationship with Jeremy Thorpe. [19] It is announced that Princess Margaret and Lord Snowdon are to separate. [23] Ian Smith rejects Wilson's conditions for a Rhodesia settlement. [24] Viscount Montgomery of Alamein dies aged 88.

Apr [5] James Callaghan succeeds as Prime Minister. [27] Britain starts exporting North Sea Oil, from Forties field.

May [10] Thorpe resigns as leader of the Liberal Party. [12] Jo Grimond agrees to act as caretaker leader of the Liberal Party. [26] There is widespread condemnation of Wilson's resignation honours list, which includes knighthoods for James Goldsmith and Joseph Kagan as well as a peerage for the Political Secretary who helped draw up the list (Lady Falkender).

Jun [1] Interim agreement is reached in Oslo between Iceland and Britain, ending the Cod War. [9] The actress Dame Sybil Thorndike dies aged 93. [28] The Seychelles become an independent republic.

Jul [1] Donald Nielson is convicted of the murder of Lesley
Whittle. [7] David Steel is elected Liberal Party leader.
[21] Christopher Ewart-Biggs, British Ambassador to the
Irish Republic, is assassinated. Donald Nielson is given
five life sentences for murder. [22] The archaeologist
who has done much to popularize archaeology, Sir
Mortimer Wheeler, dies. [30] Richard Ingrams, editor of
Private Eye, is tried on libel charges brought by Sir James
Goldsmith.

Aug [1] Trinidad and Tobago become an independent republic.
[4] Lord Thomson of Fleet, owner of *The Times*, dies.
[6] John Stonehouse begins a seven-year prison sentence
for fraud. [14] The Women's Peace Movement of Northern
Ireland, led by Betty Williams and Mairead Corrigan,
holds its first big rally. [22] The drought is the worst in
Britain for 500 years; it is also the hottest summer since at
least 1727. [25] Unemployment passes the 1.5 million
mark.

Sep [2] The European Commission on Human Rights reports on
the Irish Government's charges against Britain; the British
authorities are found guilty of torturing detainees in Ulster
following the introduction of internment in 1971, but not
guilty of discriminating between Protestant and Republican
extremists. Percy Shaw, who invented cat's eyes, dies. [20]
EEC members sign a convention in Brussels, allowing a
European Parliament to be set up. The minesweeper HMS
Fittleton sinks after colliding with the frigate *Mermaid* off the
Dutch coast: 12 die. [24] Ian Smith accepts the idea of
majority rule in Rhodesia within two years.

Oct [14] The actress Dame Edith Evans dies aged 88. [21] Michael
Foot is elected deputy leader of the Labour Party. [25] The
Queen opens the National Theatre. [26] Deryck Cooke, who
completed Mahler's 10th Symphony, dies. [29] Mining
begins on the newly-discovered coalfield at Selby. [30] EEC
agrees on the introduction of a 200 mile EEC fishing zone (in
force from 1 January 1977).

Nov [7] Crosses are planted in Belfast for the lives lost in Northern Ireland since 1969 - 1,662 in all. [19] The architect Sir Basil Spence dies. [28] The composer Harold Darke dies.

Dec [4] The composer Benjamin Britten dies. [16] It is announced that Wales and Scotland are to have referenda on devolution (a greater measure of self-government).

1977 Sir Nevill Mott (British), J. von Vleck and P. Andersen awarded the Nobel Prize for Physics.

Jan [5] Roy Jenkins resigns as MP to become the first President of the EEC Commission, but with the intention of eventually returning to form a 'third force' in British politics. [14] Lord Avon, Conservative Prime Minister 1955-57, dies. [24] The second round of Rhodesian talks fails; Ian Smith rejects British proposals for a transition to black majority rule. [29] Seven IRA bombs explode in central London without any casualties.

Feb [2] There is an important meeting of NEDC on industrial strategy to reduce strike action. [15] Statistics show that in 1976 deaths exceeded births for the first time since records began in 1837; this indicates an important trend towards demographic stability. [19] Anthony Crosland dies. [21] David Owen, aged 38, becomes Foreign Secretary. [22] The Government presses the UN to investigate reports of killings in Uganda.

Mar [3] Lord Faulkner, former Northern Ireland Prime Minister, dies. [7] The Queen arrives in Australia on her Silver Jubilee tour. [10] Callaghan arrives in Washington for talks with President Carter. [25] There is an EEC summit meeting in Rome, chaired by Callaghan. [28] The mountaineer Eric Shipton dies in Salisbury. [31] The Queen and Prince Philip arrive home at the end of their tour.

Apr [2] Red Rum wins the Grand National for the third time. [7] Margaret Thatcher begins a visit to China. [12] A new British initiative on Rhodesia begins; David Owen arrives in Tanzania on a diplomatic tour of Southern Africa, in

the hope of reaching a negotiated transfer of power in
Rhodesia.

May [13] Peter Jay, the Prime Minister's son-in-law, is named as
the next ambassador to Washington.

Jun [7] The Queen lights a bonfire in Windsor Great Park,
starting a week of Silver Jubilee celebrations.

Aug [13] The writer Henry Williamson dies.

Sep David Owen presents Ian Smith with new Anglo-American
proposals for a Rhodesian settlement. A National Front
march in Manchester is banned. [13] The London-born
conductor Leopold Stokowski dies in Hampshire aged 95.

Oct [28] Yorkshire police begin a hunt for a serial murderer, the
Yorkshire Ripper, who is making apparently random attacks
on young women.

Nov Firemen strike for a 30% pay rise. [14] The composer Richard
Addinsell dies.

Dec [12] Lady Churchill, widow of Sir Winston Churchill, dies.
[25] Charlie Chaplin dies.

1978 Liverpool Cathedral is finally completed. To celebrate Henry
Moore's 80th birthday an exhibition of his sculpture is held in
Hyde Park. Peter Mitchell is awarded the Nobel Prize for
Chemistry.

Jan The firemen's strike ends. The Government suffers a series of
defeats on its Scottish Devolution Bill; it is amended so that
devolution can only happen if a minimum of 40% of the
whole electorate votes 'yes'. [11] It is revealed that Lady
Churchill destroyed the Graham Sutherland portrait of her
husband. [30] Margaret Thatcher says that many in Britain
fear being 'swamped by people with a different culture'.

Feb [13] Heath criticizes Thatcher for causing an 'unnecessary
row' over immigration.

Mar An internal agreement is reached in Rhodesia between Smith
and three black leaders. [30] The Conservatives reveal that
they have hired the services of an advertising agency, Saatchi
and Saatchi.

May [1] The first May Day bank holiday is celebrated in Britain. [24] Princess Margaret and Lord Snowdon are divorced.

Jun [3] Jeremy Thorpe is interviewed by police investigating a plot to murder Norman Scott. [27] Evidence suggests that Britain will be self-sufficient in oil in two years' time.

Jul [25] The world's first test-tube baby is born: Louise Brown is born at Oldham General Hospital. [31] The Devolution Acts for Wales and Scotland receive the Royal Assent.

Aug [4] Jeremy Thorpe is on trial at Barnstaple for conspiracy to murder. [30] A case of smallpox is confirmed in Birmingham; Janet Parker dies on September ll.

Sep A series of strikes begins, lasting thorough the winter; people are turned away from hospitals, bodies are left unburied, and rubbish accumulates in the streets. [10] Police attribute two more murders to the Yorkshire Ripper, making a total of 10. [11] Georgi Markov, a Bulgarian defector, is stabbed in the thigh with a poisoned umbrella point at a bus stop on Waterloo Bridge. [15] Georgi Markov dies. [30] The Ellice Islands become independent as Tuvalu.

Oct [6] The unveiling of the Chagall window in Chichester Cathedral, the last of Dean Walter Hussey's remarkable commissions. [12] The *Christos Bitas* is grounded off St David's Head: an oil slick threatens the Welsh Coast.

Nov [11] Committal proceedings begin against Thorpe. The TUC refuses to endorse the Government's 5% wage limit. [30] Publication of *The Times* is suspended because of an industrial dispute.

Dec The Government introduces a plan to impose sanctions on private firms awarding pay rises above 5%; the plan is defeated in the Commons. [17] There are IRA bomb explosions in Southampton, Bristol, Manchester and Coventry. [18] Further bombs explode or are discovered in London, Bristol and Southampton.

1979 Sir Laurence Olivier receives a special Academy Award for his unrivalled contribution to theatre and cinema. Godfrey

Newbold Hounsfield (British) and Allan McLeod Cormack (American) are awarded the Nobel Prize for Physiology and Medicine.

Jan Secondary picketing in the road haulage strike creates increasing problems. 150,000 people are laid off because of the strike. [8] An oil tanker explodes in Bantry Bay killing 49 people. [31] Industrial disputes have led to accumulations of rubbish building up in the streets.

Feb A 'concordat' between the TUC and the Government depends on the Government bringing inflation down to 5% within three years. [22] St Lucia becomes independent. [26] Tom Keating's trial for art forgery ends because of his failing health.

Mar [1] 32.5% of Scots vote in favour of the devolution proposals, failing to reach the required 40%. The Welsh vote over-whelmingly against devolution. The Government is defeated in a confidence vote, necessitating a General Election. [30] The Conservative MP Airey Neave is assassinated in the car park at Westminster by the IRA. [31] The Royal Navy finally withdraws from Malta.

Apr [4] The eleventh victim of the Yorkshire Ripper dies. [23] A teacher is killed and 300 are arrested after clashes in Southall between supporters of the National Front and the Anti-Nazi League.

May [3] Jeremy Thorpe loses his seat in the General Election, marking the conclusive end of his political career. [4] Margaret Thatcher becomes the first woman Prime Minister; she leads a Conservative Government, with Lord Carrington as Foreign Secretary, William Whitelaw as Home Secretary and Geoffrey Howe as Chancellor (Conservatives 339, Labour 269, Liberals ll). [29] Bishop Abel Muzorewa becomes Zimbabwe's (Rhodesia's) first black Prime Minister.

Jun The first elections to the European Parliament are held. [22] Jeremy Thorpe is acquitted of conspiracy to murder charge.

Jul [12] The Gilbert Islands become independent as Kiribati.
Aug [8] Nicholas Montsarrat, author of *The Cruel Sea*, dies.
[14] John Stonehouse is released from prison. Gale force
winds cause havoc in the Fastnet yacht race: 17 people
are drowned. [18] A heart transplant operation is attempted
for the first time at Papworth Hospital. [27] Lord
Mountbatten is assassinated by the IRA at Mullaghmore; his
boat *Shadow V* explodes, killing him, his boatman and his
grandson Nicholas; Dowager Lady Brabourne dies the next
day.
Sep [2] The 12th victim of the Yorkshire Ripper dies. [5] State
funeral of Lord Mountbatten. [14] Plans are announced for
the redevelopment of the London docklands. [18] Corporal
punishment is abolished in all Inner London Schools. [27]
The entertainer Dame Gracie Fields dies. [29] The Pope
arrives in Ireland.
Oct [30] The inventor Sir Barnes Wallis dies.
Nov [13] *The Times* reappears after a year's absence. [21] The
House of Commons hears that Sir Anthony Blunt was the
'fourth man' in the Burgess, MacLean and Philby spy affair;
Buckingham Palace announces that Blunt has been stripped
of his knighthood. [23] Thomas McMahon is sentenced to life
imprisonment for the murder of Lord Mountbatten.
Dec UDI in Rhodesia comes to an end with an agreement on free
elections. [5] Jack Lynch resigns as Prime Minister of the Irish
Republic. [7] Charles Haughey is elected leader of Ireland's
governing party.

1980 The socket of a second Heel Stone is discovered at
Stonehenge by Michael Pitts. Frederick Sanger (British), Paul
Berg and Walter Gilbert are awarded the Nobel Prize for
Chemistry.

Jan [18] The photographer and designer Sir Cecil Beaton dies.
Feb [17] The painter Graham Sutherland dies. [28] The BBC
announces that it will scrap five of its orchestras as an
economy measure.

Mar [25] Robert Runcie is enthroned as Archbishop of Canterbury. [27] The residential North Sea oil platform *Alexander Kielland* collapses in a storm, killing 100 men.

Apr [2] There is a riot in the St Pauls area of Bristol in which 19 police are injured. [4] Argentina is reported to be increasing her links with the Falkland Islands; this turns out to be a preliminary to an invasion. [22] Unemployment passes the 1.5 million mark. [29] The film director Alfred Hitchcock dies. [30] Armed men seize 20 hostages in the Iranian Embassy in London.

May [5] SAS troops storm the Iranian Embassy, freeing the hostages. [30] EC foreign ministers agree to reduce Britain's annual payment to the EC to about 25%.

Jun [8] There is a wave of bombings in Ulster. [12] The holiday camp owner Sir Billy Butlin dies in Jersey. [30] The sixpenny piece ceases to be legal tender today.

Jul [10] Alexandra Palace is badly damaged by fire. [23] The dispute between the BBC and its musicians is resolved: three orchestras are reprieved. [24] The entertainer Peter Sellers dies. [31] Shirley Williams, William Rodgers and David Owen urge Labour MPs to join forces with them against the far left.

Aug [4] The Queen Mother's 80th birthday. [15] The wreck of the *Titanic*, which sank in 1912, is located on the seabed.

Oct [10] Margaret Thatcher makes her 'the lady's not for turning' speech at the Conservative Party Conference. [14] ICI announces that it will make 4500 of its workers redundant. [28] The Director of Public Prosecutions decides not to prosecute the National Theatre over the Howard Brenton play *The Romans in Britain*.

Nov [17] Peter Sutcliffe, the Yorkshire Ripper, murders student Jacqueline Hill.

Dec [3] Sir Oswald Mosley dies in France. [8] John Lennon is murdered outside his Manhatten apartment by Mark Chapman. Unemployment passes the two million level for the first time since 1935. There is a summit meeting in

Dublin between Mrs Thatcher and Irish Prime Minister
Charles Haughey about closer co-operation between the
UK and the Irish Republic. [17] Prof. Alan Walters is
appointed as personal economic adviser to Mrs Thatcher.

1981

Jan   [5] Peter Sutcliffe, a lorry driver, is charged with the final
      'Yorkshire Ripper' murder; he has murdered 13 women over
      the last four years. Norman St John Stevas is replaced as
      Leader of the House of Commons by Francis Pym. [6] The
      novelist A.J. Cronin dies in Switzerland. [21] Sir Norman
      Stronge and his son, both former Stormont MPs, are killed
      by the IRA. [25] The Limehouse Declaration; William
      Rodgers, Roy Jenkins, Shirley Williams and David Owen
      form a Council for Social Democracy. The break-away 'Gang
      of Four' will form a new centre party, the SDP.

Feb   [10] The National Coal Board plans to close 50 pits employing
      30,000 miners; the miners press for a national miners' strike.
      [12] Rupert Murdoch buys *The Times*. Ian Paisley is
      suspended from the House of Commons for referring to the
      Northern Ireland Secretary in unparliamentary language.
      [14] 48 young people die in a disco fire in Dublin. [20] Peter
      Sutcliffe is charged with the murder of 13 women. [24] Prince
      Charles and Lady Diana Spencer announce their
      engagement.

Mar   [9] John Lambe, the M5 Rapist, is given 12 life sentences for
      16 rapes. [26] The inauguration of the Social Democratic
      Party is seen by many people as a refreshing development in
      British politics, possibly as the beginning of the end of the
      see-saw of two-party political debate.

Apr   [3] Race riot in Southall. [4] Race riot in Brixton. [11] Start of
      a weekend of serious violence in Brixton.

May   [5] Bobby Sands dies at the end of a 66-day fast. [9] A bomb
      explodes at the Sullom Voe oil terminal while the Queen and
      King Olav are formally opening the complex. [12] The IRA
      hunger striker Francis Hughes dies. [15] Princess Anne gives

birth to a daughter, Zara. [22] Sutcliffe is sentenced to life imprisonment for the Ripper murders.

Jun [10] Eight leading IRA prisoners escape from the Crumlin Road prison. [13] Blanks are fired at the Queen in the Mall on her way to the Trooping of the Colour. [16] An alliance is formed between the Liberals and the SDP, the first of a series of muddles over the centre's political identity. [24] The Humber Bridge is opened to traffic. [30] Garret Fitzgerald becomes Prime Minister of the Irish Republic.

Jul [3] More riots in Southall. [4] Riots in Toxteth, Liverpool. [8] Riots in Moss Side (Manchester) and Wood Green (London). [15] There is another outbreak of violence in Brixton. [29] Prince Charles marries Lady Diana Spencer.

Aug [8] There are riots in Northern Ireland following the death of the ninth hunger striker and ten years of internment.

Sep [14] A 17-year-old youth is sent to prison for five years for firing blanks at the Queen. [17] The Royal Docks close, in readiness for redevelopment.

Oct [4] The hunger strike at the Maze Prison ends: ten have died. [15] Norman Tebbitt's remark that his father 'got on his bike and looked for work' angers the unemployed. [17] Lt. Gen. Sir Steuart Pringle is badly injured by an IRA car bomb.

Nov [14] Unionist MP Robert Bradford is shot dead in Belfast [25] Lord Scarman's Report on the summer race riots is published.

Dec [8] There are sudden heavy falls of snow. Arthur Scargill becomes leader of the National Union of Mineworkers. [13] The composer Cornelius Cardew dies. [17] The Law Lords rule that the Greater London Council's cheap fares policy (fares in effect subsidized from rates) is illegal. [19] The Penlee Lifeboat Disaster; the lifeboat *Solomon Browne* is lost with her crew of eight while attempting to rescue the crew of the coaster *Union Star*.

1982 Unemployment passes two million.

Feb   [5] Laker Airlines collapses with debts of more than £210 million. [19] In Belfast the De Lorean car company goes into liquidation.

Mar   [3] The Queen formally opens the Barbican Centre. [18] An Argentinian scrap metal dealer raises the Argentine Flag in South Georgia – a signal of intention from Argentina that is not correctly interpreted by the British Foreign Office.

Apr   [2] The Falklands War begins; Argentine forces invade and capture the Falkland Islands. [5] The Foreign Secretary, Lord Carrington, resigns. A British Fleet sails from Portsmouth, bound for the Falklands. [6] The importation of Argentine products is banned. [7] The Defence Secretary announces a 200-mile radius naval blockade of the Falklands. [25] British forces recapture South Georgia.

May   [1] British aircraft bomb Port Stanley in the Falklands. [2] The Argentine cruiser *General Belgrano* is torpedoed and sunk by the British submarine *Conqueror*, even though outside the 200-mile 'Exclusion Zone' and steaming away from it towards Argentina. [4] HMS *Sheffield* is destroyed by an Exocet missile from an Argentine plane; the *Sheffield* sinks with the loss of 21 lives. [7] Britain extends the total 'Exclusion Zone' to within 12 nautical miles of the coast of Argentina. [15] There is a British commando raid on the Argentine airstrip on Pebble Island. [21] The British Forces establish a bridgehead at San Carlos. HMS *Ardent* is sunk with the loss of 22 men. 21 men are killed when a Sea King helicopter crashes. [24] HMS *Antelope* is sunk after catching fire. [25] HMS *Coventry* and the *Atlantic Conveyor* are destroyed. [28] Goose Green and Darwin are captured by the British, which seems to mark a turning-point in the conflict. Pope John Paul arrives in Britain, landing at Gatwick.

Jun   [6] The British take Bluff Cove and Fitzroy. [7] The Argentines raid *Sir Tristram* and *Sir Galahad* at Bluff Cove.

[14] The Argentine forces formally surrender to troops of the British task force as British troops take Port Stanley; a ceasefire is agreed. Fighting ends in the Falklands. [17] The Argentine leader, General Galtieri, is deposed. [21] Prince Charles' son William is born in London.

Jul   [2] Roy Jenkins is elected leader of the new SDP. [7] Michael Fagan intrudes into the Queen's bedroom, exposing alarmingly poor security at Buckingham Palace. [13] The film actor Kenneth More dies at Fulham. [20] IRA bombs explode in Hyde Park and Regent's Park killing 12 people, injuring 50, and killing 7 army horses. [22] Britain lifts the 200-mile Exclusion Zone round the Falklands.

Aug   [29] Ingrid Bergman, the film actress, dies in Chelsea.

Sep   [5] Sir Douglas Bader, pilot and leader of 'The Few' in the Battle of Britain, dies.

Oct   [31] The Thames Barrier, designed to prevent London from flooding, is raised for the first time.

Nov   [1] Channel 4 Television begins transmitting. [7] The police find the trousers stolen from Sir Geoffrey Howe on a train. [10] Geoffrey Prime is gaoled for 35 years for spying.

Dec   [6] A bomb in the Droppin Well bar in Ballykelly kills 16 people and injures 66. [12] 30,000 women form a ring round the Greenham Common missile base in a protest against nuclear weapons.

Dec   [15] The border between Gibraltar and Spain is reopened after 13 years.

1983   The £1 coin comes into circulation. Sir William Golding receives the Nobel Prize for Literature.

Jan   [17] Breakfast television begins in Britain. [31] The wearing of seat belts in the front seats of cars becomes compulsory.

Feb   [9] The 1981 Derby Winner 'Shergar' is stolen in County Kildare, never to be seen again. He was killed shortly afterwards. [23] Sir Adrian Boult, conductor, dies at Tunbridge Wells aged 93. [24] The composer Herbert Howells dies.

Mar [3] The writer Arthur Koestler and his wife commit suicide.
[8] The composer Sir William Walton dies in Ischia. The spy
Donald MacLean dies in Moscow. [15] The novelist Dame
Rebecca West dies.

Apr [12] Sir Richard Attenborough wins eight Oscars for
Gandhi .

May [16] London police begin using wheel clamps in an attempt to
stop illegal parking. [21] Lord Clark, the art critic, dies. [24]
A large bomb damages the Andersonstown police station in
Belfast.

Jun [9] The Conservatives win the General Election with a
landslide majority (Conservatives 397, Labour 209,
Liberal/SDP Alliance 23); Margaret Thatcher remains Prime
Minister. [12] Michael Foot resigns as leader of the Labour
Party. [13] Roy Jenkins resigns as leader of the SDP, to be
succeeded by David Owen.

Jul [3] The home of Gerry Fitt, former Ulster MP, is destroyed by
fire. [13] Neil Kinnock escapes unhurt when his car overturns
on the M4. [16] A helicopter crashes into the sea near the
Scilly Isles, killing 20 people. [19] A new species of dinosaur
is discovered in a Surrey clay pit.

Sep [18] St Kitts and Nevis become independent. [25] 38 IRA
prisoners escape from the Maze Prison; a prison officer is
stabbed to death during the escape.

Oct [2] Neil Kinnock is elected leader of the Labour Party, Roy
Hattersley his deputy. [5] Cecil Parkinson MP admits having
had a relationship with his secretary Sarah Keays. [10] Sir
Ralph Richardson dies. [14] Cecil Parkinson resigns from the
Cabinet. [19] Maurice Bishop, Prime Minister of Grenada, is
shot by troops; General Austin takes control. [24] Dennis
Nilsson confesses to 15 or 16 murders during his trial. [25]
American troops invade Grenada, an action that is opposed
by Britain. [27] Grenadan resistance to the American troops
fails and Governor-General Sir Paul Scoon is reinstated.

Nov [4] Dennis Nilsen is sentenced to life imprisonment eight
times over, although he boasts of killing 15 young men.

[14] The first Cruise missiles arrive at Greenham Common from the USA. [18] John Habgood is enthroned as Archbishop of York. An official report accuses some police officers of being racists and bullies. [26] £26 million of gold bullion is stolen at Heathrow Airport.

Dec [3] Women peace campaigners break into the Greenham Common missile base. [10] There is a bomb explosion at the Woolwich RA barracks. [17] There is a massive IRA bomb explosion outside Harrods in London; six people are killed and many injured. [25] A bomb explodes in Oxford Street.

1984 There is a growing awareness of the dangers and causes of acid rain.

Jan [9] Sarah Tisdall, a Foreign Office clerk, is charged under the Official Secrets Act. [11] Two British lorry drivers are hi-jacked by French farmers as they drive through France in protest against foreign meat imports into France. [13] Six people die in hurricane-force winds. [25] The Government announces that workers at GCHQ may not belong to a trade union. [26] The Governor of the Maze Prison resigns after publication of a critical report on IRA prisoner escapes.

Feb [3] The Indian diplomat Ravindra Mhatre is abducted in Birmingham and later murdered. [9] Harold Macmillan accepts an earldom, becoming Lord Stockton, on his 90th birthday.

Mar [6] The National Coal Board says it will close 21 coal mines and lay off 20,000 employees. Scientists begin warning of the likelihood that burning fossil fuels will accentuate the greenhouse effect, and cause the atmosphere to become warmer. [7] Stephen Waldorf, an innocent passer-by who was shot in error by the police in 1982, is to receive £120,000 in compensation from the Metropolitan Police. [12] The miners begin their strike against the proposed pit closures, led by Arthur Scargill; mass picketing leads to violent confrontations between pickets and the police. [14] Gerry Adams, MP for West Belfast, is injured in an attempt to assassinate him. [23] Sarah Tisdall is sent to prison for six months for allegedly leaking documents to a newspaper; there are widespread protests at her sentence.

Apr [4] Bailiffs evict women from Greenham Common. [9] There is more violence on the picket lines in the miners' strike. [17] WPC Yvonne Fletcher is shot dead outside the Libyan People's Bureau in St James's Square; the Bureau is besieged by the police for ten days. [22] The British Government breaks off diplomatic relations with Libya. [27] The St James's Square siege comes to an end; 30 Libyans from the bureau are deported. The British ambassador and other diplomats return from Tripoli.

May [19] The Poet Laureate Sir John Betjeman dies.

Jun [3] Levels of childhood leukaemia are reported to be abnormally high near the Sellafield nuclear re-processing plant in Cumbria, causing renewed anxiety about the safety of nuclear plants in general. [14] Four people are killed in explosions aboard an oil tanker at Milford Haven. [28] The last issue of *Tit-Bits* is published.

Jul [5] The abducted Nigerian exile Umaru Dikko is found in a crate at Stansted Airport and rescued. [6] David Jenkins is installed as Bishop of Durham. [9] The roof of one of the transepts of York Minster is struck by lightning and destroyed by fire. [16] The High Court rules that the Government's ban on union membership at GCHQ is illegal. The Lords vote to abolish the Greater London Council and other metropolitan authorities.

Aug [5] The film actor Richard Burton dies. [15] The writer J.B. Priestley dies. [18] Clive Ponting, a civil servant, is charged with an offence under the Official Secrets Act, relating to information allegedly passed on to an MP about the circumstances surrounding the sinking of the *General Belgrano* in 1982. [26] An outbreak of salmonella poisoning at Stanley Royde Hospital in Wakefield leads to 26 deaths. [27] The actor James Mason dies in Switzerland.

Sep [15] Prince Charles' and Princess Diana's second son, Prince Henry, is born. [22] The Bishop of Durham calls the Coal Board chief, Ian MacGregor, an 'imported, elderly American'; Archbishop Runcie makes it known that he disapproves of the remark.

Oct [12] The Grand Hotel bombing; four people are killed and many injured when an IRA bomb explodes at the Grand Hotel, Brighton during the Conservative Party Conference. Mrs Thatcher, who is staying at the hotel, is unhurt but upset at the loss of her friends. [31] ACAS talks between the National Union of Mineworkers and the National Coal Board break down again.

Nov [6] The Government admits that the log of the submarine *Conqueror* relating to the sinking of the *General Belgrano* is missing. [22] The Law Lords uphold the Government's ban on union membership at GCHQ. [30] Two miners are charged with murdering a taxi-driver, David Wilkie, by dropping a concrete block on his car as he was driving other miners to work.

Dec [11] 11 die in a multiple crash on the M25 in fog. [19] Ted Hughes is appointed Poet Laureate.

1985 Spain reopens her frontier with Gibraltar after 16 years.

Jan [14] The musician and philanthropist Sir Robert Mayer dies. [29] Oxford University refuses to award Margaret Thatcher an honorary degree, because of her destructive education policies.

Feb [11] Clive Ponting is acquitted of breaching the Official Secrets Act. [20] The Irish Dail passes a Bill enabling shops to sell contraceptives. [28] Nine police are killed in an IRA bomb attack on Newry police station.

Apr [11] 24 people are killed by a Tamil bomb in Colombo shortly before Mrs Thatcher's arrival in Sri Lanka. [27] Lord Byron's publishers, John Murray, discover the manuscript of his only known short story. [30] Britain's first black bishop, the Ven. Wilfrid Wood, is appointed.

May [3] An epidemic in Stafford is identified as Legionnaire's Disease: 30 people die. [6] Four children are drowned by a freak wave during a school outing to Land's End. [11] The Bradford football stadium fire; 55 football supporters are trapped in or behind a burning stand and are burnt to death. [12] Prince Andrew opens the new Falklands airport, which has cost Britain £276 million. [16] The two miners who killed David Wilkie are sentenced to life imprisonment for murder; on appeal the charge is reduced to manslaughter. [29] The Heysel football stadium disaster; 41 Italian and Belgian supporters are killed in a riot before a Liverpool v. Juventus match. As a result of the appalling behaviour of British football supporters, British teams are afterwards banned for an indefinite period from European competition.

Jun [3] Lord George Brown of Jevington, Labour politician, dies. [5] The Government gives its approval to the development of Stansted as London's third airport, ending a long period of uncertainty not only about Stansted but about all the alternative sites. [6] A worldwide ban on British football teams is imposed by FIFA. [23] An Air India Boeing crashes into the Irish Sea, killing all 329 people on board.

Jul [2] The Church of England's general synod approves the ordination of women, although many in the church strongly oppose it. [8] Britain lifts its ban on trading with Argentina. [16] The Local Government Act; the GLC is abolished.

Aug [22] 54 people are killed at Manchester Airport when a Boeing 737 bursts into flames while on the runway.

Sep [9] There are riots in the Handsworth area of Birmingham. [28] There are violent riots in Brixton, following the shooting of an innocent black woman, Mrs Cherry Groce, by a policeman.

Oct [6] A policeman is killed during riots in the Broadwater Farm Estate in Tottenham; these riots were a reaction to the collapse and death of a black woman while police searched her home. [19] Miners in Nottinghamshire and Derbyshire vote to set up a Union of Democratic Mineworkers. [31] The

two miners sentenced to life imprisonment have their
sentences changed to eight years for manslaughter.

Dec   [2] The poet Philip Larkin dies. [7] The poet and novelist
Robert Graves dies.

1986   The Greater London Council is abolished. Corporal
punishment is abolished in all state schools. The
computerization of share transactions creates a 'big bang' of
buoyant sales. Stanley Cohen (British) and Rita
Levi-Montalcini (Italian) are awarded the Nobel Prize for
Physiology and Medicine.

Jan   [7] Thatcher refuses to join Reagan in breaking economic and
commercial links with Libya. [9] Michael Heseltine resigns
from Thatcher's Cabinet, accusing the Prime Minister of
stifling debate. [17] The Royal Yacht *Britannia* evacuates
Britons and others from Aden. [20] Anglo-French agreement
on a twin tunnel Channel rail link. [24] Leon Brittan resigns
from the Cabinet.

Feb   [14] The composer Edmund Rubbra dies. [16] The police
clash with pickets at Rupert Murdoch's printing plant at
Wapping. [26] The European Court rules that retirement age
should be the same for men and women, yet the British
Government does nothing to equalize retirement age or
pension rights.

Mar   [2] The Queen signs a proclamation which formally gives
Australia legal independence. [18] Income tax is reduced to
29%. [31] A woman dies in a fire at Hampton Court Palace.

Apr   [15] US planes bomb Benghazi and Tripoli in retaliation for
Libyan terrorist acts; the planes used in this raid take off from
British airfields, which causes widespread protests in Britain.
[17] Two British hostages are killed in Lebanon in retaliation
for British connivance at the air attack on Libya. [24] The
Duchess of Windsor, widow of ex-King Edward VIII, dies.
[26] The Chernobyl nuclear reactor in the Soviet Union
explodes; high levels of radiation affect north-west Europe,
including Britain.

May [3] There are violent clashes between police and pickets at Wapping. [16] Ex-President Galtieri is gaoled for negligence in the conduct of the Falklands War.

Jun [10] Patrick Magee is found guilty of the Grand Hotel bombing. Bob Geldof is given an honorary knighthood for his work in raising money for the starving in Africa. [20] The movement of sheep is banned in Cumbria because of the build-up of radiation levels following the Chernobyl disaster.

Jul [23] Prince Andrew marries Sarah Ferguson and is created Duke of York. [25] The Appeal Court bans publications by former MI5 officer Peter Wright.

Oct [26] Jeffrey Archer resigns as deputy chairman of the Conservative Party after rumours of scandal. [27] 'Big Bang' day in the City; there is confusion as a computer fails. [29] The M25 is finally completed.

Nov [6] 45 men from an oil rig are killed in a helicopter crash in the Shetlands. [21] The Government's AIDS advertising campaign is launched. [27] It is revealed that George V's doctor hastened the King's death, so that it would appear in the morning rather than the evening papers.

Dec [19] John Stalker announces his intention to retire from the Greater Manchester Police Force. [22] David Penhaligon, MP for Truro, is killed in a road accident. [29] Harold Macmillan, Lord Stockton, Conservative Prime Minister, dies.

1987

Jan [2] Golliwogs are banned from Enid Blyton's books by their publisher because of the offence caused to black people. [12] There are exceptionally low temperatures and heavy snowfall. Prince Edward resigns his commission in the Royal Marines. [19] Christopher Nolan, the paralyzed Irish writer, is awarded the Whitbread Prize. [20] Terry Waite, the Archbishop of Canterbury's special envoy, is abducted in Beirut while trying to negotiate the release of other hostages; now he becomes a hostage himself. [24] 300 people are injured in fierce clashes between police and pickets outside the Wapping print works.

Mar [6] The cross-channel ferry, *Herald of Free Enterprise*, capsizes outside Zeebrugge harbour because the crew leave the bow-doors open; about 200 people are drowned in the disaster. [10] Charles Haughey is elected Prime Minister of the Irish Republic on the Speaker's casting vote. [11] Dr Garret Fitzgerald resigns as leader of the Irish Fine Gael Party. [14] Roy Jenkins is elected Chancellor of Oxford University. [19] Three men are sentenced to life imprisonment for the vicious murder of PC Blakelock on the Broadwater Farm Estate. [27] 12 people are killed in violent storms.

Apr [3] In an attempt to prove rehabilitation, Myra Hindley confesses to two more murders. [7] The *Herald of Free Enterprise* is righted. [8] 104 more bodies are found inside the ship. [25] Lord Justice Gibson and Lady Gibson are killed by a car bomb in Ireland.

May [3] Peter Wright's memoirs are published in the US and Canada [8] Nine IRA gunmen are killed in a battle with police and soldiers in County Armagh.

Jun [11] In the General Election the Conservatives are returned with a majority of 101, Margaret Thatcher is Prime Minister for her third consecutive term. [12] Princess Anne is created 'Princess Royal'. [27] There is mounting controversy over the treatment of alleged child abuse cases in Cleveland.

Jul [1] One of the Moors murderers' victims' bodies is found after a search on Saddleworth Moor assisted by Ian Brady. [13] Six children who were taken from their parents by social workers in the Cleveland child abuse case are returned to their parents. [18] Oxford University refuses Thatcher an honorary degree for the second time. [24] Jeffrey Archer wins a libel action against the *Daily Star*. In the Zeebrugge Inquiry's report three crew members are blamed for leaving the doors open, and the company is accused of sloppiness.

Aug [6] David Owen resigns as leader of the SDP after a majority vote to open discussions about a merger with the Liberals. [11] The Cleveland child abuse inquiry begins. [17] Rudolf

Hess dies mysteriously in prison, apparently by his own hand. [19] Michael Ryan massacres 16 in Hungerford. [30] Three people are arrested near Tom King's home; they are later charged with conspiracy to murder the Northern Ireland Secretary.

Sep [22] The Home Secretary prohibits the sale of semi-automatic rifles.

Oct [8] An inquest finds that the victims of the Zeebrugge disaster were unlawfully killed. [15] The Queen abdicates as monarch of Fiji. [16] The hurricane: the worst storm since 1703 strikes Britain in the middle of the night. 15 million trees are blown down, revealing the poor state of English woodlands, and 17 people are killed. The Meteorological Office's failure to predict this major weather phenomenon is criticized. [19] There are floods in Wales and Cumbria; four are drowned near Llandeilo when a bridge collapses as a train crosses. The cellist Jacqueline du Pré dies. [27] Gilbert Mc Namee is sentenced to 25 years in prison for conspiring to cause bombings, including the 1982 Hyde Park bombing.

Nov [8] The Remembrance Day bombing at Enniskillen; there is widespread condemnation of this atrocity, in which 11 innocent people are indiscriminately killed. [17] The Government announces its plans to introduce the community charge in 1990 – a decision it will come to regret. [18] 31 people die in a fire on an escalator at the Kings Cross tube station. [24] A 'No Smoking' rule is in force throughout the London Underground system from today.

Dec [2] The Government announces stronger controls on firearms. [7] Dr Gareth Bennett commits suicide as it emerges that he is the author of a preface to *Crockford's* that is critical of Archbishop Runcie.

1988 Sir James Black (British), Gertrude B. Elion and George H. Hitchings (American) are awarded the Nobel Prize for Physiology and Medicine.

Jan [3] Margaret Thatcher becomes the 20th century's longest-serving Prime Minister.

Feb [7] The novelist and critic Marghanita Laski, dies; so does the actor Trevor Howard. [9] Six people die in 100 mph winds. [10] Viscount Whitelaw resigns as leader of the House of Lords owing to ill-health. He is replaced by Lord Belstead. [24] An official report on the October hurricane criticizes the Meteorological Office.

Mar [3] The Liberals and the SDP join to form the Social and Liberal Democratic Party. [6] Three members of the IRA are shot dead in Gibraltar after a bombing conspiracy is uncovered; there is controversy over the way the shootings were carried out. [10] While ski-ing, the Prince of Wales narrowly escapes death in an avalanche; the Prince's friend Hugh Lindsay dies in the accident. [16] The Loyalist gunman Michael Stone shoots three mourners dead at an IRA funeral.

Apr [14] John Stonehouse, the disappearing MP, dies. [19] Teachers are given a 4.75% pay rise. [21] Judges are given a 7.45% pay rise, nurses 15%. [23] Lord Ramsey, former Archbishop of Canterbury, dies.

May [11] The spy Kim Philby dies in Moscow.

Jun [6] Lester Piggott, the jockey, loses his OBE. [8] The broadcaster Russell Harty dies of hepatitis contracted while filming in Europe. [17] Viraj Mendis loses his appeal against deportation to Sri Lanka. [18] Mrs Marie Wilks is murdered on the M50.

Jul [6] An explosion on the North Sea oil rig Piper Alpha kills 150 men. A report on the Cleveland child abuse case is published. [28] Paddy Ashdown is elected leader of the SLD.

Aug [11] So far 6,000 seals have died in the North Sea; at first the high levels of pollution in the sea are suspected, but the cause of death is canine distemper. [19] Sir Frederick Ashton dies.

Sep [26] In a continuing muddle over names for the political centre, the SLD votes in favour of being called 'Democrats'.

[30] A jury in Gibraltar rules that the three IRA terrorist suspects were 'lawfully killed'.

Oct [31] General Galtieri of Argentina is sentenced to 12 years for his incompetent management of the Falklands War.

Nov [8] Salman Rushdie wins the Whitbread Prize with *The Satanic Verses*.

Dec [4] Edwina Currie rashly claims that most British egg production is infected by salmonella, which brings a storm of criticism from the egg producers and calls for her resignation. [12] The Clapham train crash; 34 people are killed as two trains collide. [16] Edwina Currie resigns. [21] The Lockerbie disaster: a Pan Am jumbo jet explodes in the air over southern Scotland and crashes onto Lockerbie; 270 people on board and 11 residents of Lockerbie are killed as a result of a terrorist bomb in the luggage.

1989 The introduction of the Community Charge (poll tax) as a substitute for rates meets widespread protest and defiance in Scotland.

Jan [8] A Boeing 737 crashes onto the Ml near Kegworth in Leicestershire; 47 people are killed. [18] A Manchester church is stormed to remove Viraj Mendis for deportation to Sri Lanka. [20] Field-Marshal Lord Harding dies.

Feb [14] Ayatollah Khomeini, the Iranian leader, orders Salman Rushdie's execution for blasphemy; Rushdie goes into hiding. [20] Three terrorist bombs destroy a large area of the barracks at Tern Hill in Shropshire. [28] Hereford Cathedral drops its plans to sell the medieval *Mappa Mundi* in order to raise money.

Mar [3] Michael Stone is sentenced to life imprisonment in Belfast for the Milltown cemetery murders. [4] Five people die in a train crash in Purley. [5] The Ozone Layer Conference begins in London. [6] Two people die in a train crash in Glasgow. [28] The remains of Piper Alpha are sent to the seabed.

Apr [5] President Gorbachev arrives in Britain for a three-day visit. [15] The Hillsborough football stadium disaster; 95

Liverpool supporters are crushed to death in a pen due to poor crowd control. [18] An explosion on Cormorant Alpha leads to a shut-down of 25% of North Sea oil production. [19] The novelist Dame Daphne Du Maurier dies. [28] 14 Liverpool supporters are sentenced to three years for their part in the Heysel stadium riot.

May [1] A riot starts at the Risley remand centre, in protest at the conditions at the centre; the riot ends three days later with a promise of an inquiry. [27] There is a violent Muslim protest in Parliament Square against Salman Rushdie's book.

Aug [30] Uppark House, a fine eighteenth-century mansion in Sussex, is gutted by fire. It is to be rebuilt.

Oct [19] Britain and Argentina formally end hostilities.

Dec [19] Stella Gibbons, author of *Cold Comfort Farm*, dies aged 86. [26] The composer Sir Lennox Berkeley dies.

1990 Growing disquiet over the Government's apparent callousness culminates in furious demonstrations against the Community Charge in England.

Jan [7] Terry Thomas, the film actor, and Lord Gardiner, the former Lord Chancellor, die. [9] Ruskin Spear, the portrait painter, dies. [19] The pianist Semprini dies. [25] A storm gusting to 110 mph sweeps across southern England and Wales; 46 people are killed.

Feb [1] The composer Peter Racine Fricker dies. [7] Gales sweep across southern England again; two die and there is severe flooding in river valleys. [11] There is yet another storm. [26-28] There are more storms; Towyn in North Wales is flooded when sea defences give way.

Mar The residents of Towyn are evacuated. There are widespread demonstrations against the poll tax, especially in central London. Farzad Bazoft, a 31-year-old British journalist, is accused by the Iraqis of spying and hanged. [20] Lord Rothschild, banker and Government adviser, dies.

Apr Strangeways Prison riot; the prison is taken over by the inmates for 25 days and wrecked. An earthquake centred on

Wrexham registers 5.2 on the Richter scale. The Trade and Industry Secretary, Nicholas Ridley, confirms that steel cylinders detained by customs officers are, as suspected, parts of a huge 'super-gun' bound for Iraq.

May [5] Reginald Goodall, the great Wagnerian conductor, dies.
[22] The actor and entertainer Max Wall dies aged 82.

Jun David Owen winds up the SDP. [1] Actor and comedian Eric Barker dies. [2] Sir Rex Harrison, film and stage actor, dies. [9] Photographer Angus McBean dies. [14] Comedienne Elsie Walters dies. [16] Dame Eva Turner, opera singer, dies. [21] Elizabeth Harwood, opera singer, dies.

Jul Tom King announces an 18% cut in the armed services, and a halving of the British Army of the Rhine over the next five years.
[15] Margaret Lockwood, film actress, dies in London. [24] Ian Gow MP gives a message to the IRA on television: 'they will never, never win'. A week later (July 30) he is killed by an IRA car bomb at his home in Sussex. After accusing Kuwait of stealing Iraqi oil, the Iraqi government sends thousands of troops to the Kuwait border.

Aug [2] Iraqi forces invade Kuwait. [4] The European Community joins the world blockade by freezing Kuwaiti assets. [8] Iraq announces the annexation of Kuwait. [19] Iraq orders westerners in Kuwait to assemble at three hotels preparatory to being taken to key military installations as human shields. [23] President Saddam appears on television with a group of British hostages.

Sep [6] Margaret Thatcher tells the House of Commons that British troops will be sent to the Gulf as part of a coalition force to re-establish the independence of Kuwait. [7] Historian A. J. P. Taylor dies.

Oct [2] Two suspected terrorists are arrested at Stonehenge. [21] The former Prime Minister, Edward Heath, has a three-hour meeting with President Saddam in Baghdad, in an attempt to negotiate the release of the British hostages. [24] Heath returns with 33 released British hostages.

Nov [7] The author Lawrence Durrell dies. [13] Sir Geoffrey Howe makes a dramatic and outspoken Commons speech explaining his resignation as deputy Prime Minister; the speech is decisive in bringing Mrs Thatcher's term of office to an end. [14] The journalist and broadcaster Malcolm Muggeridge dies aged 87. Michael Heseltine announces that he will challenge the leadership of the Conservative Party. [22] Margaret Thatcher resigns as Prime Minister, saying 'It's a funny old world'. [23] The author Roald Dahl dies. [28] John Major becomes Prime Minister, defeating the other candidates, Michael Heseltine and Douglas Hurd.

Dec [1] 'Breakthrough': the two sides of the Channel Tunnel are joined and people are able to walk through for the first time. [17] The Government invokes Section 10 of the Reserve Forces Act, allowing the call-up of reservists, which has not been done since the Korean War; 1500 extra personnel, mainly medics, will be needed in the Gulf. [31] Dame Joan Sutherland gives her farewell performance at Covent Garden, with Pavarotti in *Die Fledermaus*. Archbishop Robert Runcie, also shortly to retire, delivers his New Year message, praying that Terry Waite, his special envoy held in captivity in the Lebanon now for almost four years, will be released in 1991.

1991
Jan [5-6] 27 people die in gales, including two visitors to Brighton who are overtaken by a huge wave. [15] The United Nations deadline for the Iraqi withdrawal from Kuwait passes: Iraq does not withdraw. [16] The UN coalition forces launch a ferocious air attack on Iraqi forces in Kuwait and Iraq to disable the Iraqi air force and weapons factories. 'Operation Desert Storm', the Gulf War, begins. [31] Archbishop Robert Runcie retires.

Feb [7] The IRA launch a mortar-bomb attack on 10 Downing Street when the War Cabinet is in session. Windows are shattered but no one is hurt. [14] The 'Birmingham Six' are released after their convictions are overturned by the Court of Appeal. [27] Kuwait City is liberated; the Iraqi army is effectively defeated on the ground by coalition forces. [28] Ceasefire in the Gulf War follows the liberation of Kuwait.

Mar [8] The Liberal Democrats win the Ribble Valley by-election from the Conservatives. [20] Michael Heseltine announces the scrapping of the unpopular poll tax; it is to be replaced by a mainly property-based tax. [26] Norman Lamont raises VAT to 17.5% in order to take £140 per head off the Poll Tax.

Apr [2] British businessman Roger Coope is freed after spending five years in Iranian jails for alleged spying. The writer Grahame Greene dies in Vevey, Switzerland. [5] Author and illustrator Eve Garnett dies aged 91. [6] Kurdish demonstrators storm the Iraqi Embassy in London. Police find weapons and a detonator in the Embassy. Britain joins coalition forces in sending aid to the Kurds. [13] Dame Peggy Ashcroft is given an award for her lifetime achievements by the Society of the West End Theatre (Laurence Olivier awards). [16] Sir David Lean, film director, dies in London. [19] Dr George Carey is enthroned as Archbishop of Canterbury. [22] In a speech at Stratford on Avon, Prince Charles condemns low educational standards and says: 'In following fashionable trends in education, we end up with an entire generation of culturally disinherited young people.' [23] President Walesa of Poland pays a State visit to Britain and is the guest of honour at a banquet given by the Queen at Windsor Castle. [24] Gerald Ratner, Managing Director of Britain's biggest chain of jewellers, declares that his goods are 'crap'.

May [2] Missing undergraduate Rachel McLean, is found murdered under the floorboards at her Oxford lodgings. [3] Labour wins three marginal seats in local elections in Derbyshire. [6] Actor Wilfrid Hyde White dies in Los Angeles aged 87. [8] Frank Tempest is attacked by two pit bull terriers in Lincoln and receives appalling facial injuries. [13] Two-year-old Paula Holmes is attacked by a pit bull terrier in Bolton. [14] The Queen and Prince Philip are given a welcome at the White House at the start of a 10-day state visit to America during which the Queen will confer an honorary knighthood on General Schwarzkopf for his part in the Gulf War. [15] Tory MP Edwina Currie is awarded £5,000 libel damages against *The Observer* for a magazine article in which she was likened to a fictitious MP. [17] Labour wins the Monmouth by-election, with a swing of 13% from the Conservatives. [19] Britain's first woman astronaut, Helen Sharman, joins two Russian astronauts in the Soyuz TM 12 capsule on an 8-day journey to the Soviet MIR space station. Six-year-old Rucksana Khan is savaged by a pit bull terrier in Bradford, Yorkshire. Home Secretary Kenneth Baker imposes an immediate ban on the importation and breeding of pit bull terriers and the Japanese Tosas. [20] Justice Hollis allows a 12-year-old girl to have an abortion against her mother's wishes. [21] Teenager Patricia Cahill from Birmingham receives 18 years imprisonment in Thailand for alleged drug-smuggling. [23] Coral Browne, actress, dies. [24] Prince Charles and the Home Secretary Kenneth Baker attend the funeral of Rajiv Gandhi, assassinated in India on 21 May. Mrs Thatcher visits Russia as a guest of President Gorbachev. [31] Sir Angus Wilson, novelist and short-story writer, dies in Suffolk aged 77.

Jun [1] Three soldiers are killed and 18 people injured during an IRA attack on an Ulster Defence Regiment in Glennan, Co. Armagh. [3] Prince William has an operation for a fracture of the skull after being struck by a golf club at school. [3] The SAS shoot dead three IRA terrorists in the village of Coagh, Co. Tyrone. [6] Prince William leaves hospital. [7] Bill Morris becomes General Secretary of the Transport and General Workers' Union – the first black trade union leader. [10] The Duke of Edinburgh is 70 today. Britain bans a Soviet 'spyship' from carrying out research in UK waters. [11] The Maguire family's convictions for running an IRA bomb factory are quashed by the Court of Appeal. England triumph over the West Indies in the Test match at

Headingley after 22 years of trying. [14] Actress Dame Peggy Ashcroft dies aged 83. Sir Bernard Miles, actor and director, dies also aged 83. [16] Gwen Ffrangcon-Davies, the actress, is made a Dame of the Order of the British Empire; she is believed to be the first centenarian to be so honoured. [18] Foreign Secretary Douglas Hurd warns that the critical talks in Luxembourg on the future of Europe could collapse if Britain is pushed too hard: the British Government will not accept the idea of a federal Europe. [19] Mrs Thatcher speaks out on Europe again in New York and is verbally attacked by former Prime Minister Edward Heath. [21] The Queen takes the salute at the Mansion House in the City of London during a victory parade for forces who served in the Gulf War. Douglas Brand arrives in Britain after nine months in an Iraqi jail for alleged spying. [27]An IRA bomb is found in a bag outside the Beck Theatre in Hayes, Middlesex, where the band of the Blues and Royals staged a concert the day before. The bomb is safely defused. [28] At the Luxembourg summit, Jacques Delors, the European Commission president, backs down on federalism and says 'the language doesn't matter'. [29]The Queen visits Northern Ireland for the first time in 14 years to present colours to the Ulster Defence Regiment. Margaret Thatcher announces that she will resign as MP for Finchley after the next General Election but that she will still play an active part in British politics, perhaps from the House of Lords. [30] An army bomb disposal squad blows up an IRA bomb left outside the Royal Air Force careers office in Fishergate, Preston, Lancs.

Jul [1] Wearing rear seat belts in cars becomes compulsory. Thirty survivors of the Battle of the Somme gather at the Thiepval memorial for their last anniversary reunion. [3] Stormont talks on the future of Northern Ireland collapse. [7] Two suspected IRA terrorists escape at gunpoint from Brixton top-security prison, London. Home Secretary Kenneth Baker orders an inquiry into this 'grave lapse of security'. [10] The Queen opens the new Sainsbury Wing at the National Gallery. [15] The G7 Economic Summit takes place in London. [17] President Gorbachev visits London to seek economic aid for the Soviet Union. [22] John Major outlines his Citizen's Charter.

Aug [1] Flooding in SE England. [8] Hostage John McCarthy is released after being held captive in Beirut since 17 April 1986. [20] Riots at Lindholm prison in Doncaster cause widespread damage. [26] Judicial inquiry into the case of alleged ritual child abuse in the Orkneys opens in Kirkwall.

Sep [6] John Major proposes eventual full membership of the EC to eastern European states. [11] Rioting takes place in Newcastle-upon-Tyne. [24] Release of hostage Jackie Mann in Beirut. [28] Novelist and poet Roy Fuller dies.

Oct [2] Department of Health withdraws Halcion sleeping pill. [3] Allan Green, Director of Public Prosecutions, resigns after being stopped for alleged kerb-crawling. [13] Actor Donald Houston dies.

Nov [5] Businessman and newspaper proprietor Robert Maxwell is found dead at sea off the Canary Islands. Ian and Kevin Maxwell take over the chairmanship of Mirror Group Newspapers and Maxwell Communication Corporation. [18] Hostage Terry Waite is released in Beirut. [24] Rock star and Queen lead singer Freddie Mercury dies of AIDS.

Dec [4] Investigations begin into fraudulent dealings by Mirror Group Newspapers and Maxwell Communication Corporation. [7] Two trains collide in the Severn Tunnel, injuring 88 people. [9] Maastricht summit on European political and monetary union begins. [16] Stella Rimington is appointed MI5 head from February 1992. [19] Stamp duty is waived on house sales of up to £250,000 until August 1992. [23] Gales kill four people.

1992

Jan [3] Actress Dame Judith Anderson dies. [4] Toxic gas leak at Pyewipe, Grimsby, forces people to stay indoors. [8] British Steel announces the closure of Ravenscraig later in 1992 with a loss of 1,220 jobs. [11] Professor W. G. Hoskins, pioneer of landscape history, dies. [14] BCCI is put into liquidation by the High Court. [20] Northern Ireland Secretary Peter Brooke offers his resignation (in vain) following criticism for singing on television shortly after an IRA bomb had killed seven workmen near Omagh. [27] Actress Dame Gwen Ffrangcon-Davies dies, aged 101. [31] London Stock Exchange trading floor is used by dealers for the last time.

Feb [5] Paddy Ashdown confirms that he had an affair with his secretary five years previously. [6] Fortieth anniversary of Queen Elizabeth's accession to the throne. Barbara Mills QC is appointed the first woman Director of Public Prosecutions. [7] Maastricht treaty on European Union is signed by Foreign Secretary Douglas Hurd. [11] Talks are held at Downing St with the leaders of the four main political parties in Northern Ireland for the first time in 16 years. [14] Geographer Sir Clifford Darby dies. [16] Novelist Angela Carter dies. Poet George MacBeth dies. [17] IRA bomb at London Bridge station injures 29 people.

Mar [6] Thorn EMI buys the Virgin Group from Richard Branson for £560m. Government announces the foundation of a national lottery by 1994. [12] Drama critic Harold Hobson dies. [13] Eleven die in a North Sea helicopter crash. [19] Buckingham Palace announces the separation of the Duke and Duchess of York. [29] Lord Spencer, father of Diana, Princess of Wales, dies.

Apr [1] Former Attorney-General and Lord Chancellor Lord Havers dies. [8] Miners are rescued after being trapped for 15 hours in the Stillingfleet mine in North Yorkshire. [9] Conservative party wins the general election by 21 seats. [10] IRA bomb in the City of London kills three people, destroys the Baltic Exchange and causes £750m damage. [11] Cabinet reshuffle: Kenneth Baker, Tom King, Peter Brooke and Lord Waddington leave, and John Patten, Virginia Bottomley, Gillian Shephard, Michael Portillo and Sir Patrick Mayhew join. David Mellor is created National Heritage Minister; William Waldegrave is created Citizen's Charter Minister (later Public Service and Science Minister). [13] Neil Kinnock announces his resignation as leader and Roy Hattersley resigns as deputy leader of the Labour party. [19] Comedian Frankie Howerd dies. [22] Comedian Benny Hill dies. [23] The Princess Royal is permitted to divorce Captain Mark Phillips. [24] Chris Patten is appointed Governor of Hong Kong. [27] Betty Boothroyd is elected as first woman speaker of the House of Commons. [28] Artist Francis Bacon dies. [30] HMS *Vanguard*, Britain's first Trident submarine, is launched in Barrow-in-Furness.

May [12] European parliament in Strasbourg is addressed by the Queen for the first time. [18] So-called 'friendly fire' inquest, at Oxford, returns a verdict of unlawful killing in the Gulf War; the jurors evidently believed American pilots caused the deaths of nine British soldiers. [22] Cookery writer Elizabeth David dies. [25] Archbishop of Canterbury George Carey and Pope John Paul II meet for the first time. [26] Painter Sir Robin Philipson dies. [31] Erection of statue of Sir Arthur ('Bomber') Harris is met with angry demonstrations from protesters who believe it wrong to heroize a man responsible for so many civilian deaths in World War II.

Jun [3] Eleven-day Earth Summit opens in Rio de Janeiro with representatives of 178 UN countries. Actor Robert Morley dies. [5] Government decides against listing art treasures to prevent them leaving Britain. [6] Mrs Thatcher is given a life peerage. [7] *Sunday Times* begins serialisation of Andrew Morton's book *Diana: Her True Story*, exposing her unhappy marriage to the Prince of Wales. [19] Champion tennis player Kitty Godfree dies. [20] Conductor Sir Charles Groves dies. [24]Lloyd's of London report record losses of £2.6 billion. [25] Architect Sir James Stirling dies. [26] Painter and writer John Piper dies.

Jul [1] Presidency of the European Community passes to Britain. [15] Rachel Nickel is raped and murdered on Wimbledon Common during daylight hours. [16] A man manages to climb the walls and enter Buckingham Palace. [18] John

Smith is elected leader and Margaret Beckett deputy leader of the Labour Party. [19] David Mellor's offer of resignation, following newspaper reports of adultery, is refused. [20] Artist John Bratby dies. [23] Historical novelist Rosemary Sutcliff dies. [24] Final performance in the original Glyndebourne opera house. [31] Lord Cheshire, founder of the Leonard Cheshire Foundation Homes and the Memorial Fund for Disaster Relief, dies.

Aug [1] Linford Christie wins the Olympic 100m gold medal for Britain. [4] Sally Gunnell wins the Olympic 400m hurdles gold medal for Britain. [16] Government withdraws from ERM, causing effective devaluation of the pound. [18] 1,800 British troops are made available to escort aid convoys in Bosnia-Herzegovina; six RAF Tornado strike aircraft are sent to protect the Shia Muslims by means of policing an air exclusion zone in southern Iraq. [20] The *Daily Mirror* publishes compromising photographs of the Duchess of York on holiday with her friend John Bryan. [24] Extracts of an alleged conversation (the 'Squidgy' tapes) between the Princess of Wales and a male friend in 1989 are published by various newspapers. [27] Lord Owen replaces Lord Carrington as EC envoy on the Yugoslav peace conference.

Sep [19] Opera singer Sir Geraint Evans dies. [24] David Mellor resigns following revelations of his affair with actress Antonia de Sancha. [28] Playwright William Douglas-Home dies.

Oct [6] Actor Denholm Elliott dies. [14] Government plans to close 31 pits, causing the loss of 30,000 jobs, are met with widespread criticism and protest. [19] Scientist and broadcaster Magnus Pyke dies. [29] Choreographer and dancer Sir Kenneth MacMillan dies.

Nov [11] General Synod of the Church of England votes in favour of the ordination of women priests. [20] Fire at Windsor Castle causes £60m damage. [21] Public is concerned that the Queen is prepared to let the country pay for the repairs to Windsor Castle. [24] The Queen comments that 1992 has been an 'annus horribilis'. [26] It is announced that the Queen and Prince Charles have offered to pay tax.

Dec [3] Two IRA bombs in Manchester injure 64 people. [9] The Prince and Princess of Wales announce their separation. [10] Tennis player and commentator Dan Maskell dies. [11] Two-day EC summit in Edinburgh begins. [12] The Princess Royal marries Commander Timothy Laurence. [21] High Court rules proposed pit closures 'unlawful'. [25] Writer Monica Dickens dies. [31] Altogether 3,000 people in the UK have died as a result of the troubles in Northern Ireland.

APPENDICES
of Key Dates

These summaries are not comprehensive. They are meant
as a useful source of reference to direct readers to appropriate
sections of the book where the events or persons are described
in greater detail.

Wars, Battles and Conquests

BC
700-300	Celts settle in Britain
55	Julius Caesar's first expedition to Britain

AD
43	Roman Conquest of Britain begins
123	Hadrian's Wall
c. 400	Saxon raids resumed
515	Battle of Mount Badon
577	Battle of Dyrham
599-900	Viking Raids
793	Sack of Lindisfarne by Vikings
825	Battle of Ellandun
878	Battle of Ethandun: Alfred defeats the Danes
1066	Battle of Hastings (Norman Conquest)
1075	Rise of the Norman barons
1099	First Crusade: Godfrey of Bouillon takes Jerusalem
1106	Battle of Tinchebrai
1148	Second Crusade
1189	Third Crusade
1191	Capture of Acre by Crusaders
1264	Battle of Lewes
1265	Battle of Evesham
1256	Battle of Dunbar
1258	Battle of Falkirk
1314	Battle of Bannockburn
1238	Beginning of the Hundred Years War
1400	Owen Glendower leads a revolt in Wales
1403	Battle of Shrewsbury
1415	Battle of Agincourt
1455	First Battle of St Albans (Wars of the Roses)
1461	Battle of Towton (Wars of the Roses)
1471	Battle of Tewkesbury (Wars of the Roses)
1471	Battle of Barnet (Wars of the Roses)
1485	Battle of Bosworth Field
1513	Battle of Flodden Field
1513	Battle of Guinegatte
1558	Calais lost to the French

1588	Defeat of the Spanish Armada
1639	First Bishops' War
1640	Second Bishops' War
1642-6	First English Civil War
1642	Battles of Edgehill and Chalgrove Field
1642	First Battle of Newbury
1644	Battle of Marston Moor
1645	Battles of Naseby and Philiphaugh
1648	Second Civil War
1651	Battle of Worcester
1685	Battle of Sedgemoor
1672-74	Third Anglo-Dutch War
1689-97	The War of the League of Augsburg
1689	Battle of Killiecrankie
1690	Battle of the Boyne
1691	Capitulation of Limerick
1692	Massacre of Glencoe
1692	Defeat of the French off La Hogue
1701-13	The War of the Spanish Succession
1704	Capture of Gibraltar
1704	Battle of Blenheim
1706	Battle of Ramillies
1708	Battle of Oudenarde
1709	Battle of Malplaquet
1715	The 'Fifteen' (Jacobite Rebellion)
1715	Battles at Preston and Sheriffmuir
1739	War of Jenkins' Ear
1740-48	War of the Austrian Succession
1743	George II defeats the French at Dettingen
1745	Battle of Fontenoy
1746	Battles of Culloden and Falkirk
1751	Clive seizes and defends Arcot in India
1756-63	The Seven Years War
1757	Battle of Plassy
1775	American War of Independence
1798	Rebellion under the United Irishmen is put down
1800	The English take Malta
1801	Nelson destroys the Danish fleet at Copenhagen
1803	England resumes war with France

1805	Battle of Trafalgar
1808-14	Peninsular War
1809	Battle of Corunna
1812	United States declares war on Britain
1814	British defeated at New Orleans
1814	War ends with United States
1815	Battle of Waterloo
1819	Peterloo Massacre
1839	First Afghan War
1854-56	The Crimean War
1854	Battles of Alma, Balaclava and Inkerman.
1857	The Indian Mutiny breaks out
1878	The Second Afghan War
1879	Zulu War
1885	General Gordon killed at Khartoum
1898	Battle of Omdurman
1899-1903	Second Boer War (South Africa)
1900	Relief of Mafeking and Ladysmith
1914-18	First World War
1914	Battle of the Marne
1914	Battle of Mons
1914	First Battle of Ypres
1914	Second Battle of Ypres
1915	Gallipoli landings
1916	Battle of Jutland
1917	Third Battle of Ypres (22 Apr - 25 May)
1917	Battle of the Somme (21 Mar - 5 Apr)
1917	Battle of Passchendaele (26 Oct - 10 Nov)
1939-45	Second World War
1940	The evacuation of Dunkirk (29 May - 3 Jun)
1940	Battle of Britain (air)
1942	Battle of El Alamein (23 Oct)
1944	D-Day (6 Jun) - Allied landings in Normandy
1948	Emergency in Malaya
1952	Mau Mau emergency in Kenya
1956	Suez: Anglo-French attack on Egypt
1976	Cod War with Iceland
1985	Falklands War
1990-91	Gulf War

Constitutional, Legal and Religious

1086	The Domesday Survey
1100	Charter of Liberties
1164	The Constitutions of Clarendon
1166	The Assize of Clarendon
1170	Thomas Becket, Archbishop of Canterbury, is murdered
1215	King John signs Magna Carta
1258	Provisions of Oxford
1265	Simon de Montfort's Parliament
1279	Statute of Mortmain
1294	'Model Parliament' of Edward I
1297	Confirmatio Cartarum
1310	Lords Ordainers appointed
1351	Statute of Labourers
1351	Statute of Provisors
1377	First introduction of Poll Tax
1382	Wycliffe begins translating the Bible
1392	English becomes the official language in Parliament and the law courts
1393	Statute of Praemunire
1401	*De Haeretico Comburendo* – the burning of heretics – is made legal in England
1476	William Caxton sets up the first English printing press at Westminster
1494	Poynings' Law makes the Irish Parliament dependent on the English executive
1533	Act forbidding all appeals to Rome
1534	Act forbidding the Payment of Annates to Rome
1534	Act abolishing the Pope's Authority
1535	First Act of Supremacy
1535	Coverdale's English Bible is printed
1535	Sir Thomas More is executed for his refusal to recognize Henry VIII as head of the Church
1536-9	Dissolution of the Monasteries
1539	Six Articles
1549	First English Book of Common Prayer

1549	First Act of Uniformity
1559	Second Act of Supremacy
1559	Second Act of Uniformity
1563	Thirty-Nine Articles
1601	Elizabethan Poor Law
1603	Union of the English and Scottish Crowns
1605	Gunpowder Plot
1628	Petition of Right
1647	Charles I is handed over to Parliament
1649	Charles I is executed: England is governed as a Commonwealth
1660	Restoration of the monarchy
1661	Corporation Act
1662	Third Act of Uniformity
1664	Conventicle Act
1665	Five-Mile Act
1673	Test Act
1679	Habeas Corpus Act is passed
1681	Oxford Parliament
1688	The 'Glorious Revolution'
1689	Bill of Rights
1689	First Mutiny Bill
1690	Locke's *Two Treatises on Government*
1701	Act of Settlement
1707	Union of Scotland and England is effected
1711	Occasional Conformity Act
1714	Schism Act
1716	Septennial Act
1721	Robert Walpole becomes the first Prime Minister
1727	First Indemnity Act for Nonconformists
1752	Britain adopts New Style calendar
1783	American independence internationally recognized
1787	The Society for the Abolition of the Slave Trade is founded
1801	Parliamentary Union of Great Britain and Ireland is effected
1807	The Slave Trade is abolished
1824	Repeal of Combination Acts in Britain
1829	Catholic Emancipation in Britain

1832	First Reform Act
1833	Beginning of the 'Oxford Movement'
1833	First Government grant made to schools
1834	Poor Law Amendment Act
1835	Poor Law Municipal Reform Act
1846	Repeal of Corn Laws
1869	John Stuart Mill's *The Subjection of Women* is issued
1870	Irish Land Act passed
1870	Forster's Education Act
1884	Third Parliamentary Reform Act
1893	Home Rule Bill passes third reading in Commons but is rejected by Lords
1900	British Labour Party founded
1906	Mrs Pankhurst begins militant agitation
1911	Parliament Act: power of Lords reduced
1916	First Daylight Saving Act
1918	Representation of the People Act – franchise extended to most women and all men
1928	Franchise extended to all women
1972	Britain joins the EEC
1990	Community Charge (Poll Tax) introduced in England and Wales

Science and Invention

1589 Harington's 'Ajax' flushing water closet
1589 William Lee invents the knitting machine
1614 John Napier: Logarithms
1628 William Harvey describes the circulation of the blood in *Concerning the Motion of the Heart and Blood*
1636 William Gascoigne invents the micrometer
1662 Robert Boyle discovers the relation between gas pressure and volume
1665 Robert Hooke publishes *Micrographia*
1666 Sir Isaac Newton: Calculus
1668 Sir Isaac Newton constructs a reflecting telescope
1672 Newton reads his *New Theory about Light and Colours* to the Royal Society
1682 Halley's Comet so named
1684 Robert Hooke invents heliography
1687 Sir Isaac Newton: Laws of gravitation and motion, set out in his *Philosophiae Naturalis Principia Mathematica* or *Mathematical Principles of Natural Philosophy* (allegedly written after watching an apple fall in his garden in 1665)
1698 Thomas Savery invents the first steam pump
1704 Sir Isaac Newton publishes *Opticks*
1712 Thomas Newcomen invents the first steam engine
1721 Gorge Graham: the compensator pendulum for clocks
1725 William Ged: Stereotyping
1729 The astronomer James Bradley detects stellar aberrations
1730 John Hadley invents the reflecting quadrant
1733 John Kay invents the flying shuttle
1735 John Harrison invents the chronometer
1740 Benjamin Huntsman invents the crucible method of making steel from scrap
1746 John Roebuck: process for manufacturing sulphuric acid
1754 Joseph Black discovers carbonic gas
1755 Joseph Black discovers magnesium
1756 Joseph Black discovers carbon dioxide
1757 John Bird invents the sextant
1758 Jedediah Strutt invents a ribbing machine (for stockings)
1764 James Hargreaves invents the spinning jenny

1765	James Watt invents the condensing steam engine
1766	Henry Cavendish discovers hydrogen
1769	Venetian blinds patented by Edward Bevan
1772	Daniel Rutherford discovers nitrogen
1774	Joseph Priestley discovers oxygen
1785	Edmund Cartwright invents the power loom
1796	Edward Jenner pioneers vaccination
1798	Henry Cavendish determines the mean density of the earth
1800	Henry Maudslay invents the metal lathe
	Sir William Herschel discovers infra-red rays in sunlight
1804	Richard Trevithick invents the steam locomotive
1812	Bryan Donkin invents food canning
1813	Brewster's Law (Sir David Brewster)
1813	William Wollaston isolates palladium from platinum
1815	Sir Humphry Davy invents the miner's safety lamp
1817	Sir David Brewster invents the kaleidoscope
1823	Charles Babbage invents the digital calculating machine
1823	Charles Macintosh invents waterproof fabric
1823	Michael Faraday succeeds in liquefying chlorine
1824	Joseph Aspdin: Portland cement
1825	William Sturgeon: Electromagnet
1825	Michael Faraday isolates benzine
1827	John Walker: early friction match
1829	Thomas Graham formulates law on the diffusion of gases
1831	Michael Faraday – the dynamo. Electromagnetic induction.
1835	Charles Babbage: early computer
1836	Screw propeller – Sir Francis Smith
1839	William Fox Talbot invents photography
1840	Sir William Grove invents incandescent electric light
1840	MacMillan invents the first true bicycle
1845	Robert Thomson: Pneumatic tyre
1847	Dr James Simpson: first use of chloroform as anaesthetic
1852	Lord Kelvin and William Hankine invent refrigeration
1854	Sir John Elder: the compound marine steam-engine
1855	Alexander Parkes: Celluloid
1855	Sir Henry Bessemer: Bessemer converter (steel-making)
1855	Robert Bunsen: Bunsen burner
1856	Sir William Perkins creates mauve, the first artificial dye

1860   Baron Lister invents antiseptic surgery
1861   Frederick Walton: Linoleum
1864   James Clark Maxwell: electromagnetic theory of light
1864   Sir Charles Parsons invents the turbine
1868   Sir William Ramsay discovers helium
1878   Edward Hughes invents the microphone
1878   H. J. Lawson invents the modern safety bicycle
1878   Sir Joseph Swan demonstrates the filament electric lamp
1883   Sir Joseph Swan produces the first synthetic fibre
1884   Sir Charles Parsons invents the turbine
1885   Sir James Dewar invents the vacuum flask
1888   John Boyd Dunlop invents an improved pneumatic tyre
1889   Sir Frederick Abel invents cordite
1889   Friese-Green invents the cine camera
1892   Charles Cross and E. Bevan: Viscose
1894   Sir William Ramsay and Baron Rayleigh discover argon
1896   Sir William Ramsay discovers helium
1897   Sir Joseph Thomson discovers the electron
1897   J. Langley demonstrates the effect of adrenalin on the
        heart rate
1898   John P. Holland invents the submarine
1901   Cecil Booth invents the vacuum cleaner
1904   Sir John Fleming: the diode valve
1913   Hans Geiger: Geiger counter
1913   Henry Mosely: Atomic number
1914   Sir Ernest Swinton: the tank
1925   John Logie Baird discovers the proton
1928   Sir Alexander Fleming discovers penicillin
1930   Sir Frank Whittle invents the jet engine
1932   Sir James Chadwick discovers the neutron
1964   Britain starts gas and oil exploration in North Sea
1965   T. Gabor: laser holography
1967   Radio Astronomy Group, Cambridge: Pulsars
1969   Concorde makes first flight
1971   Godfrey Hounsfield: EMI-Scanner (developed from his
        invention of computed tomography in 1967)
1979   Louise Brown, the first test tube baby, is born at Oldham,
        Lancs, through methods of transplanting ovum
        developed by R. Edwards and P. Steptoe.

Exploration and Discovery

1497	John Cabot discovers Newfoundland.
1577	Francis Drake begins a voyage round the world (returns 1580).
1584	Sir Walter Raleigh discovers Virginia.
1600	The English East India Company is founded.
1610	Henry Hudson discovers Hudson Bay.
1620	The Pilgrim Fathers settle in New England.
1769	Captain James Cook visits New Zealand.
1770	Captain Cook discovers the east coast of Australia.
1796	Mungo Park explores the River Niger in Africa.
1828	Australian interior explored by Charles Sturt.
1831-6	Charles Darwin voyages round the world as a naturalist on the *Beagle*.
1841	James Ross discovers some of the coastline of Antarctica.
1848	The Franklin expedition to find the North-West Passage ends in disaster.
1851	David Livingstone discovers the River Zambezi in Africa.
1855	David Livingstone discovers the Victoria Falls in Africa.
1856	Richard Burton and John Speke discover Lake Tanganyika in Africa.
1860	Robert Burke and William Wills cross Australia (from south to north).
1877	Sir Henry Stanley traces the River Zaire (Congo) in Africa.
1912	Captain Scott reaches the South Pole (beaten by Amundsen).
1909	Sir Ernest Shackleton gets to within 100 miles of the South Pole.
1953	E. P. Hillary and Sherpa Tenzing of the Everest Expedition led by Colonel John Hunt reach the summit of Everest.
1957-8	The Antarctic Continent is crossed by Sir Vivian Fuchs, leading the British Commonwealth Trans-Antarctic Expedition.

Monarchs since the Conquest

House of Normandy

1066-1087 William I
1087-1100 William II
1100-1135 Henry I
1135-1154 Stephen

House of Plantagenet

1154-1189 Henry II
1189-1199 Richard I
1199-1216 John
1216-1272 Henry III
1272-1307 Edward I
1307-1327 Edward II
1327-1377 Edward III
1377-1399 Richard II

House of Lancaster

1399-1413 Henry IV
1413-1422 Henry V
1422-1461 Henry VI

House of York

1461-1483 Edward IV
1483   Edward V
1483-1485 Richard III

House of Tudor

1485-1509 Henry VII
1509-1547 Henry VIII
1547-1553 Edward VI
1553-1558 Mary I
1558-1603 Elizabeth I

House of Stuart

1603-1625 James I
1625-1649 Charles I
1649-1653 Commonwealth
1653-1658 Protectorate of
          Oliver Cromwell
1658-1659 Protectorate of
          Richard Cromwell
1660-1685 Charles II
1685-1688 James II
1689-1694 William and Mary
          (jointly)
1694-1702 William III (sole
          ruler)
1702-1714 Anne

House of Hanover

1714-1727 George I
1727-1760 George II
1760-1820 George III
1820-1830 George IV
1830-1837 William IV
1837-1901 Victoria

House of Saxe-Coburg

1901-1910 Edward VII

House of Windsor

1910-1936 George V
1936   Edward VIII
1936-1952 George VI
1952-   Elizabeth II

British Prime Ministers

1721-1742	Sir Robert Walpole	Whig
1742-1743	Earl of Wilmington	Whig
1743-1754	Henry Pelham	Whig
1754-1756	Duke of Newcastle	Whig
1756-1757	Duke of Devonshire	Whig
1757-1762	Duke of Newcastle	Whig
1762-1763	Earl of Bute	Tory
1763-1765	George Grenville	Whig
1765-1766	Marquess of Rockingham	Whig
1766-1767	Earl of Chatham	Whig
1767-1770	Duke of Grafton	Whig
1770-1782	Lord North	Tory
1782	Marquess of Rockingham	Whig
1782-1783	Earl of Shelbourne	Whig
1783	Duke of Portland	Coalition
1783-1801	William Pitt	Tory
1801-1804	Henry Addington	Tory
1804-1806	William Pitt	Tory
1806-1807	Lord Grenville	Whig
1807-1809	Duke of Portland	Tory
1809-1812	Spencer Perceval	Tory
1812-1827	Earl of Liverpool	Tory
1827	George Canning	Tory
1827-1828	Viscount Goderich	Tory
1828-1830	Duke of Wellington	Tory
1830-1834	Earl Grey	Whig
1834	Viscount Melbourne	Whig
1834-1835	Sir Robert Peel	Tory
1835-1841	Viscount Melbourne	Whig
1841-1846	Sir Robert Peel	Tory
1846-1852	Lord John Russell	Whig
1852	Earl of Derby	Tory
1852-1855	Earl of Aberdeen	Peelite
1855-1858	Viscount Palmerston	Liberal
1858-1859	Earl of Derby	Conservative
1859-1865	Viscount Palmerston	Liberal

1865-1866	Earl Russell	Liberal
1866-1868	Earl of Derby	Conservative
1868	Benjamin Disraeli	Conservative
1868-1874	William Gladstone	Liberal
1874-1880	Benjamin Disraeli	Conservative
1880-1885	William Gladstone	Liberal
1885-1886	Marquess of Salisbury	Conservative
1886	William Gladstone	Liberal
1886-1892	Marquess of Salisbury	Conservative
1892-1894	William Gladstone	Liberal
1894-1895	Earl of Rosebery	Liberal
1895-1902	Marquess of Salisbury	Conservative
1902-1905	Arthur Balfour	Conservative
1905-1908	Sir Henry Campbell-Bannerman	Liberal
1908-1915	Herbert Asquith	Liberal
1915-1916	Herbert Asquith	Coalition
1916-1922	David Lloyd-George	Coalition
1922-1923	Andrew Bonar Law	Conservative
1923-1924	Stanley Baldwin	Conservative
1924	James Ramsay MacDonald	Labour
1924-1929	Stanley Baldwin	Conservative
1929-1931	James Ramsay MacDonald	Labour
1931--1935	James Ramsay MacDonald	National
1935-1937	Stanley Baldwin	National
1937-1940	Neville Chamberlain	National
1940-1945	Winston Churchill	Coalition
1945	Winston Churchill	Conservative
1945-1951	Clement Attlee	Labour
1951-1955	Sir Winston Churchill	Conservative
1955-1957	Sir Anthony Eden	Conservative
1957-1963	Harold Macmillan	Conservative
1963-1964	Sir Alec Douglas-Home	Conservative
1964-1970	Harold Wilson	Labour
1970-1974	Edward Heath	Conservative
1974-1976	Harold Wilson	Labour
1976-1979	James Callaghan	Labour
1979-1990	Margaret Thatcher	Conservative
1990-	John Major	Conservative

Some British and Irish Writers

A selection only – all writers are listed in the Index of Proper Names.

Jane Austen (1775-1817)
Sir James Barrie (1860-1837)
Samuel Beckett (1906-1990)
William Blake (1757-1827)
George Henry Borrow
  (1803-1881)
James Boswell (1740-1795)
Elizabeth Bowen (1899-1973)
Rupert Brooke (1887-1915)
Anne Brontë (1820-1849)
Charlotte Brontë (1816-1855)
Emily Brontë (1818-1848)
Elizabeth Barrett Browning
  (1806-1861)
Robert Browning (1812-1889)
Edmund Burke (1729-1797)
Robert Burns (1759-1796)
Samuel Butler (1835-1902)
Lord George Byron
  (1788-1824)
Lewis Carroll (1832-1898)
Geoffrey Chaucer
  (c1345-1400)
Samuel Taylor Coleridge
  (1772-1834)
Wilkie Collins (1824-1889)
Dame Ivy Compton-Burnett
  (1892-1969)
William Congreve (1670-1729)
Joseph Conrad (1857-1924)
Sir Noël Coward (1899-1973)
William Cowper (1731-1800)
Daniel Defoe (1660-1731)
Charles Dickens (1812-1870)
Benjamin Disraeli (1804-1881)

Sir Arthur Conan Doyle
  (1832-1898)
John Dryden (1631-1700)
Daphne Du Maurier
  (1907-1989)
George Eliot (1819-1880)
T. S. Eliot (1888-1965)
Henry Fielding (1707-1754)
Ford Madox Ford (1873-1939)
E. M. Forster (1879-1970)
John Galsworthy (1867-1933)
Mrs Elizabeth Gaskell
  (1810-1865)
Edward Gibbon (1737-1794)
George Gissing (1857-1903)
Sir William Golding (1911-)
Oliver Goldsmith (1730-1774)
Kenneth Grahame
  (1859-1932)
Robert Graves (1895-1985)
Graham Greene (1904-1991)
Sir Rider Haggard
  (1856-1925)
Thomas Hardy (1840-1928)
Seamus Heaney (1939-)
Gerard Manley Hopkins
  (1844-1889)
Henry James (1843-1916)
Samuel Johnson (1709-1784)
Ben Jonson (1572-1637)
James Joyce (1882-1941)
John Keats (1795-1821)
Charles Kingsley (1819-1875)
Philip Larkin (1922-1985)
D. H. Lawrence (1885-1930)

Doris Lessing (1919-)
Christopher Marlowe
  (1564-1593)
Andrew Marvell (1620-1678)
Somerset Maugham
  (1874-1965)
A. A. Milne (1882-1956)
John Milton (1608-1674)
William Morris (1834-1896)
Dame Iris Murdoch (1919-)
Edith Nesbit (1858-1924)
Alexander Pope (1688-1744)
Beatrix Potter (1866-1943)
Anthony Powell (1905-)
J. B. Priestley (1894-1984)
John Ruskin (1819-1900)
Sir Walter Scott (1771-1832)
William Shakespeare
  (1564-1616)
George Bernard Shaw
(1856-1950)
Mary Shelley (1797-1851)
Percy Bysshe Shelley
  (1792-1822)
Richard Sheridan
  (1751-1816)

Sir C. P. Snow (1905-1980)
Edmund Spenser (1552-1599)
Laurence Sterne (1713-1768)
Robert Louis Stevenson
  (1850-1894)
Jonathan Swift (1667-1745)
Algernon Swinburne
  (1837-1909)
Alfred Lord Tennyson
  (1809-1892)
William Thackeray
  (1811-1863)
Dylan Thomas (1914-1953)
J. R. R. Tolkien (1892-1973)
William Trevor (1928-)
Anthony Trollope (1815-1882)
Sir Edgar Wallace (1884-1941)
Evelyn Waugh (1903-1966)
Mary Webb (1881-1927)
Oscar Wilde (1854-1900)
Sir Angus Wilson (1913-1990)
P. G. Wodehouse (1881-1975)
Virginia Woolf (1882-1941)
William Wordsworth
  (1770-1850)
W. B. Yeats (1865-1939)

Index of Proper Names

Index of Proper Names